THE COLD WAR

THE COLD WAR

The United States and the Soviet Union 1917–1991

Ronald E. Powaski

New York   Oxford
OXFORD UNIVERSITY PRESS
1998

Oxford University Press

Oxford New York
Athens Auckland Bangkok Bogota Bombay Buenos Aires
Calcutta Cape Town Dar es Salaam Delhi Florence Hong Kong
Istanbul Karachi Kuala Lumpur Madras Madrid Melbourne
Mexico City Nairobi Paris Singapore Taipei Tokyo Toronto

and associated companies in
Berlin Ibadan

Published by Oxford University Press, Inc.
198 Madison Avenue, New York, New York 10016

Oxford is a registered trademark of Oxford University Press

Library of Congress Cataloging-in-Publication Data
Powaski, Ronald E.
The Cold War: the United States and the Soviet Union, 1917–1991 /
by Ronald E. Powaski.
p.   cm.
Includes bibliographical references and index.
ISBN 978-0-19-507850-3
1. United States—Foreign relations—Soviet Union. 2. Soviet
Union—Foreign relations—United States. 3. Cold War. I. Title.
E183.8.S65P69 1997 327.73047—dc20 96-24691

To Stephanie and Victoria Szendrey

Geography and Vision: Seeing,

Contents

Preface

The Cold War was a struggle for global influence between the United States and the Soviet Union. To that end, the two countries employed a variety of methods, all short of a direct, all-out attack on each other's homelands. The methods they used included the creation of rival alliances, the extension of military and economic aid to client states and would-be client states, a massive and expensive arms race, propaganda campaigns, espionage, guerrilla warfare, counterinsurgency warfare, and political assassinations.

The Cold War was one of the longest conflicts in human history, over seventy years in duration, with periodic lulls in the level of hostility. It was also the widest in scope of all the world's wars; it was fought on every continent on the globe and, considering the space race, *over* every continent as well. The Cold War was also one of the costliest of the world's conflicts, not only in numbers of lives lost but also in resources expended. In the end, the Soviet Union collapsed, and communism, at least in the form that existed in the Soviet Union, expired. But, as Mikhail Gorbachev pointed out, both sides lost much in the Cold War. The United States lost many lives and consumed huge financial resources as well, and the democratic principles on which it was founded were endangered.

For decades, historians have argued about the origins of the Cold War. Who, or what, was primarily responsible? Was it inevitable?

One school of thought, the orthodox interpretation, places the major blame for the Cold War on the Soviet Union. Its proponents argue that the United States had no choice but to contain and, where possible, reverse the expansion of an aggressive communist state whose main ambition was the overthrow of capitalism, democracy, and other aspects of Western culture.

In contrast, the revisionist school places most of the responsibility for the Cold War on the United States. Revisionists argue that the Soviet Union was forced to react to an aggressive United States that was determined to expand capitalism by securing unlimited access to the world's markets and resources, and intent on crushing revolutionary movements that threatened those interests.

Another, more recent interpretation, the post-revisionist school, blames both sides for the Cold War. In essence, post-revisionists maintain that both sides took actions that prompted hostile reactions by the other, with the result that a kind of action-reaction cycle was created in which the level of animosity was periodically raised to dangerous levels, even bringing them to the brink of all-out nuclear war that neither side ever desired.

Now historians and other analysts are debating why the Cold War ended. One school of thought, the so-called Reagan victory school, attributes its end to the hard-line policies pursued by the Reagan administration during the 1980s. Reagan's "peace through strength" policy, this viewpoint argues, pushed the Soviet Union to the verge of economic collapse and, in effect, forced the Soviets to sue for peace and end the Cold War.

Not everyone accepts this interpretation. Some analysts attribute the end of the Cold War primarily to indigenous factors within the Soviet empire. These factors, they argue, compelled the last Soviet leader, Mikhail Gorbachev, to make concessions that brought an end to the Cold War, and also triggered the collapse of communism and the disintegration of the Soviet empire.

What did cause the Cold War? Why did it end? These are the principal questions this book will attempt to answer.

In a work of this scope, I am indebted to countless researchers, historians, and other analysts, of whose work this study is essentially a synthesis. I have attempted to acknowledge that debt in my end notes and suggested readings, which lists the works I relied upon in writing this book. I owe a special thanks to my editors, Nancy Lane, who encouraged me to proceed with the project, John Bauco, who helped guide it to completion, and Martha Morss, who made many helpful suggestions regarding the manuscript. I also want to thank my old friend George Barnum of Case Western Reserve's Freiberger Library for his tireless research assistance. As always, I am indebted to my best friend, and wife, Jo Ann, for her patience, encouragement, and wise counsel. This book is dedicated to my two greatest admirers, and, more rarely, severest critics, my granddaughters, Stephanie and Victoria Szendrey. They bring much joy to my life.

Euclid, Ohio   R. E. P.
January 1997

THE COLD WAR

Introduction:
The United States
and Czarist Russia

Idealism and Realism

It seems, in hindsight, that the Cold War was inevitable. From the very beginning of the Russian-American relationship, except for a brief period in 1917, the ideologies of the two nations were fundamentally incompatible. Founded in 1776, the young United States was republican and democratic; Russia, on the other hand, was an old autocracy, hostile to democracy, xenophobic, and known for ruthless suppression of its numerous subjects.

Although their political, social, and economic systems were divergent in the extreme, U.S.–Russian relations, though never really cordial, nevertheless were correct through most of their common history. To be sure, Americans were uneasy about the Holy Alliance, a union of absolutist states which Czar Alexander I fashioned in 1815 to crush liberal and national revolutions in Europe. But while Americans had the deepest sympathy for the revolutionists, they felt no compulsion to intervene on their behalf. In the minds of Americans during the late eighteenth and early nineteenth centuries, Europe was still a long way from the United States. Not only did Americans feel relatively secure being bounded by two oceans, they also were too preoccupied with their own internal affairs, including territorial expansion, industrialization, and the slavery issue, to countenance participation in foreign revolutions.

Keenly aware of these constraints on U.S. foreign policy, American leaders nevertheless appreciated the role Russia played in balancing the power of Britain and France. As a result, they did all they could, in this age of rising revolutionary fervor, to keep America's relations with autocratic

Russia courteous. The United States was benevolently neutral toward Russia during the Crimean War (1844–1845), when the Russians fought Britain, France, and the Ottoman Empire. The Russians reciprocated by following a policy of benevolent neutrality toward the American Civil War, a conflict in which the sympathies of the British and French governments leaned toward the South.

Expansionism

Despite the initial ability of Russians and Americans to overcome their ideological, political, and social differences, there was another factor that seemed to make eventual conflict between the two nations inevitable. Both were expansionist states whose respective spheres of interest eventually would expand to global dimensions.

From a small duchy centered on the city of Moscow in the fourteenth century, Russia had expanded to the Baltic Sea and across the vast expanse of Siberia by the time of the American Revolution. By the end of the nineteenth century, the Russian Empire extended from Central Europe to the Pacific Ocean and from the Arctic to Turkestan.

Tracing its origin to a small English settlement at Jamestown, Virginia, that was established in 1607, the United States by the end of the American Revolution extended from the Atlantic Ocean to the Mississippi River and from the Great Lakes to Florida. By 1900 the United States had completed its expansion to the Pacific Ocean, declared the Western Hemisphere to be an American sphere of influence, and, thanks to a victorious war with Spain, acquired a major colony in the Far East, the Philippine Islands.

Such ambitious nations seemed destined to collide. Still, Americans and Russians saw too little of each other to create much friction. American and Russian territory touched only at the Alaskan boundary, and in 1867 Russia agreed to sell Alaska to the United States.

By the end of the nineteenth century, however, Russia's expansion to the Pacific made it the major threat to the continued territorial integrity and independence of the Chinese empire, at a time when the United States had begun to look upon China as a major arena of American trade and investment. Taking advantage of China's defeat by Japan in 1895, the Russians slowly took control of China's Manchurian provinces.

In response to the threat posed by the establishment of foreign spheres of influence in China, in 1899 Secretary of State John Hay issued his first Open Door note, calling on the major foreign powers to recognize the right of all nations to trade with China. Of the six nations to whom Hay sent the note—Britain, France, Germany, Italy, Japan and Russia—only the latter equivocated in its response. Although Hay considered the ambiguous Russian response as an affirmation of the Open Door policy, it nevertheless indicated that American and Russian ambitions in China were diametrically opposed.

In what proved to be a major transformation of the international scene, the clash of American and Russian interests in China was complemented by a diplomatic rapprochement between Britain and the United States. Thus, the major factor that had made possible relatively good relations between the United States and Russia for over a century, that is, common antipathy toward Britain, disappeared. Russia, rather than Britain, was now regarded by the United States as the major threat to the balance of power in the Far East. In contrast, Britain and Japan were now looked upon as the major obstacles to the seemingly limitless expansion of the Russian empire.

Motivated by a desire to check Russian ambitions in the Far East, President Theodore Roosevelt applauded the conclusion of the Anglo-Japanese alliance in 1902 and welcomed the Japanese attack on Russian forces in Manchuria in 1904. Only after Japan began to threaten the balance of power in the region, after a series of stunning victories over Russia's army and navy, did Roosevelt attempt to mediate an end to the Russo-Japanese War, an effort that succeeded in 1905 with the conclusion of the Treaty of Portsmouth.

While the Russians were happy to get out of the conflict with Japan, and with their sphere of influence still intact in northern Manchuria, they resented America's tacit support of Japan during that conflict. Ironically, once the war was over, Russia and Japan combined to resist the efforts of President William Howard Taft's administration (1909–1913) to expand American investments in Manchuria. Thus, by the eve of World War I, the geopolitical ties that had linked Russian and U.S. interests for over a century had almost totally disappeared.

The Revival of American Idealism

Russo-American relations deteriorated not only because of commercial or geopolitical factors but because of increasing American emphasis on the ideological differences between the two countries. While Americans had never been comfortable with Russian autocracy, the government of the United States had never allowed it to disrupt the relations between the two countries.

Americans grew less and less tolerant of Russian autocracy, however, particularly after the assassination of Czar Alexander II in 1881 inaugurated a period of extreme reaction in Russia. The new czar, Alexander III, fell under the influence of Constantine P. Pobedonostsev, the Procurator of the Holy Synod. To save Russia from the evils of liberalism, Pobedonostsev revived the old reactionary formula of "Orthodoxy, Autocracy, and Nationality." Political oppression, religious persecution, and efforts to "Russify" non-Russian minorities all increased during Pobedonostev's tenure in office.

By the early twentieth century, it was impossible for the U.S. government to ignore internal conditions in the Russian empire. More and more

Jews were fleeing Russia and coming to the United States, where they became the catalyst behind rising public pressure against Russian anti-Semitism, particularly the murderous pogroms aided and abetted by the czar's government.

In 1903, in what amounted to an abandonment of the traditional U.S. policy of nonintervention in the internal affairs of European states, Theodore Roosevelt's administration (1901–1909) bowed to public pressure and signed a petition criticizing the government of Czar Nicholas II for failing to prevent a pogrom at Kishenev, the capital of Bessarabia (now Moldova), where forty-five Jews were killed and hundreds more were injured and left homeless. American opinion was aggrieved further by the refusal of the Russian government to allow the victims of the pogrom to receive American relief supplies. Unswayed by American opinion, the czarist government took no steps to prevent additional pogroms. As a result, in 1911, the administration of William Howard Taft bowed to overwhelming public and congressional pressure and abrogated the Russo-American Commercial Treaty of 1832.

A complete breakdown in U.S.–Russian relations did not occur while Russia was under monarchical rule. This was due partly to the reforms Czar Nicholas II was forced to introduce in the wake of another Russian revolution, in 1905. The czar established a parliament (the Duma), extended the franchise, and promised to protect civil liberties. These measures blunted the revolutionary impulse, split the opposition, and won some grudging support from the Russian middle class. These limited reforms enabled the czar to remain in control of the country until the monarchy was overthrown in March 1917. Few Americans lamented its demise.

1

The United States and the Bolshevik Revolution, 1917–1933

The Provisional Government

World War I was the catalyst of the Russian Revolution. Repeated mobilizations of some 15 million men during the war contributed to the disruption of industrial and agricultural production, the breakdown of the transportation network, and severe shortages of food and fuel, especially in the cities. All of these problems were aggravated by the ineptitude and corruption of Czar Nicholas II's regime, which rendered it incapable of solving them.

In early March 1917 the country finally exploded in revolution. A series of strikes and demonstrations in Petrograd (as St. Petersburg was renamed in 1914), protesting food shortages in the capital, quickly spread to Moscow and other Russian cities. On March 11 the czar responded by dissolving the parliament and ordering troops to break up the demonstrations. But when the soldiers refused to obey Nicholas' order, and then joined the demonstrators, the monarchy lost its primary support. On March 16 Nicholas abdicated, bringing the 300-year-old Romanov dynasty to an end. That day a provisional government was proclaimed under the leadership of a moderate conservative, Prince George E. Lvov. The new government promised to convene a constituent assembly to determine Russia's permanent form of government, as well as implement an ambitious program of social and economic reforms. However, in what would prove to be its death warrant, the Provisional Government also promised to keep Russia in the war.

President Woodrow Wilson hailed the March Revolution as a major step toward achieving the kind of postwar world order he hoped to build.

5

With the despotic czar replaced by a pro-democratic and pro–Allied government in Russia, Wilson plausibly could portray the war as a legitimate struggle between the forces of democracy and those of reaction and militarism. On March 22, only a week after the revolution, the president granted recognition to the Provisional Government. In his message to Congress requesting a declaration of war on Germany on April 2, the president referred to Russia as a "fit partner for a league of honor."[1] Between March and November 1917 the United States would advance the new Russian government $450 million in credits (only $188 million of that amount would be used before the Provisional Government itself was overthrown).

The root cause of the Provisional Government's failure was its refusal to end Russia's participation in the war. By the spring of 1917 the Russian army and people were exhausted by the conflict. Consequently, the demands of the Bolshevik faction of the Russian Social-Democratic Labor Party for an immediate end to the conflict and the redistribution of land to the peasants became increasingly appealing. Realizing this, the Germans, on April 16, 1917, allowed the Bolsheviks' leader, Vladimir Lenin, to return to Petrograd from his place of exile in Switzerland. The Germans hoped that Lenin's agitation would further disrupt the Russian war effort and perhaps even knock Russia out of the war. Lenin immediately obliged the Germans by launching a program to overthrow the Provisional Government. He argued that it represented only the bourgeoisie, not the masses of the Russian people, who, he insisted, were more equitably represented by the councils (soviets) of workers and soldiers that had sprung up throughout Russia. Rather than supporting the war, Lenin worked to bring about Russia's defeat, arguing that only defeat would produce the conditions necessary to topple the Provisional Government.

The failure of the great Russian offensive in July 1917 helped to bring about the conditions Lenin desired. The ensuing disintegration of the army enabled the Germans to capture Riga, in Latvia, on September 3, thereby leaving the road to the Russian capital, only some three hundred miles distant, wide open. Six days later, General Lavr Kornilov, the commander-in-chief of the Russian army, tried to reverse the military collapse by staging a coup against the government of Alexander Kerensky, a moderate socialist who had replaced Prince Lvov as prime minister on August 6. Kornilov's attempted coup failed only because the Bolshevik-dominated Red Guards, as well as soldiers and sailors loyal to the Petrograd soviet, came to Kerensky's rescue and prevented Kornilov's troops from marching on the city. Kerensky responded by formally proclaiming a Russian republic on September 27. But the gesture proved to be a case of too little and too late. Deserted by the army, deprived of real authority in the cities by the increasingly pro-Bolshevik soviets, and bypassed by the peasantry, which began to seize land without governmental authorization, Kerensky's government quickly became irrelevant.

The government's demise was assisted by the Allies, who would not allow the Provisional Government to take Russia out of the war out of fear that this would enable the Germans to transfer millions of troops to the western front. In so doing, the Allies allowed the Bolsheviks to retain a major weapon with which they continued to attack Kerensky. While the United States did not directly participate in the Allied pressure to revive the eastern front, both President Wilson and Secretary of State Robert Lansing were confident that they could keep Russia in the war. With this end in mind, in June they sent a commission headed by former Secretary of State Elihu Root to assure Russia of continued American support. In the same month, the administration also dispatched a team of experts, under the direction of John F. Stevens, to help keep Russia's railroads running. In addition, the American Red Cross and the Young Men's Christian Association undertook humanitarian programs in Russia. But none of these steps could halt the deterioration of social and economic conditions that the war had aggravated. In the end, the refusal of the Provisional Government to terminate Russian participation in the war was directly responsible for its overthrow by the Bolsheviks on November 7, 1917.

The Bolshevik Revolution

On November 8, one day after the overthrow of the Provisional Government, the second All-Russian Congress of Soviets (without the representatives of the moderate parties, who had walked out of the congress the previous day) approved the formation of the Council of Peoples' Commissars, with Lenin as chairman, Leon Trotsky as commissar for foreign affairs, and a little-known Georgian, Josef (Vissarionovich Djugashvili) Stalin, as commissar of nationalities. The congress also unanimously approved a decree abolishing private ownership of the soil and another calling for the immediate opening of peace negotiations with the Germans. On November 20 the new Soviet government proposed an immediate armistice with the Central Powers. One week later, a preliminary cease-fire was signed between Russia and its enemies. The two sides agreed to begin negotiations for a formal peace treaty at Brest-Litovsk in Poland on December 22.

The Bolsheviks attempted to place on the Allies the entire blame for the separate peace these negotiations eventually produced. On November 27 Trotsky demanded that the Allies "declare, clearly, precisely, and definitely in the name of what aims must the nations of Europe shed their blood during the fourth year of the war."[2] He then defiantly announced the publication of the incriminating secret treaties that the Allies had concluded with the czarist regime. The treaties called for massive cessions of territory by the Central Powers and, had Russia been victorious, would have given it control of the strategic Straits of the Bosporus and Dardanelles, which connect the Black and Mediterranean Seas. Trotsky then invited the Allies to participate in the Brest-Litovsk negotiations, believing that their refusal to do so would trigger the world revolution the Bolsheviks believed was imminent.

The Wilson administration was stunned by the turn of events in Russia. On December 2, the day the Brest-Litovsk talks began, Secretary of State Lansing wrote Wilson a memorandum in which he stated that the Bolshevik faction was of such a nature politically and ideologically that it was impossible to extend recognition to it. The Bolsheviks were characterized, Lansing asserted, by "a determination, frankly avowed, to overthrow all existing governments and establish on their ruins a despotism of the proletariat in every country."[3] To recognize the Bolsheviks, he warned, would be to encourage their followers in other countries.

Wilson fully agreed with Lansing on the issue of recognizing the Soviet government. He regarded the Bolshevik regime as a demonic conspiracy that had destroyed the democratic promise of the Provisional Government. And he found particularly offensive its doctrine of class warfare, the dictatorship of the proletariat, its suppression of civil liberties, and its hostility toward private property. Like Lansing, Wilson believed that Bolshevism could not long survive in Russia or anywhere else. Nor could Wilson accept the Bolshevik invitation to participate in the Brest-Litivosk negotiations, arguing that the Allies could not conclude a "premature peace" before German "autocracy had been taught its final and convincing lesson."[4]

Yet neither Wilson nor Lansing was content to follow the "do-nothing" policy the secretary of state had recommended in his December 2 memorandum. As their support for the Provisional Government had demonstrated, both men were most eager to keep Russia in the war, to prevent the Germans from transferring substantial numbers of troops to France before the American Expeditionary Force (then mobilizing under General John J. Pershing) was ready to deal with them. This objective became even more important after the Bolsheviks and the Central Powers signed a preliminary armistice at Brest-Litovsk on December 15. Lansing concluded that the only hope for keeping Russia in the war, and thereby avoiding a prolonging of the conflict by two or three years, was "a military dictatorship backed by loyal disciplined troops."[5] On December 10 he suggested that the United States help General Alexis M. Kaledin, the leader of the Don Cossacks, play this role.

From the first, Wilson was opposed to direct American involvement in the Russian civil war. His caution was prompted by recollection of his decision to intervene in the Mexican civil war in 1914. Mexicans of all political persuasions had responded to the intervention by rallying around their previously unpopular government in order to oppose American "imperialism." The Mexican experience made Wilson highly sensitive to the negative consequences of intervening in the domestic affairs of other nations. Nevertheless, despite his high regard for the principle of self-determination, Wilson did not consider the Soviet government as representing the will of the Russian people. Moreover, Wilson believed, giving clandestine assistance to Kaledin would serve the purpose of keeping Russia in the war, without committing the United States to direct involvement in its civil war. It was this consideration influenced the president when he met with Lansing on December 11 and agreed to give financial assistance to Kaledin. Since the administration had no legal authority to aid an unrecognized political regime, Wilson and Lansing decided to lend the money to the British or the French and let them pass it on to Kaledin. But before Kaledin could receive this assistance, he was deposed by his own troops, on January 28, 1918.

In late December 1917, before Kaledin was overthrown, Britain and France, who were encouraged by the United States' willingness to support Kaledin, concluded a secret bilateral convention that specifically defined the geographic areas in southern Russia in which they would assist the anti-Bolshevik forces. The British were allotted the Transcaucasus and North Caucasus regions, while Bessarabia, Ukraine, and the Crimea were given to the French. While there is no evidence indicating that the U.S. government was formally consulted about the Anglo-French convention, Washington was informed of the general nature of the Allied agreement and apparently made no objection to it. In effect, the Allies, with the tacit support of the United States, entered the Russian civil war on the side of the opponents of the Bolsheviks.

The Fourteen Points

Not everyone, however, believed that it was impossible for the West to work with the Bolsheviks. Among those who believed that Allied and Bolshevik cooperation was possible were William Boyce Thompson, the head of the American Red Cross mission in Russia and his assistant, Major (later Colonel) Raymond Robins. While directing the Red Cross assistance program to Russia, Thompson and Robins had been serving as surreptitious American conduits to Kerensky's government, as well as to the opposition Social Revolutionary Party. After Kerensky's overthrow, Robins, without authorization from Washington, began talking to Trotsky. As a result of their discussions, Robins, as well as Thompson, was led to believe that it was possible, even after the Brest-Litovsk negotiations had begun, to keep Russia in the war and on the side of the Allies.

After the Brest-Litovsk talks broke off on December 29 (because the Bolsheviks wanted the negotiations relocated to a neutral site), the U.S. ambassador in Petrograd, David R. Francis, came to the same conclusion reached by Robins and Thompson. On January 2, 1918, Francis approved a memorandum to Robins permitting him to inform Lenin and Trotsky that "if the Russian armies now under the command of the people's commissaries commence and seriously conduct hostilities against the forces of Germany and her allies," he would recommend to Washington that the United States grant formal recognition to the Soviet government.[6] However, Francis never sent the memorandum to Robins, apparently because he could not obtain State Department authorization to do so. On January 8 the Bolsheviks returned to Brest-Litovsk to resume peace negotiations with the Germans.

That day Wilson delivered his famous Fourteen Points peace plan to a joint session of Congress. The address was designed not only to counter the Bolsheviks' call for a general armistice but also, by offering the terms of an ostensibly just peace, to promote the overthrow of the Kaiser's government. In addition, the Fourteen Points were designed to create a world characterized by greater economic interdependence, that is, one open to unrestricted flows of trade and investment. The president's plan attempted to supersede Trotsky's publication of the secret Allied treaties by demanding "Open Covenants of peace, openly arrived at."[7] In addition, Wilson was anxious to preserve Russia's right of self-determination and territorial integrity. Here, the president had as much to fear from his allies as he did his enemies. Not only, were the Allies supporting reactionary "White" (anti-Bolshevik) leaders, but the British and the Japanese were not adverse to the idea of breaking up Russia in order to advance their own respective imperial agendas. Point six of the Fourteen Points specifically addressed this threat. It called for the withdrawal of all foreign troops from Russia and recognized the right of the Russian people to determine their own government.

Although those who advocated cooperation with the Bolsheviks thought that Wilson's reference to Russia "under institutions of her own choosing" indicated a retreat from the administration's nonrecognition policy, the president still did not regard the Soviet government as representing the will of the Russian people. This impression was reinforced after the Bolsheviks, on January 20, 1918, dissolved the Russian Constituent Assembly, which had been elected the previous November to create a permanent, representative government for Russia. The Bolsheviks decided to dissolve the assembly primarily because they had won only 168 of the 703 seats contested in the election.

In a further slap at Western values, on February 10, 1918, the Bolsheviks repudiated all debts to the Allies that had been incurred by the previous Russian governments, including the money extended to the Provisional Government by the United States. On January 20, 1918, Wilson wrote Lansing that fidelity to debts should be a requirement for recognizing any Russian government.[8] In the same month, the Bolsheviks began to remove Allied war supplies from Archangel, a major port in northern Russia. Allied efforts to regain these supplies, which had never been paid for by the Provisional Government, ended in failure. As a result of these actions by the Bolsheviks, Wilson concluded that they were irresponsible and untrustworthy.

The Treaty of Brest-Litovsk

In the meantime, the peace talks between the Bolsheviks and Central Powers at Brest-Litovsk continued to run into difficulties. The Germans demanded that the Soviet government renounce Russian sovereignty over Poland, Lithuania, and most of Latvia, and recognize the independence of Finland and Ukraine. Finding it impossible either to accept the German peace conditions or to resume hostilities, Trotsky announced to an astonished world on February 10 that the Soviet government was walking out of the war as well as the Brest-Litovsk talks. The Germans quickly brought the Bolsheviks back to reality. On February 16 they terminated the armistice and, two days later, resumed their virtually unhindered advance toward Petrograd and Kiev.

The resumption of the German offensive quickly brought the panic-stricken Bolsheviks back to their senses. On February 19 they announced that they were prepared to accept the German peace terms. On March 3 they signed the Brest-Litovsk Treaty. In doing so, the Bolsheviks accepted the loss of 780,000 square kilometers of territory formerly held by the Russian empire. The treaty also reduced Russia's population by 56 million people, its railway network by one-third of its former length, its iron ore production by 73 percent, and its coal supply by 89 percent.

The Bolsheviks' signatures on the peace treaty did not end Russia's humiliation, however, for the Germans continued their military offensive, in the process gobbling up additional territories once held by the Russian empire. Having taken Kiev on March 1, the Germans continued their advance across the Ukraine, captured the Crimea in late April, and reached the Don River near Rostov in early May. The German conquest of the Ukraine exposed the entire southern flank of greater Russia, and left vulnerable to German attack the city of Moscow, which the Bolsheviks made the new capital of Russia on March 6. In the north, German troops landed in Finland on April 3 and helped the Finns clear their country of Bolshevik forces. As a result, the Russian northern front became as vulnerable to German attack as its southern flank.

The Last Chance for Allied-Soviet Collaboration

During the weeks before the Bolsheviks returned to Brest-Litovsk, Allied representatives in Russia continued to receive indications that the Bolsheviks might resume hostilities with the Central Powers if they could count on meaningful Allied military support. On January 28, 1918, Captain E. Francis Riggs, the U.S. assistant military attaché in Petrograd, cabled that the Bolshevik leaders appeared to feel that "the three powers— the United States, Britain, and France—should be tolerated in order to be used against Germany."[9] On February 18, after the Germans resumed their offensive in Russia, the French military attaché, Jacques Sadoul, was able to persuade his government to reverse—if only temporarily—its hostile policy toward the Bolsheviks and to accept his argument that Allied cooperation with them offered the only realistic possibility of maintaining an eastern front against Germany. Sadoul was authorized to approach the

Bolsheviks to determine if there was in fact any basis for bringing Russia back into the war.

The French government also asked the United States if it would join France in collaborating with Lenin and Trotsky. Lansing personally took the French request to President Wilson. Lansing's brief, penciled notation on the document revealed their mutual disgust with the French request: "This is out of the question. Submitted to [President] who says the same thing."[10] Although both men were obviously interested in reestablishing the eastern front, they were not prepared to do so by supporting the Bolsheviks. Lansing emphasized that the Bolsheviks were ultimately more dangerous to American security than were the Germans, since Bolshevism denied both nationality and property rights and threatened to spread revolution worldwide.

Uninformed about Wilson's decision, Raymond Robins nevertheless continued to pressure the Bolsheviks to cooperate with the Allies. By late February 1918 his efforts appeared to be close to fruition. On February 22 the Bolshevik Central Committee voted 6 to 5 to accept an offer of military assistance from France and Britain (with Lenin casting the crucial vote). The Bolshevik leader apparently was convinced that Germany was determined to crush Russia and destroy the revolution, and, while he did not trust the West, he felt that the Allies were likely to help Russia if only to revive the eastern front. Consequently, on March 2, the eve of the signing of the Brest-Litovsk Treaty, Lenin prepared for the possibility of resuming the war with Germany. He issued an order to delay the demobilization of the Russian army and intensified preparations for blowing up railways, bridges, and roads that could be used by the Germans.

Even the Bolshevik signature on the Brest-Litovsk Treaty the next day did not preclude the possibility of Russia reentering the war, since the treaty had to be ratified by the Central Committee of the Bolshevik Party and then by the Congress of Soviets. The Bolsheviks attempted to take advantage of the time this required by intensifying their efforts to get Allied assistance. On March 4 Trotsky sent a message to Ambassador Francis stating that, even if the peace treaty were ratified, hostilities between Russia and the Central Powers would resume in April or May. Trotsky wanted to know what help Russia could count on from the Allies. In response, Francis authorized Colonel James A. Ruggles, the U.S. military attaché, to go to Petrograd, along with Captain Riggs, to discuss the possibility of American military assistance to Russia. Two days later, on March 8, Ruggles and Riggs reported back to Francis that "all Bolshevik leaders were of the opinion that they must make war on Germany—only differences of opinion were whether it should be tomorrow or today. The question of ratification of peace was really immaterial."[11] The same day, the Central Committee voted 30 to 12, with four abstentions, to accept the treaty of peace with the Central Powers.

On March 5 Robins also saw Trotsky. The Bolshevik leader handed him an unsigned document that asked how much support the Soviet government could expect from the Allies against Germany "particularly and especially from the United States." Later in the day, Robins saw Lenin, who indicated that he approved Trotsky's questionnaire. However, while Robins was certain that the Bolsheviks were ready to enter the war on the Allied side, it seems more likely that they were only gauging the extent of Allied interest in that possibility, rather than making a definite commitment to implement it. In fact, Trotsky's document contained a statement, probably drafted by Lenin, that seemed to rule out any possibility of Allied-Bolshevik collaboration. It said that all questions raised in the document were "conditioned with the self-understood assumption that the international and foreign policies of the Soviet Government will continue to be directed in accord with the principles of international socialism and that the Soviet Government retains its complete independence of all non-socialist governments."[12]

However, instead of collaborating with the Bolsheviks, Wilson decided to go over their heads with a direct appeal to the Russian people. On March 11, 1918, he sent a message to the Congress of Soviets in which he bluntly told the Russian people that the United States, despite its great sympathy for their travail, was "unhappily not . . . in a position to render the direct and effective aid it would wish to render."[13] The implication of Wilson's message was that the Bolsheviks were in league with the Germans. When Trotsky's March 5 document finally reached Washington (on March 16), the State Department responded by stating that it considered Wilson's message to the Russian people an "adequate answer" to the questions it contained.[14]

After Wilson's message was read to the Soviet Congress on March 15, that body passed a resolution advocating the overthrow of all bourgeoisie governments, including that of the United States. Commenting on the resolution's passage, one Bolshevik leader, Gregory Zinoviev, said: "We slapped the President of the United States in the face."[15] On March 17 the Soviet Congress ratified the Brest-Litovsk Treaty by a vote of 784 to 261.

Given the vast ideological gulf that divided the Bolsheviks and the Allies, there was little possibility of even a limited collaboration between them. Nor was there any chance, even if the Allies had been inclined to help, of rendering effective assistance to the Bolsheviks given the distances involved and the Allied preoccupation with the Germans on the western front. Lenin fully realized this, and, more importantly, he knew that he had much more to fear from the far more proximate German military power. Moreover, Lenin realized that peace and immediate land reform were the only ways to maintain peasant support for his regime. Given these considerations, there was little likelihood, short of a German attack on Moscow or Petrograd, that the Bolsheviks would make a commitment to the Allied cause. Nevertheless, Lenin and Trotsky tried to keep their Allied option alive, not only because the Germans might attack the Russian heartland but also because the Allies might intervene directly on behalf of the Bolsheviks' White opponents.

Allied Pressure for Intervention

Lenin had every reason to fear the prospect of Allied intervention. The conclusion of the Brest-Litovsk Treaty coincided with the launching of an all-out German offensive in the west on March 21, which was designed to divide the British and French armies and thereby carry the Germans to the sea. In the following forty days the British army, which bore the brunt of the German attack, suffered 300,000 casualties, more than a fourth of its entire strength. The German offensive was not blunted until mid-June, when the full weight of the American Expeditionary Force finally came into play and threw the Germans onto the defensive. Until then, the fate of the Allied armies in France hung by a thread, thus contributing to the belief that even a token revival of resistance in the east might spell the difference between victory and defeat.

As a way of reviving the eastern front, the Allies had been pressuring the United States since December 1917 to permit the Japanese to intervene in Siberia, by way of the port of Vladivostok. Japanese intervention ostensibly would prevent Allied supplies located in that city from falling into Bolshevik hands. Japanese expansionists, who were strongest in the army and the foreign office, saw the Bolshevik Revolution as a splendid opportunity to expand Japanese control of Manchuria, and possibly eastern Siberia as well. When disorder broke out in Vladivostok in early January 1918, both the Japanese and the British sent warships to the city, ostensibly to protect foreign property and their nationals. But Japanese Foreign Minister Viscount Motono Ichiro really did not want British or other Allied assistance at Vladivostok. On January 15 he informed the American ambassador in Tokyo, Roland S. Morris, that if it became necessary to occupy Vladivostok and the Chinese Eastern Railway, "Japan asks that this task be left to her alone."[16]

The Wilson administration was extremely apprehensive about the prospect of unilateral Japanese intervention in Siberia. Both the president and Lansing feared that it would not only endanger Russia's territorial integrity—and thereby drive the Bolsheviks into the arms of the Germans—but also possibly the Open Door policy in China, which attempted to preserve China's independence and territorial integrity, as well as the right of all nations to trade with and invest in China. Japan had already taken advantage of the war in Europe to force China to accept twenty-one exorbitant demands that threatened to destroy China's economic and political integrity. And although Japan had promised to uphold the Open Door in the Lansing-Ishii understanding of November 1917 (in exchange for a vague recognition by the United States of Japan's "special interest" in Manchuria and China), neither Lansing nor Wilson completely trusted the Japanese. Consequently, the administration refused to accept Japan's right to intervene unilaterally in Siberia. If Allied intervention in Siberia should become necessary—and neither Wilson nor Lansing at this point believed it was—then, the British were informed, it should "be undertaken by international cooperation and not by any one power acting as the mandatory of the others."[17]

In late February, however, the administration temporarily bowed to Anglo-French pressure and reversed its opposition to Japanese intervention in Siberia. To Lansing, it seemed inevitable that the Japanese were going to intervene regardless of American protests, and he believed it might be wiser to make Japan a mandatory of the Allies rather than to watch it act unilaterally. Swayed by Lansing's argument, Wilson, on March 1, 1918, reluctantly approved a message to the Allies stating that the United States "assures the Japanese government that it has entire confidence that, in putting an armed force into Siberia, it is doing so as an ally of Russia, with no purpose but to save Siberia from the invasion of the armies and intrigues of Germany, and with entire willingness to leave the determination of all questions that may affect the permanent fortunes of Siberia to the Council of Peace."[18]

Wilson's turnabout shocked his confidante and chief diplomatic adviser Colonel Edward House, who was appalled by the ethical implications of appearing to give the Japanese a foothold in Siberia. Emphasizing the moral argument, House was able to persuade the president to reverse himself once again. As a result, Wilson canceled the dispatch of his March 1 note and substituted another one on March 5. The new note stated that "the wisdom of intervention seems . . . most questionable." If undertaken, it would "appear that Japan was doing in the East exactly what Germany is doing in the West."[19]

Allied Intervention Begins

Wilson's refusal to approve Japanese intervention did not mean that he had abandoned the hope of influencing events in Russia. Far from it, on March 14 he told Lord Reading, the British ambassador, that he was "endeavoring to find a way both to reconcile [the] American people to the need for intervention and to allay Russian fears of it."[20]

The British were more than eager to find a way to bring this about. And in their attempt to do so, they received unexpected assistance from Germany. After the Germans resumed hostilities with Russia in late February, anti-Bolshevik Finns, supported by Germany, were reported to have crossed the Finnish border into Russian territory west of the northern port of Murmansk. Faced with this new German threat, the Murmansk soviet appealed to Trotsky for help on March 1. In response, Trotsky, with Lenin's approval, informed the Murmansk soviet that it was "obliged to accept any help from the Allied missions."[21] Consequently, the next day, the Murmansk soviet concluded a mutual defense agreement with the British and the French. It permitted the British to land 200 marines at Murmansk on March 6. This step was the beginning of direct Allied military intervention in Soviet Russia, and it came at the invitation of the Soviet government. The British, seeking American support for this venture, requested the participation of a U.S. warship at Murmansk and pointed out to Wilson that Trotsky had requested the Allies to intervene.

Wilson was in sympathy with the Allied mission to Murmansk. On April 4 he agreed to dispatch an American cruiser, the *Olympia,* to the port after learning that Trotsky had requested Allied intervention. Yet he was not yet ready to send American troops to Murmansk. U.S. military intervention, he realized, would risk not only driving the Bolsheviks into the arms of the Germans but also alienating American support for the war by widening the breach in the nation's isolationist tradition caused by its intervention in the European war.

The British, however, did not give up. They devised a new plan, which proposed Allied intervention in Siberia, by way of the port of Vladivostok, as well as in northern Russia. While British and French forces would occupy Murmansk and Archangel, the Japanese would bear the main military burden at Vladivostok. Eventually, it was hoped, the eastern front would be reconstituted as Anglo-French forces from the north of Russia linked up with anti-Bolshevik armies in the south and east of Russia as well as Japanese troops advancing from Vladivostok. It was obvious to the British that Wilson would never support such an elaborate plan of intervention, but they apparently believed he could be pulled into it piecemeal, as indeed he eventually was.

To secure Wilson's support for this scheme, the British and French proposed, as a substitute for unilateral Japanese intervention in Siberia, an inter-Allied expedition to Vladivostok, one that would include U.S. and British forces as well as those of Japan. In this way, they hoped to overcome not only Bolshevik objections to Allied military action in Siberia but Wilson's opposition as well. The Japanese government, which rejected Motono's earlier call for unilateral Japanese intervention, cooperated with the Anglo-French scheme by agreeing to participate in the inter-Allied expedition. Nevertheless, the Japanese reserved the right to intervene unilaterally if their national interests were endangered. In such an event, the Japanese informed the State Department, they were confident that they could "count on the friendly support of the American Government in the struggle which may be forced upon them."[22] In spite of this loophole in the Japanese position, on March 20 Wilson instructed Ambassador Morris to tell the Japanese government that their response was "most gratifying" and that it removed any possibility of misunderstanding "which might otherwise arise."[23]

Only two weeks later, the Japanese took advantage of the loophole in their nonintervention promise to Wilson. On April 4 several Russian soldiers shot and killed three Japanese civilians in Vladivostok. The next day, without the approval of his government, the Japanese naval commander at Vladivostok put 500 men ashore to protect Japanese civilians and property in the city. The British followed suit the same day by putting 50 men ashore to guard their consular establishment. On April 8 the British ambassador, Lord Reading, urged Lansing to order the U.S. cruiser *Brooklyn,* which was anchored in Vladivostok harbor, to deploy ashore its contingent of marines. Lansing, who discussed the issue with Wilson the next day, refused to do so, arguing that "the state of affairs in Russia proper is . . . against such a policy."[24] And this remained the administration's position all through the month of April.

The Bolsheviks quite naturally regarded the Anglo-Japanese landings at Vladivostok as the first step in a more expansive plan for the Allied occupation of eastern Siberia. On April 5 the new Soviet foreign minister, Georgii Chicherin, demanded an explanation of the Allies' intentions. Without authorization from Washington, Ambassador Francis announced on April 9 that the Anglo-Japanese landing at Vladivostok was simply a precautionary move by the Japanese and British authorities at Vladivostok and was "not a concerted action between the Allies."[25]

The Japanese nevertheless were offended by the ambassador's implication that the move did not have the support of the United States. Francis was reprimanded for his unauthorized statement, but it was not disavowed by Washington. The fact is, the United States tried to persuade the Japanese to withdraw their marines from Valdivostok. Nevertheless, years later, Stalinist-Soviet historians, pointing to the presence of the *Brooklyn* in Vladivostok harbor, would portray the United States as one of the instigators of the landing.

The Road to American Intervention

In spite of the refusal of the United States to participate in the landings at Vladivostok, the British did not give up their effort to secure American intervention in Russia. On April 8 they presented a draft note to the Supreme Allied War Council, calling for joint intervention in Russia to prevent Allied military supplies stored at Murmansk and Archangel from falling into German hands. However, the British effort was blocked by the U.S. military representative, General Tasker H. Bliss. As a result, in mid-April the British War Cabinet decided to send a military mission of their own to Murmansk for the express purpose of preparing for "cooperation in any Allied intervention in Russia."[26] But the British quickly realized that they did not have sufficient resources of their own to make the mission effective. Consequently, on April 17 the British War Cabinet approved a plan to transfer to northern Russia 20,000 troops of the Czechoslovak Legion, a force of some 70,000 men who had been taken prisoner by the Russians, or had deserted from the Austro-Hungarian army, and who had been fighting in Russia on the Allied side. On May 2 the Supreme War Council approved the British plan.

Confronted with increasing British pressure, American opposition to Allied intervention in northern Russia began to weaken. On May 11 Lansing told Lord Reading that action at Murmansk and Archangel would receive "far more favorable consideration" on the part of the United States than intervention in Siberia, primarily because the former offered military advantages to the Allies, while the latter did not.[27] After being informed about this conversation, Wilson responded on May 20 by agreeing that the two regions had to be treated differently, but he still opposed intervention in either. In defending his position, Wilson relied on the argumentation of General Peyton C. March, the chief of the Army's general staff: "(1) that no force strong enough to amount to anything can be sent to Murmansk without subtracting just that much shipping and man power from the western front, and (2) that such a subtraction at the present crisis would be most unwise. . . ."[28]

The British still did not give up. On May 28 British Foreign Secretary Arthur Balfour sent Wilson a note in which he called American assistance "essential" to the success of the mission to Murmansk and vital as a demonstration of Allied unity.[29] Balfour's plea was reinforced by alarming, but erroneous, messages from Ambassador Francis on May 29 and May 30 to the effect that the Finns had cut the Murmansk Railway. On June 1, one day after receiving Balfour's message, Wilson met with Lansing and agreed to send U.S. troops to Murmansk, provided such a diversion of Allied resources was approved by Allied Supreme Commander General Ferdinand Foch. On June 3 the Supreme War Council quickly took advantage of Wilson's concession and formally called for intervention in northern Russia. On June 17 Foch approved the mission. Yet it was not until the end of June that Wilson agreed to the size of the U.S. military contribution, that is, three battalions of infantry, or some 5,700 troops, far fewer than the Supreme War Council had requested. Although Wilson still had serious misgivings about his decision, he finally had decided to take the plunge into Russia.

Wilson's cave-in on intervention was prompted primarily by his growing concern that a revival of the eastern front was necessary to prevent the imminent collapse of the western front. On May 27 the Germans launched a new offensive on the western front. In less than a week they were able to break through the Allied lines and advance to Chateau Thierry, on the Marne River, not far from Paris. With the French preparing to abandon their capital, the president appreciated, more than ever, the advantage the Germans possessed by having a relatively inactive Russian front on their rear. For Wilson, action in Russia now had become a psychological and political necessity. He desperately needed a large intervention force to prevent the Germans from transferring an additional forty divisions to the western front.

Throughout April and May, Wilson had tried to get as much information as possible about the anti-Bolshevik groups in Siberia. While he still opposed direct U.S. military intervention in Siberia, as his support for Kaledin had demonstrated, he clearly was willing to assist indirectly the indigenous forces opposing the Bolsheviks. On April 18 he wrote Lansing: "I would very much value a memorandum containing *all* that we know about these several *nuclei* of self-governing authority that seem to be springing up in Siberia. It would afford me a great deal of satisfaction to get behind the most nearly representative of them if it can indeed draw leadership and control to itself."[30]

Wilson was prepared to assist the anti-Bolshevik forces even if it could not be determined whether they had the overwhelming support of the Russian people. On May 29 he told a British diplomat, Sir William Wiseman, that he was willing to intervene, even in opposition to the wishes of the Russian people if it was for their own eventual good. "If we could have put a large British-American force into Vladivostok, and advanced along the Siberian railway," the president told Wiseman, "we might . . . have rallied the Russian people to assist in the defense of their country." But Wilson did not believe the Allies could afford to divert forces from the western front for this purpose. He also feared that Japanese intervention in Siberia would simply drive the Russians into the arms of the Germans. When Wiseman asked the president if this meant that the Allies should "do nothing at all," Wilson replied: "No. We must watch the situation carefully and sympathetically, and be ready to move whenever the right time arrived."[31]

Then, on June 2, Wilson received the break he had been hoping for. News arrived that fighting had broken out between the Bolsheviks and the Czechoslovak Legion. In mid-March, after the Treaty of Brest-Litivosk had been signed, the Czechoslovaks received Bolshevik permission to withdraw to Vladivostok by way of the Trans-Siberian Railway. Nevertheless, fighting erupted between the two forces on May 26, after the Czechoslovaks rejected a Bolshevik demand that they disarm first before moving to Vladivostok. Anti-Bolshevik elements quickly rallied to the Czechoslovaks, and by the end of June their combined forces had brought most of Siberia east of the Ural Mountains under their control. By June 17, Wilson saw the Czechoslovaks, whom he called "the cousins of the Russians," as a strong, effective force that he could legitimately support "with Japanese and other assistance" against the Germans, as well as the Bolsheviks, and he thought he could do so without alienating the Russian masses.[32]

On July 3 the Czechoslovaks captured Vladivostok by ousting the Bolshevik forces in the city. This action offered the Allies a secure base for operations in Siberia. The previous day, the Supreme War Council had appealed to the president to approve the immediate dispatch of 100,000 Allied troops to Vladivostok. It listed three objectives for the mission: (1) to enable the Russians "to throw off their German oppressors," (2) "to reconstitute the Russian front," and (3) "to bring assistance to the Czechosolvak forces."[33]

On July 6, Wilson informed Lansing, Secretary of War Newton D. Baker, Secretary of the Navy Josephus Daniels, Admiral William Benson (the Chief of Naval Operations), and General March that he had decided to propose to the Japanese government a joint Japanese-American expedition to Vladivostok. But instead of the 100,000 troops proposed by the Supreme War Council, Wilson limited the contribution of each nation to 7,000 troops. They ostensibly would guard the line of communications of the Vladivostok Czechoslovaks as they advanced westward to rescue their comrades, who were trapped by the Bolsheviks at Irkutsk. The British and French, who obviously wanted a far more expansive intervention than Wilson desired, would not be invited to participate in the expedition.

Only General March argued against the mission. He pointed out that there was no way to reconstitute Russia into a military machine and that the only purpose intervention would serve would be to give the Japanese a foothold in Siberia.[34] Wilson admitted that it was physically impossible to reestablish an eastern front against the Germans, but he was willing to risk the possibility of Japanese aggrandizement at Russia's expense to support the Czechoslovaks and to maintain Allied unity. He evidently believed that there was less risk that the Japanese would overrun Siberia if they intervened with the United States than if they did so alone.

Wilson's decision was subsequently restated, in his own typewritten words, in an *aide-mémoire* that was presented to the Allied envoys in Washington on July 17. Portions of the president's statement were released to the press in paraphrased form on August 3. In it, Wilson stated: "Military action is admissible in Russia . . . only to help the Czechoslovaks get their forces into successful cooperation with their Slavic kinsmen and to steady any efforts at self-government or self-defense in which the Russians themselves may be willing to accept assistance." He added: "Whether from Vladivostok or from Murmansk and Archangel, the only legitimate object for which American or Allied troops can be employed . . . is to guard military stores which may subsequently be needed by Russian forces and to render such aid as may be acceptable to the Russians in the organization of their own self-defense." In a warning to the Allies, Wilson added that any other plan inconsistent with these limited objectives would oblige the United States to withdraw its forces from Russia. He also stated that he had asked the Allies to give "the most public and solemn" assurances that they did not contemplate "any interference of any kind with the political sovereignty of Russia, any intervention in her internal affairs, or any impairment of her territorial integrity either now or hereafter."[35] Wilson said nothing at this point—although he would later—about evacuating the Czechoslovaks from Russia. On August 20 he deferred "a consideration of the future movements of the Czechoslovaks, whether eastward to France or westward to Russia, until after eastern Siberia had been cleared of enemies."[36]

The president's memorandum left unsaid that the American forces would be guarding the supply lines of not only the Czechoslovaks but also their "Slavic kinsmen," that is, the anti-Bolshevik forces who were fighting along side them. Moreover, it was clear that the arms and ammunition that the United States was sending the Czechoslovaks would also find their way to the Whites. Wilson obviously realized this and accepted it. As the earlier Kaledin episode indicated, Wilson was prepared to support the effort to bring about "self-government" in Russia, which, in his opinion, the Bolsheviks did not represent. But he was not prepared to use U.S. troops to do the Whites' fighting for them.

Needless to say, the president did not seek Soviet permission to send U.S. military forces to Russia. On July 29, after Allied ambassadors had left Russia—an action the Soviets interpreted as the prelude to war—the Soviet Central Executive Committee passed a resolution declaring "the socialist fatherland in danger" and calling on the "toiling masses" in the Allied countries to stop the military intervention in Russia by their governments.[37] In effect, the Allies and the Soviets had entered a de facto state of war.

Wilson's effort to limit Allied intervention in Russia began to fall apart almost immediately. The British and French were offended by the president's failure to inform them of his decision, and they had no intention of being excluded from the operation. The British ordered a battalion stationed in Hong Kong to go to Vladivostok, and the French simply declared that they considered the Czechoslovak Legion an integral part of the French army. The Chinese and Italians also sent detachments to Vladivostok. The scale of the Allied intervention clearly had become more than Wilson had intended, though it still was far short of the size desired by the Allies.

More ominously, the Japanese also refused to comply with the limitation Wilson sought to place on the expedition to Vladivostok. Instead of observing the 7,000-troop ceiling set by the president, the Japanese government, on July 24, proposed to send to Vladivostok an entire division (approximately 12,000 men) and additional troops later if they were needed. Equally portentous were Japanese references to their "special position" in Siberia. Irked by the Japanese response, which he believed would create the impression that the Allies were interfering in Russia's internal affairs, Wilson threatened to cancel U.S. participation in the expedition. But he could not abandon the Czechoslovaks. Consequently, he accepted a purposely vague Japanese promise to maintain "harmony" with their allies and decided to go ahead with the expedition, undoubtedly hoping that the presence of U.S. troops at Vladivostok would serve to restrain Japanese ambitions in Siberia.[38] The first U.S. troops landed at Vladivostok on August 16 and at Archangel on September 4, 1918.

The War in Russia

Now that Japan's intervention in Siberia had Wilson's blessing, the Japanese military, which hoped to use the expedition as a way of expanding its hold on Manchuria, quickly imposed its own agenda on the Japanese government. The government approved the army's recommendation to send an independent Japanese force to protect the Manchurian border against an alleged invasion of Chinese territory by Bolsheviks and organized German war prisoners, the occurrence of which the Chinese government emphatically denied. By August 21 the Japanese had stationed 12,000 troops along the Chinese Eastern Railway. By the middle of September, the Japanese had some 62,000 troops in Siberia and in northern Manchuria.

Wilson did everything he could to restrain the Japanese. Viscount Ishii Kikujiro was informed of the president's displeasure with the size of the Japanese military buildup. At the same time, Wilson also placed the general direction of the Trans-Siberian and Chinese Eastern Railroads in the hands of an American, John Stevens, the director of the Russian Railway Service Corps. In addition, Wilson, who initially had forbidden General William S. Graves, the commander of the American Siberian Expeditionary Force, to advance beyond Vladivostok, now agreed to a Chinese request to permit U.S. troops to advance to Harbin in Manchuria. The move was made ostensibly to expedite the eastward movement of the Czechoslovaks, but it obviously served to curb Japanese ambitions in Manchuria as well. And, needless to say, maintaining the railroads of eastern Siberia also served to supply the forces fighting the Bolsheviks as well.

While the Japanese were attempting to carve out a sphere of influence in Siberia, the British and French pursued their own agenda in northern Russia. General Frederick Poole, the British commander at Murmansk, drew up a plan for an invasion of northern Russia by 5,000 Allied troops, which he predicted would be quickly joined by some 100,000 anti-Bolshevik Russians. As the first step in Poole's plan, on August 1 an Allied flotilla sailed into Archangel harbor with some 600 British troops, one French colonial battalion, and (without Wilson's foreknowledge) the U.S.S. *Olympia*. Quickly routing the Bolshevik garrison, Poole's force advanced 140 miles to the south within one week, without encountering any significant opposition.

As soon as the American units (commanded by Colonel George E. Stewart) arrived at Archangel on September 4, Poole immediately dispatched them to the front, where they became involved in a number of small-scale engagements with Soviet forces, again without the foreknowledge of the president. However, when the Supreme War Council received a request from Poole for additional troops on September 2, General Bliss, the American representative, responded negatively. Wilson supported Bliss's decision. On September 26 Lansing sent a circular note to the major Allied governments in which he insisted that "all military effort in northern Russia be given up except guarding of the ports themselves and as much of the country round about them as may develop threatening conditions. . . . No more American troops will be sent to the northern ports."[39]

In spite of the note's categorical tone, U.S. troops remained prominent on the front in northern Russia, where they continued to engage Bolshevik forces in sporadic clashes. In response, the United States government protested vigorously and demanded the replacement of General Poole. Giving in to the American pressure, the British recalled Poole on October 14 and replaced him with a distinctly less politically motivated commander, General W. Edmund Ironside.

Wilson also resisted Allied efforts to expand the Allied intervention in Siberia. He wrote Lansing: "It was out of the question to send reinforcements from eastern Siberia. . . . the Czechoslovaks must (so far as our aid was to be used) be brought out eastward, not go westward. Is there no way—no form of expression—by which we can get this comprehended?"[40] Lansing informed the British that after U.S. troops in Siberia had completed their mission "to rescue the Czechs," they, along with the Japanese forces, would evacuate Russian territory.[41]

At long last, the war with Germany ended with the signing of an armistice on November 11, 1918. But the fighting in Russia continued. On the very day the war ended in Western Europe, Allied troops, including two companies of Americans, fought a savage battle with Red Army units at Tulgas, a village on the North Dvina River. Two months later, on January 25, 1919, the Allied forces were placed on the defensive by an emboldened Red Army, which attacked an exposed Allied salient around Shenkursk, some 200 miles south of Archangel; the hard-pressed Allied troops were compelled to withdraw some fifty miles to the rear. As the aggressiveness of the Red Army increased, the morale of Allied and American troops began to decline.

Shortly after the German armistice was signed, both General Graves and Colonel Stewart had requested permission to begin the immediate withdrawal of U.S. forces from their respective theaters of operation. While Wilson was very much inclined to get U.S. troops out of Russia, for a variety of reasons he believed he still could not do so. For one, he did not believe he could abandon the Czechoslovaks, who by now were thoroughly demoralized after suffering a series of stunning defeats at the hands of the Red Army during the fall. And he was not prepared to allow the Japanese a free hand in Siberia, which he feared would have been a major result of the prompt withdrawal of U.S. troops from Russia. More importantly, Wilson believed that a precipitous withdrawal of American troops would jeopardize Allied unity at a time when he needed Allied support to implement his plan for the League of Nations. Wilson privately acknowledged that it was "harder to get out [of Russia] than it was to go in."[42] Consequently, on December 4 the State Department informed its chargé d' affaires in Archangel, Dewitt Poole, that there would be no change in U.S. policy until the question of how further to assist Russia was discussed by the Allies at the impending Paris peace conference.

A Diplomatic Interlude

Needless to say, the end of World War I only increased the Bolsheviks' sense of peril. "Now world capitalism will advance against us," Lenin told Chicherin.[43] In an attempt to prevent an all-out Allied invasion in support of the White forces that were arrayed against the Red Army, the Soviet government launched a peace initiative shortly before the war ended. On November 3 Chicherin addressed a note to the Western powers stating that the Soviet government was "prepared to go very far with regard to concessions to the entente powers with a view of arriving at an understanding."[44]

The concept of appealing to the West in the name of economic advantage would remain a central premise of Soviet diplomacy well into the 1920s.

But the Soviet peace proposal received a very cold reception in the Western capitals. "Now that our enemies are defeated," wrote Lord Robert Cecil, British Assistant Secretary for Foreign Affairs, "the chief danger to this country is Bolshevism." Stephen Pichon, the French foreign minister, shared this sentiment. On the telegram bearing the Soviet peace proposal, he wrote: "We do not have the least desire to enter into talks with the Bolsheviks."[45] Rather than negotiating with the Bolsheviks, the British and French were preparing to increase their assistance to the Whites.

Unlike his allies, however, Wilson by this time was eager to bring direct American military involvement in the Russian conflict to an end, and therefore was less willing to dismiss the Soviet peace feelers as were the British and the French. Accordingly, at the beginning of January 1919 he authorized William Buckler, a special assistant at the U.S. embassy in London, to meet with a Bolshevik representative, Maxim Litvinov, in Stockholm. After meeting with Litvinov on January 14–16, Buckler reported that the Bolshevik diplomat displayed a "conciliatory attitude."[46] It was reflected in Litvinov's willingness to negotiate an armistice with the Allies and his promise that the Soviet government would demonstrate greater moderation in its domestic and foreign policies. In return, Litvinov expected the Allies to "discontinue all direct or indirect military operations against Soviet Russia, all direct or indirect material assistance to Russian or other forces operating against the Soviet government, and also every kind of economic warfare and boycott."[47]

By this time, Wilson was in Paris leading the U.S. delegation to the peace conference. On January 21 he read Buckler's report to the Council of Ten, which was composed of representatives from the victorious powers. The concessions offered by Litvinov had a significant impact on their deliberations. As a result, the Council authorized Wilson to draw up a proposal (first suggested by British Prime Minister David Lloyd George in early December 1918) to invite all the warring parties in Russia, including the Bolsheviks, to attend a peace conference on Prinkipo Island (in the Sea of Mamora, near Istanbul, Turkey) beginning on February 15. Wilson hoped that, by bringing the Bolsheviks to the negotiating table, he could persuade them to accept a democratic settlement of the Russian civil war. At the very least, he hoped to prevent Lenin from posing as the defender of a Russia endangered by foreign intervention. But the Prinkipo proposal collapsed after the Whites, at the urging of the bitterly anti-Bolshevik French, refused to attend the conference.

Lenin, believing that the Allies were prepared to recognize the Bolshevik regime, accepted the Prinkipo invitation. But he clearly was not prepared to abandon his revolutionary agenda to achieve peace with the Allies. On January 23, 1919, only one day after receiving the Prinkipo proposal, Lenin called for the establishment of the Third International, or Comintern, to run the international communist movement. In early March the

Comintern held its first meeting in Moscow, where it began to plan the intensification of revolutionary propaganda and agitation around the world. Later in March, Soviet-style governments came to power in Hungary and in Bavaria, reinforcing Lenin's belief that the rest of Europe soon would rise in revolution.

The Bullitt Mission

In February 1919, after Wilson had returned to Washington from Paris, to attend to congressional matters, another attempt to communicate with the Bolsheviks was undertaken by William Bullitt, a young member of the State Department. Bullitt firmly believed that U.S. recognition of, and aid to, the Bolshevik regime would persuade it to moderate its behavior.

Actually, the idea of making another attempt to accommodate the Bolsheviks was the brainchild of British Prime Minister Lloyd George, who persuaded Colonel House to support the initiative. House went along with Lloyd George's proposal because he believed an accommodation with the Bolsheviks was necessary to keep Soviet Russia from becoming a German client state. Lansing, who still opposed recognition of the Bolshevik regime, authorized the Bullitt mission, but only to get additional information on the political and economic conditions in Russia.

Bullitt, however, was under the impression that he had been authorized to do considerably more than that, in fact, to find out if peace between the Bolsheviks and the Allies was possible. Shortly before he left for Moscow, he was given a proposal drafted by Colonel House and Philip Kerr, Lloyd George's secretary, which indicated an Allied willingness to grant the Bolsheviks de facto recognition in exchange for a moderation of their behavior. Apparently, neither Wilson nor Lansing had any foreknowledge of the House-Kerr proposal. While the president had told the Council of Ten on February 14 that "informal American representatives should meet representatives of the Bolsheviks," he made it clear that all he sought was information for a Russian settlement, not a rapprochement with the Bolsheviks.[48] Not surprisingly, Lenin, now desperate for peace, not only agreed to accept a cease-fire but also expressed his willingness to pay Russia's debts, to recognize the independence of the former Russian empire's subject nationalities, and to declare a general amnesty in return for an end to Allied intervention.

When Bullitt returned to Paris on March 25, with what he believed was a plan to end the fighting in Russia, he received a cold shoulder. Lansing flatly opposed Lenin's offer, and Wilson, who by this time had arrived back in Paris from the United States, shunned an appointment with Bullitt with the excuse that he had a headache. (It is quite probable that the president was telling the truth, considering the severe case of flu and possible minor stroke he suffered soon thereafter.) Clearly, though, Wilson, whose League of Nations plan was under attack at home, was reluctant to risk another fight over an effort to reach an accommodation with Soviet Russia. Without Wilson's support, and faced with French opposition to the idea of any understanding with the Bolsheviks, both House and Lloyd George abandoned Bullitt.

The Hoover-Nansen Plans

While Wilson was not prepared to recognize the Bolshevik regime, he was also increasingly less interested in using military means to overthrow it. Shortly before returning to Washington on February 15, 1919, Wilson had an encounter with Winston Churchill, the British minister of war. Churchill wanted to send a British army of a few thousand volunteers to Russia as well as accept a Japanese offer to aid the White forces under Alexander Kolchak, Admiral of the Black Sea Fleet, which controlled much of central and western Siberia. In return for Japanese assistance, Churchill suggested giving Japan part of Sakhalin Island, Kamchatka Peninsula, and control of the Manchurian railroads. Churchill wanted a decision from the Supreme War Council before Wilson left Paris. But the president rejected Churchill's scheme. Allied intervention, he argued, was doing "no sort of good" in Russia, since there were not enough troops there to defeat the Bolsheviks and no one, except the Japanese, was prepared to send more.[49] It was clear, Wilson added, that the Allies would have to leave Russia some day, and his inclination was to do so at once.

The next day, after Wilson had left Paris, Churchill renewed his effort to gain the approval of the Supreme War Council for Allied military intervention in Russia. When Wilson was informed about Churchill's continued effort to intervene in Russia, he was furious. He instructed House to make clear to the Council that "we are not at war with Russia and will in no circumstances that we can now foresee take part in military operations there against the Russians."[50] As a result, Churchill's intervention proposal was rejected once and for all.

Rather than military force, Wilson accepted Lansing's statement "Empty stomachs mean Bolsheviks. Full stomachs mean no Bolsheviks."[51] Food, trade, and democracy, Wilson believed, were the only effective ways to prevent the communization of Europe. To save Europe from starvation as well as Bolshevism, Wilson appointed Herbert Hoover the coordinator of America's postwar European relief programs. In Hungary, Hoover used the pressure of American food, in conjunction with an invasion of that country by the Romanian army, to help overthrow the communist government of Bela Kun.

Russia was also offered food relief, through the person of Fridtjof Nansen, a Norwegian polar explorer, but the Nansen Plan stipulated conditions that were bound to be rejected by the Bolsheviks. One was that Allied agents must have the right to supervise distribution of the food relief inside Russia, thereby removing from Bolshevik hands a vital instrument of popular control. The second condition required the Bolsheviks to cease hostilities against their White opponents and stop their efforts to overthrow foreign governments. Lenin replied that he was prepared to meet with representatives of the Allies to open peace negotiations, but he could not stop fighting the "tools" of the Allied governments. As a result, the Nansen Plan was never implemented, and an economic blockade of Bolshevik Russia, which went into effect shortly after the Treaty of Brest-Litovsk, was permitted to continue. In effect, since the Bolsheviks would not accept economic aid on Allied terms, the Allies would continue their effort to strangle Soviet Russia economically.

Withdrawal

In the meantime, congressional opposition to the U.S. military presence in Russia began to increase. On January 13, 1919, Republican Senator Hiram Johnson of California introduced a resolution that declared "in the opinion of the Senate, the soldiers of the United States, as soon as practicable, should be withdrawn from Russia."[52] Only the vote of Vice President Thomas Marshall, which broke a tie vote on the resolution, prevented its passage. Nevertheless, Wilson was moved by the congressional pressure. On February 24, 1919, the State Department informed the Allies that the president had ordered "the prompt withdrawal of American and Allied troops in North Russia at the earliest possible moment that weather conditions in the spring will permit."[53] The evacuation began in June 1919 and by July 23 the last American troops had left northern Russia. A total of 222 Americans had been killed in northern Russia fighting the Bolsheviks.

While Wilson had agreed to withdraw U.S. forces from northern Russia, extracting them from Siberia proved more difficult. During the winter of 1919, the British and French had given Admiral Kolchak considerable support, with the result that he had achieved a series of stunning victories over Bolshevik forces in western Siberia. Under pressure from the Allies, Wilson, on May 26, 1919, agreed to cooperate with them in providing food, supplies, and munitions to Kolchak. Though Wilson was taken aback by Kolchak's extreme conservatism, the Russian admiral had the advantage of being opposed by the Japanese, who preferred to work with the more pliable Cossack general Grigorii Semenov, whose forces controlled eastern Siberia. Nevertheless, Wilson did not agree to assist Kolchak until after the admiral had promised that he would create a freely elected constituent assembly, bring Russia into the League of Nations, and assume the legal debts of former Russian governments.

By this time the president was seriously disabled by a series of strokes, and the fate of his Russian policy was tied to the debate on the Treaty of Versailles, especially its provision calling for U.S. membership in a League of Nations. Progressive opponents of the League, led by Republican Senator William E. Borah of Idaho, charged that U.S. involvement in the Russian civil war was only the beginning of what he predicted would become a never-ending effort to maintain the status quo throughout the world. At the other end of the political spectrum, conservatives wanted to withdraw U.S. troops from Russia because they believed their presence encouraged radicalism at home by increasing public sympathy for the Bolsheviks.

In March 1919, the same month in which the Comintern was established, a congressional committee was set up to investigate the extent of communist subversion in the United States. In May, 5 million copies of Lenin's letter "To the American Worker" were distributed, and in August 1919 the Communist Labor Party of the United States was organized under the leadership of native-born Americans John Reed, Benjamin Gitlow, and William Lloyd. Other radicals, who were mainly foreign-born Americans, formed the Communist Party.

Spurred by these events, as well as a series of strikes and race riots that many blamed on communist agitation, the nation was in the grip of its first Red Scare in the summer of 1919. Wilson's attorney general, A. Mitchell Palmer, attempted to exploit the frenzy as a way of winning the Democratic nomination for president in 1920. Palmer established the General Intelligence Division within the Justice Department and appointed as its head J. Edgar Hoover, later the director of the department's Federal Bureau of Investigation. Under Palmer's orders, thousands of aliens suspected of engaging in communist activities were arrested and hundreds were deported. While Palmer did not win the Democratic presidential nomination, he did increase the public's fear of a Bolshevik revolution in the United States and aroused support for withdrawing U.S. troops from Russia to the safety of the U.S. homeland.

While the Red Scare was raging in the United States, the fortunes of the White resistance in Russia were taking a definite turn for the worse. Kolchak's forces were decisively defeated by the Red Army in the autumn of 1919, and the admiral was executed by the Bolsheviks on February 7, 1920. With Kolchak's collapse, it became clear that American troops could no longer be left in Siberia without their becoming embroiled in clashes with the advancing Red Army. As a consequence, the last American troops were withdrawn from Vladivostok in April 1920.

With the withdrawal of British and French troops during 1920, and the conclusion of a truce agreement in October of that year ending a Polish-Soviet war, the Red Army was able to concentrate on the remaining White forces in southern Russia. By the middle of November 1920, as a result of a series of decisive Soviet victories in the Crimea, the Russian civil war was over. The Japanese, however, kept troops in Siberia until late 1922, when domestic opposition to their continued presence, and steady diplomatic pressure from the Western nations, finally forced their withdrawal. With the Allied forces withdrawn and the Whites crushed, the Soviets were able to gain control of all the territories of the former Russian empire by 1922, with the exception of Finland, Estonia, Latvia, Lithuania, Bessarabia (Moldova), and parts of Poland.

Nonrecognition

The Bolshevik victory led to demands within the United States for recognition of the Soviet government, but Wilson was not about to change course. On September 27, 1920, the president provided the rationale for what later would become the country's post–World War II containment policy. "Bolshevism," he said," is a mistake and it must be resisted as all mistakes must be resisted. . . . It cannot survive because it is wrong."[54]

A month earlier, on August 10, Bainbridge Colby, Wilson's new secretary of state, issued a statement which said that it was not possible for the United States to recognize the Soviet government because "the existing regime in Russia is based upon the negation of every principle of honor and good faith, and every usage and convention underlying the whole structure of international law. . . ."[55]

Even though the Wilson administration refused to recognize the Soviet government, on July 8, 1920, it lifted the embargo on U.S. trade with the Soviets. The move was prompted by the termination of the Allied trade embargo earlier in the year. However, the State Department warned "that individuals or corporations availing themselves of the present opportunity to trade with Russia will do so on their own responsibility and at their own risk."[56] The department also stated that it would retain a number of impediments to trade, such as passport and visa restrictions, prohibitions on long-term loans, and a ban on the acceptance of Soviet gold in payment for purchases. While Washington did not prohibit commercial credits to the Soviet Union, by direct and indirect means it did discourage them. For example, the Commerce Department recommended that firms dealing with Russia should not grant credit for any sale more than the anticipated gross profit. The department also suggested that American businessowners collect 50 percent cash advances before sending goods to Russia and the rest in six to nine months. As a result, several years would pass before Soviet-American trade began to flow.

Harding and the New Economic Policy

Lenin had hoped that the election of the Republican administration of Warren G. Harding in November 1920 would bring to the White House more practical leaders whose interest in promoting business profits would not only stimulate trade with and investment in Russia but also lead to Washington's recognition of the Soviet government. But only a few days after taking office in March 1921, Charles Evans Hughes, Harding's secretary of state, announced that the Soviets would have to meet certain basic conditions if they expected diplomatic recognition, including payment of the czarist debt and halting their efforts to overthrow foreign governments. Since the Bolsheviks were not prepared to satisfy either condition, nonrecognition would remain the basic Soviet policy of the United States under Harding as well as his Republican successors, Calvin Coolidge and Herbert Hoover.

Nonrecognition did not prevent the American Relief Administration (ARA) from sending $50 million worth of food, clothing, and medicine to Russia during the devastating famine of 1921, which was in part a consequence of the civil war and the Bolsheviks' attempt to socialize the economy. Although an implacable foe of the Soviet regime, the ARA's director, then Secretary of Commerce Herbert Hoover, believed the relief mission would succeed where Allied armies had failed in rescuing Russia from the Soviets. While millions of Russians were saved from starvation by the American assistance, the ARA did not contribute to the overthrow of the Soviet regime. Indeed, its relief efforts may have saved the Bolshevik regime from a counterrevolution.

In 1921 Americans were encouraged by Lenin's apparent abandonment of the Bolshevik effort to communize Russia with the promulgation of the so-called New Economic Policy (NEP). The NEP was designed to save the country from economic disaster by temporarily encouraging the development of private enterprise and by attempting to attract badly needed foreign investment and technology. Only after Russia had been restored to economic health, Lenin argued, could socialization of the economy resume.

To win foreign assistance in rebuilding Russia, Lenin asserted, the Bolsheviks must be able "to exploit the contradictions and antagonisms among the imperialists." In his view, one of the most important of these contradictions was the one he believed existed between the United States and the Western European countries. "America is strong," Lenin explained, "everybody is now in its debt, everything depends on it, everybody hates America more and more . . . because America is richer than the others."[57] To maintain its status as the leading capitalist country, Lenin believed the United States could be persuaded to rebuild the Soviet economy, provided that lucrative profit-making opportunities were offered. The initial scheme for doing so consisted of concessions, that is, joint ventures between foreign businesses and Amtorg, the Soviet economic development agency. Lenin expected the capitalists nations to fall all over themselves in a race for concessions in Russia.

Most capitalists, and especially American capitalists, however, did not respond to the Soviet bait. In 1925 Americans held just eight out of ninety active concessions in Russia. Among them were W. Averell Harriman, later ambassador to the Soviet Union, and Armand and Julius Hammer, who received concessions for asbestos mining and pencil manufacturing. Except for Hammer's pencil factory, the returns, if any, on the U.S. investments were small. Foreigners found it difficult to deal with the Soviet bureaucracy and worried about losing their investments through eventual nationalization. The Russians also became disillusioned with the concessions program, particularly because they feared that the joint ventures with capitalists would undermine their effort to socialize Russia. Even Lenin finally had to admit, shortly before his death in 1924, that concessions were "a foreign thing in our system."[58]

Hoover and the First Five-Year Plan

In 1928, after Josef Stalin had emerged triumphant from a succession struggle with Leon Trotsky (who wanted to emphasize the international effort to spread communism rather than Stalin's plan to build socialism in Russia first) and the so-called Right Revisionists (who wanted to preserve some of the capitalistic features of the NEP), the Soviet government inaugurated the First Five-Year Plan. It dropped the concessions program and shifted to a policy of relying on domestic, rather than foreign, capital in industrializing the Soviet Union. Instead of concessions, the First Five-Year Plan employed the contract method to acquire foreign technical assistance. Given the poor record of American investment in Russia under the concession system, technical assistance provided on a contractual basis was more attractive to American businesses. As a result, large quantities of U.S. goods and technical aid began to flow into the Soviet Union for the first time since the Bolshevik Revolution. During the First Five-Year Plan, as many as 1,000 American engineers worked in the Soviet Union under individual technical aid contracts, and many more were in Russia under contracts signed with American corporations.

Among the most significant of the U.S. companies that operated in the Soviet Union during the First Five-Year Plan were the Albert Kahn Company, an industrial architecture firm that designed some 600 plants in Russia, the General Electric Company, which built the massive Dneiprostroy dam and provided substantial technical assistance to the Soviet electrical industry, and the Ford Motor Company, which not only sold thousands of automobiles, trucks, and tractors to the Soviet Union, but also virtually created the Soviet automobile industry. Ford gave the Soviets full rights to make or use Ford machinery, inventions, and technical advances, and provided the Soviets with detailed drawings of a complete factory. Russian engineers also were given access to Ford's American plants so that they could acquire practical training, while the company sent its own engineers and crew leaders to the Soviet Union to help in the planning and operation of the new works.

Like other American businessowners who participated in the First Five-Year Plan, Henry Ford was not only motivated by a desire to make a profit in the Soviet Union but also by a belief that American know-how would prompt the Soviets to abandon socialism and convert to American-style capitalism. But Stalin accepted Western aid only to help Russia to become a self-sufficient industrial power, not to learn how to become a capitalist nation. After the Soviets had received the know-how they needed to make their own automobiles and tractors, they terminated their working relationship with Ford in 1934. Ironically, capitalists like Ford had unconsciously contributed to the success of the First Five-Year Plan as well as Stalin's ability to consolidate his dictatorship.

Other American capitalists helped build socialism in Russia by extending short-term credit to the Soviet government, which in turn enabled the Soviets to purchase badly needed American products. As a result, trade between the two countries, mainly in the form of American exports to the Soviet Union, increased twentyfold between 1923 and 1930, when it reached $114,399,000. By 1930 the United States had become the leading exporter to the Soviet Union, furnishing 25 percent of total Soviet purchases, while the Soviet Union had become America's eighth-largest customer and the single largest foreign purchaser of American agricultural and industrial equipment.

Nevertheless, the Soviets were upset about their inability to gain long-term credits from American banks. The U.S. government discouraged such credits, not only because the Soviet Union refused to pay the czarist debt but also because there were no formal diplomatic relations between the two countries. As a way of pressuring Washington to change its policy, the Soviet government in 1931 began to shift most of its orders to other countries, particularly Germany. As a result, Soviet-American trade declined abruptly during the following year. By 1932 the U.S. share of Soviet imports had fallen from 25 percent to only 4.5 percent, an 82 percent decline from the previous year.

The decline in Soviet-American trade during 1932, the worst year of the Great Depression, only increased the pressure on the United States to recognize the Soviet government and thereby normalize economic as well as political relations between the two countries. A poll of fifty of the largest companies doing business with the Soviet Union indicated that twenty-two of them favored immediate recognition and another eleven wanted President Hoover to send a trade commission to explore solutions to the economic and political problems the two countries were experiencing. Only four of the respondents flatly opposed recognition.

Another factor favoring the normalization of Soviet-American relations was that the United States was the only major country that had not established an embassy in Moscow; this situation became somewhat of an embarrassment as the Soviets began to play a more active role in international affairs during the late 1920s. When Hoover's secretary of state, Henry Stimson, reminded both China and the Soviet Union of their obligation under the 1928 Kellogg-Briand Pact to refrain from aggressive actions during a dispute over Manchuria, Soviet Foreign Minister Maxim Litvinov responded that the United States was hardly in a position to give "instructions" to the Soviet Union, a country whose existence it refused to recognize officially.[59]

More than embarrassing was the growing realization among some Americans, including Stimson, that nonrecognition of the Soviet Union deprived the United States of the ability to enlist Soviet support in maintaining not only the Open Door in China but also a balance of power in the Far East, which was increasingly being threatened by the revival of Japanese militarism. Both the Soviet Union and the United States opposed the Japanese military occupation of Manchuria in 1931, but, without diplomatic relations, they were unable to act in concert to prevent or reverse it.

Acting on this realization, Stimson met secretly with Karl Radek, one of Litvinov's lieutenants, at the Geneva Disarmament Conference, to discuss the possibility of U.S. recognition of the Soviet Union. He also ordered his subordinates in the State Department to study the impact recognition would have on curbing Japan's aggressive appetite. But the State Department's Division of East European Affairs, which was largely staffed with diplomatic holdovers from the early years of the Bolshevik Revolution, opposed recognition, arguing that Japan would interpret it as a hostile act.

Ideological considerations, however, were more important than Japanese sensitivity in explaining why the State Department opposed U.S. recognition of the Soviet government. As Robert F. Kelley, the influential chief of the State Department's Division of East European Affairs, put it in an internal memorandum in April 1929: "The essential difficulty lying in the way of the recognition of the Soviet government is not certain acts of the Bolshevik regime, such as repudiation of debts, the confiscation of property, and the carrying on of propaganda in the United States; but the Bolshevik world revolutionary purpose, of which these acts are manifestations."[60]

Kelley's views were shared by President Hoover. Despite his willingness to feed Bolshevik Russia and even trade with it, Hoover believed that recognition of the Soviet government would advance the cause of communism, which he strenuously opposed. As a result, the normalization of Soviet-American relations would have to wait until a less doctrinaire president sat in the White House. That president was Franklin D. Roosevelt.

Assessment

Historians have debated for years the significance of the factors that motivated American intervention in the Russia civil war. One interpretation, popularized by John A. White and Betty Miller Unterberger, emphasizes Wilson's desire to check Japanese expansion in the Far East. Another interpretation, of which William Appleman Williams was a leading exponent, sees American intervention as motivated primarily by a desire to overthrow the Bolshevik regime. The latter interpretation was supported by Soviet historians, some of whom argue that Wilson was determined from the beginning to crush the Soviet republic. On the other hand, historian John W. Long has argued that "there is simply no evidence to support the contention that President Wilson was motivated by an ideological desire to crush Bolshevism and convert the Russians to his own political convictions."[61]

It seems that Wilson was motivated at least in part by a desire to overthrow the Bolshevik regime, but he was opposed to using U.S. and Allied military forces to achieve this end. He feared that direct Allied military intervention, particularly unilateral Japanese intervention, would throw the Russian people into the laps of the Bolsheviks, who posed as the defenders of Russia's independence and territorial integrity. He also feared that Allied intervention would compel the Bolsheviks to turn to the Germans for assistance against the Allies. Rather than direct military intervention against the Bolsheviks, therefore, Wilson preferred to intervene indirectly by assisting the anti-Bolshevik White forces and their Czechoslovak allies. He also kept the pressure on the Soviet government through a policy of political isolation and economic strangulation.

Despite his reservations, Wilson slowly and reluctantly agreed to send U.S. troops to Russia. With respect to northern Russia, his decision was motivated primarily by a desire to maintain the unity of the Western allies at a time when their armies on the western front were in danger of being overrun by the Germans. He also was concerned about the possibility that Allied military supplies stored in northern Russia might be seized by the Germans or the Bolsheviks. He came to the conclusion that a U.S. military presence in Siberia was necessary not only to save the Czechoslovak Legion and assist anti-Bolshevik Russians but also to prevent unilateral Japanese intervention in eastern Russia and northern Manchuria. After Germany was defeated, Wilson was slow to pull troops out of Russia because he feared that such a move would disrupt Allied unity at a time when it was vital to the successful implementation of his primary goal, the creation of the League of Nations.

Although Wilson attempted to restrict the mission of U.S. forces in both northern Russia and Siberia to essentially that of performing guard duty, he was patently unsuccessful in doing so. American troops, especially those in northern Russia, frequently came into conflict with Bolshevik forces. The ensuing collapse of their morale and rising public and congressional opposition to an American military presence in Russia after the war with Germany was over ultimately forced Wilson to pull the troops out of northern Russia. However, the withdrawal of U.S. forces from Siberia took place only when it became glaringly obvious, after the defeat of Kolchak, that further effective White resistance was no longer possible.

In 1933, when negotiations to establish diplomatic relations between the United States and the Soviet Union began, Roosevelt's secretary of state, Cordell Hull, showed the Soviet negotiator, Maxim Litvinov, documents which, Hull argued, proved that U.S. intervention in Russia was motivated solely by a desire to protect its territorial integrity against Japan. Since the Soviets were eager to obtain U.S. recognition, Litvinov accepted Hull's argument and the Soviet government agreed to drop all claims against the United States for its part in the intervention.

Still, America's involvement in the Russian civil war was not forgotten. Stalin would refer to it repeatedly during the 1930s and 1940s, and allude to it several times during World War II conferences with his American allies. Wilson's decision to intervene in the Russian civil war no doubt deepened Stalin's suspicions about America's ultimate objectives. For this reason, the origins of the Cold War can be traced to this period.

2

Franklin D. Roosevelt and the Grand Alliance, 1933–1945

U.S. Recognition of the Soviet Union

By the time Franklin D. Roosevelt entered the White House in March 1933, it had become obvious that the U.S. nonrecognition policy was a failure. Not only did the policy fail to change the internal structure of the Soviet Union, it did not dissuade the Soviets from engaging in anticapitalist activities abroad. Nor did it prevent other countries from establishing diplomatic relations with the Soviet government. Indeed, of all the world's major countries only the United States did not recognize the Soviet Union at the time of Roosevelt's inauguration.

Perhaps even more important, nonrecognition prevented the United States from fully exploiting an expanding Soviet market. In 1931 the Soviets had shifted their trade to other countries, not only because they wanted to obtain more favorable trade terms but also because they wanted to pressure the United States into recognizing their government. With the United States sliding into the Great Depression, congressional pressure to recognize the Soviet Union mounted as the scale of U.S.–Soviet trade declined.

But there was a more important factor working toward U.S. recognition of the Soviet Union. After the Versailles treaty was rejected by the Senate in 1920, the United States withdrew into relative isolation. With Germany prostrate in defeat and Japan still on friendly terms with the Western powers, the United States was secure behind its two oceans. As a result, it could afford to ignore the Soviet Union diplomatically, if not commercially. However, America's sense of security began to diminish in the early 1930s. In 1931 the Japanese army revived its plan to conquer China. Within two years it had succeeded in expelling the Chinese from their Manchurian provinces. In 1933 Adolf Hitler came to power in Germany. His vow to destroy the system established by the Versailles treaty and restore German military supremacy in Europe threatened to upset the balance of power in Europe.

Like his distant cousin, Theodore Roosevelt, Franklin Roosevelt insisted that the United States must play a major role in maintaining not only the European balance of power but a global one as well. He was also one of the few Americans who realized the crucial role the Soviet Union could play in checking the aggressive designs of both Germany and Japan. Still, Roosevelt could not forget the humiliation Woodrow Wilson suffered when the Senate rejected the League of Nations. As a result, the new president was reluctant, indeed fearful, of getting too far in front of American public opinion. Not surprisingly, his approach to the Soviet Union was cautious.

The Soviets, for their part, also appreciated the potential strategic importance of the United States. Shortly after Roosevelt entered the White House, the Soviets abandoned the isolationist policy they had been following since the early twenties. They embarked on a campaign to create an effective collective security system, one that would help to check both Germany and Japan. In 1934 the Soviet Union joined the League of Nations and in the following year concluded alliances with France and Czechoslovakia. Nevertheless, in Soviet eyes, only the United States had the potential to restrain Japan's ambitions in the Far East, which, until Hitler displayed his aggressive designs in the mid-thirties, were the major focus of Soviet concern. Not surprisingly, then, the Soviets eagerly accepted the president's October 10, 1933, invitation to end "the present abnormal relations" between their two countries.[1] Maxim Litvinov, the Soviet commissar of foreign affairs, was dispatched to the United States to personally conduct the recognition negotiations.

Despite the eagerness of both sides to begin the negotiations, two major obstacles stood in the way of recognition. One was the Comintern; the other was the unpaid Russian debt. To remove the first obstruction Litvinov signed a statement, drafted by the State Department, promising that the Soviet Union would not "permit the formation or residence on its territory of any organization or group whose objective is the overthrow of the political or social order of . . . the United States."[2] The statement did not specifically mention the Comintern because the State Department feared that the Soviets could evade the agreement by simply changing that organization's name.

The two sides were unable to agree on the terms for repaying the Russian debt. The best they could do was reach an understanding, fashioned personally by Roosevelt and Litvinov, that made recognition possible. They agreed that the Soviet government would pay no less than $75 million, and not more than $150 million of the total debt that the U.S.

Treasury Department estimated to be $636 million. The final amount would be settled through additional negotiations and would be repaid through extra interest on a loan granted by Washington or by private sources. All other official and private claims would be eliminated. On this less than precise basis, the agreement establishing diplomatic relations between the two countries was signed on November 17, 1933. William C. Bullitt, who had unsuccessfully championed recognition during the Wilson administration, was named the first U.S. ambassador to the Soviet Union.

Disillusionment

Despite the apparently satisfactory beginning to formal Soviet-American diplomatic relations, both sides soon became disillusioned. Clearly, each government had misunderstood what the other had been offering in signing the Roosevelt-Litvinov agreements. The Soviets thought that recognition would gain them the support of the United States against Japan. But Roosevelt had told Litvinov that, while the United States was prepared to give the Soviet Union "100 percent moral and diplomatic support" in their effort to curb Japanese ambitions in the Far East, the American people were not willing to risk war with Japan.[3] The farthest he could go, Roosevelt had hinted, was to suggest the possibility of a tripartite nonaggression pact involving the United States, the Soviet Union, and Japan. Litvinov believed—incorrectly—that, if Japan refused to sign such a pact, the United States would conclude it with the Soviets alone.

In reality, Roosevelt in 1933 was not prepared to go even this limited distance toward cooperating with the Soviet Union. Restricted by isolationist sentiment in the Congress and in the nation, Roosevelt was compelled to reassure the American people that the United States "intend and expect to remain at peace with the world."[4] Litvinov shrewdly and accurately analyzed the president's attitude: "Roosevelt, afraid of every double sided obligation, . . . prefers to make unilateral statements" rather than cooperate with other nations in deterring aggression.[5]

Once the Soviets realized that "moral support" was all they could expect from the United States, progress on resolving the debt issue ground to a halt. The Soviets argued that the only obstacle to a debt settlement was the Roosevelt administration's refusal to grant the Soviet Union a $100 million credit, which they insisted was necessary to deter other nations from demanding unreasonable debt settlements from the Soviet Union. Roosevelt, for his part, believed the Soviets were duty bound to fulfill the "commitment" that he believed they had made to settle the debt issue quickly. Convinced that the Soviets needed the United States more than America needed them, and afraid that further compromise would alienate Congress, which passed a law (the Johnson Act of 1934) prohibiting U.S. loans to nations in default of their debt payments, Roosevelt refused to budge.[6] In January 1935 the United States closed its consulate-general in Moscow and reduced its embassy staff to protest Soviet intransigence on the debt issue.

In spite of the failure to resolve the debt problem, the Roosevelt administration nevertheless hoped to expand Soviet-American trade. However, the expected surge in Soviet-American trade did not material-ize, primarily because the debt imbroglio had rendered Soviet credit-worthiness virtually nonexistent. As a result, Soviet-American trade after 1935 was even less than it had been in the 1920s.

Ostensibly, the inability to resolve the debt issue was the only obstacle to improved Soviet-American relations. Yet there was a more pervasive impediment to closer relations between the two countries: their ideologi-cal incompatibility. It was manifested, in one way, by the U.S. reaction to the Soviet announcement that the Comintern would convene in 1935. The Comintern had not met since 1928, partly because Stalin had decided to play down the Soviet effort to promote world revolution in order to concentrate on building socialism in the Soviet Union first. But after Soviet efforts to conclude an anti-aggression system with the capitalist nations made little headway, Stalin decided to revive the Comintern. He saw it as an instrument to promote the creation abroad of left-liberal coali-tions willing to cooperate with the Soviet Union in establishing an antifas-cist collective security system.

The State Department responded by warning Moscow that it would consider the participation of American communists in the Comintern meeting a violation of the understanding reached by Roosevelt and Litvi-nov during the recognition negotiations. The Soviets, however, ignored the warning, and American communists participated in the Comintern proceedings. The State Department reacted with another note threaten-ing the "most serious consequences" if the Soviet Union continued to violate the Roosevelt-Litvinov agreement.[7]

The Comintern incident did much to reinforce the State Depart-ment's belief that the Soviets would not observe agreements they had concluded. "It is perfectly clear," Ambassador Bullitt wrote in July 1935, "that to speak of 'normal relations' between the Soviet Union and any other country is to speak of something which does not and cannot exist."[8] The Soviets, for their part, had come to much the same conclu-sion. Since the United States wanted "to remain aloof from all active interest in international affairs," Litvinov said, "friendly relations with the United States were not of great importance to the Soviet Union."[9]

The anti-Soviet hostility of the State Department was reinforced by reports from the staff of the U.S. embassy in Moscow, particularly from two of its members, George F. Kennan and Loy Henderson, both of whom would play a significant role in formulating America's post–World War II policy toward the Soviet Union. The gist of their reports was epit-omized by Kennan's later statement: "Never—neither then nor at any later date—did I consider the Soviet Union a fit ally or associate, actual or potential, for this country."[10] While Kennan saw communist ideology simply as a means to an end for the Soviets, that is, Soviet aggrandizement, Henderson considered ideology the primary engine of Soviet foreign policy. He wrote that "the establishment of a Union of World Soviet Socialists Republics is still the ultimate objective of Soviet foreign policy."[11]

Clearly, Stalin posed as a revolutionary leader who was well-versed in Marxist-Leninist theory. But, as Kennan believed, he generally used ideology as a way of advancing the national interests of the Soviet Union, as well as augmenting his own power, rather than as an end in itself. Still, Stalin was skillful in disguising his realistic ambitions in ideological trappings, thereby promoting disagreement among American analysts regarding his ultimate objectives. Furthermore, Soviet policy had an ambiguous quality all of its own. Despite its support for collective security, the Soviet Union in the 1930s, like the Western powers, was much more interested in avoiding war than in overthrowing Hitler or driving the Japanese out of China. Soviet spokesmen would rail publicly against the aggressive designs of Germany and Japan while privately engaging in secret diplomacy with those two powers.

The anti-Soviet hostility of the U.S. embassy in Moscow was only exacerbated by the purges of the Soviet government and military that Stalin inaugurated in 1936. In an attempt to eliminate real and imaginary opposition to Stalin's dictatorship, hundreds of old-Bolsheviks, members of the Soviet foreign ministry, and the top leadership of the armed forces were executed. By the end of 1938 about 35,000 Red Army officers had been purged, including 80 percent of the colonels, 90 percent of the generals, and 100 percent of the deputy-commissars for war. It has been estimated that as many as 10 million people died as a result of the purges.

In the opinion of the U.S. embassy staff, the purges had so weakened the Soviet Union militarily that it would not be able to play a major role in world affairs for the foreseeable future, and therefore it had nothing of value to offer U.S. diplomacy. Roosevelt, however, had little use for the opinions of the professional diplomats. He was determined to do all he could to create the foundation for Soviet-American collaboration to counter the growing threat posed by the Axis powers.

The Growing Axis Threat, 1935–1936

By 1935 few Americans doubted Hitler's aggressive intentions. In March of that year, the Nazi dictator violated the disarmament clauses of the Treaty of Versailles by announcing the formation of a German air force and his intention to increase the size of the German army to 550,000 men. A year later, on March 7, 1936, the Führer again violated the Versailles treaty by sending German troops into the demilitarized Rhineland. Britain, which was not prepared to go to war over territory in Germany's "own back garden," did not oppose the Rhineland occupation. Although the French army was still stronger than Germany's, France was also politically unstable, economically weak, deeply divided on social and economic issues, and, like the British, intensely fearful of another war. Consequently, without British support, which was not forthcoming, the French refused to force a German withdrawal from the Rhineland.

While Hitler was tearing up the Treaty of Versailles in Europe, Italy's fascist dictator, Benito Mussolini, embarked on a course of aggression in Africa. On October 3, 1935, as a first step in a bid to recreate an Italian empire in Africa, Mussolini's troops invaded Ethiopia. The League of Nations condemned the Italians as aggressors and prohibited arms shipments, loans, and credits to Italy, and then placed an embargo on Italian imports, but the league's attempt to punish Italian aggression was undermined by Britain and France. They attempted to dissuade Mussolini from joining Hitler by offering him a deal that would have allowed Italy to keep a part of Ethiopia. Faced with no effective opposition from either the West or Ethiopia, the Italians completed their conquest of that country in May 1936. Two months later, the league voted to end its sanctions against Italy. The inability of the league to prevent and then reverse Italy's aggression in Ethiopia convinced Roosevelt that a general war was probable.

No sooner did the war in Ethiopia end, than another crisis erupted, in July 1936: the Spanish Civil War. On one side of this bloody conflict was a popular-front coalition of socialists, liberals, and communists loyal to Spain's republican government; the other side, led by General Francisco Franco, was supported by conservatives, monarchists, fascists, the armed forces, and the Catholic Church. Both Germany and Italy intervened quickly, and probably decisively, on the side of Franco. Some 50,000 Italian troops and 10,000 German soldiers and airmen saw action in Spain. The republican or "Loyalist" side, on the other hand, received considerable—but, as it turned out, insufficient—support from the Soviet Union, primarily in the form of supplies and weapons. Both the French and the British governments adopted a hands-off attitude toward the conflict. Ultimately, their refusal to support the Loyalists was a major factor in the republican defeat in 1939.

The Spanish Civil War emboldened the aggressors. In October 1936 Hitler and Mussolini signed a treaty that became known as the Axis Pact. Although not yet an alliance, the pact pledged both states to collaborate against international communism, not only in Spain but elsewhere in the world. On November 25, 1936, Japan aligned itself loosely to Germany by concluding the Anti-Comintern Pact. Publicly, this agreement committed Japan to the Axis struggle against world communism, but a secret provision of the pact also obliged each party to refrain from concluding any agreement with the Soviet Union that would impair the other's interests. When Mussolini joined this treaty a year later, the Rome-Berlin-Tokyo axis was complete.

Britain and France, by failing to support the Soviet Union in Spain and by appeasing rather than confronting the aggressors elsewhere, was directly responsible for the isolation of the Soviet Union, but the United States contributed to the weakness of the Western response to the Axis challenge. While Americans were quick to condemn the Anglo-French appeasement of the aggressors, they were even more determined to stay out of the conflict themselves. With this objective, Congress passed the first of a series of neutrality acts in 1935. The 1937 version embargoed the shipment of arms, ammunition, and implements of war in the event of foreign wars or civil wars, recognized as such by the president. In addition, the act prohibited loans to belligerents and travel by Americans on the ships of belligerent nations.

Roosevelt's Effort to Collaborate with the Soviets, 1937–1938

Although Roosevelt was hamstrung by isolationist sentiment in the Congress and the nation, by the anti-Soviet attitude of the State Department, and by Anglo-French efforts to appease Hitler and Mussolini, he was still determined to create a working relationship with the Soviets. With this end in mind, shortly after his reelection in November 1936, Roosevelt replaced William Bullitt (who had worn out his welcome in Moscow as a result of fighting with the Soviets over the debt issue) with Joseph E. Davies, a wealthy lawyer with no diplomatic experience. While Davies was in many respects diplomatically naive, particularly in his assessment of the nature of the Soviet regime, like Roosevelt, he believed that good relations with the Soviet Union would pay dividends to the United States in the future. Sharing this belief, Roosevelt was not only receptive to Davies's optimistic assessment of conditions in the Soviet Union, he took steps to ensure that it would shape the conduct of the administration's Soviet policy. In the spring of 1937, the State Department's Division of East European affairs, a hotbed of anti-Soviet opinion, was eliminated, and its Russophobe head, Robert Kelley, was transferred to the U.S. embassy in Turkey.

Nevertheless, Roosevelt still was not able to overcome opposition within the U.S. government to the idea of improved Soviet-American relations. Its strength was demonstrated by Roosevelt's inability to satisfy Stalin's November 1936 request to allow U.S. companies to construct a battleship for the Soviet navy. The president reacted favorably to the project, considering it a low-risk way to demonstrate U.S. solidarity with the Soviet effort to oppose Axis aggression. But the project died after it was blocked by anti-Soviet hard-liners in the U.S. Navy, led by Admiral William Leahy, the chief of naval operations. Leahy opposed any American effort that might enhance the international prestige or the military power of the Soviet Union. Fearing hostile congressional and public reaction if the Soviet request leaked to the news media, Roosevelt, for the time being, abandoned this attempt to collaborate with the Soviets.

During 1937, however, Roosevelt intensified his effort to educate the American people about the growing Axis threat. On October 5, almost three months after Japan began an undeclared war with China, he delivered a speech in Chicago in which he said that it might be necessary for the "peace-loving nations" to "quarantine" the aggressor states. Despite the favorable reaction that the speech received in the press, the president's extreme sensitivity to isolationist sentiment in the nation, and in the State Department, prevented him from initiating a more forward U.S. policy toward the Axis powers. The Soviet government, which had permitted *Pravda* to print the president's Chicago speech in its entirety, was disappointed by the absence of meaningful action in its wake.

Privately, Roosevelt did press the State Department to examine the possibility of U.S. collaboration with the British, the French, and even the Soviets to check Japan. But Secretary of State Hull and his advisers suspected Soviet motives in the Far East; they believed Moscow was trying to embroil the United States in a war with Japan and, considering Stalin's purges, doubted that the Red Army could be effective in any conflict with Japan. Faced with this opposition, the president backed off again. He did not oppose the State Department's unsuccessful effort to block Soviet participation in the Brussels Nine Power Conference on the Far East, nor did he object when U.S. representatives at that conference rebuffed inquiries by Litvinov about the possibility of Soviet-American action against Japan.

The Soviets, apparently, were not making idle inquiries. They had potent military power in the Far East, and they had demonstrated a willingness to use it. The Red Army reacted with force when the Japanese army attacked Soviet forces on the Amur River in 1937. They would also deal forcibly with the Japanese army at Lake Khasan in 1938 and at Khlakin-Gol in 1939. These incidents were not mere skirmishes between border guards but full-scale battles involving whole divisions, tanks, artillery, and aircraft. In effect, the Soviets had called the Japanese bluff and demonstrated what could be done to deter aggression—if the will to do so existed.

After an unprovoked Japanese air attack on a U.S. gunboat, the *Panay*, on December, 12, 1937, Roosevelt made another approach to the Soviets. He asked Davies to propose to the Kremlin the establishment of a liaison system, by which the two countries could exchange data concerning the military situation in the Far East. Roosevelt warned the ambassador to keep this matter strictly confidential, particularly from the U.S. Moscow embassy. On June 5,1938, Stalin gave his support to Roosevelt's military liaison proposal, provided that it were kept secret.

Roosevelt's liaison offer also encouraged the Soviet leader to seek a settlement of the debt issue as a way of removing the major obstacle to closer collaboration between the two countries. He offered to pay $50 million toward the Kerensky debt in exchange for a ten-year credit of $150 million. In response, Davies attempted to get the Soviets to agree to pay interest on the debt. But Stalin responded by raising the ante. He now wanted an American credit of $200 million. The continuing inability to resolve the debt problem prompted Roosevelt to drop his military liaison proposal. Once again, the president's attempt to establish a collaborative relationship with the Soviet Union was blocked by the debt imbroglio.

The Turn of Austria and Czechoslovakia, 1938–1939

Without effective opposition from the Western powers, the Axis nations continued their aggressive ways. On March 12, 1938, the German army occupied Austria, and Hitler announced that nation's unification (*Anschluss*) with the Reich.

After Austria, Czechoslovakia was Hitler's next target. In the spring of 1938, the Führer demanded the absorption into Germany of the Czech Sudetenland, which had a large German population. The Czechoslovaks, whose army was one of the best in Europe, rejected Hitler's demand and turned to France and England for support, but the French, who were committed by treaty to defend Czechoslovakia, would not act without the cooperation of Britain. As result of a Czechoslovak-Soviet alliance in 1935, the Soviets were also obliged to defend Czechoslovakia, but their commitment was dependent on prior action by France. Thus, ultimately, the fate of the Czechs was in the hands of the British, who were not obliged by any treaty to come to Czechoslovakia's assistance.

Winston Churchill called for Britain and France to join with the Soviet Union in a "grand alliance" to check further German expansion. British Prime Minister Neville Chamberlain, however, believed that Hitler's aims were limited to the acquisition of lands inhabited by Germans. He also feared that Churchill's call for a grand alliance with the Soviet Union would only enhance that country's status while jeopardizing his plan to appease Hitler. The alternative to appeasement, a war with Germany over Czechoslovakia, was unthinkable to the prime minister, and many other Britons as well.

Rather than allying with France and the Soviet Union to uphold Czechoslovakia, Chamberlain capitulated to Hitler. At Munich, on September 29–30, 1938, he and French Premier Edouard Daladier met with Hitler and Mussolini and agreed to hand over the Sudetenland to Germany. In return, Hitler pledged that he would not seek an additional foot of European territory. The Czechoslovaks pleaded for U.S. intervention in the crisis, but Roosevelt had no intention to become involved. In fact, he was relieved that a peaceful solution to the crisis had been found.

Roosevelt's hopes for the Munich settlement proved illusory. On March 15, 1939, German troops occupied what remained of Czechoslovakia. Hitler then made it clear that Poland would be his next victim by increasing pressure on the Poles to accept German annexation of the free city of Danzig, on the Baltic coast, and to grant Germany exclusive road and railroad rights across the so-called Polish corridor, which separated East Prussia from the rest of Germany. The Poles rejected the German demands and turned to France and Britain for support. Badly burned by Hitler's violation of the Munich agreement, Chamberlain on March 31 promised to come to Poland's assistance, as well as Romania's, if their independence or vital interests were endangered by another power. In response, Germany and Italy concluded a formal alliance, the "Pact of Steel," in May. The Nazi dictator clearly intended to test the newly found assertiveness of the British.

The Soviet-German Nonaggression Pact

By the spring of 1939 it was obvious that, because of U.S. isolationism, the most effective way of saving Poland and checking Axis aggression in Europe would be an alliance of Britain, France, and the Soviet Union. In April 1938 Joseph Davies had warned that "the Nazi objective was to split the Western powers, isolate the Russians from their potential allies, and pick off the democracies, piecemeal."[12] Blocked in his own efforts to strengthen Soviet-American ties, Roosevelt encouraged the British to conclude an alliance with the Soviet Union.

Chamberlain, however, feared that Hitler would use an Anglo-French-Soviet alliance as an excuse for dragging Britain into a war both he and a majority of the British people were determined to avoid. Moreover, Britain's new protectorates, Poland and Romania, feared the Soviets as much as the Germans and, as a result, flatly refused to permit Soviet troops to enter their territory, even after a German attack began.

Nevertheless, at the insistence of his cabinet, which believed an alliance with the Soviets would be vital to the defense of Poland, Chamberlain agreed in May 1939 to begin joint Anglo-French talks with the Soviets. But the most the British prime minister would offer the Soviets was a consultative pact that would come into operation only if Britain, France, or the Soviet Union became involved in war directly or as the result of aggression against another European state that offered resistance. This arrangement would remove the appearance of a Soviet threat to Poland and Romania while avoiding any British guarantee to the Soviet Union. However, the two Western powers refused to accept the Kremlin's demands for boundary adjustments or grant the Soviets the right to occupy the Baltic states. Obviously, Chamberlain's offer did not go far enough to satisfy Soviet security concerns

The inability of the Soviets and the Western Allies to agree gave Hitler an opportunity that he skillfully exploited. Putting aside, for the time being, the hostility he felt for communism, in early August 1939 he responded to earlier Soviet suggestions for an understanding by instructing his ambassador in Moscow to propose a political agreement between the two governments. Stalin, who by this time had given up on the prospect of a meaningful alliance with the Western Allies, or aid from the United States, jumped at the German offer. On August 20 a Soviet-German commercial agreement was concluded. Three days later, both countries startled the world by signing a nonaggression treaty. It required both to refrain from attacking each other and to remain neutral if either became involved in a war with other countries. In a secret protocol to the treaty, Germany recognized Finland, Latvia, Estonia, and the eastern half of Poland to be within the Soviet sphere of influence.

In the short term, the German-Soviet Nonaggression Pact was extremely advantageous to both parties. The agreement enabled Hitler to attack Poland, on September 1, without having to fear Soviet opposition. Stalin, on the other hand, was able to put more territory between Germany and the Soviet heartland. On September 17 the Red Army invaded eastern Poland and seized almost half the country. By the end of October, the Soviets had demanded and obtained bases in Latvia, Lithuania, and Estonia. When the Finns refused to grant similar rights and boundary concessions, the Soviets invaded their country on November 30. After unexpected resistance on the part of the Finns, the Soviets forced them to cede the entire Karelian Isthmus, several islands in the Gulf of Finland, as well as territory in Finland's north. In June 1940 the Soviets annexed the Baltic states of Latvia, Lithuania, and Estonia. On June 27 Stalin forced Romania to cede to the Soviet Union northern Bessarabia and northern Bukovina.

The Nonaggression Pact convinced the State Department's Soviet specialists that any agreement with Stalin was not worth the paper on which it was written. To them, there was no limit to the depth Stalin would sink to advance the interests of the Soviet Union. The implications of this assessment were not very promising for the long-term success of Soviet-American relations. George Kennan, for one, "could see little future for Russian-American relations other than a long series of misunderstandings and disappointments and recriminations on both sides."[13] It was a prediction that was destined to come true.

But Roosevelt had not given up on the possibility of eventual Soviet-American collaboration against the Axis powers, even after the Nonaggression Pact was concluded. Thus, U.S. reaction to Soviet aggression in Eastern Europe was relatively mild. While an arms embargo was placed on Germany and its allies, it was not imposed on the Soviets. And while Roosevelt invoked a "moral" embargo on the Soviet Union after its invasion of Finland, cutting off the shipment of aircraft and strategic metals to the Soviet Union, other Soviet purchases were allowed to more than double over the previous year. Then, in December 1939, Roosevelt removed the embargo and again permitted strategic materials to be sold to the Soviet Union. The president clearly was trying to keep open the possibility that Stalin would eventually join with the West against Hitler. While Roosevelt would not condone Soviet expansion, as long as Stalin did not threaten Britain and France, he would not do anything meaningful to oppose it.

Lend-Lease

Because of Germany's brutal conquest of Poland, American opinion was increasingly sympathetic to the idea of helping the Allies, short of direct

U.S. military involvement. As a result, Roosevelt was finally able to persuade the Congress to revise the Neutrality Act in November 1939. The new version replaced the arms embargo with a "cash and carry" provision: belligerent powers could purchase arms if they paid for them and carried them away in their own ships. Although Roosevelt did not say so publicly, he realized that the cash-and-carry feature of the bill would help the Allies more than Germany because Britain and France controlled the high seas. In this way, cash and carry represented the first meaningful step toward U.S. aid to the countries fighting Hitler.

But the new American assistance proved to be pitifully insufficient in helping the Western powers halt the blitzkrieg that Hitler unleashed upon them in the spring of 1940. Denmark, Norway, Belgium, Luxembourg, the Netherlands, and even France were quickly overrun by the German army. The armistice signed by the French on June 22 left the northern two-thirds of their country occupied by the Germans but permitted the French to establish a pro-Nazi government at Vichy, which controlled the southeastern third of the country.

With France out of the war, Britain stood alone to face the full fury of the German onslaught. Fortunately, Britain had an aggressive new leader in the person of Winston Churchill, who had replaced Neville Chamberlain as prime minister on May 10, 1940. But the British were hard-pressed to prevent German submarines from cutting their economic lifelines to the outside world. In an obviously unneutral action, Roosevelt, by executive order, gave the British fifty over-age U.S. destroyers. In return, the British transferred to the United States British air and naval bases in Newfoundland and Bermuda, and leased to the United States, for ninety-nine years, additional bases in the Caribbean.

While Churchill appreciated immensely the gift of the U.S. destroyers, their arrival did not measurably relieve the acute financial crisis Britain faced in trying to pay for American war materiel. In a novel approach to the problem, Roosevelt decided that he would simply lend or lease Britain the supplies it needed. As passed by Congress in March 1941, the Lend-Lease Act authorized the president to sell, transfer, exchange, lease, or lend—under such terms as he thought suitable—supplies of munitions, food, weapons, and other defense articles to any nation whose defense he deemed vital to the security of the United States. Shortly thereafter, Congress approved an initial Lend-Lease appropriation of $7 billion.

While the United States was acting to keep Britain in the war against Germany, Hitler invaded the Soviet Union on June 22, 1941. The German invasion ended the brief, unnatural period of cooperation between Hitler and Stalin that had begun with their nonaggression pact in August 1939. Although Stalin had observed the collateral Soviet-German trade agreement by providing Germany with strategic raw materials until the very day of the invasion, Hitler had become alarmed by Soviet territorial ambitions. In November 1940, Soviet Foreign Minister Vyacheslav Molotov declared that Bulgaria, Turkey, Hungary, Romania, Yugoslavia,

Greece, and Finland were all within the Soviet sphere of interest. Hitler responded by ordering his generals to prepare for the invasion of the Soviet Union. As a prelude to it, the following spring, German troops occupied Romania and Bulgaria, and conquered Yugoslavia and Greece.

The Roosevelt administration warned the Soviets that the German attack was coming. As early as January 1941, the U.S. embassy in Berlin had learned from a disaffected German foreign ministry official that Hitler was planing to move east. But Stalin ignored the warnings, believing that he could buy additional time by continuing to appease Hitler. Thus, he made no protest when Hitler invaded Yugoslavia, only one day after the Soviets had signed a treaty of friendship with that country. In May the Soviets even withdrew recognition from the Norwegian, Belgian, and Yugoslav governments-in-exile, all victims of German aggression. Rather than admit that his effort to appease Hitler had failed, Stalin refused until the very night of the attack to allow defensive preparations to begin. As a result, the Soviet Union suffered enormous losses of men, equipment, and territory during the early months of the war.

In spite of Stalin's past duplicity and his complicity with Hitler's aggression, Churchill extended Britain's unsolicited offer of help to the Soviet Union. To his secretary he said, "If Hitler invaded Hell, I would at least make a favorable reference to the Devil in the House of Commons."[14] The Soviets enthusiastically accepted Churchill's offer.

Churchill also asked Roosevelt to join him in helping the Soviets. The State Department, however, reacted coolly to the request. George Kennan wrote that welcoming the Soviet Union "as an associate in defense of democracy" would identify the United States with a regime "which is widely feared and detested throughout the world."[15] Motivated by this same line of reasoning, the State Department favored giving the Soviets only minimal assistance, suggesting a relaxation of export restrictions to permit the Soviets to buy supplies not needed by either the United States or Britain. However, the State Department did not believe that any assistance should be given to the Soviet Union without obtaining Soviet political concessions first. The War Department, on the other hand, felt that any U.S. assistance to the Soviets would be wasted because it believed that the Red Army could not survive for more than three months.

Roosevelt ignored the War Department's dire prognostications and the State Department's hostility toward the Soviets. He preferred to believe the prediction of Ambassador Davies that Soviet resistance would "amaze the world." He also agreed with Davies's assessment that, if the United States withheld assistance to the Soviet Union, Stalin might conclude a separate peace with Hitler. Unlike the State Department's Soviet specialists, Davies dismissed the menace of Soviet communism. He did not believe that it would be possible "for many years, for the Soviets to project communism, even if they wished, into the United States or even Europe."[16]

While Roosevelt was not ignorant about the nature of the Soviet regime or communist ideology, he believed that the Soviet Union under

Stalin had become a conventional imperialist power with ambitions not unlike those of czarist Russia. Consequently, he was convinced that he could deal with Stalin as a realist rather than a revolutionary. The primary focus of Roosevelt's Soviet policy, then, was not Soviet ideology but Soviet military power. To the president, Hitler's preoccupation with the Soviet army would not only save Britain from the full force of German power but possibly preclude the necessity of U.S. military involvement in the war as well. The defeat or neutralization of the Red Army, on the other hand, would not only endanger Britain but also encourage Japanese expansion in the Far East. With the prospect that the Axis would dominate the entire Eastern Hemisphere, Roosevelt could see no way for the United States to stay out of the conflict.

Not surprisingly, then, Roosevelt was determined to do all he could to keep the Soviet Union in the war against Germany. He immediately unfroze Soviet assets in the United States and refrained from invoking the Neutrality Act to permit American ships to deliver supplies to Vladivostok. By the end of July, Roosevelt's close aide, Harry Hopkins, was in Moscow laying the foundation for long-range U.S. aid to the Soviet Union.

Stalin, with his armies reeling from the German onslaught, feared that U.S. economic aid would not arrive in time to avert disaster. What he wanted immediately—and he pressed this request incessantly throughout the early years of the war—was the creation of a second front, either in France or in the Balkans, that would divert German divisions from the Russian front. He even told Hopkins that he would welcome the presence of U.S. troops in the Soviet Union. But in the summer of 1941 the United States was not yet at war with Germany, and Roosevelt had no intention of sending U.S. troops to the Soviet Union. Rather, Roosevelt intended to use U.S. economic aid as the primary way of keeping the Soviet Union in the war. Stalin, of course, had no choice but to accept the aid alternative. That fall, an agreement was concluded in which the United States promised to provide the Soviets with 1.5 million tons of supplies, valued at $1 billion, over a nine-month period.

American public and congressional opinion at first resisted the idea of giving aid to the Soviets. More than a few Americans shared the sentiments of Senator Harry S. Truman of Missouri, who suggested: "If we see that Germany is winning, we ought to help Russia and, if Russia is winning, we ought to help Germany, and that way let them kill as many as possible."[17] As a result, although Roosevelt had the authority to extend Lend-Lease aid to the Soviet Union, he did not do so without first preparing the ground of public opinion carefully. One reason for the president's caution was his appreciation of the fact that Congress, which retained control of Lend-Lease appropriations, could have blocked aid to the Soviets simply by not funding it.

Besides popular hostility toward the Soviets, another factor complicating Roosevelt's effort to aid the Soviet Union was an issue that would haunt the Grand Alliance throughout the war, and eventually contribute to its demise once the Axis powers were defeated: postwar territorial boundaries. Almost immediately after Churchill had offered help to the Soviets, Stalin began pressing the British and the Americans to recognize the gains the Soviet Union had made in Eastern Europe, gains that were facilitated by his nonaggression pact with Hitler. No matter that these territories were at the time being overrun by the Germans! Simultaneously, however, the Polish government-in-exile (the so-called London government) was pressuring both Churchill and Roosevelt to recognize Poland's prewar boundaries, including territory seized by the Soviets in September 1939. From the very first, Roosevelt realized the disruptive nature of the postwar boundary issue. Consequently, he would insist, until the very end of the war, that postwar boundaries must be dealt with only after the conflict had ended. As a result, the Polish-Soviet alliance of July 30 made no mention of Poland's postwar boundaries.

But Roosevelt could not completely avoid postwar issues. His ability to obtain public and congressional support for aiding the Soviet Union depended largely on the ability of the American people to understand why the conflict was being fought. Consequently, Roosevelt secretly met with Churchill in Placentia Bay, off the coast of Newfoundland, near Argentia, on August 9–12, 1941, in the first of a series of wartime conferences of the two leaders. There they drew up, at the president's suggestion, the Atlantic Charter. It stated that the two powers sought no territorial aggrandizement or territorial changes that were not in keeping with the freely expressed wishes of the concerned peoples. Both leaders also promised to respect the right of all peoples to choose their own form of government and to live in freedom from want and fear. Although no one believed the Atlantic Charter would be adequate in addressing the actual postwar conditions, its principles nevertheless were accepted as the basis of America's policy toward Eastern Europe. In September 1941 all the governments at war with Germany, including the Soviet Union, approved the charter. Following America's entrance into the war, the principles of the Atlantic Charter would be incorporated in the Declaration of the United Nations.

In drafting the Atlantic Charter, however, Roosevelt blundered by not mentioning religious freedom as a war aim. It was an omission opponents of aid to the Soviet Union were quick to condemn. In an attempt to correct his error, the president informed Soviet Ambassador Constantine Oumansky that "if Moscow could get some publicity back to this country regarding the freedom of religion in Russia, it might have a very fine educational effect before the next Lend-Lease bill comes up in Congress."[18] Not surprisingly, on October 4, 1941, the Soviets publicly proclaimed that freedom of worship was guaranteed in the Soviet Union as long as it did not challenge the authority of the state. When the pope made no objection to U.S. assistance to the Soviet Union, a relieved Roosevelt believed he could go ahead with Lend-Lease to the Soviets without fear of major religious opposition in the United States.

After preparing the ground of public opinion, in September 1941 the administration introduced a second Lend-Lease bill in the Congress, one that did not specifically mention — but did not exclude — aid to the Soviet Union. The bill passed the House on October 10, 1941, by a vote of 328 to 67 and the Senate on October 23 by a vote of 59 to 13. A week later Roosevelt informed Stalin that the United States would provide the Soviet Union with $1 billion of supplies under Lend-Lease. In return, the Soviets agreed to repay this amount, without interest, over a ten-year period once the war was over. On November 4 Stalin replied that the Soviet government "accepted with sincere gratitude" the U.S. assistance.[19]

The passage of the Lend-Lease bill, in effect, made the United State a de facto ally of the Soviet Union as well as Great Britain. It was only a matter of weeks before the Grand Alliance became a reality. The Japanese attack on Pearl Harbor on December 7, 1941, brought the United States into the war against the Axis powers along side Great Britain and the Soviet Union.

Anglo-American Strategic Planning

Shortly after the Japanese attack on Pearl Harbor, from December 22, 1941, to January 14, 1942, Churchill and Roosevelt discussed military strategy in Washington. The president assured the prime minister that the defeat of Germany, rather than Japan, was the first American priority, but Roosevelt's military advisers, led by Army Chief of Staff General George C. Marshall, disagreed with the British regarding the best strategy for defeating the Germans. The Americans wanted the allies to concentrate on preparations for an invasion of France in early 1943, which they believed was the quickest way to relieve the German pressure on the Russian front.

Churchill, on the other hand, believed that too few troops would be available in 1943 for an early and successful invasion of France across the English Channel. The result, he believed, would be a sacrificial venture in which British troops would be called upon to do most of the sacrificing, since too few U.S. troops would be combat-ready by then. Instead of an invasion of France, Churchill argued that a North African campaign should be the first Anglo-American operation. It would not only put U.S. troops into action faster than a cross-channel invasion but would also remove the threat posed to the Suez Canal, Britain's lifeline to India and the oil of the Middle East, by German General Erwin Rommel's Africa Corps, which was advancing across Libya toward Egypt.

Roosevelt accepted Churchill's argument that an invasion of North Africa should occur first. The president believed it was necessary to engage the Germans in ground combat during 1942 to raise American morale. Equally important, a campaign in North Africa would relieve German pressure on the Russian front much sooner than a cross-channel operation.

As a result, the president ordered the preparation of an invasion of North African (Operation Torch), which was initially scheduled to take place in May 1942.

Stalin, had he been invited to participate in the Churchill-Roosevelt discussions, undoubtedly would have supported the argument of the U.S. military chiefs that an invasion of France was the most effective way of assisting the Soviet war effort. And he would have been furious had he known (as he later would) that the earliest that he could hope for a cross-channel invasion was early 1943. But after the German advance was stopped at the gates of Moscow, in early December 1941, Stalin's need for a second front lost some of its urgency. As a result, he once again made the conclusion of a satisfactory postwar settlement the immediate focus of his discussions with his British allies. Late in that month, Stalin told British Foreign Secretary Anthony Eden that the conclusion of a formal treaty of alliance between their two countries depended on the willingness of the British to recognize the territorial gains made by the Soviet Union since 1939, namely the annexation of the Baltic states as well as parts of Finland, Poland, and Romania.

The British feared that their recognition of these conquests would alienate the Americans, and consequently they at first balked at the Soviet threat. However, after Stalin hinted, in a speech on February 23, 1942, that he might conclude a separate peace with the Germans, the British became more amenable to the idea of recognizing all the post-1939 Soviet acquisitions, with the exception of the annexation of eastern Poland. On March 7 Churchill asked Roosevelt to give him "a free hand to sign the treaty which Stalin desires as soon as possible," to prevent the Soviets from leaving the war.[20] Roosevelt was inclined to approve Churchill's request provided that the Soviets permitted the Baltic peoples to leave their occupied countries. But when Secretary of State Hull refused to recognize any Soviet gains, and even warned the British against doing so, Roosevelt backed off and supported Hull's stand.

Blocked by Hull's opposition to territorial concessions to the Soviets, the president instead offered Molotov, in a White House meeting on May 29, 1942, the prospect of "a second front this year." Bothered by such a definite commitment, General Marshall urged the president to remove all reference to a specific date for the invasion. Roosevelt refused to do so. He believed that a definite commitment was the only way to ensure continued Soviet participation in the war and avoid making the territorial concessions that Stalin demanded. It was bad enough that Roosevelt had to tell Molotov that, to free shipping for the invasion of North Africa, it would be necessary to reduce Lend-Lease shipments to the Soviet Union from 4.1 to 2.5 million tons in the coming year. Molotov sarcastically replied that "the second front would be stronger if the first front still stood." He then asked what would happen if the Soviets accepted these reductions "and then no second front eventuated?" To reassure him, Roosevelt agreed to Molotov's suggestion that the communiqué released after their meeting would include a specific reference "to the urgent task of creating a second front in Europe in 1942."[21]

The British, however, were not about to permit Roosevelt to commit them to a premature cross-channel operation. Churchill personally informed Molotov that Britain could make no commitment to a specific date for the invasion, but the Soviets ignored Churchill's qualification and instead emphasized Roosevelt's promise. This prompted the U.S. ambassador in Moscow, William H. Standley, to warn "that if such a front does not materialize quickly and on a large scale, these [Soviet] people will be so deluded in their belief in our sincerity of purpose that inestimable harm will be done."[22]

It was soon apparent that a cross-channel operation could not take place in 1942. The failure of an Anglo-Canadian raid on the French port of Dieppe in August 1942, and the heavy Allied casualties it produced, convinced the British that the Allies would not be ready soon for a massive invasion of France. Moreover, in June Rommel scored a stunning victory in Libya by capturing Tobruk with a force inferior in size to that of its British defenders. With Egypt in danger of being overrun, Roosevelt was forced to agree with Churchill that the cross-channel invasion would have to be delayed.

When Stalin received this news, he complained that the Soviet Union was being betrayed by its allies. This view was reinforced by the British decision in July to suspend the convoys to northern Russia for the rest of the summer. The disaster that struck one British convoy (PQ 17)—the Germans sank twenty-three of its thirty-four merchant ships—convinced the British that it was not safe to send convoys to northern Russia during the long days of summer. With the German army once again racing across the plains of southern Russia, Stalin found the postponement of the cross-channel invasion and the suspension of the northern convoys bitter pills to swallow. Nor did he buy Roosevelt's argument that the successful allied invasion of North Africa in November 1942 fulfilled the president's promise of a second front that year. The duplicity practiced by Roosevelt in 1942 would not be forgotten by the Soviet leader.

The Casablanca Conference, January 1943

Churchill wanted to preclude the possibility that the Americans would turn their attention to the cross-channel invasion, or to the Pacific theater, now that Operation Torch had been successfully launched. In late November 1942 he outlined a three-part strategy designed to keep the Mediterranean theater as the main focus of Anglo-American energies. One part called for an invasion of Sicily and Italy after the completion of the North African campaign. The second part called for an invasion of the Balkans from Turkey, assuming that the Turks could be persuaded to enter the war against the Germans. Even at this early date, Churchill saw a Balkan operation as the primary way to prevent the postwar domination of Eastern Europe by the Soviet Union. The third part of the prime minister's strategy called for a limited invasion of France in August or September 1943, but only after Germany was weakened by Allied attacks along the Mediterranean coast and on the Soviet front and by intensified Allied bombing of the German homeland.

Even though U.S. military planners realized that adoption of Churchill's Mediterranean strategy would delay the cross-channel invasion further, they reluctantly accepted it for a number of reasons. For one, the conclusion of the North African campaign would free a large number of veteran Allied troops to attack Sicily without creating major demands on scarce Allied shipping. In addition, the North Africa invasion suggested that more than twice the men, and far more landing craft, would be needed for a major cross-channel operation than originally had been anticipated. Both Marshall and General Dwight D. Eisenhower, who was the designated Allied supreme commander in Europe, reluctantly admitted that it was unlikely that this force could be assembled before 1944.

With the Soviet army tying down almost three-quarters of the German army, the thought of doing nothing until 1944 was unthinkable to Roosevelt. As a result, he essentially accepted Churchill's strategy at a conference they attended in Casablanca, Morocco, on January 14–25, 1943. The two leaders decided that Sicily would be invaded as soon as possible after the North African campaign had ended, and U.S. air power in Britain would be increased substantially to permit the heaviest possible bombing of Germany. At the same time, however, the buildup of ground forces in Britain would be accelerated to make possible an invasion of France by August or September 1943 if the Soviets needed more immediate Anglo-American help.

The terms of Axis surrender were also determined for the first time at Casablanca. At Roosevelt's insistence, the Axis would be offered only "unconditional surrender." Unlike after World War I, this time the Germans would realize that they had been soundly defeated. Moreover, Roosevelt believed the unconditional surrender formula would persuade Stalin not to seek a separate peace with the Axis powers, especially after he learned that the cross-channel invasion would have to be postponed once again, this time for over a year.

Some historians have called the unconditional surrender policy a mistake, arguing that it only strengthened the enemy's will to resist. But Roosevelt did not want to deal with the German army, as Woodrow Wilson did during World War I. Instead, he wanted the German General Staff dissolved. In vain did Churchill, and even Stalin, who felt that the unconditional surrender policy would prolong the war, attempt to change his mind. As a result, the total defeat of the Axis powers became the ultimate war aim of the Grand Alliance, eclipsing in importance even the implementation of the Atlantic Charter.

In reporting the results of the Casablanca talks to Stalin, Churchill and Roosevelt were deliberately evasive on the matter of a second front.

With the president's approval, Churchill informed the Soviet leader: "We are pushing preparations to the limit of our resources for a cross-channel operation in August [1943]."[23] Stalin was not pleased with the news. On February 16, shortly after the great Soviet victory at Stalingrad, he insisted to Churchill that the cross-channel operation should begin that spring, or in early summer at the latest. Moreover, he would not consider an invasion of Sicily a substitute for a second front in France. Stalin would be angered further when Churchill informed him, on March 30, that convoys to Murmansk would again be suspended, this time until the fall of 1943, because of the demands the Sicilian campaign was placing on Allied shipping.

The Soviet Threat to Eastern Europe

Relations between the Soviets and the West were also strained by the growing animosity between Moscow and the London Poles. On April 13, 1943, the Germans announced the discovery of a mass grave in the Katyn Forest, near Smolensk in the Soviet Union, where, they alleged (an allegation that was later substantiated) that ten thousand Polish soldiers had been slaughtered by the Soviets after they had occupied eastern Poland in 1939. (In October 1992 the Russian government released documentation which revealed that more than 20,000 Poles, including nearly 5,000 Polish officers, were executed at Katyn. The executions were ordered by the Soviet Politburo, over which Stalin presided.) After the Polish government in London demanded an investigation of the event by the International Red Cross, the Soviets responded by breaking diplomatic relations with the London Poles on April 26.

Fearing that the Katyn massacre would disrupt the Grand Alliance, both Roosevelt and Churchill dismissed it as German propaganda. Nevertheless, the Katyn massacre reinforced the arguments of those who believed that the West must make a strong stand during the war to block Soviet expansion after the conflict. In a long memorandum to Roosevelt on January 29, 1943, former ambassador William C. Bullitt warned the president that postwar Soviet expansion could extend "as far west as the Rhine, perhaps even beyond." He wanted Roosevelt to act immediately to prevent the Soviets "from replacing the Nazis as the masters of Europe."[24] Bullitt suggested, as Churchill had, that the Anglo-American armies invade the Balkans as soon as possible to check Soviet postwar expansion.

"I don't dispute your facts," Roosevelt responded to Bullitt. "They are accurate. I don't dispute the logic of your reasoning." But the president rejected Bullitt's advice. "I just have a hunch," he said, "that Stalin is not that kind of man. Harry [Hopkins] says he's not, and that he doesn't want anything but security for his country, and I think that if I give him everything I possibly can, and ask nothing from him in return, *noblesse oblige*, he won't try to annex anything and will work with me for a world of democracy and peace."[25]

In hindsight, Roosevelt's response to Bullitt appears the height of naiveté. But, as historian John Lewis Gaddis has pointed out, Roosevelt's hunch was based on sound reasoning. A precipitous move against the Soviets in the Balkans could have jeopardized the ultimate outcome of the war by encouraging the Soviets to make a separate peace with Germany, as well as risking their continued neutrality in the war with Japan. As a result, Roosevelt did not anticipate, nor did he implement for the remainder of his life, a confrontational policy toward the Soviet Union. Instead, he attempted to accommodate Soviet security demands, particularly in Eastern Europe, where, he realized, Soviet military power was certain to predominate after the war.[26]

In early May 1943, Roosevelt sent former ambassador Joseph Davies to Moscow with a personal message for Stalin to reaffirm his continued support for the cross-channel invasion at the earliest possible date and suggest that they meet that summer to plan the defeat of Germany. Stalin replied that he would be pleased to attend a summit meeting that year, and, as a good-will gesture he dissolved the Comintern later that month.

The Tehran Conference, November–December 1943

By the time the Big Three summit convened in Tehran, Iran, in November 1943, Italy had been invaded by the Anglo-American forces and forced to surrender. (Nevertheless, most of Italy was quickly occupied by the Germans, who effectively slowed the Allied advance up the Italian peninsula.) Surprisingly, the Soviets did not allow their exclusion from an occupation role in Italy to impair their relations with their Western allies. Stalin approved the Italian surrender terms and even empowered General Eisenhower to sign for the Soviet Union.

Stalin's new amity toward his allies was a direct response to signs that they would finally open a second front in France. At a preparatory conference of foreign ministers (Hull, Eden, and Molotov) in Moscow during October, the Soviets were informed that the cross-channel invasion (code-named Overlord) would begin in May 1944. As a result, the Soviets signed the Four Power Declaration on General Security at the Moscow Conference, in which they promised to fight to the war's end and to cooperate afterward to create a new international peace organization, as proposed by Roosevelt, the United Nations.

Roosevelt and Churchill arrived in Tehran on November 27, where they met with Stalin until December 2. Much to the chagrin of Churchill, who had hoped that Stalin might be persuaded to support an Anglo-American invasion of the Balkans, the Soviet leader decisively threw his weight behind Overlord, which was rescheduled to begin no later than June 1, 1944. Rather than a Balkan operation, however, Stalin supported the U.S. plan to divert some Allied troops from Italy for an invasion of southern France (Operation Anvil).

Having settled the matter of Allied strategy, the Big Three turned their attention to political issues. With respect to Germany, Roosevelt proposed to divide that country into five independent states. Churchill, on the other hand, already thinking that postwar Germany must be strong enough to check Soviet expansion while not too strong to dominate Europe, favored carving Germany into only two states, Prussia and a Danubian confederation. Stalin strenuously opposed any Germanic confederation, arguing that the Germans would simply create another powerful state. Unable to agree on the partition of Germany, the Big Three referred the German problem to the newly created European Advisory Commission.

The Big Three also failed to agree on Poland's future at Tehran. The Soviets wanted to move Poland's boundaries to the west by giving it German territory east of the Oder River and annexing to the Soviet Union eastern Poland. While Roosevelt sympathized with this transfer of territory, he feared that the opposition of the London Poles to such an arrangement would cause him to lose Polish-American votes in the next presidential election. Stalin expressed his sympathy with the president's predicament and, as a result, a settlement of Poland's boundaries was postponed. However, Stalin rejected Roosevelt's request to permit a plebiscite in the Baltic states, realizing all too well that their people would vote for independence.

In an attempt to assure Stalin that the United States would not be a postwar threat to the Soviet Union, Roosevelt informed him that neither the Congress nor the American people would condone a long-term U.S. occupation role in postwar Europe; the occupation would be a year or maybe two years at most. If peace were ever threatened again in Europe, Roosevelt told Stalin, Britain and the Soviet Union would have to provide the ground forces, although the United States might send planes and ships. Stalin, in all likelihood, was not disappointed by this information.

Neither Stalin nor Churchill was enthusiastic about Roosevelt's proposal to give the new United Nations the major responsibly for maintaining world peace. The UN, Roosevelt suggested, should have three parts: a thirty-five- to forty-member body that would meet periodically in different places to make recommendations; an executive committee of ten nations, including the great powers, that would deal with all nonmilitary problems; and a third group, "the Four Policemen"—the United States, Britain, the Soviet Union, and China—that would have the power to deal immediately with any threat to the peace or any sudden emergency requiring action. Stalin told the president that he preferred regional police forces to a global one. Roosevelt replied that the American people and Congress would regard regional security arrangements as spheres of influence and would oppose them. Probably believing that Roosevelt's conception of the UN was unworkable, Stalin in the end accepted a worldwide, rather than a regional, peacekeeping body.

The Tehran Conference marked the high point of Allied political unity during the war. The Big Three drafted the outlines of postwar Europe and East Asia, accepted a major peacekeeping role for the United Nations, and approved plans for the invasions of northern and southern France. By accepting Soviet control of the Baltic states, altered boundaries for Poland, the need for permanent restraints on German and Japanese power, and a predominant role for the Big Four in maintaining world peace, Roosevelt believed that he had established the foundation for stable Soviet-American relations after the war.

But others were not so sure. Churchill did not believe that Stalin would be as cooperative after the war as he was while he needed Anglo-American help. One State Department analyst, Charles Bohlen, predicted that, as a result of the Tehran agreements, after the war "the Soviet Union would be the only important military and political force on the continent of Europe." [27] Now that the Allies agreed on military strategy, the political issues raised at Tehran would move to the forefront in the months ahead. Ultimately, they would tear apart the Grand Alliance.

Churchill's Containment Policy

In June 1944 the armed forces of the Western allies, under General Eisenhower's command, finally began the cross-channel invasion of France. By August they had broken out of their Normandy beachheads and driven the Germans back across the Seine River, capturing Paris in the process. The Allies had also continued their slow progress up the Italian peninsula and entered Rome in June.

While the Allied armies advanced in France and Italy, the Soviet juggernaut continued its inexorable march from the east. On August 1, 1944, the Red Army reached the suburbs of Warsaw. But the Soviet forces did not enter the city until the Germans had first crushed the Polish Home Army, which had staged an uprising to coincide with the arrival of the Soviets. The betrayal of the Home Army, which was loyal to the Polish London government, demonstrated again the ruthlessness Stalin could employ in the pursuit of Soviet self-interest.

The Red Army also advanced rapidly into the Balkans. On August 25, 1944, Romania deserted Hitler and joined the Soviet side, followed on September 9 by Bulgaria. By October 1 the Red Army crossed into Yugoslavia, where it made contact with communist partisans under Josip Broz Tito. Two weeks later, on October 15, Belgrade was liberated. By the end of November, Budapest, the Hungarian capital, was also under Soviet control.

The rapid Soviet advance into Eastern Europe alarmed Churchill. In an attempt to restrain Soviet postwar ambitions in that region, the prime minister tried to revive his idea of a Balkan campaign during the summer of 1944. He argued that, since the Allied armies in northern France were progressing rapidly, an invasion of southern France was no longer necessary.

Consequently, Churchill wanted Anvil canceled and its troops shifted to Yugoslavia, from where they could drive into Austria and southern Hungary. But Roosevelt refused to be diverted from the strategy agreed to at Tehran. The shortest path to victory, the president insisted, was to drive into the heart of Germany from France while the Soviets invaded from the east. As a result, Anvil proceeded as scheduled, with the allied forces landing in southern France on August 15.

Unable to enlist Roosevelt's assistance in blocking Soviet domination of Eastern Europe, Churchill developed a multifaceted containment strategy of his own. First, he tried to establish, or reestablish, and aid pro-Western governments in Eastern Europe. Second, in September, at a meeting at the president's home in Hyde Park, New York, he persuaded Roosevelt not to share the secret of the atomic bomb with the Soviets. The bomb, Churchill believed, might be the only way to prevent postwar Soviet domination of Europe. Third, in a display of classic realpolitik, he tried to gain an agreement with Stalin that would define their respective spheres of influence in Eastern Europe. To Churchill, it was better to deal with the Soviets on a quid pro quo basis—getting something in return for handing over to them Eastern Europe—which he believed Roosevelt was willing to do "noblesse oblige." Stalin was more than willing to reach an understanding with Churchill that would recognize Soviet domination of most of Eastern Europe. At a meeting in Moscow during October 1944, he and the British prime minister agreed that Britain would have paramount influence in Greece, while Soviet influence would predominate in Romania and Bulgaria. Britain and the Soviet Union would have equal influence in Hungary and Yugoslavia.

Roosevelt, who was informed about the nature of the Anglo-Soviet spheres-of-influence agreement, did not publicly endorse it, primarily because it was opposed by Secretary of State Hull. The Anglo-Soviet agreement confirmed Hull's suspicion that Churchill was determined to restore the old diplomacy, with its secret deals, balances of power, and spheres of influence, rather than back the new diplomatic order he was trying to fashion based on the principles of the Atlantic Charter and the United Nations. In spite of Hull's opposition, Roosevelt did not condemn the Anglo-Soviet agreement. In fact, he cabled Stalin that he was "delighted" with the outcome of the conference. In the president's opinion, it would help to build a "satisfactory and a durable peace."[28] Stalin, no doubt, was pleased by Roosevelt's reaction. Soviet postwar dominance in Eastern Europe apparently would not be opposed by either Britain or the United States.

The Yalta Conference, February 1945

Roosevelt had been trying since July 1944 to arrange another summit meeting with Stalin, either in Scotland or in the Mediterranean, but the Soviet leader said that his poor health made it impossible for him to leave the Soviet Union. By the beginning of 1945 Roosevelt's own health was not good. When Lord Moran, Churchill's physician, saw him in February 1945, he thought the president displayed all the symptoms of hardening of the arteries in the brain. Moran, quite prophetically, gave him only a few months to live. Against the wishes of his advisers, who could not understand why the president of the United States had to travel halfway around the world to see Stalin, Roosevelt agreed to meet with him, at Yalta, in the Soviet Crimea.

Germany was the first issue the Big Three addressed at Yalta. With the Red Army on the Oder River, only forty miles from Berlin, while the Anglo-American forces were still on the west side of the Rhine, it appeared as though the Soviets would end the war themselves. As a result, before the Red Army could advance into western Germany, Roosevelt and Churchill accepted the German occupation zones recommended by the European Advisory Commission, which gave the Soviets a zone in eastern Germany. But the Allies were not able to agree on the partition of Germany. The Soviets now wanted Germany divided into several small states. Churchill, fearing that a dismembered Germany would become easy prey for Soviet subversion, opposed a draconian partition. As a result, the conference could only agree that Germany would be dismembered after the war without saying how it would be done.

The Big Three also were not able to agree on the amount of reparations Germany would be required to pay. The Soviets wanted to exact $20 billion from the Germans. They recommended that half this amount should consist of movable capital, including machinery and rolling stock, which would be seized within two years of the war's end. The balance would be taken from current German production over a period of ten years. The Soviets wanted half of Germany's reparation payments. To the displeasure of Churchill, who blamed reparations for the collapse of the peace after World War I and thought the Soviet reparations proposal excessively severe, Roosevelt supported the Soviet proposal as a basis for discussion.

Even so, the president refused to approve a massive U.S. loan to the Soviet Union, which Molotov had proposed shortly before the conference, and which might have reduced the amount of reparations the Soviets were seeking. Remembering the Soviet-American debt imbroglio, the president apparently was unwilling to disregard the advice of the State Department that the loan should not be offered until the Soviets had made concessions on other issues. In the end, neither Roosevelt nor Stalin was able to win Churchill's support for stringent German reparations, and therefore, no final agreement on the issue was possible at Yalta. Instead, the Big Three agreed to establish a Reparation Commission in Moscow that would study the matter further.

Poland proved to be the most troublesome problem at Yalta. Stalin demanded Anglo-American recognition of a Polish puppet government created by the Soviets, the so-called Lublin government. In addition, the

Soviet leader wanted Poland's eastern boundary moved west to the so-called Curzon Line and its western boundary to the Oder and West Neisse Rivers. Neither Roosevelt nor Churchill was willing to recognize the Lublin government or the Oder-Neisse Line as the western boundary of Poland, although they did accept the Curzon Line as its eastern border. Unable to agree on Poland's western border, the Big Three decided to resolve the issue at the final peace conference.

Roosevelt feared that the inability to resolve the dispute over the composition of the Polish government would wreck the Yalta conference and cripple his effort to lay the foundation for friendly Soviet-American relations after the war. As a way out of the stalemate, the president suggested that Stalin permit the creation of a new Polish provisional government, one that would include both the London Poles and the Lublin group. Stalin rejected the president's request, insisting that a friendly Poland was vital to the security of the Soviet Union and arguing the London Poles were anti-Soviet. However, as a concession to the president, he promised that "all democratic and anti-Nazi parties" could participate in "free and unfettered elections."[29] Yet Stalin refused to permit Western observations of the Polish elections designed to ensure that they were really free. Instead, he proposed the creation of a tripartite commission, composed of Molotov and the U.S. and British ambassadors in Moscow, with the authority to enlarge the Polish government.

Roosevelt and Churchill accepted this arrangement. When Admiral William Leahy, Roosevelt's chief of staff, was informed about the Polish arrangement, he reacted: "Mr. President, this is so elastic that the Russians can stretch it all the way from Yalta to Washington without ever technically breaking it." "I know Bill," Roosevelt replied. "I know it. But it's the best I can do for Poland at this time."[30] Nevertheless, to cover himself from any criticism that he had sold out Poland and the rest of Eastern Europe, Roosevelt persuaded Stalin and Churchill to accept a State Department-drafted Declaration on Liberated Europe. It committed the Allies to assist liberated peoples in solving their political and economic problems by democratic means, including free elections.

Roosevelt's policy of avoiding a confrontation with Stalin over Eastern Europe was partly motivated by his desire to win Soviet support for the United Nations. Stalin wanted the Soviet Union to have three seats in the General Assembly. Churchill supported Stalin's request because the British Commonwealth had already been allotted multiple assembly seats. Roosevelt reluctantly accepted the idea of seating the Soviet republics of Ukraine and Byelorussia (later Belarus) but only after Churchill and Stalin promised to raise no objections to giving two additional seats to the United States. Roosevelt also required them to keep this concession secret until the first session of the UN, which the Big Three agreed would begin in San Francisco on April 25, 1945.

With respect to the Far East, in a private meeting with Stalin, the president questioned the right of Britain and France to have any influence in Asia after the war. Although he had made it clear that Japan would be occupied by the United States, Roosevelt proposed to Stalin that Korea should be established as a trusteeship under U.S., Soviet, and Chinese, but not British or French, supervision. Stalin said that, if the British were denied a role in Korea, Churchill might "kill us."[31] As a result, Roosevelt agreed that Korea should be ruled by a trusteeship in which Britain and China would participate, along with the Soviet Union and the United States, for an indefinite period before being granted independence. As for the French, Roosevelt told Stalin that they were unfit to govern Indochina, which he felt should become a UN trusteeship.

In this meeting, Stalin repeated an earlier statement on the political conditions under which the Soviet Union would enter the war against Japan. The Soviet Union, he said, must be given back the southern part of Sakhalin Island, which Japan had gained after the Russo-Japanese War of 1904–1905, as well as the Kurile Islands. Stalin also wanted access to two Chinese ports in Manchuria—Darien and Port Arthur—and joint ownership with China of the Chinese Eastern and Southern Manchurian Railroads. Stalin also demanded that China make no attempt to end Soviet hegemony over Outer Mongolia. Roosevelt raised no objection to Stalin's territorial demands on Japan but he said he would support the concessions from China only if its leader, Jiang Jeshi (Chiang Kai-shek), agreed to make them. Stalin accepted this condition and promised to enter the war against Japan, two or three months after the defeat of Germany. The Far Eastern agreement, which was supported reluctantly by Churchill, was made a top secret; not even Edward Stettinius, who succeeded Hull as secretary of state, was informed about it.

Although, in hindsight, Roosevelt's concessions to Stalin in the Far East appear excessive, with the collapse of the Japanese military inevitable, the territory demanded by the Soviets was theirs for the taking. Moreover, Roosevelt was not sure that the atomic bomb would work, and therefore he accepted General Marshall's argument that Soviet participation in the war against Japan would be vital to the success of the planned U.S. invasion of the Japanese home islands. Roosevelt was also not particularly bothered by the concessions he had made at China's expense. In return for them, Stalin had promised to sign a treaty of friendship with Nationalist China, which might prove important to Jiang Jeshi in his approaching life-and-death struggle with the Chinese Communists led by Mao Zedong.

Stalin was less successful in getting the United States and Britain to acquiesce to other Soviet ambitions. While both Roosevelt and Churchill accepted, in principle, a revision of the Montreaux Convention, which gave Turkey the right to close the straits of the Dardanelles and Bosporus to foreign warships, nothing was finalized on this matter at Yalta. It was, however, agreed that the issue would be considered later at a conference of the foreign ministers.

An even more potentially explosive issue at Yalta was Iran. This country was occupied during the war by U.S., British, and Soviet troops to ensure safe passage of Lend-Lease supplies to the Soviet Union. At Yalta both the British and the Americans tried to get the Soviets to sign a document renewing their earlier pledge to withdraw their troops from Iran at war's end. But the Soviets refused to do so until they received oil concessions from the Iranian government commensurate with those granted to Britain and the United States. While the British and Americans recognized the Soviet Union's right to Iranian oil concessions, they refused to make the withdrawal of the Red Army from Iran contingent on Soviet success in getting them. The unresolved Iranian problem would erupt into a major Soviet-American crisis a year later.

The Aftermath of Yalta

After his return to Washington, Roosevelt told Congress that the Yalta agreements represented a major step toward peace. Privately, however, he expressed less confidence in the results of the conference. Upon seeing Adolph Berle, a State Department member and old friend who feared Soviet postwar ambitions, Roosevelt threw his arms up and said: "Adolph, I didn't say the result was good. I said it was the best I could do."[32] The alternative was to risk the breakup of the Grand Alliance before the war was over. Until then, Roosevelt hoped that Stalin would cooperate by curbing his territorial appetite and by preserving the facade of democracy in Eastern Europe that was created at Yalta.

But this was asking too much of the Soviet dictator. The Soviets violated the Declaration on Liberated Europe within two weeks of signing it by forcing a subservient government on Romania. The negotiations to broaden the Warsaw government by including non-Communists made little progress, and the Soviets proceeded with the liquidation or deportation of Poles who opposed Communist rule. Roosevelt was embarrassed further, in late March 1945, when news of his acquiescence to Stalin's demand for three UN seats leaked to the press. Americans began to wonder what other secret agreements had been concluded at Yalta.

With the waning of Yalta's glitter, Churchill concluded that there was little likelihood that Stalin would cooperate with the West after the war. On March 8, 1945, he cabled the president urging a harder line toward Soviet policy in Eastern Europe. But Roosevelt wanted to avoid any kind of ultimatum to the Soviets, not only because he believed that there was no way to enforce it but also because he was unwilling to do anything that might jeopardize the approaching UN conference in San Francisco. Rather than confronting Stalin over Poland, Roosevelt preferred to pressure the Warsaw government to observe the Yalta accord.

By April, however, Roosevelt seemed to be moving in the direction favored by Churchill. He approved a State Department-drafted message to Stalin on April 1 suggesting that the Soviets were violating the Declaration on Liberated Europe by their actions in Romania. The statement added that "a thinly disguised continuation of the present Warsaw regime would be unacceptable and would cause the people of the United States to regard the Yalta agreement as having failed."[33]

Still, there are reasons to believe that Roosevelt intended to continue to avoid a confrontation with the Soviet Union for as long as possible. Much to Churchill's chagrin, the president supported Eisenhower's decision to allow the Red Army to capture Berlin, primarily to save American lives. On April 11, 1945, in his next to last message to Churchill, a cable that he personally drafted, the president wrote: "I would minimize the general Soviet problem as much as possible because these problems, in one form or another, seem to arise every day and most of them straighten out. . . ."[34] On the next day, April 12, while resting at his vacation home in Warms Springs, Georgia, Roosevelt suffered a cerebral hemorrhage and died.

Roosevelt's Wartime Diplomacy: An Assessment

The main goal of Roosevelt's Soviet policy was to enlist the aid of the Soviet Union in checking and later defeating the Axis powers. In the thirties, Roosevelt recognized the Soviet government, took the first steps toward military collaboration with the Soviets at a very low level, by offering a military liaison and the construction of a battleship, and encouraged the British and French to conclude an alliance with the Soviet Union. But Roosevelt's effort to create a collaborative relationship with the Soviet Union was blocked by anti-Soviet hard-liners in the State and War Departments as well as isolationists in the Congress who opposed American involvement in Europe's military affairs. Roosevelt also was hampered by the appeasement policies of the British and French and by their unwillingness to work with the leading communist country against the fascist powers. In their defense, however, the British and French were unwilling to stand up to the Axis without American support, which was not forthcoming. Nevertheless, when Stalin did not obtain from the Western powers what he wanted, a military alliance and a free hand in Eastern Europe, he turned to Hitler and signed the infamous Soviet-German Nonaggression Pact.

Despite Stalin's perfidy in the wake of his pact with Hitler, Roosevelt did not lump the Soviet Union with the Axis powers. He realized that the Soviet-German arrangement could not last and that the Red Army would be necessary to defeat Hitler. After the German invasion of the Soviet Union, Roosevelt gave the Soviets massive Lend-Lease assistance. Also, after considerable and inevitable delay, U.S. forces, along with their British, French, and Canadian allies, finally gave Stalin the second front, in France, that he had been denied for the bulk of the war. While Roosevelt was successful in creating and maintaining the Grand Alliance until Allied victory in World War II was assured, he felt compelled to make political concessions to the Soviet Union in Europe and Asia that would eventually tear apart the Grand Alliance.

After Roosevelt's death, conservative critics argued that the concessions he made at Yalta demonstrated that he was a naive dupe of the Soviet dictator. In a more recent and sophisticated analysis, Frederick Marks has argued that, instead of pursuing the chimera of a cooperative Soviet-American relationship after the war, Roosevelt should have prepared the nation for an inevitable breakdown of the Grand Alliance. Had he been so inclined, Marks writes, the president "might have sided with Churchill on the value of Germany and France as potential make-weights against Soviet power."[35]

Other historians regard Roosevelt as a shrewd statesman who based his Soviet policy on a realistic assessment of the balance of power that would prevail in postwar Europe. According to this interpretation, Roosevelt was correct in making the defeat of Germany, rather than the prevention of Soviet occupation of Eastern Europe, the major priority of his wartime policy. His approval of the cross-channel assault, rather than Churchill's Balkan strategy and his decision to postpone territorial decisions as much as possible to the end of the war preserved the Grand Alliance until ultimate victory over the Axis powers was achieved. Churchill's alternative, this view contends, may have delayed final victory without standing any chance of halting the inexorable march of the Red Army. By following the cross-channel strategy, major Anglo-American armies were able to meet the Soviets deep in Germany, on the Elbe River, rather than farther west.

To be sure, Roosevelt overestimated his own ability to influence Stalin. Indeed, his attempt to accommodate the Soviet Union's security concerns undoubtedly gave Stalin the impression that Soviet occupation of Eastern Europe was acceptable to the United States as long as it could be made palatable to American public opinion. In this sense, Roosevelt was Stalin's accomplice in the Soviet occupation of Eastern Europe. As Frederick Marks implies, by failing to prepare American opinion for the type of policy the Soviets would follow in Eastern Europe, Roosevelt bears his share of the responsibility for the subsequent Cold War.

Still, Roosevelt was not as naive as he has appeared to be concerning the inevitability of continued good relations between the United States and the Soviet Union. His refusal to share the atomic bomb with the Soviets and his decision to tie U.S. postwar economic assistance to the willingness of the Soviet Union to comply with the Yalta accords indicate that he did not completely trust Stalin. Moreover, as John Lewis Gaddis has pointed out, "When Roosevelt did make concessions, it was generally in areas where Anglo-American power could not feasibly be brought to bear to deny the Russians what they wanted."[36]

Shortly before Roosevelt died, rising Soviet-American tensions over Eastern Europe produced the first tangible indication that he was prepared to adopt a more confrontational policy toward the Soviet Union once victory over Germany and Japan had been achieved. Ultimately, however, this transition in policy would be made by his successor, Harry S. Truman.

3

Truman and
Containment, 1945–1953

Harry S. Truman entered the White House in April 1945 expecting to
continue Roosevelt's effort to build a collaborative relationship with the
Soviet Union. Yet, within a year, the Grand Alliance was in shreds and the
United States and the Soviet Union had again become enemies. Primarily
because of a drastic intensification of the Cold War during Truman's presidency, the United States would abandon its prewar isolationism once and
for all and adopt a policy of containing the expansion of communism in
Europe and the Far East. Historians have argued about the reasons for
the breakdown of the Grand Alliance ever since.

The New President

Truman was at least partially responsible for the postwar breakdown of
Soviet-American relations. With almost no experience in international relations, the new president was much more susceptible to the anti-Soviet views
of former Roosevelt advisers who stayed on in Truman's administration,
particularly Admiral William Leahy, the military chief of staff, Secretary of
the Navy James V. Forrestal, and Moscow ambassador Averell Harriman,
than the deceased president had been. Along with Winston Churchill, they
pressed Truman to take a tougher stance against the Soviets.

At first Truman complied. On April 16 he joined Churchill in sending a
message to Stalin insisting that the Soviets abide by the Yalta accord on
Poland. In a White House meeting on April 23, Truman personally berated
Soviet Foreign Minister Molotov for failing to observe that agreement. On

May 11 the United States abruptly ended Lend-Lease shipments to the Soviet Union, except aid that would be used for the anticipated Soviet war effort against Japan.

The Soviets responded with increased hostility of their own. On April 24 Stalin accused the United States and Britain of trying to "dictate" Soviet policy toward Poland. Shortly afterward the Soviets arrested sixteen leaders of the Polish underground who had been lured out of hiding by a promise of safe passage out of the country. The Soviets also intensified their effort to communize Bulgaria and Romania. As a result, the United Nations organizational conference that met in San Francisco was disrupted by acrimonious exchanges between the Soviet and U.S. delegations.

The rapid deterioration of Soviet-American relations after Truman's ascendancy to the White House alarmed Secretary of War Henry Stimson and former U.S. Ambassador to Moscow Joseph E. Davies. They pointed out to the new president that, even though Germany had surrendered on May 8, it was essential to maintain the Grand Alliance to ensure peace in postwar Europe and the defeat of Japan, which was still fighting. Even though the United States was developing the atomic bomb, in the spring of 1945 it was still only a hypothetical weapon. Truman accepted Stimson's and Davies's argument that everything possible must be done to secure Soviet participation in the war against Japan.

With this aim in mind, on May 19 Truman persuaded the ailing Harry Hopkins, the personification of Roosevelt's conciliatory Soviet policy, to travel to Moscow to try to resolve the administration's differences with Stalin. Hopkins's mission, from May 25 to June 6, was successful, and Soviet-American tensions diminished appreciably during the late spring and early summer of 1945. Stalin told Hopkins he would allow five non-Lublin Poles and three London Poles to participate in the communist-dominated Polish government. This arrangement gave Truman a face-saving way to recognize the Polish government on July 5. In return, Stalin did not object to the continuation of U.S. hegemony in the Western Hemisphere through a regional alliance between the United States and the nations of Latin America, the Rio Pact of 1947. The Soviet leader also recognized the predominant interests of the United States in Japan and China, and agreed to participate in an international trusteeship in Korea. In addition, Stalin dropped his earlier demand that the Soviet Union must have a veto over UN Security Council discussions as well as its actions. As a result, the San Francisco conference was able to complete its work on the UN charter, which went into effect on December 20, 1945. Stalin also reacted favorably to Truman's request to meet with him and Churchill at Potsdam, near Berlin, from July 17 to August 2.

The Potsdam conference was, on the whole, a success. The Big Three agreed to establish a Council of Foreign Ministers to draft the peace treaties for the defeated Axis powers and address territorial and other issues that would arise after the war. They also agreed to demilitarize, de-Nazify, and democratize Germany and to put the surviving Nazi leaders on trial (at Nuremberg, Germany) for war crimes. A compromise on the thorny problems of German reparations and boundaries was also reached at Potsdam. The Western allies accepted Polish occupation of German territory east of the West Neisse line. In return, the Soviets reluctantly agreed to the Western demand that the final determination of Germany's eastern boundary should await a formal peace conference. The Soviets also dropped their Yalta demand for $10 billion in German reparations and accepted a formula whereby each power would extract reparations from within its respective occupation zone.

At Potsdam, Stalin also reaffirmed the promise he had made to Roosevelt at Yalta (which he reaffirmed to Hopkins in May) that the Soviet army would invade Japanese-held Manchuria by mid-August. Truman, in turn, nonchalantly informed the Soviet leader that the United States had a weapon of great destructive capability, without specifically mentioning the atomic bomb, which had been tested successfully in the desert of New Mexico on July 16. Stalin tried to downplay the significance of the president's message by telling Truman that he hoped that the United States would make good use of the new weapon against Japan, but he also ordered his scientists to speed up their work on a Soviet atomic weapon. Truman and Secretary of State James Byrnes, for their part, hoped that the Americans' atomic bomb would force Japan to surrender before Stalin could make good on his pledge to enter the war against the Japanese.

That expectation was not fulfilled. On August 8, two days after an atomic bomb destroyed Hiroshima, the Soviet Union declared war on Japan. Not until August 14, five days after a second U.S. atomic bomb devastated Nagasaki, and with Soviet troops overrunning Manchuria, did Japan surrender.

The Decline of the Grand Alliance

The need for the Big Three to cooperate to defeat the Axis powers was the cement that held together the Grand Alliance, but once Japan had surrendered, the bonds forged by necessity began to crumble. Secretary of State Byrnes, who traveled to the London Conference of Foreign Ministers in September 1945, naively believed that the military and economic superiority enjoyed by the United States at the war's end would enable him to dictate the terms of the peace treaties. But Molotov ignored America's power and informed Byrnes that, unless Britain and the United States accepted Soviet versions of the Romanian and Bulgaria peace treaties, he would not accept the Italian treaty drafted by the Anglo-American side. Molotov also shocked the Americans by demanding a role for the Soviet Union in the occupation of Japan. The London conference broke up in disarray after Byrnes rejected Molotov's proposals.

In the wake of the failure of the London conference, the Soviets appeared increasingly menacing to the West. They began to pressure Turkey to grant the Soviet Union an unconditional right to send warships through the straits of the Bosporus and the Dardanelles. They also launched a campaign of intimidation against Iran designed to win for the Soviet Union oil concessions comparable to those granted by the Iranians to Britain and the United States. John Foster Dulles, who had attended the London conference as a Republican observer, could only conclude that it was "no longer necessary, nor was it healthy, to hide the fact that fundamental differences now existed between the United States and the Soviet Union."[1]

However, while Byrnes was increasingly disturbed by the Soviet Union's behavior, he was not yet ready to abandon the effort to work out Soviet-American differences. Apparently, Stalin wasn't either. In mid-December 1945 Byrnes traveled to Moscow and, seemingly, was able to patch up differences with the Soviets. Stalin agreed to token representation for the pro-Western parties in the Communist-dominated governments of Romania and Bulgaria. In return, Byrnes stated that the United States was prepared to recognize these governments. The foreign ministers also agreed that a conference to complete the peace treaties would be held in Paris beginning in May 1946. In addition, Byrnes agreed to create an Allied Control Council, which would consult with and advise, but not direct, General Douglas MacArthur on occupation measures in Japan. As a result of these agreements, the Americans and the Soviets were able to fashion a face-saving way of recognizing their respective spheres of influence.

Byrnes and the Soviets also reached a compromise agreement creating a UN atomic energy commission, but in doing so, the secretary of state ignored an agreement Truman had concluded with Britain and Canada on November 15. That agreement called for nuclear disarmament and the sharing of atomic information with the Soviets, but only after an international inspection system had been put into operation. While Byrnes eventually was able to persuade the Soviets to accept this condition, he nevertheless alarmed anti-Soviet hard-liners in the Truman administration and the Congress, who felt that his work in Moscow amounted to a sellout. The president apparently accepted their viewpoint, and Brynes's influence abruptly declined during the winter. In April 1946 the secretary of state told Truman that he would resign after the completion of the Axis peace treaties later in the year.

American hard-liners were not the only forces pressuring Truman to break with the Soviets. At the London meeting of the United Nations in January 1946, Britain's foreign minister, Ernest Bevin, took the lead in resisting the Soviet effort to intimidate Turkey and Iran. Bevin hoped his example would prompt the Truman administration to collaborate with Britain in the defense of Western interests. *Time* magazine compared Byrnes, "a habitual compromiser," with the British foreign minister, who "spoke up to the Russians as a great many plain people in pubs and corner drugstores had often wanted to speak."[2]

Stalin also inadvertently pushed Truman in the direction desired by Bevin. In an address on February 9, 1946, the Soviet leader called for a new five-year economic program that would prepare the Soviet Union for an inevitable conflict with the capitalist world. U.S. Supreme Court Justice William O. Douglas called Stalin's speech "the Declaration of World War III."[3] Other observers, however, interpreted Stalin's speech as merely an attempt to mobilize the Soviet people for the sacrifices that postwar reconstruction would require, not as a preparation for a war with the West.

Yet Americans were agitated by Soviet behavior, which seemed to belie Stalin's pacific intentions. Soviet troops were still in Iran, and they continued to occupy Chinese Manchuria long after the Japanese surrender. Furthermore, much to the embarrassment of the Truman administration, the Soviets invoked the Yalta agreements to defend their occupation of Japan's Kuril Islands. As a result, Byrnes was compelled to release the text of the Yalta accords in late January. The congressional and public outcry they produced, particularly against the Far Eastern concessions Roosevelt had made to win Soviet participation in the war against Japan, forced Truman to try to distance himself not only from the Soviets but also from Byrnes, who until this time had prided himself on being at Roosevelt's side at Yalta.

Growing American suspicion of Soviet intentions was aggravated further by a news report on February 3, 1946, that a Soviet spy ring had successfully transmitted secret information about the U.S. atomic bomb to the Soviet Union. The news did much to dampen public enthusiasm for any plan to abandon the American atomic monopoly. Republican leaders, like Michigan Senator Arthur Vandenberg, warned Truman that the Republican Party would no longer support the kind of conciliatory approach toward the Soviet Union that Byrnes had pursued in Moscow.

But the administration was already moving toward a more confrontational policy toward the Soviets. On February 12 the State Department informed them that the United States was deferring recognition of the Bulgarian government until Bulgaria reached a reparations agreement with Greece. On February 22, in a major reversal of the administration's hands-off policy toward Iran, Byrnes informed the Iranians that the United States would actively support their independence and territorial integrity. The loss of Iran's oil, Truman admitted in his memoirs, "would be a serious loss for the economy of the Western world."[4] Even more important than Iran's oil, however, were the far vaster oil reserves of nearby Saudi Arabia, which the State Department called "a stupendous source of strategic power, and one of the greatest material prizes in world history."[5]

The apparent Soviet threat to the Middle East's oil also made the defense of Turkey a vital American interest for the first time. In late February Byrnes decided to send the U.S.S. *Missouri*, the world's most powerful warship, to Istanbul as a warning to Moscow that the United States would not tolerate Soviet aggression against Turkey.

Thus, in the space of a few days in February 1946, the Truman administration gave up, once and for all, the idea of attempting to accommodate the desires of the Soviet Union. The rationale for the new policy was provided on February 22 in an 8,000-word "Long Telegram" that was drafted by George Kennan. From his post in the U.S. embassy in Moscow, Kennan warned the State Department that Soviet hostility toward the capitalist world was inevitable and immutable because it provided the justification for the oppressive totalitarian system the Communists had imposed upon the Soviet people. Instead of trying to accommodate the Soviet regime, Kennan recommended that the United States concentrate on containing the expansion of Soviet power until such a time that a more moderate form of government came into being in the Soviet Union.

In an address on February 28, Byrnes announced the administration's new confrontational approach. In a phrase Truman had underlined in the text of the speech before its delivery, Byrnes stated that "we cannot allow aggression to be accomplished by coercion, or pressure, or subterfuges, such as political infiltration."[6] In delivering this address, historian Robert Messer has observed, "Byrnes announced, with Truman's blessing, his personal declaration of the Cold War."[7]

Less than a week later, on March 5, Winston Churchill, now leader of the opposition party in Parliament, delivered a commencement address in Fulton, Missouri. With Truman present on the speakers' dais, Churchill declared that an "Iron Curtain" had descended from "Stettin in the Baltic to Trieste in the Adriatic." He called for the creation of a "fraternal association of the English-speaking peoples" to keep the peace. He concluded, "I am convinced that there is nothing they [the Soviets] admire so much as strength, and there is nothing for which they have less respect than for military weakness."[8] Stalin took the speech as a sign that Churchill wanted a war with the Soviet Union.

Following up on his new, tougher line toward the Soviet Union, Byrnes publicized, on March 5, a note he had sent Moscow demanding Soviet withdrawal from Iran. Three days later, he asked British Foreign Secretary Ernest Bevin if Britain would be willing to join the United States in placing the Iranian issue before the Security Council. Responding to the embarrassing exposure of their attempts to intimidate Iran, the Soviets agreed on April 4 to withdraw their troops from that country by early May. In exchange, the Soviets received oil concessions in northern Iran from the Iranian government. However, after Soviet troops had left Iran, the Iranian parliament, with U.S. support, canceled its oil concessions to the Soviets.

The Soviet withdrawal from Iran appeared to confirm the wisdom of the tougher U.S. policy. In the face of a resolute stand by the United States and Britain, the Soviets demonstrated that they would back down. Years later, Truman said the administration's response to the Iranian crisis was the first of a series of initiatives that, as he put it, "saved the world."[9]

The crisis also marked the end of the Grand Alliance. Within a three-week period after Churchill's Fulton speech, Stalin terminated his effort to secure a $1 billion U.S. loan, rejected membership in the World Bank and the International Monetary Fund, timed the withdrawal of Soviet troops from Manchuria to support the infiltration of the Chinese Communist forces of Mao Zedong, and launched an ideological purge of the Kremlin leadership designed to remove pro-Westerners from positions of influence. By March 1946, in short, the Grand Alliance was dead.

The Baruch Plan

As Soviet-American relations deteriorated during 1946, so, too, did the prospects for preventing a nuclear arms race. On June 14, 1946, Bernard Baruch, the U.S. representative to the UN Atomic Energy Commission, presented the U.S. plan for international control of atomic energy. Not surprisingly, the Baruch plan was unacceptable to the Soviet Union. While it would have given the Soviets some information concerning atomic energy—information they probably already possessed—and a vague promise to destroy the U.S. nuclear arsenal in the indefinite future, it would have required the Soviets to assume major risks: loss of the veto on atomic energy matters, international inspection of Soviet scientific, industrial, and military facilities, and the possible curtailment of Soviet atomic energy development.

The Soviet counterproposal, which was presented to the UN by Andrei Gromyko on June 19, 1946, was equally unacceptable to the United States. The Soviets insisted that the United States must surrender its nuclear advantage in exchange for a vague Soviet promise to participate in a system of international control. Gromyko also stated bluntly that the Soviet Union would not accept any curtailment of its Security Council veto power.

While the Baruch plan was approved by the UN Atomic Energy Commission on December 30, 1946, its rejection by the Soviet Union made this U.S. victory meaningless and a nuclear arms race inevitable. Moreover, by rejecting the Baruch plan, the Soviets reinforced the impression that they were the primary obstacle to world peace. As a result, most Americans slowly accepted the contention of the Truman administration that confrontation must take precedence over a conciliatory policy toward the Soviet Union.

Not everyone was ready to abandon the effort to reach an understanding with the Soviets. In a 5,000-word letter to Truman on July 23, Commerce Secretary Henry Wallace asserted that the Soviets had legitimate reasons for fearing the United States, including its possession of the atomic bomb and the development of U.S. military bases around the periphery of the Soviet Union. To Wallace, the only solution to an otherwise inevitable nuclear arms race was "atomic disarmament" and an effective system of enforcing it. When Wallace continued his criticism of the administration's foreign policy in a speech at Madison Square Garden on September 12, Truman fired him eight days later. In response, Wallace challenged Truman, unsuccessfully, in the presidential election of 1948.

The Truman Doctrine

In 1947 Greece became another theater of the Cold War. Occupied by Britain after the war, Greece was overwhelmed by major problems of relief and reconstruction, paralyzed by an economy on the verge of collapse, threatened by hostile Balkan neighbors, and fractured by a civil war that pitted the supporters of the right-wing government of Constantine Tsaldares against a coalition of socialists, communists, and liberals.

In February 1947 the British, who were hard-pressed by an acute economic crisis, informed the United States that they could no longer bear the burden of trying to keep order in Greece. The Truman administration decided to assume the responsibility the British were about to surrender. Before a joint session of Congress on March 12, 1947, Truman declared that "it must be the policy of the United States to support free peoples who are resisting attempted subjugation by armed minorities or by outside pressure." The president requested congressional approval for $300 million in aid for Greece and another $100 million for Turkey to help them meet the communist challenge. He asserted that giving aid to Greece and Turkey was part of a global struggle "between alternative ways of life" and that the "fall" of these nations to communism would produce similar results elsewhere.[10]

The Truman Doctrine proved to be the first step in a global ideological crusade against communism. "By presenting aid to Greece and Turkey in terms of ideological conflict between two ways of life," historian John Lewis Gaddis has observed, "Washington officials encouraged a simplistic view of the Cold War which was, in time, to imprison American diplomacy in an ideological straitjacket " that "may well have contributed to the perpetuation of the Cold War."[11]

The Rio Pact

While the United States was taking steps to safeguard the eastern Mediterranean region from communism, it was also moving to protect Latin America. In September 1947 the United States and nineteen Latin American states signed the Inter-American Treaty of Reciprocal Assistance at Rio de Janiero, Brazil. The Rio Pact was an open-ended alliance, designed to cover aggression from any quarter, even from signatories of the treaty. The treaty's security zone encompassed both North and South America. On December 8 the Senate approved the treaty without amendment by the overwhelming vote of 72 to 1.

In April 1948 the Rio Pact was complemented by the Organization of American States (OAS), which was created at the Ninth International Conference of American States in Bogota, Colombia. The OAS charter contained procedures for the settling of disputes between its members before they were referred to the Security Council of the United Nations. The charter of the OAS went into force in December 1951 after two-thirds, or fourteen, of the members had ratified it.

The Marshall Plan

Besides the Truman Doctrine and the Rio Pact, the other component of the emerging Truman containment strategy was the Marshall Plan. Named after General George C. Marshall, who succeeded James Byrnes as secretary of state in January 1947, the Marshall Plan was designed as a massive economic aid program (over $12 billion by 1952) to rebuild war-torn Europe. The economic recovery of Europe, administration officials realized, would help ensure that Western Europe remained politically stable, sufficiently conservative to protect America's European economic investments, and, as a result, less susceptible to Soviet pressure.

Although the Soviet Union and its East European satellite states were invited to participate in the Marshall Plan, it was soon apparent that their involvement would seriously compromise Soviet economic and political interests. In return for U.S. economic assistance, the Soviets feared the United States would require a Soviet withdrawal from Eastern Europe. Consequently, on July 2, 1947, the Soviet Union rejected the Marshall Plan and subsequently pressured its satellites to follow suit. As an alternative

Europe, 1955

to the Marshall Plan, on October 5 the Soviets announced the creation of their own economic assistance program, the so-called Molotov Plan.

The rival economic plans reinforced the existing military division of Europe by creating competing economic spheres of influence. In the West, Marshall Plan economic assistance either revitalized or created for the first time democratic governments, that were based upon, or at least tolerant of, free market principles. In the East, the Molotov Plan became the basis of COMECON, which welded the economies of Eastern Europe to the Soviet economy.

The economic regimentation of Eastern Europe was accompanied by intensified political repression, since the Soviets saw no further need to placate Western opinion. By the spring of 1948, when a Communist coup brought Czechoslovakia firmly into the Soviet bloc, the last vestiges of democracy had vanished in Eastern Europe.

The German Problem

Germany was the issue that finalized the breakup of the Grand Alliance, just as it had been the primary reason for bringing the Big Three together in the first place. At the Potsdam conference, Truman, Churchill, and Stalin had decided that Germany would remain one economic entity, in spite of its division into military occupation zones. However, this decision was ignored by the French, who continued to rule their occupation zone independently of the other allied zones. The French not only wanted to keep Germany weak, they also wanted to ensure that German reparation payments would be obtained from current German production. While the Soviets also wanted to keep Germany weak, they believed that it would be easier to collect reparation payments from a unified Germany than one divided into separated economic entities.

U.S. policymakers, on the other hand, came to regard Stalin's support for a unified German economic entity as a Soviet plot to dominate the entire country. Accordingly, in May 1946 the United States and Britain halted the payment in kind of German reparations from their respective zones to the Soviet Union. In addition, on September 6, 1946, Secretary of State Byrnes promised the German people the restoration of self-government and suggested that the ceding of German territory to Poland would not be permanent. He also indicated that U.S. troops would remain in Germany indefinitely.

The United States and Britain then proceeded to take the first steps toward creating a West German state that would be sufficiently strong to block further Soviet expansion into Western Europe. On January 1, 1947, the U.S. and British occupation zones were fused into one administrative entity, called Bizonia. In February 1948 the Western powers instituted a program of currency reform in Bizonia as a preparation for its participation in the Marshall Plan. Moreover, the Western powers, without the concurrence of the Soviet Union, decided to convene an assembly to draft a constitution for a West German state.

The Soviets naturally regarded the prospect of a West German state with ties to the enormously powerful United States as a new German menace. To prevent it, the Soviets applied pressure on the divided city of Berlin, 125 miles deep inside the Soviet zone. In March 1948 the Soviets began to restrict Western ground travel into West Berlin, and on June 24 they brought it to a complete halt.

The Truman administration regarded the Berlin blockade as a major test of the West's determination to defend the freedom of not only West Berlin but all of Western Europe. Accordingly, the United States took vigorous countermeasures. Traffic into West Berlin from the Soviet zone was halted. In addition, the United States undertook a monumental airlift of supplies into West Berlin that enabled the city to withstand the Soviet stranglehold. Moreover, in an obvious demonstration of U.S. atomic power, sixty B-29s were dispatched to Britain by the president. Although the B-29s were called "atomic bombers," they carried no atomic weapons. Nevertheless, the action made the previously tacit threat of U.S. nuclear retaliation against the Soviet Union explicit for the first time.

It was not the threat of nuclear devastation, however, that moved the Soviets to end their blockade of West Berlin. Instead, they came to see that the blockade of Berlin would probably hasten the formation of a unified West German state rather than forestall it. Moreover, the Soviet blockade of West Berlin produced an economically painful Western counterblockade of the Soviet zone. In addition, the Berlin blockade was a monumental propaganda defeat for the Soviet Union, for it gave additional substance to the U.S. hard-line interpretation of Soviet intentions. In May 1949 the Soviets ended their blockade after the Western powers agreed to lift their counterblockade.

Despite the pacific termination of this first Berlin crisis, its occurrence nevertheless destroyed any remaining hope for the rapid reunification of Germany. In 1949 the Western powers transformed their occupation zones into a West German state, the German Federal Republic. The Soviets responded in the same year by establishing a communist puppet state in their zone, which they styled the German Democratic Republic. The division of Germany sealed the postwar division of Europe into rival American and Soviet spheres of influence.

Deterrence

The Berlin blockade completed the transformation in America's approach to the Soviet Union that had begun with Truman's presidency in April 1945. At the time of the Yalta Conference, in February 1945, Soviet objectives were seen by Americans as essentially defensive, but by 1948 a study of the newly created National Security Council, NSC-20, viewed the Soviet goal as nothing less than the domination of the entire world. It insisted that America's primary objective must be one of reducing "the power and influence of Moscow" by all means possible, including the "liberation" of Eastern Europe, the dismantling of the Soviet military establishment, and the dissolution of the Soviet Communist Party.[12] While NSC-20 stated that these goals could be achieved without force, it did not preclude the possibility of war. In the event of hostilities, according to another National Security Council Study, NSC-30, the atomic bomb could deter the Soviet Union from overrunning Western Europe.

The adoption of a nuclear deterrent strategy by the Truman administration revolutionized the U.S. approach to war. In the past, Americans had generally prepared for war only after a war had begun. Now, the advocates of deterrence argued, the United States would have to prepare for war before its outbreak, in order to prevent it. However, it was never quite clear how much force would be needed to deter the start of a war. This ambiguity would ultimately do much to stimulate the production of nuclear weapons.

The U.S. nuclear threat, in turn, spurred the Soviet atom bomb project. In August 1949 the Soviets succeeded in detonating their first nuclear device. The threat of nuclear annihilation, once an American monopoly, now became mutual. Five months later, in January 1950, Truman approved the development of a U.S. fusion weapon, the hydrogen bomb. Its successful test, in November 1952, would make the threat of nuclear devastation a global phenomenon.

NATO

The Soviet atomic bomb directly contributed to the creation of America's first entangling European alliance, NATO, in 1949. The North Atlantic alliance was a product of what came to be called the Cold War consensus. It held that, if the United States again withdrew into isolation, Western Europe would fall under the domination of another aggressive power, the Soviet Union, and this situation would again require U.S. military intervention. The American people, influenced largely by the aggressiveness displayed by the Soviet Union after World War II, came to believe that it would be far less expensive in lives and wealth to prevent another global conflagration than it would be to win one after it had begun.

Another factor that encouraged the United States to abandon its isolationist tradition was a growing realization that the oceans no longer offered the nation much protection against attack. This was even more obvious after the Soviets developed an atomic bomb of their own and the means to deliver it (a long-range bomber modeled closely on the American B-29).

Still, even after the Soviet Union's aggressive tendencies had been confirmed in the eyes of most Americans, the Truman administration at first sought to limit the U.S. commitment to European security primarily to economic assistance, as expressed in the Truman Doctrine and the Marshall Plan. The administration initially believed that Britain could and would bear the major military responsibility for defending the continent against the Soviets. However, the British government was eventually able to convince the administration that Britain could not do so, even with massive U.S. economic assistance. The United States would have to make a military commitment to Europe's defense.

The first step toward the North Atlantic alliance, which was first proposed by Britain's foreign secretary, Ernest Bevin, was the creation of an Anglo-French alliance. This step was taken with the signing of the Treaty of Dunkirk in 1947. Although directed at Germany, the Dunkirk treaty also served as the nucleus of the Brussels Pact of 1948, which bound Britain and France to the defense of the Benelux countries. The Brussels Pact, in turn, served as the nucleus for the broader North Atlantic Alliance, which united the United States, Canada, and fourteen European nations or mutual defense. The heart of the North Atlantic Treaty, Article 5, provided that an attack against any one of the signatories would be regarded as an attack against all, requiring the parties to respond to any such aggression by taking appropriate individual and collective action.

A practical U.S. military commitment to Europe's defense did not exist until September 1950. In that month Truman decided to return U.S. combat troops to Europe to reinforce the American occupation troops that had been stationed in Germany since the end of the war. Their arrival, in the following year, created the possibility of an effective ground resistance to a Soviet attack on Western Europe. Needless to say, the new U.S. military presence only reinforced Soviet fears of America's aggressive intentions and prompted a new Soviet military buildup in the early 1950s.

The "Loss" of China

The Cold War also spread to China during Truman's administration. For decades Jiang Jeshi's (Chiang Kai-shek's) Nationalist forces had been battling the Chinese Communists under the leadership of Mao Zedong (Mao Tse-tung), but the two sides agreed to a tenuous truce after the Japanese invaded China in 1937. In the face of the Japanese onslaught, the Nationalists retreated to the western and southern parts of China, while the Communists consolidated their strength in China's rural northwest. Once the United States entered the war against Japan in 1941, the Nationalists armies allowed the Americans to play the major role in defeating the Japanese, while they marshaled their resources for the inevitable postwar showdown with the Communists.

By June 1944 Franklin Roosevelt was thoroughly disgusted with Jiang's lackluster prosecution of the war. He sent then Vice President Henry Wallace to China to pressure Jiang to negotiate a settlement with the Communists that would enable the Nationalists to do more against the Japanese. The Wallace mission was unsuccessful, primarily because Jiang demanded nothing less than a Communist surrender. Nevertheless, Roosevelt was stuck with the Nationalist leader since he believed the U.S. Congress and the American people would not accept a Communist alternative. Therefore, Roosevelt ignored a proposal (dated January 9, 1945) from Mao Zedong and his de facto foreign minister, Zhou Enlai (Chou En-lai), that they be invited to Washington to discuss with the president a settlement of the Chinese civil war.

Stalin, likewise, did not give the Chinese Communist leaders much support. During the war, he did not want the Chinese civil war to disrupt the Grand Alliance. In April 1945 he assured the Truman administration that he would abide by his pledge to Roosevelt (at the Yalta conference) that he would not assist the Chinese Communists to subvert Nationalist authority in China. True to his word, on August 14, 1945, Stalin concluded a Treaty of Friendship and Alliance with the Nationalist

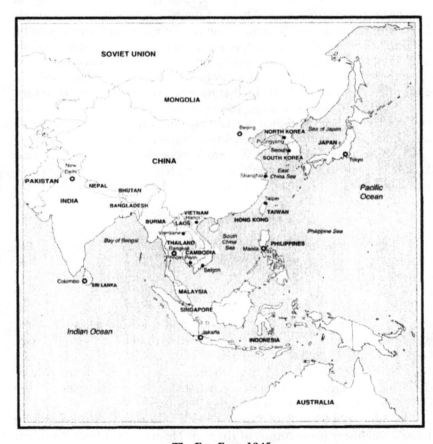

The Far East, 1945

government. By signing the treaty, the Nationalists accepted the loss of Outer Mongolia, granted the Soviets access to the port facilities of Dairen, and permitted the construction of a Soviet naval base at Port Arthur. They also agreed to joint Soviet-Chinese ownership of the Manchurian railways. The Nationalists obviously thought these concessions were worth the Soviet Union's pledge to refrain from assisting the Chinese Communists and to withdraw Soviet troops from Manchuria as soon as Japanese forces had surrendered.

Why did Stalin prefer dealing with the Nationalists rather than the Communists? The Soviet leader probably assumed that, at least in the near future, the Communists were too weak to overthrow the Nationalists, while the latter were not strong enough to threaten Soviet interests in East Asia. Moreover, there was little love lost between Stalin and the Chinese Communists. Mao Zedong had repudiated Soviet control of the Chinese Communist Party in 1935 and then turned Marxist theory upside down by attempting to build communism in China on the support of the peasants rather than the industrial proletariat. As a result, Stalin called Mao a "margarine Marxist" who was afflicted by "chauvinism" and a "petty bourgeois ideology."[13] Apparently, Stalin preferred to deal with a weak Nationalist China that was willing to cooperate with the Soviet Union than a China ruled by Communists who refused to follow the Soviet pattern.

In spite of Stalin's preference for the Nationalists in China, rather than the Communists, the difficulties the Truman administration had experienced with the Soviets in Eastern Europe and the Middle East caused it to distrust Soviet motives in East Asia as well. Ignoring the differences that separated the Chinese and Soviet Communists, the administration considered Mao Zedong merely a Soviet puppet who would do Stalin's bidding without hesitation. Consequently, Truman, like Roosevelt, ignored the efforts of the Chinese Communists to achieve a modus vivendi with the United States. While the State Department realized that Jiang Jeshi's government was hopelessly corrupt and unrepresentative of the masses of the Chinese people (over 90 percent of whom were peasants), the Truman administration rallied to the Nationalists as the best way of blocking Soviet penetration of Eastern Asia.

Accordingly, the United States went out of its way to help Nationalist forces regain control of Chinese territory that was occupied by the Japanese army during the war. Japanese forces outside Soviet-occupied Manchuria were instructed to surrender only to Nationalist commanders, and not to the Chinese Communists. The administration also ordered Lieutenant General Albert C. Wedemeyer, the U.S. chief of staff to Jiang, to airlift and sealift the best Nationalist divisions to Japanese-occupied areas as rapidly as possible. In addition, 53,000 U.S. Marines were ordered to occupy key cities in northern China to ensure that they would not fall under Communist control before Nationalist forces arrived. Some of these U.S. forces skirmished with Communist troops in Shanghai.

On September 14, 1945, Truman also approved a plan proposing extended U.S. military assistance to the Nationalists, including equipment for thirty-nine Nationalist divisions and eight air wings. The United State also continued to provide the Nationalists with economic aid after the war. In fact, more U.S. assistance arrived in Nationalist China after the war with Japan was over—about $3 billion between 1945 and 1949—than had been delivered to the Nationalists during that conflict.

U.S. assistance to Jiang Jeshi no doubt contributed to Stalin's decision to provide some assistance to the Chinese Communists. Accordingly, Soviet forces facilitated the movement of Communist forces into Soviet-held Manchuria. The Soviets also equipped the Chinese Communists with weapons seized from the Japanese. As a result, by November 1945 the Communists had 215,000 troops in Manchuria. When the Soviets finally withdrew from China in May 1946, the Communist forces were in an incontestable position in northeastern China, from which they later launched an offensive that would eventually (in 1949) drive the Nationalists from the mainland of China.

While the Truman administration did what it could to help Jiang Jeshi, it nevertheless preferred to avert an all-out civil war in China, believing that only the Soviet Union would benefit from such a conflict. Accordingly, in November 1945 Truman sent then Army Chief of Staff General George Marshall to China to try to mediate a settlement of the Nationalist-Communist conflict. In addition to playing a mediatory role, Marshall was instructed to facilitate the ongoing U.S. supply of the Nationalist forces, in the hope that they would be able to reestablish control over Manchuria. Hampered by the less-than-neutral role he was asked to play, not to mention the hostility of the contending parties for one another, Marshall was unable to negotiate an end to the civil war.

In July 1946 Jiang launched an all-out offensive against his Communist antagonists. However, while the Nationalists forces were able to make some gains against the Communists in the major cities, Communist strength in the countryside grew. Jiang's dependence on the landlords and the rural gentry made it impossible for him to address effectively the needs of the peasantry, needs that the Communists at least attempted to satisfy. As a result, by 1947 the Nationalist offensive had sputtered out and the initiative had shifted to the Communists. Advancing from their bases in Manchuria and northern China, the Communist armies swept southward against the crumbling Nationalist lines.

Faced with the prospect of disaster, Jiang, on January 8, 1949, pleaded for military intervention by the United States, Britain, France, and even the Soviet Union. The Soviets still had not abandoned the Nationalists because Stalin feared that a China ruled by Mao Zedong would be more difficult to deal with than a weakened Jiang Jeshi. Thus, the Soviet leader urged Mao to halt his forces on the Yangtze River and form a coalition government with the Nationalists. But Mao would not be denied his ultimate triumph. He ignored Stalin's demand and ordered his armies across the Yangtze, from where they quickly advanced into southern China. On October 1, 1949, Mao Zedong proclaimed the establishment of the People's Republic of China, with Beijing (Peking) its capital. Faced with this fait accompli, the Soviet Union became, on the next day, the first nation to recognize the new government. In December 1949 what remained of the Nationalist government and Jiang Jeshi's forces fled to the island of Taiwan, some 200 miles to the east of the Chinese mainland.

A New U.S.–China Policy

The Truman administration attempted to absolve itself of responsibility for the Communist victory even before it was accomplished. On August 5, 1949, the administration issued a long defense of its China policy, known as "The China White Paper." In a letter of transmittal that accompanied it, Secretary of State Dean Acheson blamed the Communist victory on the shortcomings of the Nationalists themselves. He stated that U.S. military intervention on their behalf would only have antagonized the Chinese people without saving the Nationalists. Acheson clearly hoped that the new Chinese regime would follow the Tito model and stay out of the Soviet bloc. For this reason, and because the Joint Chiefs of Staff agreed that the strategic importance of Taiwan was not sufficient to "justify overt military action" in its support, on January 5, 1950, Truman announced that the United States would not intervene on behalf of the Nationalists.[14] In effect, the administration indicated that it would not contest a Communist attempt to occupy that island.

Truman's decision was amplified in a speech delivered by Acheson on January 12. The secretary of state assured the nation that the Communist victory in China did not constitute a threat to the rest of Asia. But he excluded both Taiwan and South Korea, as well as the Southeast Asian mainland, from a U.S. strategic defense line that he said extended from the Aleutian Islands to Japan, the Ryukyu Islands, and south to the Philippines. As far as the United States was concerned, Acheson said, the military security of countries beyond the defensive perimeter "lay beyond the realm of any practical relationship." Should an attack on these areas occur, "the initial reliance must be on the people attacked to resist it and then upon the commitments of the entire civilized world under the charter of the United Nations." The administration would, however, give the countries outside the U.S. defensive perimeter economic aid and advice, but only if there were a "fighting chance" they could emerge without turning communist.[15]

The Truman administration did not immediately rule out the possibility of conducting normal relations with the new Communist regime in China. Rather, it hoped to use the prospect of recognition, trade, and a seat in the United Nations as inducements for "good behavior" by the Chinese Communists. Consequently, U.S. consular and embassy officials did not immediately leave their posts in Communist-occupied China, although they studiously avoided treating the Communists as the de facto authorities.

For a number of reasons, however, U.S. recognition of the Communist regime became politically impossible for the Truman administration. One was the hostile reaction of Republican congressmen to the "loss" of China. They called The China White Paper "a 1,054 page whitewash of a wishful, do-nothing policy which has succeeded only in placing Asia in danger of Soviet conquest, with its ultimate threat to the peace of the world and our own national security."[16] Republicans could not understand why containment was a feasible policy for Europe but not for Asia. Republican Senator William F. Knowland of California declared that, since communism was global in character, "it did not make sense to try to keep 240,000,000 Europeans from being taken behind the Iron Curtain, while we are complacent and unconcerned about 450,000,000 Chinese going the same way."[17]

The negative impact of Knowland's criticism of the administration's China policy was augmented by the virulent attacks of Republican Senator Joseph McCarthy of Wisconsin. Beginning in February 1950, McCarthy charged that the loss of China, as well as Eastern Europe, was a result of communist infiltration of the U.S. State Department. McCarthy's unsubstantiated charge that card-carrying communists were working in the State Department not only created a numbing atmosphere of fear and suspicion, but also helped to make recognition of Communist China politically impossible for three decades.

The Chinese Communists were also partially responsible for Washington's inability to follow a realistic policy toward them. In March 1948 the Chinese Communists announced that they would not recognize treaties concluded by the Nationalist government nor would they recognize foreign diplomatic officials until after their governments had recognized the Communist regime. On October 24, 1949, the Chinese jailed U.S. Consul General Angus Ward for a month on charges—apparently true—that his consulate was a nucleus of a U.S. espionage network. Truman called the arrest an outrage. Acheson said the Ward incident was one of the major reasons, along with the new government's refusal to recognize the international agreements of the old regime, why the United States could not recognize the Chinese Communist government.

The Ward case, at the same time, convinced Mao Zedong that the United States and Communist China could not have a friendly relationship. As a result, Mao gave up the prospect of U.S. recognition and adopted a virulently anti-American posture. With only the Soviet Union as a potential ally, Mao traveled to Moscow in December 1949 to assure Stalin that he was not another Tito. On January 14, 1950, the Chinese Communists seized American, Dutch, and French diplomatic property in

Beijing, which had been awarded to them by the "unequal treaty" of 1901. The United States responded by closing all its consular offices in China and recalling its diplomats.

Any remaining possibility of an improvement in America's relations with Communist China was clearly ruled out by the Sino-Soviet Treaty of Friendship, Alliance, and Mutual Assistance, which Mao and Stalin concluded on February 14, 1950. In it the Soviets promised to provide the Chinese with technical help and $300 million in loans, far less than the Chinese had expected. Getting money from Stalin, Mao later recalled, was like taking "meat out of a tiger's mouth."[18] In return, the Soviets were allowed to retain their previous rights over the Manchurian railways and their bases in Port Arthur and Dairen, although they promised to relinquish them eventually. Acheson, having given up his hope for a Titoist China, denounced the Sino-Soviet Treaty as "an evil omen of [Soviet] imperialistic domination" of China.[19]

Japan

The "loss" of China prompted the Truman administration to develop Japan as a bulwark against further communist advances in East Asia. This had not been one of the original objectives of the U.S. occupation policy. Rather, the Truman administration had planned initially to transform Japan into a peaceful state that would not threaten its neighbors. To this end, General Douglas MacArthur, the commander of U.S. occupation forces in Japan, instituted a virtual revolution in Japan's political, economic, and social systems.

The Japanese emperor was compelled to renounce the theory of his own divinity. Japan's new constitution, written in part by the Americans, reduced him to a constitutional figurehead. The new constitution also required Japan to renounce war as a sovereign right. It also granted the Japanese people comprehensive rights, including freedom of the press, education, representation, and free elections. In addition, with the exception of the imperial family, the Japanese nobility was abolished.

In addition to the constitutional strictures, the United States sought to prevent the revival of Japanese militarism by reducing the country's industrial production to the level of the 1930s. But Japan's industrial infrastructure was so badly damaged by the war, that the initial U.S. program became almost impossible to implement. To avert starvation and long-term economic dependence on the United States, MacArthur, over the objections of the Soviet Union and China, was compelled to reverse U.S. policy and help Japan to rebuild its industrial base.

To rebuild Japan, MacArthur decided, the Allied occupation of Japan had to end as quickly as possible. Accordingly, in July 1947 the United States proposed holding a preliminary conference of the Allied Far Eastern Commission to discuss peace terms for Japan. But when the Soviets made it clear that they would veto any peace treaty that would align Japan permanently with the West, the Truman administration dropped the treaty proposal. Although the administration at this early date did not see Japan as a potential ally of the West, this view changed after the Communists' victory in China. American planners now concluded that Japan had become essential to the defense of the Far East, particularly as a forward base for American military power in the western Pacific. This new policy of building up Japan as an Asian bulwark against communism heightened the tension between the Soviet Union and Communist China, and was a contributing element to the Sino-Soviet alliance.

Indochina

The victory of communism in China also spurred American fears of a "domino effect" in Southeastern Asia, and particularly in French Indochina, China's neighbor. Throughout World War II, Franklin Roosevelt had attempted to prevent the French from regaining control of their colony after the Japanese surrender by trying to make Indochina a trusteeship of the Chinese. But Roosevelt buckled in the face of pressure from the Pentagon and the State Department, as well as the British and French, and gradually modified his anti-colonial position. In March 1945 he informed a State Department official that he would agree to allow the French to return to Indochina if they promised the colony eventual independence. He also reluctantly permitted U.S. air support for French forces fighting the Japanese in Indochina. While Roosevelt, by the time of his death, may not have totally abandoned his goal of ending French rule in Indochina, he nevertheless left his successor an ambiguous legacy with respect to his ultimate intention.

Before the Communists' victory in China, however, the Truman administration had demonstrated little interest in Indochina, but this changed after Mao Zedong's triumph. On December 23, 1949, a National Security study, NSC-48/1, concluded that the Soviet Union was determined to dominate all of Asia. The victory of communism in China, it stated, was the first step toward that goal. "If Southeast Asia also is swept by communism, we shall have suffered a major political rout the repercussions of which will be felt throughout the rest of the world."[20]

Since 1946 a Moscow-trained, Marxist Vietnamese by the name of Ho Chi Minh had been leading his Vietminh forces in a war of national liberation against the French. In January 1950, after unsuccessfully attempting to obtain U.S. support for his struggle, Ho announced that his nation would "consolidate its friendly relations" with the Soviet Union, China, and other "Peoples' Democracies" that were actively supporting national liberation movements in the colonial world.[21] Before the end of the month, both China and the Soviet Union had recognized Ho's Democratic Republic of Vietnam.

The French responded to Ho's de facto alliance with the Soviet Union and China by recognizing Vietnam, Laos, and Cambodia (Kampuchea) as independent states within the French Union. However, the French recognized their puppet, Bao Dai, as the legitimate ruler of Vietnam, rather than Ho Chi Minh. On February 6, 1950, the United States said that it would view any armed communist aggression against these new states (whose governments it recognized the next day) as a matter of grave concern. U.S. support for the French effort in Indochina was motivated not only by a desire to halt communist expansion in Southeast Asia, but also to ensure that France would follow America's lead in Europe, particularly in NATO. That alliance clearly was beginning to make claims on U.S. policy that had not been foreseen when NATO was created. For the purpose of containing communism in Europe and in Asia, the United States had wedded itself, even if reluctantly, to the cause of French imperialism in Indochina.

NSC-68 and Point Four

The U.S. decision to support the French position in Indochina was a part of a revised containment strategy, which was drafted by the State Department's Policy Planning Staff during the spring of 1950 and adopted in June of that year by the National Security Council. Designated NSC-68, the new, top-secret strategy (it was not declassified until the 1970s) was based on the premise that "a defeat of free institutions anywhere is a defeat everywhere." In effect, NSC-68 was another major step in the process, which began with the Truman Doctrine, of making the United States the policeman of the world. It would serve as the blueprint for waging the Cold War for the next twenty years

NSC-68 estimated that the Soviet Union would not have enough atomic weapons to risk an attack on the West until 1954, which the study called the "year of maximum danger." The Soviet atomic threat, NSC-68 stated, could be countered by the hydrogen bomb, whose development Truman had approved in January 1950. But the authors of NSC-68 also expected the Soviets to promote and support limited wars by its satellite states, which would need to be countered by larger U.S. and Allied conventional forces. With the objective of "frustrating the Kremlin design," NSC-68 called for an enormous increase in U.S. defense spending, roughly 350 percent more per year, and higher taxes to pay for it. The implementation of NSC-68, the study advised, would require the mobilization of American society and the creation of a "consensus" that "sacrifice" and "unity" were necessary to counter the communist challenge.[22]

In addition to considering the Soviet Union as the primary threat, the writers of NSC-68 viewed China as a "springboard" for Communist penetration of Southeast Asia. To meet this challenge, in May 1950 Secretary of State Acheson signed a military aid agreement with France and the French Indochinese states. Earlier in 1950 U.S. economic and military aid was provided to Burma and Thailand. Holding that any shift in the global military balance could imperil the United States, NSC-68 also encouraged a new view of Taiwan's importance. In late May 1950 the administration decided to expedite the shipping of military aid committed, but not yet delivered, to the Nationalists. It also intensified covert operations in China and Taiwan. In effect, the Truman administration decided to intervene again in the Chinese civil war, and again on the side of the Nationalists.

The Truman administration also adopted a program of technical assistance not only for Taiwan but also for other, less-developed nations. Called the Point Four Program, it was designed primarily to combat the spread of communism in the Third World by ameliorating the effects of poverty. Point Four also encouraged American businessowners to invest in the underdeveloped countries to ensure that they would continue to serve as a market and source of raw materials for the United States. The initial allocation for the program (in 1950) was $34.5 million, but by 1953, the annual appropriation was raised to $155.6 million. By then, scores of countries, including India, Iran, Paraguay, and Liberia, were hosting American technical experts. U.S. Point Four assistance was provided for a variety of purposes, including agriculture, health care, transportation, finance, irrigation, and vocational training.

While Congress agreed to increase funding for the Point Four Program, the Truman administration hesitated before requesting the huge outlays for new weapons the implementation of NSC-68 would require. Administration supporters believed that only a crisis would loosen Congress's purse strings and persuade it, and the American people, to support the radical expansion of the protective role of the United States called for in NSC-68. "Thank God Korea came along," one of Truman's advisers later recalled.[23]

The Korean War

The Korean War began on June 25, 1950, when the Soviet-equipped armies of North Korea crossed the 38th parallel, its border with non-Communist South Korea. The North Koreans quickly captured Seoul, the South Korean capital, and advanced to the southern part of the Korean Peninsula.

The available evidence indicates that both the Soviets and the Communist Chinese were aware of, and probably approved, the North Korean plan to reunify Korea by force. Nevertheless, the Soviets seemed to have been surprised by the timing of the attack. In fact, the Soviet UN delegate was still absent from the Security Council (because the UN had refused to seat Communist China) when that body considered North Korea's aggression.

The Truman administration almost immediately included South Korea in its Pacific defense perimeter. Acheson now regarded the North Korean attack as "an open, undisguised challenge to our internationally accepted position as the protector of South Korea, an area of great importance to the security of American-occupied Japan"[24] The administration wanted to strengthen the U.S. position not only in the Far East but, more importantly, in Europe, where American interests were far more vital. "You may be sure," one member of the State Department, Charles Bohlen, advised George Kennan, "that all Europeans, to say nothing of the Asiatics, are watching to see what the United States will do."[25]

A failure to resist aggression in South Korea could encourage another Soviet proxy attack in Western Europe, the administration believed, perhaps by East Germany against West Germany. The result, Truman feared, would be "a third world war, just as similar incidents had brought on the Second World War." [26] The fact that the North Korean attack posed a direct challenge to the UN's ability to resist aggression was another factor behind Truman's decision to intervene. "We can't let the UN down!" the president exclaimed to his advisers.[27]

On June 25 Truman authorized U.S. naval and air forces to assist the South Koreans. However, he did not order U.S. combat troops into Korea until five days later, on June 30, and only after General Douglas MacArthur, the commander of the U.S. forces in the western Pacific, warned that the South Koreans would be defeated without them. Truman's action was authorized by the UN Security Council on July 7, by a vote of 7 to 0, with Yugoslavia abstaining and the Soviet Union not participating. In all, nineteen countries ultimately contributed personnel to the UN side, but the United States provided, by far, the largest number of troops and the overwhelming bulk of war materiel. Truman's decision to commit combat troops to Korea was the beginning of America's crusade to contain communism in the Third World by direct U.S. military involvement.

War with China

The intervention of the United States prevented the North Koreans from defeating the South Koreans and reuniting the country under communism. On September 15 General MacArthur launched a brilliant amphibious operation behind the North Korean lines at Inchon, near Seoul. Simultaneously, U.S. and South Korean forces pushed north from the so-called Pusan perimeter, to which they had retreated before the North Korean onslaught. To escape destruction in this allied pincer, the North Korean army retreated across the 38th parallel.

At this point, Truman made a fateful decision: he allowed U.S. and UN forces to invade North Korea to reunify the peninsula under the Seoul government. Truman made his decision after MacArthur had assured him, in an October 15 meeting with the president on Wake Island, that Communist China would not enter the war. However, both Truman and MacArthur ignored warnings from the Chinese that they would intervene if the UN forces crossed the 38th parallel. The Chinese apparently feared that an anti-Communist Korea would serve as a springboard for a

U.S. attack on Manchuria. On November 25, after some UN units had approached the Yalu River, the border of China and North Korea, the Chinese army attacked. The UN forces were forced to make a hasty retreat below the 38th parallel.

China's intervention in the Korean War initiated a major debate between General MacArthur and President Truman. MacArthur, seeking to reverse his humiliation at the hands of the Chinese, wanted to retaliate by bombing their bases in Manchuria, blockading the coast of the Chinese mainland, and enlisting the forces of Jiang Jeshi to fight in Korea. The general was even prepared to use the atomic bomb against the Chinese. Truman, on the other hand, did not want to expand the war beyond the borders of Korea for fear that it would bring in the Soviets and possibly initiate a general war, one involving the use of nuclear weapons. Moreover, Truman's advisors, both military and civilian, feared getting tied down in a war with China when they considered the real danger to be a Soviet incursion into Europe or Japan. General Omar Bradley, chairman of the Joint Chiefs of Staff, called a larger war in East Asia "the wrong war, at the wrong place, at the wrong time, and with the wrong enemy."[28] In April 1951, after MacArthur made a number of publicized statements criticizing the president's conduct of the war, Truman relieved him of his command.

After MacArthur's dismissal, the administration decided to make no further attempt to "liberate" North Korea and instead concentrated on pushing back the Communist forces to the 38th parallel. After this was achieved, in May 1951 the administration proposed negotiations designed to end the fighting and restore the prewar status quo.

The armistice talks began the following month, but both sides immediately took uncompromising positions and stuck to them for the next two years. The United States demanded a demilitarized zone along the existing battle line and an armistice commission with unrestricted right to monitor any military buildup. The Communists called for the withdrawal of all foreign troops, both Chinese and United Nations, from Korea and for a demarcation line at the 38th parallel. Even though the Chinese proposal conformed to one endorsed by the United States in January 1951, the Americans turned it down. The Joint Chiefs of Staff and General Matthew Ridgway, who succeeded MacArthur as the UN commander, feared that, if U.S. forces pulled out of Korea, the South Koreans alone would be unable to fend off another Chinese invasion. On the other hand, the Chinese were equally afraid that, if U.S. forces were permitted to remain in South Korea, North Korea would be invaded again.

When the armistice talks began, the Chinese were willing to accept a cease-fire, but the Joint Chiefs of Staff, who were backed by Truman, refused to stop the fighting until an armistice agreement was signed. They believed the Chinese would drag out the talks if UN forces were removed. As a result, the fighting in Korea went on as the armistice talks continued, and an additional tens of thousands of soldiers and civilians would lose their lives before an agreement was concluded.

Another issue that delayed an armistice agreement in Korea was the Chinese demand that all prisoners of war be returned to their homelands regardless of whether they wanted to go back. The United States flatly refused to repatriate Chinese and North Korean prisoners who did not want to return to their homelands. This issue was not resolved until Dwight Eisenhower became president in January 1953. Eisenhower made veiled threats to expand the war, perhaps with nuclear weapons. This, and the death of Stalin in March 1953, persuaded the Chinese to drop their demand for the forced repatriation of prisoners of war. As a consequence, an armistice agreement was signed in June 1953.

This agreement, while it ended the fighting in Korea, did not drastically alter the prewar status quo. Korea remained divided, north and south, with the boundary of the two Koreas still extending roughly along the 38th parallel. Nor did the armistice agreement require the withdrawal of foreign troops from the peninsula. As a result, the United States retained, and still retains today, almost 40,000 troops in Korea.

The Impact of the Korean War: The Far East

The Korean War froze Sino-American relations into a pattern of hostility that would last two decades. About 142,000 Americans were killed or wounded in Korea as well as four million Koreans on both sides. An estimated 900,000 Chinese were wounded or killed, including Mao Zedong's son. The United States branded China as an international aggressor, imposed a tighter economic embargo on trade with the Chinese, and banished any thought of giving the Communists China's seat in the United Nations. With the Chinese and Americans at each other's throats, Stalin became convinced that Mao was not about to become another Tito. As a result, Soviet military and economic aid to China increased after the Korean War.

Sino-American relations were also exacerbated by America's defense of Taiwan. On June 27, two days after the Korean War began, Truman ordered the U.S. Seventh Fleet to patrol the Taiwan Strait, thus blocking the possibility of a Chinese Communist invasion of the Nationalist-held island. The administration also expanded economic and military aid to Taiwan. On May 1, 1951, a U.S. military mission arrived in Taiwan to help rehabilitate the Nationalist military establishment. Taiwan quickly became a vital link in the American "island defense chain" in the Western Pacific. But U.S. policy toward Taiwan was not purely defensive in purpose. During the Korean War, the Central Intelligence Agency and Taiwan initiated small-scale guerrilla operations against the Chinese mainland. These would continue until the Nixon Administration entered office in 1969.

The Korean War also served as a catalyst for expanded U.S. involvement in Indochina. On December 4, 1950, Truman told British Prime Minister Clement Attlee that "the only way to meet communism is to eliminate it. After Korea, it would be Indochina, then Hong Kong, then

Malaya."[29] To prevent the dominoes from falling, on June 27, 1950, Truman announced that he would increase U.S. military assistance to the anti-Communist forces and install a new permanent U.S. military mission in Saigon. Along with the $10 million he approved on May 1, Truman allocated $5 million for military assistance on June 27 and an additional $16 million on July 8. By the time of the Korean armistice, the United States had assumed 80 percent of the cost of the French war with Ho Chi Minh.

Truman was also prepared to intervene militarily in Indochina in the event the Chinese army came to the assistance of the Vietminh. On June 25, 1952, the president approved NSC-124/1. It stated that, in case of overt Communist Chinese aggression against Indochina, "the United States should take air and naval action in conjunction with at least France and the United Kingdom against all suitable targets in China." In the event Britain and France refused to take military action against China, NSC-124/1 added, "the United States should consider taking unilateral action."[30]

The Korean War and the conflict in Indochina also underscored the growing strategic and economic value of Japan as a bulwark against communist expansion in Asia. To that end, the Truman administration spurred the signing of a peace treaty in September 1951 to restore Japan's complete sovereignty. A security treaty, committing the United States to the continued defense of Japan, was signed the same day. In return for U.S. military protection, the Japanese gave the United States the continued use of bases and logistic facilities in Japan. The treaties were ratified by the Japanese parliament in late 1951 and by the United States in early 1952. American occupation of Japan ended on April 28, 1952.

In addition to signing a treaty with Japan, in 1951 the United States concluded alliances in the Pacific area with Australia and New Zealand (the ANZUS Pact) and with the Philippines, thereby completing the Pacific island defense chain.

The Impact of the Korean War: Europe

In spite of the U.S. military buildup in East Asia, Europe remained the major area of the Truman administration's concern. The Korean War seemed to confirm European fears that the Soviets were prepared to use their satellite states to fight proxy wars against the West. While the United States was now firmly committed, through the North Atlantic Treaty, to come to the assistance of Western Europe in the event of a Soviet attack, the United States had few forces on the continent to implement that commitment. Before the Korean War, the United States had two under-strength occupation divisions in West Germany. The European forces on the continent, the Pentagon believed, could not fill that gap. The European forces consisted of British occupation forces in Germany and poorly armed and ill-trained Benelux and French divisions scattered throughout West Germany and Western Europe.

To meet what was perceived as an expanded Soviet threat to Western Europe in the wake of the Korea War, NATO took steps to enhance its military capabilities. It created a unified command structure in 1951, which Truman appointed General Eisenhower to lead. At the Lisbon conference in 1952, the alliance agreed to build a ninety-six-division ground force to counter the Soviet military presence in Eastern Europe. To strengthen NATO's Mediterranean flank, Greece and Turkey were accepted as full alliance members in 1952, and the United States reestablished diplomatic relations with Franco's Spain and Tito's Yugoslavia.

The United States also provided an additional $4 billion of military assistance in fiscal year 1951 to help their European allies rearm, but the allies insisted that an augmented U.S. military presence was also necessary. Accordingly, in September 1950, Truman broke the long-standing tradition against a peacetime U.S. military presence in Europe. He announced that he would send four U.S. divisions to the continent, bringing the total deployed there to six divisions. No one considered this a permanent arrangement, yet U.S. troops would remain in Europe over four decades later. The dispatching of combat troops to Europe transformed the American commitment to the continent's defense. What had been essentially only a promise to defend Western Europe now became a commitment backed by sufficient military power to ensure that that pledge could be implemented.

To gain the Pentagon's support for the commitment of U.S. troops to Europe, however, Truman felt compelled to accept its demand for the rearmament of West Germany and the eventual incorporation of West German forces into NATO. It would take another five years of delicate diplomacy to convince the other allies, particularly the French, that Germany's rearmament could be accomplished safely. In fact, without the assignment of U.S. combat troops to Germany and their incorporation into an integrated NATO command structure, France would not have accepted German rearmament. In effect, the United States had to commit its military power to Europe not only to restore a European balance of power that was threatened by the Soviet Union but also to provide a guarantee that a rearmed Germany would not attack its uneasy neighbors.

The Militarization of U.S. Foreign Policy

In the end, the Korean War confirmed the basic thesis of NSC-68, which held that the United States needed larger and more effective mobile striking forces to demonstrate America's resolve to counter communist aggression anywhere on the globe. Accordingly, the size of the U.S. Army was increased from ten understrength divisions to eighteen full-strength divisions, with air- and seapower increased proportionally. As a result, the total number of U.S. military personnel rose from 1,460,000 to 3,555,000 between June 1950 and June 1954. The strength of U.S. forces stationed in foreign countries also increased during this period, from 280,000 to 963,000 personnel. With much justification, historians consider the Korean War as important as World War II in shaping the character of international relations during the second half of the twentieth century.

Assessment

There have been three major interpretations regarding the origins of the post–World War II Cold War: the so-called orthodox, the revisionist, and the post-revisionist interpretations.

The first, the orthodox interpretation, assigns major responsibility for the breakdown of the wartime Grand Alliance to the Soviet Union. The refusal of Stalin to abide by the Yalta accords and his efforts to expand communism in Europe, the Middle East, and the Far East, historians of this school of thought argue, made the collapse of the Grand Alliance inevitable. The United States, under Truman's leadership, had no choice but to make every effort to check Soviet expansionism.

Some orthodox historians, such as Arthur M. Schlesinger, Jr., argue that the ideological incompatibility of the two superpowers made the revival of the Cold War in the late 1940s inevitable:

> Stalin and his associates, whatever Roosevelt or Truman did or failed to do, were bound to regard the United States as the enemy . . . because of the primordial fact that America was the leading capitalist power and thus, by Leninist syllogism, unappeasedly hostile, driven by the logic of its system to oppose, encircle and destroy Soviet Russia. Nothing the United States could have done . . . would have abolished this hostility . . . nothing short of the conversion of the United States into a Stalinist despotism; . . . and even this would not have sufficed, unless accompanied by total U.S. subservience to Moscow.[31]

On the other hand, political scientist Hans Morgenthau argues that the traditional goals of Russian expansionism, rather than communist ideology, was Stalin's guiding light. For Stalin, Morgenthau argues, "communist orthodoxy was a means to an end, and the end was the power of the Russian state, traditionally defined." Morgenthau sees Soviet moves against Turkey and Iran, as well as in the Far East, as marking the "traditional limits of Russian expansionism." As Stalin told Eden during World War II: "The trouble with Hitler is that he doesn't know where to stop. I know where to stop."[32] Americans, however, failed to appreciate the limited nature of Stalin's ambitions, Morgenthau argues, while the Soviet leader could not understand the cause of American sensitivity. As a result, in Morgenthau's opinion, the Cold War was to some extent the product of mutual misunderstanding.

Soviet historians, for their part, have argued that the United States exaggerated and overreacted to any threat the Soviet Union may have posed to the United States at the end of World War II.[33] The Soviet

Union, they point out, was too crippled by the war to pose any significant threat to the United States for years. Supporting this view, one revisionist historian, Michael Parenti, has written: "The Soviets lost more than 20 million citizens in World War II; fifteen large cities were either completely or substantially ruined; 6 million buildings were obliterated, depriving 25 million people of shelter. Some 31,000 industrial enterprises, 65,000 kilometers of railway, 56,000 miles of main highway, and thousands of bridges, power stations, oil wells, schools, and libraries were destroyed; tens of thousands of collective farms were sacked and millions of livestock slaughtered." After a trip to the Soviet Union in 1947, British Field Marshal Montgomery wrote to General Eisenhower: "The Soviet Union is very, very tired. Devastation in Russia is appalling and the country is in no fit state to go to war."[34]

By contrast, the United States emerged from the war not only with the world's strongest economy but with military superiority as well. Even without the atomic bomb, Parenti points out, "the United States possessed 67 percent of the world's industrial capacity within its own boundaries, and had 400 long-range bomber bases, in addition to naval-carrier forces around the Eurasian perimeter. In contrast, the Soviets had no strategic air force, meager air defenses, and a navy that was considered ineffective except for its submarines."[35]

Some revisionist historians, such as Gabriel and Joyce Kolko stress economic factors as being the most important causes of the Cold War. The Kolkos charge that the Truman administration fabricated the myth of a hostile Soviet Union to win public support for a new interventionist strategy designed to make the world safe for American capitalism. The Truman administration, they argue, sought a global open door policy of equal trade and investment opportunity, private enterprise, multilateral cooperation in foreign commerce and freedom of the seas.[36] The refusal of the Soviet Union to subordinate its economic system, and the political structure that supported it, to U.S. influence, revisionists conclude, is the main reason why the Cold War continued.

Supporting this view, Fred Block argues that "American policy-makers were more concerned about national capitalism in Western Europe than they were with a possible invasion by the Red Army or successful socialist revolution. . . . It is necessary to place the Cold War in the context of the American effort to create a certain type of world economy."[37] Elaborating upon this view, Parenti argues that U.S. defense officials in the postwar era did not expect a Soviet military attack. Their real fear was that they would lose control of Europe and Asia to revolutions caused by widespread poverty and economic instability. "The 'Giant Red Menace,'" Parenti says, "was conjured up to win public support for military and economic counterrevolutionary aid to European and Asian capitalist-dominated nations. While protecting the West from an impending but nonexistent Soviet invasion, U.S. forces and U.S. aid bolstered conservative political rule within Greece, Turkey, Egypt, and Kuomintang [Nationalist] China."[38]

Another, more recent, post-revisionist interpretation, incorporates ideas from both the orthodox and the revisionist interpretations. John Lewis Gaddis, the author of the first major post-revisionist account, considers both internal and external influences important in explaining the breakdown of the Grand Alliance. To Gaddis, domestic politics, bureaucratic inertia, quirks of personality, and inaccurate as well as accurate perceptions of Soviet intentions were all important in shaping U.S. policy.[39]

Another post-revisionist analysis, by Robert Pollard, challenges the importance of economic factors in the revisionist interpretation. In Pollard's view, "the original impulse behind American multilateralism was neither anticommunism nor a need to sustain world capitalism. Instead, American officials backed the Open Door largely because they were determined to prevent a revival of the closed autarkic systems that had contributed to world depression and split the world into competing blocs before the war." In other words, strategic security interests, not economic interests, drove U.S. policy; the United States relied upon "economic power to achieve strategic aims."[40]

More recently, in a work based on enormous research, Melvyn Leffler argues that both security and economic concerns were important in formulating U.S. strategy, and that U.S. officials acted not to balance and contain Soviet power but rather to achieve a preponderance of power.[41]

Needless to say, there is much to be gained by studying all these interpretations. They reveal the complexity of the forces, and personalities, that were at work after World War II. As the orthodox interpretation emphasizes, and the events of the pre–World War II era demonstrate, ideological differences were certainly an important, if not the primary, cause of the Cold War. That these differences were submerged during the war was a product of necessity: the defeat of a common enemy required cooperation, not ideological conflict. Once that goal was achieved, the old ideologically based perceptions that had governed pre–World War II Soviet-American relations began to take precedence again and the distrust and suspicion that had characterized the relationship before the war were revived.

Still, ideological differences are insufficient to explain the intensification of the Cold War after World War II. The fact that the United States and the Soviet Union emerged from that conflict as the world's two strongest military powers only aggravated their ideological incompatibility. Relatively isolated from one another before the war, with vast geographical buffers and powerful military forces between them, Soviet and American interests now collided as both nations attempted to fill the power vacuum created by the collapse of Germany and Japan.

Nor can economic factors be ignored in any explanation of the Cold War. As revisionists have asserted, the United States clearly used its preeminent economic power to fashion a world friendly to American capitalism. The Truman administration did attempt to modify Soviet policy by suspending Lend-Lease aid and by refusing to offer the Soviets a postwar reconstruction loan. While the United States invited the Soviets to participate in the Marshall Plan, it is also clear that Soviet acceptance of the American terms for doing so would have made their economy, not to mention their foreign and domestic policies, susceptible to U.S. manipulation.

Revisionists are also correct in asserting that Stalin's immediate postwar aims were limited. American intelligence was aware that the Soviet Union was greatly weakened by the war and probably desired at least a temporary détente with the United States, not only to gain time for reconstruction but also to procure American financial assistance to support that effort. Rather than attempting to conquer Western Europe, the Soviets displayed a cautious attitude, not only in their dealings with the West but in their handling of Eastern Europe, where the imposition of totally communist governments was not foreordained, at least not until the hard-line attitude of the Truman administration became blatantly obvious.

To a lesser extent, Stalin was as much a victim of American—primarily Roosevelt's—duplicity as the West was of Soviet dishonesty. During the war Stalin repeatedly attempted to gain American and British recognition of a Soviet sphere of influence in Eastern Europe, and he apparently believed he had succeeded in doing so. Roosevelt, at least tacitly, was prepared to recognize the predominant influence of the Soviet Union in that region while paying lip service to the Wilsonian principle of self-determination, which was exemplified in the Declaration on Liberated Europe. Truman, with almost no diplomatic experience, at first tried to follow his predecessor's conciliatory policy. In return, Stalin gave both tacit and formal recognition to U.S. predominance in Latin America, Italy, Japan, China, and the Pacific, as well as British predominance in Greece and Western Europe. Had matters stood there, perhaps the revival of the Cold War could have been avoided, or at least postponed.

But, in the eyes of anti-Soviet hard-liners within the Truman administration, the Republican Party, and the news media, Stalin overreached himself by making demands upon Iran and Turkey. Stalin's speech of February 9, 1946, Kennan's Long Telegram, the revelation of a Soviet atomic spy ring operating in the United States, and Churchill's Fulton address all contributed to growing fear of the Soviet Union. It appeared to an increasing number of Americans that there were no limits to Stalin's territorial ambitions.

The growing U.S. antagonism toward the Soviets was also fueled by Soviet-American differences over Germany, international control of atomic energy, and the role of the United Nations. As a result, Truman's early effort to maintain the Grand Alliance by negotiating a settlement of U.S. differences with the Soviets came to be regarded as synonymous with the Western effort to appease Hitler before World War II. Facing a presidential election in 1948, which Truman believed he could not hope to win if he continued a conciliatory policy toward the Soviet Union, the president adopted the containment policy. The Truman Doctrine, the

Marshall Plan, and NATO followed in succession. The Soviets, in turn, reacted with the Molotov Plan, the Berlin blockade, and a rival alliance, the Warsaw Pact (in 1955), and extinguished the last flicker of national self-determination in Eastern Europe.

With the status quo frozen in Europe, the Third World quickly became the main arena of superpower competition. Blinded by ideological considerations that were reinforced by the postwar Red Scare and the failure of the accommodationist policy toward the Soviet Union, the Truman administration refused to recognize the communist takeover of China. Instead, it expanded the containment policy to the Far East, intervening in the Korean War, providing military and economic aid to Taiwan, Thailand, and French Indochina, and forming a network of alliances with Japan, Australia, and New Zealand. By the time Harry Truman left office in 1953, the foundations for the next four decades of the Cold War were firmly established.

4

Eisenhower and the Globalization of the Cold War, 1953–1961

The Cold War deepened and expanded during the administration of Dwight D. Eisenhower. While the superpower stalemate was maintained in Europe, the rearmament of West Germany, the Hungarian Revolution, and the status of Berlin were among the issues that aggravated Cold War tensions on that continent during the Eisenhower years. Although Eisenhower kept his promise to end the Korean War, Sino-American relations remained frigid, and, in fact, were aggravated during two crises in the Taiwan Strait. During the Eisenhower years, the United States also became more deeply involved in Indochina and took the first steps down the slippery slope to the Vietnam quagmire.

The Cold War also intensified in the Middle East, as a result of Egypt's increasing dependence on the Soviet Union, and in Latin America, culminating in the establishment of the first Soviet client state in the Western Hemisphere, Cuba. During Eisenhower's presidency, the Cold War spread even to sub-Saharan Africa, when the superpowers intervened in the internal affairs of the Congo (now Zaire). The Cold War truly became global in scope during the Eisenhower years. The friction between the United States and the Soviet Union in the Third World became increasingly dangerous as a result of a mushrooming nuclear arms race during Eisenhower's years.

Death of Stalin: A Lost Chance for Accommodation?

On March 5, 1953, shortly after Eisenhower entered the White House, Joseph Stalin died. Some historians believe Stalin's death created the opportunity for a Cold War thaw. Stalin's successor, Premier Georgi Malenkov, sought to relax superpower tensions in order to be free to concentrate on the Soviet Union's internal problems. On March 15 Malenkov declared that there were no existing disputes that could not be decided by peaceful means. In April he called for East-West talks on reducing armed forces in Europe.

Initially, Eisenhower believed that Stalin's death might clear the way for fundamental changes in Soviet behavior and an improvement in East-West relations. In a speech on April 16, 1953, he expressed his willingness to begin arms reduction talks if the Soviets would take concrete steps to resolve outstanding differences with the West. To test Soviet good will, Eisenhower proposed that the Soviets allow free elections in Eastern Europe, sign an Austrian peace treaty, and stop supporting anticolonial rebellions in Asia.

Winston Churchill, who was again (since October 1951) Britain's prime minister, publicly praised Eisenhower's speech, but privately he said that it did not go far enough. As early as February 1950, Churchill had called for a return to the high-level diplomacy that he had participated in at Tehran, Yalta, and Potsdam. On May 11, 1952, shortly after Eisenhower's speech, Churchill proposed a summit conference of world leaders to resolve Cold War differences. He was motivated not only by a belief in the flexibility of the new Soviet leadership but also by a growing fear of nuclear war, enhanced by the development of the hydrogen bomb.

Any inclination that Eisenhower may have had to accept Churchill's summit proposal was squashed by his secretary of state, John Foster Dulles. While Dulles acknowledged that it was possible for Soviet behavior to change, he did not think it was likely to occur soon. He believed the latest Soviet peace offer was simply an attempt to disrupt the U.S. effort to rearm West Germany and admit it into NATO. Therefore, for Dulles, a rapprochement with the Soviet Union at this time could have come only at the expense of weakening the West.

Dulles's fear was shared by West German Chancellor Konrad Adenauer. He feared that, to reduce the tensions of the Cold War, Churchill might be prepared to sacrifice the military integration of Western Europe and accept a permanent Soviet presence in Eastern and Central Europe. Adenauer urged Eisenhower to permit nothing—not even the prospect of German reunification—to stand in the way of the restoration of West Germany's sovereignty and its integration into the Western community.

Dulles also feared the domestic repercussions of negotiating with the Soviets. The Republican Party, and especially Senator McCarthy, had pilloried Truman for "appeasing" the communists. Dulles was unwilling to add fuel to that fire by appearing eager to negotiate with the Soviets. As a result, the secretary of state downplayed the significance of Eisenhower's April 16 speech. The Soviet peace initiative, he added, was simply another "tactical move of the kind for which Soviet communism has often practiced."[1]

While Eisenhower undoubtedly had the final say on the direction his administration's foreign policy would take, and increasingly asserted himself with Dulles as time passed, he was reluctant early in his presidency, when McCarthyism was in full stride, to challenge his more diplomatically experienced secretary of state on an issue as politically sensitive as negotiations with the Soviet Union As a result, nothing came of Malenkov's peace initiative.

The Red Scare

While Eisenhower personally was immune to McCarthy's charges, he nevertheless tried to insulate his administration against the senator's witchhunt in the federal bureaucracy by instituting an antisubversive program of his own. In April 1953 the president signed an executive order authorizing the heads of all federal departments and agencies to fire any employee whose loyalty, reliability, or "good conduct and character" were in doubt. Hundreds of federal employees lost their jobs under the new security system, but not a single traitor, spy, or subversive was indicted by the government.[2]

The Department of State was particularly hard hit by the Eisenhower security program. Among those who lost their jobs were a number of experts in Chinese affairs, including John Patton Davies and John Carter Vincent. However, they were dismissed, not because they were subversives, but because they had predicted the collapse of the Nationalist government in China and had favored a more realistic policy toward the Chinese Communists. The decline of expertise and morale in the foreign service that resulted from this purge did much to prevent the formation of a realistic policy toward communism, particularly Asian communism, in the years ahead.

Perhaps the most prominent victim of the witchhunt was J. Robert Oppenheimer, the father of the atomic bomb. Oppenheimer was denied his security clearance by the administration on the grounds that he had associated with communists. Although Oppenheimer did have personal relationships with American communists, an investigation by the Atomic Energy Commission failed to prove that he had ever been disloyal to the United States. A testament to his innocence was the restoration of his security clearance by President John F. Kennedy in 1963. Rather than disloyalty, the prime reason for Oppenheimer's disgrace was his unrelenting opposition to the development of thermonuclear weapons. By fighting the decision to develop the hydrogen bomb, Oppenheimer made enemies of influential individuals, including his erstwhile friend, Edward Teller, the father of the hydrogen bomb and the most prominent scientist who testified against him in the AEC investigation.

While Oppenheimer was exonerated, Julius and Ethel Rosenberg were executed for their ties to communism. The Rosenbergs had been sentenced to death in 1951 for providing atomic secrets to agents of communist countries. While the guilt of Julius, if not his wife, seems well-founded, their case nevertheless raised a storm of controversy. Many believed that the Rosenbergs were victims of the McCarthyite hysteria, but Eisenhower refused to commute their sentences, saying their activities on behalf of the Soviet Union had "immeasurably increased the chances of atomic war."[3]

McCarthy was at least indirectly responsible for the ruined careers of hundreds of government employees. But in the end, during April 1954, he went too far by launching a televised investigation of alleged communist subversion of the U.S. Army. The unscrupulous methods the senator employed in these hearings provoked widespread public revulsion. Fearing voter retribution in the approaching congressional election, about half of the Senate's Republican members decided to support a resolution censuring McCarthy for "obstructing the constitutional processes of the Senate" and acting in a manner that "tended to bring the Senate into dishonor and disrepute."[4] While McCarthy's power was finally broken, the pall he had cast over America would last for years.

Eastern Europe

Rather than seeing Stalin's death as an opportunity for easing tensions with the Soviet Union, Dulles viewed it as a chance to throw world communism on the defensive. In place of what he called the "negative, futile, and immoral" containment strategy of the Truman administration, Dulles proposed a more dynamic policy that would "liberate" the "captive peoples" under communist control. While Dulles was usually careful to qualify his calls for liberation with phrases like "by all peaceful means" and rejected a strategy inciting armed revolt in Eastern Europe, many nevertheless gained the impression that the new administration would attempt to "roll back" communism in that region of the world.[5]

It soon became apparent, however, that the Eisenhower administration had no intention of fomenting revolution in the Soviet empire. Soviet military preponderance in Eastern Europe combined with the continuing development of the Soviet nuclear arsenal made the thought of U.S. intervention in that region unthinkable. Indeed, from the first, the administration adopted a cautious policy toward Eastern Europe. It refused to support congressional resolutions calling for the repudiation of the 1945 Yalta agreements, in which the Soviet Union had promised to allow free elections in the East European nations it had occupied during the war. Furthermore, when Soviet tanks quelled workers' riots in East Berlin in June 1953, the administration did nothing more than deplore the Soviet repression and praise the heroism of the workers.

One thing that the United States could do, safely, to undermine Soviet hegemony in Eastern Europe was to support the continued independence from Moscow of Josip Tito's Yugoslavia. Even though Tito was a communist, he was not a Soviet puppet, and the administration hoped that assistance to Yugoslavia would encourage the Soviet satellites to follow a more independent line. Although Tito's brand of neutralism was not emulated elsewhere in Eastern Europe, U.S. support for Yugoslavia increased during the Eisenhower years.

The Berlin Conference, 1954

The brutal Soviet intervention in East Berlin in 1953 ruled out the possibility of an East-West summit that year. Nevertheless, in late January and early February 1954, the foreign ministers of Britain, France, the United States, and the Soviet Union met in Berlin to discuss Central European issues. Georges Bidault, the French foreign minister, made it clear to Dulles that his parliament would not pass an American-backed effort to create a European Defense Community (EDC) unless the West made a good-faith effort to negotiate a resolution of the German problem first. This consideration—and not the change in Soviet leadership—was the most important reason why Dulles agreed to participate in the Berlin conference.

Dulles was not surprised that no agreement on Germany was reached. The Western powers insisted that German reunification could only result from free elections in both Germanys, but this demand was rejected out of hand by the Soviets. Equally unacceptable to the West were Soviet demands that a reunified Germany be neutralized, the effort to create a European Defense Community abandoned, and NATO dissolved. In their place, the Soviets proposed the creation of a European security pact in which both the United States and China would have observer status. The Berlin conference, like all previous meetings on Germany, ended in failure.

Unable to resolve the German problem with the Soviets, the Western allies implemented their own solution. They granted West Germany full sovereignty and, after France rejected the EDC proposal in 1954, permitted the West Germans to rearm and (along with Italy) join NATO the following year. The Soviets in 1955 retaliated by creating the Warsaw Pact, an alliance that bound East Germany and the other satellite states to the military doctrine of the Red Army. The division of Germany, as well as Europe, would continue to be major features of the Cold War for another thirty-five years.

Dulles considered the failure of the Berlin conference a vindication of his belief that nothing productive could result from negotiations with the Soviet Union. But Charles E. Bohlen, the U.S. ambassador to Moscow, believed that, had Eisenhower immediately accepted Churchill's call for a summit early in 1953, "there might have been opportunities for an adjustment of some outstanding issues, particularly regarding Germany."[6] By the time the Berlin conference was held, in early 1954, however, Malenkov's leadership was under challenge from Nikita S. Khrushchev, who became the head of the Soviet Communist Party during the summer of 1953. Khrushchev accused Malenkov of being too eager to appease the

Western "imperialists." When Khrushchev finally became the dominant figure in the Soviet leadership (after Malenkov was replaced as premier in February 1955 by a Khrushchev ally, Nikolai Bulganin), the West would be confronted with a far more formidable, and often unpredictable, Soviet leader than Malenkov had been.

Massive Retaliation and The New Look

On January 12, 1954, shortly before the Berlin conference closed, Dulles announced a new U.S. military strategy for dealing with the communist challenge. He said the United States would react massively, with nuclear weapons, in the event of communist aggression at any level, strategic or tactical. The president told congressional leaders that the general idea was "to blow [the] hell out of them [the communists] in a hurry if they start anything."[7]

Both Eisenhower and Dulles were aware of the risks involved in threatening to use nuclear weapons in response to localized communist aggression, but, Dulles stated, "you have to take chances for peace just as you must take chances for war. . . . if you are scared to go to the brink, you are lost."[8] Both Eisenhower and Dulles believed that showing a willingness to wage nuclear war would make it unnecessary to wage any war, whether nuclear or conventional. In addition, relying on nuclear rather than conventional forces would be cheaper. Nuclear weapons, Defense Secretary Charles Wilson said, would give the United States "a bigger bang for the buck."[9]

To back up the massive retaliation strategy, the administration intended to give the nation's armed forces a "New Look." It called for major cuts in conventional forces and a massive buildup of nuclear weapons. During the Eisenhower years, the size of the army and navy was reduced, while that of the air force increased—a reflection of the fact that air power, and particularly strategic air power, was going to be the primary component of the administration's massive retaliation strategy. In June 1953 the U.S. Air Force began ordering the nation's first intercontinental jet bomber, the B-52, which had a capability to deliver hydrogen bombs on Soviet targets.

For long-term deterrence, however, the Eisenhower administration placed major emphasis on developing ballistic missiles. In 1955 the president approved the development of the Atlas missile, America's first intercontinental ballistic missile (ICBM), and its first intermediate-range ballistic missile (IRBM), the Thor. In 1957 the president approved still another air force ICBM, a solid-fueled missile, Minuteman, which in the 1960s replaced the manned bomber as the primary component of the nation's strategic forces.

Both the army and the navy were also equipped with low-yield tactical nuclear weapons (with firepower equivalent to less than twenty kilotons of TNT). They were seen as a relatively inexpensive way to offset the perceived Soviet superiority in conventional forces. For this reason primarily, in December 1954 NATO agreed to integrate tactical nuclear weapons, including atomic cannons, missiles, and even land mines, into its defense system. NATO's conventional ground forces would remain an integral part of the alliance's defenses during the Eisenhower administration, but they would serve as a tripwire for triggering the use of nuclear weapons, rather than as the primary means of defending Western Europe.

The Soviet Nuclear Weapons Program

Khrushchev called Dulles's brinkmanship strategy nothing but "barefaced atomic blackmail."[10] However, more than the diplomatic consequences of the U.S. nuclear buildup, Khrushchev feared the growing U.S. capability to destroy the still embryonic Soviet nuclear force. Consequently, he accelerated the Soviet nuclear weapons program. By 1955 the Soviet nuclear arsenal would number some 300 to 400 atomic and thermonuclear weapons.

Americans, in general, overreacted to the growing Soviet nuclear arsenal. When the first Soviet intercontinental bombers appeared, in "waves," during the July 1955 Moscow air show, U.S. Air Force spokesmen claimed the Soviets would soon have an impressive lead in bombers. The consequence was the first of a series of "gap" scares that would sweep the United States during the nuclear arms race. In this case, the "bomber gap" scare of 1955 turned out to be nothing more than a myth fabricated by the air force and U.S. intelligence, with the assistance of the Soviets. The waves of bombers that flew in the Moscow air show were actually the same planes repeatedly flown over the spectator stands to create an illusion of massive Soviet strategic air power.

In reality, the Soviet Union never achieved the number of long-range bombers predicted by the air force and U.S. intelligence. Like Eisenhower, Khrushchev did not believe defense spending should take precedence over a healthy economy, and already in the mid-1950s the Soviet economy was suffering from declining industrial productivity and agricultural inefficiency. Rather than building expensive, long-range bombers in significant numbers, the Soviet leader decided to concentrate his country's economic resources on the development of ballistic missiles.

The New Look and the Third World

While dealing with the possibility of overt Communist aggression in Europe, the Eisenhower administration's New Look also addressed the threat of Communist expansion into the developing nations, the so-called Third World. There, the Soviets posed as the friends of colonial nations struggling to free themselves from the rule of Britain, France, Belgium, Portugal, and the Netherlands. By so doing, the Soviets not only hoped to undermine Western influence in these areas but also to block the allegiance of the Third World countries to an anti-Soviet alliance system that the Eisenhower administration was attempting to build.

The Central Intelligence Agency became the favored instrument for the growing U.S. involvement in the Third World. Under the leadership of Allen Dulles (brother of the secretary of state), the CIA expanded its activities beyond its original statutory responsibility for gathering foreign intelligence. Under Eisenhower the CIA would intervene not only to shore up shaky regimes friendly to the United States but also to overthrow objectionable governments as well. Covert CIA-directed operations were preferred to overt military operations by the armed forces because they were relatively inexpensive and also less likely to be exposed to congressional and public scrutiny.

Iran

The first CIA-directed covert operation during Eisenhower's presidency was conducted in Iran. On May 28, 1953, the Iranian prime minister, Dr. Mohammed Mossadeq, cabled Eisenhower to ask him for U.S. help in counteracting a boycott of Iranian oil by the international oil companies. The boycott was instituted after Mossadeq nationalized the Anglo-Iranian Oil Company in 1951. Mossadeq told the president that, if he did not receive U.S. assistance, Iran might be forced to turn to the Soviet Union.

Mossadeq's threat turned on Eisenhower's alarm bell. Only two weeks after entering the White House, the new president accepted the advice of the U.S. national security bureaucracy, which insisted that Mossadeq had to be overthrown to ensure continued Western access to Iranian oil and to prevent Iran from becoming a Soviet satellite. Accordingly, on May 28, 1953, Eisenhower rebuffed Mossadeq's plea for assistance, stating that all that was required to settle the crisis was "a reasonable agreement" with the British. Then Eisenhower added a warning of his own. He expressed his hope that, "before it is too late, the Government of Iran will take such steps as are in its power to prevent a further deterioration of the situation."[11]

Mossadeq decided to ignore Eisenhower's subtle threat. In July 1953 he dissolved the Iranian parliament, received a Soviet aid mission, and, while he was not a Marxist himself, began to accept support from the Marxist Tudeh party. Mossadeq's actions, in turn, provided Eisenhower with the justification he believed he needed to overthrow the Iranian leader. The CIA-sponsored operation was placed under the direction of a grandson of President Theodore Roosevelt, Kermit Roosevelt. Roosevelt arrived in Tehran in early August 1953 and won the support of General Fazlollah Zahedi and the pro-Western shah, Mohammed Reza Pahlavi, who was more than eager to get rid of Mossadeq to restore absolute monarchy. However, in attempting to replace Mossadeq with Zahedi, the shah acted prematurely. After street riots broke out in Tehran on August 16, 1953, the shah was forced to flee the country.

Just three days later, Kermit Roosevelt orchestrated a countercoup, sending paid anti-Mossadeq rioters into the streets and promising money and equipment to the Iranian army to ensure its loyalty to the shah. After several hundred Iranians lost their lives, the Mossadeq government capitulated and Zahedi took over the premiership. The shah then made a triumphant return to Tehran and with U.S. support became the real ruler of Iran.

During the next year, the new Iranian government negotiated an agreement creating an international oil consortium that broke the British monopoly and gave American companies a 40 percent interest in Iranian oil operations. Over the next twenty-five years, the international oil industry exported 24 billion barrels of oil from Iran on favorable terms for the involved companies and Western consumers. In return, the United States gave $85 million in economic and military aid to Iran during 1954 and much more over the next two decades. As a result, the shah's army would become one of the largest and best equipped in the Middle East, and Iran, a country that bordered the Soviet Union, one of America's most important client states.

The success of the Iranian intervention encouraged Eisenhower to support covert operations elsewhere in the Third World, in Guatemala, Egypt, Syria, Indonesia, and Cuba. But ultimately, the United States would pay a steep price for its Iranian success. America's reimposition of the shah aborted the development of a moderate form of Iranian nationalism. When nationalism finally triumphed in Iran, as a result of the revolution of 1978–1979, it would take a much more xenophobic, extremist, and anti-American form.

Guatemala

As in the Middle East, Eisenhower's primary objective in Latin America was, as one high-ranking State Departmental official put it, "to keep the area quiet and keep communism out."[12] But Latin America was ripe for communist penetration. Poverty, illiteracy, disease, and a rapidly growing population were only some of the problems that plagued the region. An extremely unjust distribution of wealth—with a small upper class controlling the government, the army, and most of the wealth and property— was the rule rather than the exception in the countries of Latin America. Resistance to reform by the elites who ruled these countries strengthened the appeal of communism among their impoverished and landless peasants. Unfortunately, to prevent communists from controlling these countries, the Eisenhower administration, more often than not, sided with the ruling elites who were indifferent to the plight of the poor.

In 1953 Guatemala's popularly elected president, Jacobo Arbenz Guzmán, attempted to alleviate the misery of the country's peasants by initiating a program of land reform. (In Guatemala, 70 percent of the land was owned by only 2 percent of its population.) In the process, the

Arbenz government expropriated 234,000 acres of uncultivated land belonging to the U.S.–owned United Fruit Company, one of the largest landholders in the country. The company insisted that the financial compensation offered by the government was too little, and it pressured the Eisenhower administration for assistance. Ignoring the need for land reform in Guatemala, and the initial success of Arbenz in implementing it, both Eisenhower and Dulles (who as a lawyer had done legal work for United Fruit) concentrated on the fact that Guatemalan communists supported Arbenz and therefore concluded that he was a Communist tool who was willing to turn his country into a client of the Soviet Union. If the Soviets were successful in Guatemala, Eisenhower and Dulles feared, both the Monroe Doctrine and U.S. predominance in Latin America would be undermined, and the whole effort to roll back communism would become a sham. The president and his secretary of state were not prepared to allow this to happen.

During the summer of 1953, Eisenhower authorized the CIA to develop a plan to overthrow the Arbenz government. About one hundred Americans, and an equal number of mercenaries recruited from Guatemala and neighboring Central American nations, were placed under the leadership of a U.S.-trained Guatemalan, Carlos Enrique Castillo Armas. Suspecting that the United States was plotting to overthrow his government, Arbenz sought military aid from Communist countries. The Soviets, eager to embarrass the Americans in their own hemisphere, authorized a shipment of Czechoslovak weapons to Arbenz.

News of the Czech arms shipment, which the CIA learned was due to arrive in Guatemala on May 15, produced a predictable reaction. A resolution introduced by Senate Minority Leader Lyndon Johnson (Dem.–Tex.), which reaffirmed the Monroe Doctrine and labeled the Guatemalan situation an instance of "Soviet interference" and "external aggression," quickly passed in the Senate, by a vote of 69 to 1. On June 18, Castillo, at the head of about 150 troops, crossed into Guatemala from Honduras and began a desultory march on Guatemala City. The capital was bombed and strafed by American aircraft of World War II vintage, which were flown by CIA pilots. On June 27, after his army abandoned him, Arbenz fled the country.

After arriving in the capital in a U.S. plane, Castillo formed a military junta. Opposition parties were banned, thousands of suspected political enemies were jailed, hundreds were murdered, the land reform program was canceled, and the expropriated lands, including those of the United Fruit Company, were restored to their original owners. Castillo became the recipient of U.S. military and economic assistance. When he was assassinated in 1957, a pro–U.S., right-wing dictatorship continued to control the country. During Eisenhower's last year in office, Guatemala would become a staging area for a CIA-directed invasion of Cuba.

Dien Bien Phu

The Eisenhower administration also felt compelled to deal with the threat of communist expansion in Indochina. In the spring of 1954, the long struggle between France and the communist Vietminh reached a climax. On April 26, a French garrison at Dien Bien Phu, in northern Vietnam, was surrounded by Vietminh forces. Both Eisenhower and Dulles were determined to avoid the loss of Indochina to communism. Comparing the nations of East Asia to a row of falling dominoes, Eisenhower warned that Burma, Thailand, and Indonesia would be the next victims if communism were permitted to triumph in Indochina. Their conquest, in turn, he believed, would endanger the so-called U.S. defensive chain of Japan, Taiwan, and the Philippines, as well as threaten Australia and New Zealand.

To prevent a French collapse, Eisenhower initially was prepared to commit U.S. air and naval forces to the defense of Indochina and, if necessary, a small contingent of marines. As a trial balloon, on April 16 Vice President Richard Nixon suggested that the United States intervene to check communist expansion, but the reaction to Nixon's suggestion was so hostile that Dulles was compelled to deny any administration intention of sending U.S. troops to Indochina.

Instead of ground forces, Admiral Arthur W. Radford, chairman of the Joint Chiefs, favored using tactical nuclear weapons, delivered by U.S. carrier–based aircraft. But neither the president, nor any other top administration official, seriously considered using nuclear weapons at Dien Bien Phu. Only if the Chinese intervened in Indochina, as they had in Korea, was Eisenhower prepared to introduce nuclear weapons. In an oblique warning to the Chinese, in early June 1954, Dulles declared that China's involvement in Indochina "would be a deliberate threat to the United States itself," and thus "we could not escape ultimate responsibility for decisions closely touching our own security and self-defense."[13]

Despite the hostile reaction to Nixon's trial balloon, Eisenhower did not abandon his inclination to assist the French with U.S. conventional forces. He approved a secret air strike, scheduled for April 28, and was prepared to go before Congress to obtain authorization for conducting it. However, Dulles was more sensitive than Eisenhower to the possibility of Chinese involvement in the conflict. He was able to persuade the more hawkish president to accept that U.S. military intervention in Indochina could only take place as a part of "united action." What he had in mind was a coalition of states comprising the United States and the Associated States of Vietnam, Laos, and Cambodia with France, Britain, Australia, New Zealand, Thailand, and the Philippines.

In an attempt to round up congressional support for—or, as historian Frederick Marks III, recently argued, to restrain the president from—committing U.S. forces to the conflict, Dulles met privately with congressional leaders on April 3.[14] However, the Congressmembers clearly opposed involving the United States in another Asian land war so soon after Korea. Their stance was reinforced by the Joint Chiefs of Staff, who informed the president that "Indochina is devoid of decisive military objectives and that the allocation of more than token U.S. armed forces in Indochina would be a serious diversion of limited U.S. capabilities."[15]

While Eisenhower said later that he would not have intervened in Indochina without congressional approval, there is some evidence that he was prepared to do so regardless of congressional opinion, that is, had he been able to obtain the support of America's key allies, particularly Great Britain. But the British feared a wider war in Asia and consequently refused to intervene in Indochina. Churchill told his physician, Lord Moran: "I don't see why we should fight for France in Indochina when we have given away India."[16]

While the French were eager to obtain U.S. military assistance for their struggle against the Vietminh, they were unwilling to meet the conditions set by the United States for obtaining it. The Eisenhower administration wanted France to grant independence to the states of Indochina, pledge to "stay in the fight" against the communists, and not negotiate away too much at the impending Geneva peace conference. In addition, the administration wanted the French to permit the United States to train the noncommunist Vietnamese forces. However, following the fall of Dien Bien Phu on May 7, 1954, and the consequent collapse of the government of French Premier Joseph Laniel, which had prosecuted the war, even the French realized that the independence of the Indochinese states was inevitable. As a result, the French joined the Geneva talks, whose Indochina phase began on May 8, with the hope of limiting the gains of the Vietminh while preserving their own influence in an independent Indochina.

The Geneva Conference

The Eisenhower administration disliked the idea of negotiating with communists at Geneva and especially with the Chinese, but in deference to America's allies, who wanted to end the conflict, the administration agreed to participate in the talks, along with Britain, France, China, and the Soviet Union. The administration explicitly stated that its participation should not be an indication that the United States was moving toward recognition of the Beijing government.

In July 1954 the Geneva conference produced a settlement that temporarily ended the conflict in Indochina. France recognized the independence of Vietnam, Cambodia, and Laos. However, Vietnam was partitioned at the 17th parallel until elections could be held (scheduled for June 1956) to choose a government for the entire country. The communists had control of the area north of the 17th parallel, where they established the Democratic Republic of Vietnam, with its capital at Hanoi. The territory south of the 17th parallel, the State of Vietnam, with its capital at Saigon, remained under the control of the French puppet emperor Bao

Dai. The Geneva agreement also called for national elections in Laos and Cambodia and prohibited the Indochinese states from joining a military alliance or permitting foreign military bases to be established on their soil.

The participants in the Geneva conference were asked to give their oral assent to the accords. France, Britain, the Soviet Union, China, and North Vietnam agreed to do so. The Soviet Union supported the Geneva accords because it was eager to win French support against West Germany's rearmament. The Chinese, on the other hand, approved the Geneva settlement primarily because they believed it would keep the United States out of Indochina. With considerable reluctance, and under Soviet and Chinese pressure, the Vietminh agreed to the temporary division of Vietnam, but only because they believed the election scheduled for 1956 would give them control of the entire country. Both the United States and South Vietnam refused to give their assent to the Geneva accords, although the U.S. delegate promised that the United States would refrain from the use of force to undermine them. More bluntly, President Eisenhower announced that the United States "has not itself been party to, or bound by, the decisions taken by the conference."[17]

Indochina

Eisenhower was disappointed that the Geneva accords recognized communist control of North Vietnam, but he was determined to prevent a communist victory in South Vietnam. As a result, the president refused to accept the Geneva ban on military assistance to the contracting parties and quickly moved to fill the military void created by the withdrawal of France. By the time the last French military units left Vietnam in early 1956, the United States had replaced France as South Vietnam's protector. In November 1954 U.S. military advisors began training a South Vietnamese army, styled the Army of the Republic of Vietnam (ARVN). Between 1954 and 1959 U.S. assistance to South Vietnam would total $1.2 billion and would finance about 80 percent of South Vietnam's military expenditures and nearly 50 percent of its nonmilitary spending.

The Eisenhower administration also tried to circumvent the Geneva ban on military alliances. In September 1954 Dulles negotiated the creation of a Southeast Asian counterpart to NATO. Called SEATO (South East Asian Treaty Organization), its members—the United States, Britain, France, Australia, New Zealand, Thailand, the Philippines, and Pakistan—promised to cooperate to prevent the extension of communism in Southeast Asia. Even though Laos, Cambodia, and South Vietnam were forbidden by the Geneva accords from entering any military alliance, a protocol to the SEATO treaty extended its protection to those states.

The Eisenhower administration sabotaged the Geneva accords in yet another way: it encouraged the South Vietnamese premier, Ngo Dinh Diem, to cancel the all-Vietnam election that had been scheduled for 1956. Both Diem and the U.S. administration feared that Ho Chi Minh, the hero of the national struggle against French imperialism, would win the election and thereby bring all of Vietnam under communist control. In place of the all-Vietnam election, Diem conducted a tightly staged "national referendum" in South Vietnam during October 1955. Supposedly 98 percent of the voters approved the removal of Emperor Bao Dai and the establishment of the Republic of Vietnam, with Diem as president. The Eisenhower administration quickly recognized the new regime and, in effect, attempted to make the 17th parallel an international boundary between two independent Vietnamese states, rather than the temporary demarcation line called for in the Geneva accords.

With the support of the landlord class, the army, and a notoriously corrupt bureaucracy, Diem quickly moved to crush opposition to his personal dictatorship. It was composed primarily of Buddhists, Montagnard mountain tribesmen, middle-class liberals, and the remnants of the southern Vietminh, all of whom were indiscriminately and inaccurately labeled "Vietcong," or Vietnamese communists. With, at first, modest amounts of assistance from North Vietnam, the Vietcong instituted a campaign to oust Diem and reunify the country. By 1958 the second Indochina war, a conflict to which the United States was already deeply committed, was well under way.

China

Despite the public animosity that Eisenhower and Dulles displayed toward the Chinese communists, they privately realized that it was inconsistent to maintain diplomatic relations with a communist government in the Soviet Union but not one in China. Both men believed that a two-China policy was inevitable and that both Chinas should be given membership in the United Nations when that body's charter was updated in 1955. Soon after the Korean War ended in June 1953, Dulles, with Eisenhower's approval, instituted plans for implementing a two-China policy, including a policy of gradually expanding U.S. trade with Communist China, in the hope of modifying its behavior.

But both the president and his secretary of state soon realized that any attempt to implement a two-China policy would be virulently, and probably successfully, opposed by the China Lobby, a pro-Nationalist coalition of Americans, both inside and outside the Congress, who regarded any moves toward improved relations with Beijing as tantamount to the "appeasement" policy followed by the Truman administration. Already beset by the McCarthy hysteria, the Eisenhower administration was not inclined to take on the China Lobby. As a result, the administration believed it had no alternative but to maintain a hostile policy toward the Beijing regime. Thus, it refused to recognize the Beijing regime as the legitimate government of China and blocked it from assuming China's seat in the United Nations. It also continued the Truman-initiated embargo on U.S. trade with China.

The administration became even more hostile to the Communist Chinese as time passed. During the last months of the Korean War, the president withdrew the U.S. Seventh Fleet from the Taiwan Strait — a move many regarded as a green light for Jiang Jeshi to invade the mainland. Dulles also attempted to expand the U.S. alliance system around China's southern periphery. The United States concluded a defense pact with South Korea in 1953 and one with Taiwan the following year. Eisenhower also approved a campaign of covert operations, conducted by the CIA, against the Chinese mainland.

At the Berlin conference in January 1954, Soviet Foreign Minister Molotov had privately warned Dulles that U.S. policy toward China was "bankrupt" because it "merely forced China closer to the Soviet Union."[18] Paradoxically, Dulles believed that making the Chinese more dependent on the Soviet Union was the best way to split the Sino-Soviet alliance. He was convinced that the Soviet economy could not bear the added burden of assistance to China, considering that the Soviets were already giving economic aid to Eastern Europe, Korea, and North Vietnam. The result, he predicted, would be Chinese disillusionment with their Soviet ally.

The Offshore Islands Crisis, 1954

With no prospect of a Sino-American rapprochement possible at the Geneva conference in 1954, and fearing that the Nationalists would attempt an invasion of the mainland with U.S. support, the Communist Chinese initiated their own campaign of pressure against Taiwan. On September 3, 1954, they began shelling Jinmen (Quemoy) and Mazu (Matsu), two of twenty-five Nationalist-held islands lying five to twenty-five miles from the mainland of China. In addition, Communist Chinese airplanes attacked the Dachen (Tachen) Islands, 200 miles north of Taiwan.

Admiral Radford, speaking for the Joint Chiefs of Staff, advocated an all-out defense of the offshore islands, including the use of atomic weapons. While Eisenhower was skeptical about the military importance of the islands, he nevertheless believed that their loss would be a serious blow to the Nationalists. Yet he was also reluctant to risk war with China to defend them. Accordingly, he tried to defuse the crisis by dispatching Dulles to Taiwan, both to indicate America's determination to defend Nationalist China and to restrain Jiang Jeshi from triggering an all-out war.

On November 23, 1954, Dulles and Nationalist Chinese Foreign Minister George K. C. Yeh initialed a mutual defense treaty. The treaty, which was approved by the U.S. Senate on February 9, 1955, extended a guarantee of U.S. military support to Taiwan and the Penghu (Pescadores) Islands (but not the other offshore islands). While Jiang Jeshi was pleased by the protection offered to his regime by the treaty, he sensed, correctly, that it was meant to win his acceptance of Taiwan, rather than the Chinese mainland, as his permanent home. While a two-China policy became the de facto policy of the United States, neither the Beijing nor the Taipei government was prepared to give up its claims to the Chinese territory it did not control.

The Chinese Communists, furthermore, regarded the U.S.–Taiwan Mutual Defense Treaty as a threat to China's sovereignty and territorial integrity. Particularly alarming to them was Article 6 of the treaty, which stated that the treaty might be extended to "other territories" by mutual agreement of the contracting parties. The article reinforced Beijing's suspicion that the United States was preparing to support a Nationalist invasion of the mainland—a suspicion the Eisenhower administration, which was trying to deter a communist invasion of Taiwan, purposely did nothing to dispel.

The Nationalist-held islands were not specifically protected by the U.S. defense pact with Taiwan. Nevertheless, as the situation in the strait grew more tense, in January 1955 the president requested, and received, unprecedented authority from Congress to employ U.S. armed forces to protect them. The Formosa Resolution authorized the president to use the armed forces of the United States to protect Taiwan and "related positions and territories of that area now in friendly hands." In exchange for its expanded defense commitment to Jinmen and Mazu, the United States received Jiang's agreement to withdraw his forces from the Dachens.

Eisenhower was fully prepared, but reluctant, to use nuclear weapons in the Taiwan Strait crisis. On March 15 he publicly stated that he saw no reason why nuclear weapons "shouldn't be used just exactly as you would use a bullet or anything else."[19] Soon thereafter, Vice President Nixon warned the Chinese that the United States would use nuclear weapons in the defense of Taiwan and the offshore islands. In the meantime, plans were under way to use several atomic bombs, with a yield of ten to fifteen kilotons—about the yield of the bomb that destroyed Hiroshima—on Chinese coastal air bases.

The Chinese, apparently believing that the administration was not bluffing, pulled back from the brink of war. In April 1955 Zhou Enlai, the Chinese foreign minister, indicated that his government was willing to enter into direct discussions with the United States to resolve the Taiwan Strait problem. The following month, a cease-fire went into effect in the Taiwan Strait and, while the United States did not officially recognize the existence of the Beijing government, representatives of the two countries began meeting in Geneva. While the Geneva talks (which were transferred to Warsaw later in the year) dragged on inconclusively, the first Taiwan Strait crisis came to an end.

The Emerging Sino-Soviet Split

The strong U.S. stand during the offshore island crisis was designed not only to prevent the humiliation of Jiang Jeshi but also to drive a wedge between the Chinese Communists and the Soviets. By threatening to conduct a nuclear war with China, Eisenhower and Dulles purposely tried to put the Soviets in a position where they either would have to abandon their Chinese ally or risk nuclear devastation from the far superior U.S. nuclear arsenal. If the Soviets refused to honor their treaty commitments to help the Chinese, the president told the National Security Council, "the Soviet empire would quickly fall to pieces."[20]

The Soviets, however, were already busy trying to shore up their relationship with China. In October 1954, at the height of the Taiwan Strait crisis, Khrushchev led a high-level Soviet delegation to Beijing to negotiate a new series of political and economic agreements. The Soviets agreed to (1) evacuate all of their military units from Port Arthur by May 31, 1955, (2) transfer entirely to the Chinese, by January 1, 1955, the Soviet share of four mixed Sino-Soviet companies operating in Sinkiang Province and Dairen, (3) acknowledge Chinese hegemony in Manchuria, and (4) give greater assistance to Chinese industrialization. The Soviets also promised to give more consideration to Beijing's views on international communist strategy in general and on Asian affairs in particular.

Despite these agreements, the Soviets did not give the Chinese all the support they expected to receive during the offshore islands crisis. This was due in part to the Soviet preoccupation with a Kremlin power struggle, from which Khrushchev emerged triumphant over Malenkov on February 8, 1955, with the latter having been removed as premier and replaced by Nikolai Bulganin. Determined to put more emphasis on domestic reform, Khrushchev and Bulganin quickly signaled their interest in improving relations with the West. They even hinted to U.S. officials that they were trying to restrain their Chinese allies during the offshore islands crisis. Khrushchev personally warned Zhou Enlai, who secretly visited Moscow in April 1955, that the Soviet Union would not risk war with the United States over the offshore islands. The lack of Soviet support for China during the crisis proved to be a major reason for the subsequent Sino-Soviet split.

It also reinforced the Chinese in their conviction that they must accelerate their own nuclear weapons program. Ironically, the Eisenhower administration's threat to use nuclear weapons against China, to protect territory that even Dulles admitted was never considered essential to U.S. interests, in the end would create a problem far out of proportion to the one it was designed to address: a Chinese nuclear weapon capability.

The Spirit of Geneva, 1955

Dulles openly played upon the emerging differences between the Soviets and the Chinese by offering the new Soviet leadership the prospect of worthwhile negotiations. The Soviets responded with a proposal to conclude a peace treaty with Austria, which they had studiously blocked for ten years. The Austrian treaty, which was signed on May 15, 1955, ended the postwar occupation of that country by Britain, France, the United States, and the Soviet Union. It also established Austria as an independent county, forbade its reunification with Germany, and guaranteed its neutrality.

The Austrian treaty also provided the impetus for the first major East-West summit since the end of World War II. So, too, did an escalating Soviet-American nuclear arms race. On March 1, 1954, the U.S. Atomic Energy Commission detonated a thermonuclear device at Bikini Atoll, in the South Pacific. By the fall of 1954, the Soviets had exploded their own hydrogen device, thereby eliminating very quickly America's thermonuclear monopoly.

Eisenhower's desire to constrain the nuclear arms race prompted him to meet with the new Soviet leaders in Geneva, Switzerland, in July 1955. They were joined by Anthony Eden, who succeeded Churchill as British prime minister in April 1955 and French premier Edgar Faure. Despite the genial atmosphere that enveloped the summit participants, the Geneva talks quickly became stalemated due to the inability of the two sides to resolve the disarmament and German problems.

Concerning the first issue, the Western powers would not accept a modified version of a Soviet disarmament plan, first submitted on May 10, 1955. The initial version had called for the liquidation of all foreign military bases and a general disarmament agreement as prerequisites to a settlement of the Cold War. The new version of the Soviet plan, which was presented at Geneva, dropped these prerequisites and substituted a proposal for a ceiling of 150,000 to 200,000 troops on the armed forces of the smaller nations. This was an obvious Soviet attempt to scuttle NATO's plan to create a 500,000-troop West German army, and therefore was unacceptable to the West. Also rejected by the Western leaders was a Soviet proposal for a ban on the first use of nuclear weapons, which was an option NATO wanted to retain to deter a Soviet invasion of Western Europe.

The Soviets also renewed their earlier proposal for the creation of an all-European security pact that would have replaced both the NATO alliance and the Warsaw Pact. It also would have permitted a reunified, but neutralized, German state. However, the Western powers turned down the security pact proposal because they refused to contemplate either the dissolution of NATO or the neutralization of West Germany, both of which were considered vital to the preservation of democracy in Western Europe.

The United States still wanted Germany reunified through free national elections, which obviously would bring all of Germany firmly into the Western camp. To preclude this outcome, the Soviets preferred to keep Germany divided. To this end, in September 1955 they extended formal diplomatic recognition to the Federal Republic of Germany and later that year admitted East Germany into the Warsaw Pact. The Soviets also planted the seeds of future crises with the West by proclaiming that the East German government now had full control over East Berlin.

In an attempt to break the disarmament stalemate, on the fourth day of the conference Eisenhower proposed an "Open Skies" plan. It called for aerial inspection of both the Soviet Union and the United States, as well as the exchange of blueprints of U.S. and Soviet military installations.

However, the plan was unacceptable to the Soviets. They feared that its implementation would reveal to the United States the location of Soviet nuclear and military installations, thereby guaranteeing that U.S. nuclear bombs would be targeted on them. Little did the Soviets suspect, though, that within a year of the Geneva conference the ingenious Americans would begin a unilateral and secret version of the Open Skies plan, when U-2 photo-reconnaissance planes began flying over Soviet territory.

Even though the Geneva conference produced only a cultural exchange agreement, Eisenhower said that it had produced "a new spirit of conciliation and cooperation" between the two superpowers. At Geneva, historian Stephen Ambrose observes, "the West had admitted that it could not win the Cold War, that a thermonuclear stalemate had developed, and that the status quo in Europe and China . . . had to be substantially accepted."[21] Nevertheless, the Geneva conference did not end the Cold War. Indeed, the "spirit of Geneva" survived barely a year.

De-Stalinization

In February 1956 Khrushchev attempted to consolidate his leadership of the Soviet Union with a seven hour, 26,000-word, secret speech before the Twentieth Congress of the Soviet Communist Party. In the speech, the Soviet leader attacked his hard-line opponents by denouncing the crimes of their mentor, Josef Stalin. The late tyrant, Khrushchev charged, had executed thousands of "honest communists" and other innocent people, on the basis of false confessions exacted by torture. Khrushchev denounced Stalin's "megalomania" and said that his penchant for self-glorification had led to a "cult of the individual." He attacked Stalin's foreign policies. "During Stalin's leadership," Khrushchev said, "our peaceful relations with other nations were often threatened, because one-man decisions could cause, and often did cause, great complications." Khrushchev accused Stalin of saying "I shall shake my little finger and there will be no more Tito" and of making demands of a "colonial nature" on China.[22]

In other speeches to the party congress, Khrushchev outlined bold new directions for Soviet policies. In foreign affairs he accepted the possibility of different roads to socialism, thus tacitly conceding that Tito had been right all along in his dispute with Moscow. In enunciating a doctrine of "peaceful coexistence," Khrushchev stated that war between capitalism and communism was no longer inevitable. He pledged that the Soviet Union would engage the West in "peaceful competition." To Washington, it appeared that Khrushchev was willing to subordinate, or even sacrifice, Soviet support for the expansion of communism in order to promote peace with the United States.

Reinforcing this hope in the West was the announcement, on April 17, 1956, of Khrushchev's decision to dissolve the Cominform (Communist Information Bureau). The move apparently had been demanded by Tito as the price for ending his strained relationship with the Soviet bloc. The

Kremlin invited Tito to Moscow in June 1956, not only to patch up
Soviet-Yugoslav relations but also to reduce the risk of unrest in the other
Soviet satellites, which had increased in the wake of Khrushchev's de-Stalinization speech. The Soviets hoped to use Yugoslavia as an example of
how the East European satellites could enjoy national freedom while
remaining communist. As further inducement to the Yugoslav leader, on
June 1, just one day before Tito's arrival in Moscow, Stalin's long-time
accomplice, Vyacheslav Molotov, resigned as Soviet foreign minister. The
change was viewed not only as a sop to Tito but as a sign of Moscow's
eagerness to promote détente with the West.

The Eisenhower administration welcomed Khrushchev's de-Stalinization campaign and Soviet rapprochement with Yugoslavia. It hoped that
these moves would lead to a loosening of the Soviet grip on Eastern
Europe and improved East-West relations as well. Eisenhower wanted to
give the Soviets every possible chance to prove the sincerity of their professed interest in détente. In response to Soviet protests, he temporarily
suspended flights over Soviet territory by U.S. spy planes. At the same
time, the administration pressed Khrushchev to continue his liberalization
program. On June 4, 1955, the State Department released to the public a
document, obtained by the CIA, that purported to be a copy of the text of
Khrushchev's de-Stalinization speech. Dulles called it "the most damning
indictment of despotism ever made by a despot." [23]

The Hungarian Revolution

The publication of Khrushchev's secret speech only fueled already long-
seated resentment against Stalinism in the Soviet satellite states. In June
1955 riots erupted in Poland, where opponents of the communist regime
demanded the ouster of Polish Stalinists. With Khrushchev's reluctant
support, an anti-Stalinist and "national communist," Wladislaw Gomulka,
came to power after promising his people that he would end the most
oppressive features of Polish communism. By the fall, however,
Khrushchev thought Gomulka's reform program had gone too far, and
he ordered the Polish leader to constrain it. But Gomulka refused to
comply and instead threatened to call upon the Polish people to resist the
Soviet pressure. Unwilling to use force against Poland, Khrushchev
backed down, and in effect permitted Gomulka's brand of national communism to survive.

The so-called Polish solution, however, was not acceptable to Hungarian students. They saw the Polish crisis as an opportunity to rid their
country of communism completely. By October 23, 1956, student-led
demonstrations escalated into an armed revolt against the communist
regime and the Soviet military presence in Hungary. On October 30 and
31 the reform-minded government of Imre Nagy announced that Hungary would cease to be a one-party state and would leave the Warsaw Pact.
In the meantime, after several days of fighting with Hungarian rebels,

Soviet troops were withdrawn from Budapest. The Soviet withdrawal, however, proved to be only a tactical maneuver. Early on November 4 an estimated 200,000 Soviet troops and 5,500 tanks mounted a powerful assault on the unsuspecting Hungarians. By November 8 virtually all resistance was crushed: 20,000–25,000 Hungarians and several thousand Soviet troops were dead, and some 200,000 Hungarians had fled, or were fleeing, across the Austrian border. Nagy was arrested (and subsequently executed) and replaced by Janos Kadar, who would rule Hungary until 1989.

The Eisenhower administration had repeatedly encouraged the people of Eastern Europe to shake off the Soviet yoke. When the people of Hungary attempted to do so, though, they received no meaningful assistance from the United States. The administration obviously was not prepared to risk a nuclear war with the Soviet Union by intervening on behalf of the Hungarian freedom fighters. Instead of intervening militarily, the administration continued its effort to promote the development of Tito-like national communism in Eastern Europe, as a first step toward the eventual overthrow of communism.

In the aftermath of the Hungarian Revolution, the Soviets did all in their power to suppress the growth of national communism in Eastern Europe. While there was no new break with Tito, Titoism was no longer favored by Moscow as an antidote for Stalinism. Instead, the Soviets attempted to cement their hold on Eastern Europe—and forestall the necessity of Soviet military intervention in the future—by expanding economic assistance to the satellite governments.

Nasser and the Bagdhad Pact

While the Hungarian Revolution was playing out to its tragic end, another crisis was brewing in the Middle East. Following the reestablishment of a pro-Western government in Iran in 1953, the Eisenhower administration attempted to prevent the expansion of Soviet influence in the Middle East by enlisting the Arab states in an anti-Soviet alliance. To this end, the United States adopted a more neutral attitude toward the Arab-Israeli dispute than had been followed by the overtly pro-Israeli Truman administration.

The new U.S. stance, however, was only partially successful. In February 1955 only one Arab state, Iraq, joined the new Baghdad Pact, an alliance that included Turkey, Iran, Pakistan, and Britain. While the United States never joined the Baghdad Pact, to avoid antagonizing Arab states that opposed British hegemony in the region, Washington sponsored its creation. Moreover, the United States immediately established a military liaison with the organization, whose name was changed to the Central Treaty Organization (CENTO) after Iraq withdrew in 1958. On February 1, 1958, the U.S. strengthened its affiliation with CENTO by becoming a full member of its military planning committee. Dulles believed that this "northern tier" of allied states would be an effective bulwark against Soviet expansion into the Middle East.

But the Bagdhad Pact was soon undermined by Gamal Abdel Nasser, who became president of Egypt after overthrowing King Farouk in July 1952. Initially, the Eisenhower administration was favorably disposed to Nasser, believing he would bring stability to Egypt and thereby to the Arab world. Consequently, the United States facilitated the conclusion of a new Anglo-Egyptian treaty in 1954. Britain agreed to withdraw all its troops from Egypt over a twenty-month period, but Nasser's ambitions reached beyond the expulsion of the British from his country. He saw himself as a modern Saladin who would unite the Arab world and destroy Israel. By challenging Western hegemony in the Middle East, Nasser soon became a hero to the Arab masses.

Nasser refused to join the Baghdad Pact and instead turned to the Soviets for the assistance he would need to crush Israel. The Soviets quickly obliged the Egyptian leader; they saw assistance to Egypt as way to leapfrog Dulles's "northern tier." In September 1955 Czechoslovakia, acting at the behest of the Soviet Union, agreed to provide Egypt with a large quantity of arms, including planes and tanks. The Czech arms deal was followed, in April 1956, by the conclusion of a military alliance between Egypt, Saudi Arabia, Syria, and Yemen, the obvious target of which was Israel. In the following month Nasser broke off diplomatic relations with Nationalist China and recognized the communist govern- ment in Beijing. The new Cairo-Moscow axis effectively bypassed the Bagdhad Pact and gave the Soviet Union its first client state in the Middle East; the relationship would last until the early 1970s.

The Suez War

On July 19, 1956, the Eisenhower administration reacted to Nasser's turning to the Soviet bloc by informing the Egyptian government that the United States would not help finance construction of the Aswan High Dam, a pet project of the Egyptian leader. A few days later, on July 26, he retaliated by announcing that he would nationalize the Suez Canal and use the revenues collected from it to finance the Aswan Dam.

The governments of Britain and France were horrified at the thought that Egyptian control of the canal would give Nasser the ability to stran- gle Middle Eastern oil shipments to Western Europe. Without the knowl- edge of the Eisenhower administration, on October 22 and 23, 1956, Britain, France, and Israel agreed on a scheme to bring Nasser down. It called for Israeli forces to drive to the canal, thereby providing the excuse for Anglo-French military intervention. The Israeli attack began on Octo- ber 29. Two days later, after Egypt refused to permit Anglo-French inter- vention to "protect" the canal, British and French war planes started bombing Egyptian bases. On November 5 Anglo-French paratroopers were airdropped into the canal zone.

The Suez campaign soon became a disaster for Britain and France. Rather than gaining complete control of the canal, the allied forces captured only its northern terminus, Port Said. Nasser reacted by scuttling ships in the canal, a move that effectively closed it to world commerce. Nasser's action, combined with the shutting down of the Iraq-Syria-Lebanon oil pipeline, created an oil crisis for Western Europe.

Eisenhower was infuriated by the allied attack on Egypt. Privately, he expressed his amazement at the way the British and French could make "such a complete mess and botch of things." It was, he said, "the damnedest business I ever saw supposedly intelligent governments get themselves into."[24] The president realized that there would be no chance either to end the oil crisis or to stabilize the Middle East unless the British, French, and Israelis withdrew from Egyptian territory. To that end, the United States introduced a UN resolution, which was supported by the Soviet bloc, calling for a cease-fire. As a way of pressuring the occupying forces to leave Egypt, the administration also delayed the implementation of an emergency plan to meet Europe's oil needs by diverting to that continent production from the Persian Gulf and the Western Hemisphere.

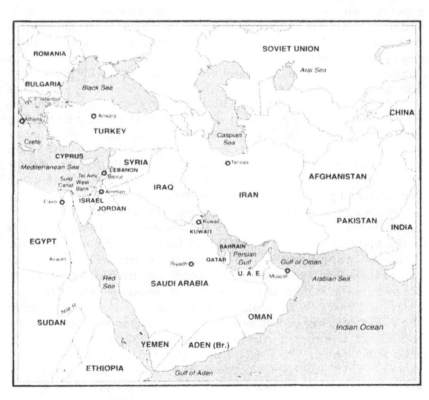

The Middle East, 1956

In the end, Britain and France succumbed to U.S. pressure. On November 6 they accepted a cease-fire. They also agreed to withdraw their military forces from Egypt, a move that was completed on December 22, 1956. The Israelis, however, withdrew only after the Eisenhower administration assured them that the United States would guarantee the principle of "free and innocent passage" through the Strait of Tiran, Israel's major water thoroughfare to the Indian Ocean.

The Eisenhower Doctrine

By all logic, for foiling the aggression against Egypt the United States should have emerged from the Suez crisis with an enhanced image in the Middle East. Instead, at the very time the Red Army was crushing the Hungarian Revolution, the Soviet Union reaped most of the propaganda benefits from the termination of the Suez War. After it had become clear that the Eisenhower administration would not support the allied invasion of Egypt, thereby reducing the risk of a conflict between the Soviet Union and the United States, the Soviets engaged in a campaign of "rocket rattling" against Britain, France, and Israel. Soviet Premier Bulganin also warned Eisenhower that the fighting in the Middle East could lead to a "world war" and suggested that the United States should join with the Soviet Union in military action designed to curb the allied aggression. Eisenhower angrily rejected the Soviet proposal, calling it "unthinkable." Instead, he placed U.S. forces on a worldwide alert to deter Soviet military intervention in the conflict.

The Suez War, much to the chagrin of the Eisenhower administration, also enhanced the prestige of Gamal Nasser. Despite the humiliating defeat of his army by the Israelis, Nasser's ability to reverse their military gains, albeit with crucial support from the United States and the Soviet Union, only wetted his ambition to lead the Arab world. Shortly after the war, Nasser concluded a second arms deal with the Soviet Union and strengthened Egypt's commercial ties with the Soviet bloc.

Because the Eisenhower administration now believed that Soviet and Egyptian "subversive activities" were the key threats to Western interests in the Middle East, it felt compelled to fill the vacuum caused by the decline of British power in that region. In January 1957 Eisenhower asked Congress to approve a resolution endorsing the president's right to use force in the Middle East against "overt armed aggression from any nation controlled by International Communism." The administration also requested congressional approval for $200 million a year in economic and military assistance to Middle Eastern countries that were willing to resist Soviet inroads. The House quickly approved the president's request by a vote of 355 to 61, but the Senate, more sensitive to extending U.S. aid to Arab enemies of Israel, refused to grant the president specific authorization to use troops. The amended version of the administration's

Middle Eastern resolution that eventually passed in the Senate simply stated that the United States "is prepared" to employ force if the president "determines the necessity thereof."[25]

The Eisenhower Doctrine, as the administration's resolution was soon dubbed, was the concluding link in the chain of security commitments the United States had fashioned since the end of World War II. By 1958 the United States had assumed the explicit obligation of defending some forty-five countries and, by implication, several more. Critics charged that the administration was suffering from "pactomania," an unwarranted expansion of U.S. military commitments. The administration rebutted the charge by insisting that America's alliances (all but four of which were concluded by the Eisenhower administration) helped to maintain the independence of the free world and the security of the United States.

The critics were on the mark when they identified the fallacy that underlay the philosophy of the Eisenhower Doctrine. The main threat to the independence of pro-Western countries in the Middle East, such as Iraq, Jordan, and Lebanon, came not from international communism but from Nasser. On July 14, 1958, the pro-Western government of Iraq was toppled by General Abdel Karim Kassim, who quickly announced his intention to take Iraq into the United Arab Republic, a union of Egypt, Syria, and Yemen that was created in February of that year.

On the same day that news of the Kassim coup reached Washington, the United States received a request from the pro-Western president of Lebanon, Camille Chamoun, to help put down an alleged Nasserite attempt to overthrow his government. Eisenhower immediately ordered 14,000 U.S. soldiers to Lebanon to prevent a "communist-inspired" coup d'état. The administration also supported a British effort to prop up Jordan's King Hussein, whose cousin, King Faisal, was assassinated in the Iraqi coup. Fifty U.S. fighters accompanied an airlift of British troops to Amman, Jordan's capital, and the United States agreed to supply the petroleum requirements of the British forces engaged in the operation. In October, with both governments stabilized, the British forces were withdrawn from Jordan and the U.S. Marines from Lebanon.

The Anglo-American interventions in Jordan and Lebanon achieved their major objectives. They not only shored up pro-Western governments in these countries, they also helped to diminish the threat of rampant radical nationalism elsewhere in the Arab world. Kassim dropped his bid to take Iraq into the United Arab Republic and assured Western oil companies that their properties in his country were safe. As a consequence, Egypt and Iraq became bitter enemies in the waning years of the Eisenhower administration. So, too, did Syria and Egypt, with the result that the Syrians left the UAR in 1961. With their departure, Nasser's dream of dominating the Arab world collapsed.

The Anglo-American intervention in the Middle East also demonstrated the limits of the Soviet Union's influence in the region. The Soviets were willing to provide military and economic assistance to Nasser and his allies, but they were unwilling to risk a military confrontation with the United States in the Middle East. Moreover, intervention in the region embroiled the Soviets in intra-Arab disputes—they were aiding two regimes that hated each other (Egypt and Iraq)—and placed them in a quandary over whether to aid local communists in these and other Middle Eastern countries, at the risk of alienating their noncommunist governments.

While the Eisenhower administration had achieved its goal of filling the Middle Eastern vacuum created by the humiliation of Britain and France in the Suez War, it was unable to resolve the main threat to Middle Eastern stability, the dispute between Israel and the Arab world. On August 26, 1955, Dulles proposed a peace settlement that linked the formal fixing and guaranteeing of borders between Israel and its Arab neighbors with the resettlement and repatriation of thousands of Palestinian refugees who had fled their homeland during the 1948–1949 war. But the proposal went nowhere, primarily because the administration did not put the same degree of political weight behind it that it did to other Middle Eastern problems, such as getting the Israelis to withdraw from Egypt. As a result, the Palestinian problem endured as the greatest single threat to stability in the region long after Eisenhower left office in 1961.

Sputnik and the Missile Gap

Although the prestige of the Soviet Union in the Arab world increased following the Suez War, Khrushchev's standing at home plummeted in the wake of the Hungarian Revolution. A coalition of Stalinists, led by Molotov and Malenkov, blamed his de-Stalinization campaign for weakening the Soviet hold on Poland and almost losing Hungary and the rest of Eastern Europe as well. However, in June 1957 Khrushchev was able to foil an attempt by the Molotov-Malenkov coalition to overthrow him by relying on the support of the Central Committee and Defense Minister Georgi Zhukov. Then, in October 1957, four months after the Molotov-Malenkov coalition was ousted from the Presidium, Khrushchev dismissed Zhukov. The following March, he also ousted Nikolai Bulganin and assumed his position as chairman of the Council of Ministers. Now, as both head of the government as well as the party, Khrushchev resumed his program to reform the Soviet system and enhance the status of the Soviet Union in the world community.

Khrushchev's prestige, and that of his country, received a major boost after the Soviet Union launched the first earth-orbiting satellite, *Sputnik I*, on October 4, 1957. The weight of the Soviet satellite, 184 pounds, was six times heavier than *Vanguard*, the satellite the United States was preparing to launch. Even more impressive was the November 3 launch of *Sputnik II*, a dog-carrying satellite weighing 1,120 pounds. The failure of the

U.S. Navy to launch *Vanguard* on December 6 and the meager weight of America's first successful satellite, the Army's thirty-pound *Explorer*, which was placed into orbit on February 1, 1958, shocked the American people. To Americans, it was unbelievable that a people supposedly as backward as the Soviets could demonstrate such technological prowess. However, scientific, political, and military leaders in the United States realized that the launching of the satellites validated Khrushchev's boast of the previous August that the Soviet Union had developed an intercontinental ballistic missile. Obviously, a missile that could launch satellites into orbit could also deliver nuclear warheads to U.S. targets.

To overcome the alleged Soviet technological superiority, an alliance of educators, defense contractors, and congressional Democrats passed the National Defense Education Act in 1958. It called for spending $5 billion on higher education in the sciences, foreign languages, and humanities to counter the perceived Soviet threat. Meanwhile, a coalition of defense contractors, Democratic politicians, and the Pentagon — the so-called military-industrial complex, a term coined by Eisenhower in his farewell address — accused the administration of wholesale neglect of national defense and called for a massive increase in spending on missile development.

However, the president knew, on the basis of secret U-2 surveillance intelligence, augmented later by CIA radar and electronic eaves-dropping installations in Turkey and Iran, that the Soviets were not undertaking a massive ICBM deployment. As U.S. intelligence data accumulated, even Eisenhower's initial belief that the Soviets enjoyed a small missile lead proved false. Department of Defense intelligence spokesmen stated that, as late as September 1959, when the first U.S. ICBM, the Atlas, became operational, the Soviets had still not deployed any operational missiles. But it was not until early in 1961, after John F. Kennedy entered the White House, that a National Intelligence Estimate stated that the Soviets possessed only a small number of operational ICBMs.

In short, during the Eisenhower years, there never was a missile gap, at least not one favoring the Soviet Union. While the Soviets deployed more operational IRBMs in Europe than the United States, until the early 1970s they never had more operational ICBMs than the Americans. Nevertheless, despite the overwhelming nuclear superiority the United States enjoyed in the late fifties, the pressure generated by the military-industrial complex compelled Eisenhower to accelerate the U.S. missile program. Ironically, Khrushchev's boasting about Soviet missile superiority backfired; it prompted the Americans to augment their already overwhelming nuclear superiority, thereby enhancing the nuclear vulnerability of the Soviet Union. The growing imbalance in Soviet-American strategic power, some historians believe, was the major factor behind Khrushchev's decision to place ballistic missiles in Cuba in 1962 — an action that nearly produced a nuclear war.

The Test Ban Talks

Flushed with the *Sputnik* successes, on December 10, 1957, the Soviets proposed a two- to three-year suspension of nuclear weapon tests beginning January 1, 1958. But, in the wake of *Sputnik*, the Eisenhower administration feared that a suspension of tests would be politically unacceptable. Therefore, on January 12, 1958, the administration responded to the Soviet initiative by renewing its offer of the preceding August, which linked a test suspension to a weapons production cutoff. Probably, the administration was neither surprised nor terribly disappointed when the Soviets again rejected that offer. The administration was still free to accelerate the U.S. missile program, while it had shown that it was responsive to world opinion.

However, on March 31, 1958, the Soviets surprised the United States by announcing that they were beginning an indefinite suspension of their nuclear test program, and they called on the United States and Britain to follow suit. When the Americans and British refused to comply, the Soviets resumed testing on September 30. But, again, they said that they favored an "immediate" and "universal" cessation of nuclear tests.

Faced with public pressure to end testing, the United States and Britain announced on October 31, 1958 that they were suspending nuclear tests for a year, on the condition that the Soviet Union did likewise. The suspension of testing by the Soviets on November 3 set the stage for the longest moratorium on nuclear testing in the Cold War, which lasted almost three years, and also for the beginning of negotiations, in Geneva, Switzerland, for a permanent ban on all nuclear testing.

The Geneva test ban conference, which began on October 31, 1958, was soon deadlocked over the inspection issue. The Soviets insisted that each of the nuclear powers was entitled to a veto over the activities of the control commission that would police the test ban. The Americans and British disagreed. They feared that a Soviet veto would make the inspection system meaningless. Nor could the two sides agree on the number of seismological stations that would be permitted to check for surreptitious underground tests on the territory of each participant. A report of the Geneva scientific panel recommended the construction of 170 to 180 seismological stations, 100 to 110 of which were to be located in continental areas, while the remainder would be placed on oceanic islands. The Soviets considered the number of required inspections unacceptable.

Khrushchev then tried to break the inspection impasse by proposing a small number of annual inspections. Eisenhower accepted the Soviet proposal contingent on Khrushchev's willingness to modify his position on the veto in the control commission and his acceptance of the need for further technical talks on the problem of detecting high-altitude tests. On May 14 Khrushchev agreed to continue Soviet participation in the technical talks but said nothing about the veto issue. Eisenhower ignored the omission and the technical talks resumed in July 1959. However, progress in the technical talks ground to a halt by the end of the year after Edward

Teller, the leading scientific proponent of the hydrogen bomb, insisted that the Soviets could cheat by testing nuclear devices in large caverns beneath the surface of the earth. While other scientists disputed Teller's assertion, it nevertheless stalled progress in the technical talks.

The only bright spot in what otherwise was a dismal autumn for arms control was the signing, on December 1, 1959, of the Antarctic treaty by twelve countries, including Britain, France, the Soviet Union, and the United States. The treaty demilitarized the Antarctic, provided for full multilateral inspection, and prohibited the dumping of radioactive wastes on the polar continent.

The Second Taiwan Strait Crisis, 1958

In spite of the Soviet Union's nuclear inferiority, Khrushchev could not ignore the opportunities provided by the inclination of Americans to minimize their own nuclear strength. When a second Taiwan Strait crisis erupted in August 1958, after the Chinese resumed the bombardment of the offshore islands in an attempt to force a resolution of Taiwan's status, Khrushchev sent Eisenhower a letter stating that the Soviet Union would "do everything" to defend China if the United States attacked the Chinese mainland.[26] He also went out of his way to warn the West Germans that in the event of war they would have "no chance of survival."[27] Khrushchev promised that even the distant United States would not escape nuclear devastation.

Eisenhower responded by ignoring Khrushchev's threats and ordering warships of the U.S. Seventh Fleet to escort Nationalist Chinese supply ships from Taiwan to within three miles of the offshore islands. Although mainland batteries drove off several resupply efforts, the Communists were careful not to fire on U.S. vessels. But the United States wanted no wider war with China. Dulles stated that, if the Chinese Communists agreed to a de facto cease-fire, Nationalist forces on Jinmen and Mazu could be reduced. On October 6 the Communists reacted by announcing a one-week suspension of their bombardment provided that the United States stopped escorting Nationalist ships. After Washington agreed to this arrangement, the Communists extended their cease-fire by two weeks. In return, Dulles flew to Taiwan later that month and persuaded Jiang Jeshi to pull back some of his troops from the offshore islands and to renounce the use of force to regain control of the mainland. With the expiration of the two-week cease-fire, the Communists said that they would shell Jinmen only on alternate days of the month. On this basis, the second Taiwan Strait crisis ended.

In spite of the diplomatic support that Khrushchev gave China during the second Taiwan Strait crisis, Chinese suspicion of their Soviet ally deepened. Khrushchev's guarantees to the Chinese and warnings to Eisenhower were made only after it had become obvious that the United States was not preparing to attack China. Clearly, in the wake of the Soviet

Sputnik triumph, the Chinese hoped to use the growing Soviet nuclear arsenal as a shield to protect themselves against U.S. retaliation while they attacked the remaining offshore islands.

Khrushchev was not willing to risk a nuclear war with the United States for the benefit of his Chinese allies. Indeed, the Soviets were increasingly worried about the flippant attitude that the Chinese were displaying toward a nuclear war. When Mao Zedong visited Moscow in November 1957, he shocked the Soviets by saying that a nuclear war would not be the end of communism. China would still have some hundreds of millions of people who would probably survive, while the populations of the capitalist countries—he did not mention the Soviet Union—would be wiped out.

Still, the Soviets, after the Hungarian Revolution, were eager to keep China in the Soviet camp. For that reason primarily, they agreed to provide the Chinese with nuclear assistance, and even, according to some sources, a sample nuclear weapon. While the Soviets did help China put into operation its first nuclear reactor, they never made good on their promise to deliver a nuclear weapon. In 1959, as Soviet fears of Chinese nuclear recklessness revived, the Soviet Union terminated all nuclear assistance to China.

Moscow was also not prepared to underwrite China's effort to acquire economic independence. During his November 1957 visit to Moscow, Mao Zedong learned that the Soviets still expected China to repay the $2.4 billion in debts it owed the Soviets, which was largely money borrowed during the Korean War. Partly to achieve greater economic independence, and partly to distance himself from Soviet "revisionism," Mao in 1958 launched his "Great Leap Forward," an all-out attempt to quickly transform the basically agrarian Chinese economy into an industrial giant. The effort turned into a disaster that set back China's economic development for years and again forced the Chinese to turn to the Soviets for economic assistance. To the Soviets, the Great Leap Forward carried an unmistakable warning: the Chinese were in a hurry to emancipate themselves from their economic and technological dependence on the Soviet Union. Thus, the Soviets not only felt a sense of urgency about forestalling China's nuclear development but wanted to squeeze the maximum possible benefit from the Chinese alliance before its fragility became apparent to the West.

The Berlin Crisis, 1958

For the Soviets, the growing Chinese threat made a resolution of the German problem all the more urgent. They could not deal safely with the Chinese, they believed, with a growing military threat in West Germany. In the wake of the Soviet space triumph, the Eisenhower administration tried to reassure America's NATO allies that its nuclear commitment to Western Europe's defense remained strong. Therefore, it announced its intention to place U.S. intermediate-range missiles in Western Europe and share their control with the European allies, including the West Germans. Although both the United States and the West Germans would have a veto on the use of nuclear weapons deployed on West German soil, the Soviets feared that the West was facilitating the emergence of an independent West German nuclear arsenal.

In an attempt to prevent the West Germans from gaining access to nuclear weapons, in March 1958 the Soviets supported a plan by Polish Foreign Minister Adam Rapacki to create a nuclear-free zone in Central Europe. In this zone, which included Poland, Czechoslovakia, and the two Germanys, the manufacture and deployment of nuclear weapons would have been prohibited. However, the United States and its NATO allies rejected the Rapacki plan because they feared that its acceptance would have left West Germany vulnerable to Soviet conventional forces.

The refusal of the West to accept the Rapacki plan prompted the Soviets to launch a campaign of intimidation that was aimed at the weakest link in the West's defenses, and a major thorn in the sides of the Soviet Union and the East German regime, the city of West Berlin. By 1958, thanks in part to $600 million in U.S. economic aid, West Berlin had become a showcase of democratic capitalism. The city had attracted over two million East Germans, most of whom were young and professionally trained, reducing the population of East Germany to about 16 million.

In a note delivered to the Western powers on November 27, 1958, Khrushchev proposed an agreement that would transform the former German capital into a demilitarized "free city," with access to both East and West Germany guaranteed by the Soviets and the three Western powers. If no solution to the Berlin "problem" were reached within six months, Khrushchev threatened to terminate Soviet occupation of East Berlin and transfer to the East German government control of the West's air, highway, and railroad access routes to West Berlin. Such a move would not only have imperiled the Western presence in Berlin but also acknowledged the legitimacy of the East German regime, and thereby the permanent division of Germany; thus, the proposal was unacceptable to the Western powers.

Not willing to go to the brink of nuclear war with the Soviets over Berlin, however, the Eisenhower administration offered to discuss the city's status. As a result, four-power negotiations on Berlin were held in Geneva from May 11 to August 5, 1959. The allies offered to limit their garrisons in West Berlin and to forego placing nuclear weapons into the city if the Soviets agreed to allow free elections in East Germany. However, the allies said they were willing to defer the elections until after German reunification occurred. In return they expected the Soviets to guarantee Western access to Berlin until the city became the capital of a reunited Germany. While the Geneva conference on Berlin failed to agree on the city's status, it did serve to defuse the crisis. The Soviets allowed their six-month deadline to pass without carrying out their threat to transfer control of the Western access routes to the East Germans.

In July 1959 Khrushchev invited himself to the United States. Fearing that the Soviet leader would turn the trip into a propaganda bonanza, the Eisenhower administration reluctantly received him. Khrushchev arrived in the United States the following September and, after touring an Iowa corn farm and unsuccessfully seeking admission to the newly opened Disneyland, met with Eisenhower at the presidential retreat, Camp David.

While the two leaders were unable to resolve their differences at Camp David, Khrushchev announced that the Western powers could stay in West Berlin for another eighteen months, as long as progress toward a final settlement of the city's status was being made. The two men agreed to another summit in Europe the following spring, after which Eisenhower planned to travel to the Soviet Union. The president gave the impression that the Soviet retreat on Berlin had ended the issue, but Khrushchev would revive it two years later, when Eisenhower's successor, John F. Kennedy, was in the White House.

The Paris Summit, May 1960

Besides the Berlin problem, the other major issue that was expected to be discussed at the summit meeting was the nuclear test ban. Faced with the Geneva conference's inability to work out a comprehensive test ban agreement, the Eisenhower administration, on February 11, 1960, proposed a partial ban on nuclear weapons tests and a phased approach to the inspection problem. Prohibited in the first stage, the administration suggested, would be all atmospheric and underwater tests, as well as tests in space above an unspecified height where detection procedures were considered unreliable. Underground tests that produced seismic signals greater than 4.75 on the Richter earthquake magnitude scale would also be prohibited. The administration also made an important concession by indicating its willingness to accept a limited number of annual inspections. It now considered a quota of twenty annual on-site inspections sufficient to deter Soviet cheating.

On March 19, 1960, the Soviets responded by saying that at least three modifications of the U.S. proposal would be necessary before they could accept it. First, all tests in space would have to be prohibited, regardless of whether or not they could be detected. Second, a four- to five-year moratorium on all underground tests below the 4.75 Richter-scale threshold would have to be observed. Third, a smaller number of "symbolic" inspections would be required, to simply express the good intentions of the parties to uphold a test ban treaty rather than to determine with scientific preciseness whether violations had occurred.

At the end of March 1960, British Prime Minister Harold Macmillan and the president agreed to accept the Soviet conditions. Britain and the United States would continue to observe the moratorium on underground tests beneath the 4.75 threshold, but for only one or two years, provided that the Soviets agreed to sign a treaty barring all verifiable tests and creating a coordinated seismic research program. When the Soviets reacted favorably to the Western proposition, the general anticipation was that a test ban treaty could be concluded at the Paris summit meeting, which both Eisenhower and Khrushchev had agreed to attend in May.

However, just as the superpowers appeared to be moving toward a test ban agreement, an event occurred that derailed it for three more years. On May 7 Khrushchev announced that six days earlier the Soviet Union had shot down an American U-2 spy plane deep inside Soviet territory. The aircraft's pilot, Francis Gary Powers, the Soviets boasted, had survived the crash and was being held in captivity. The U-2 incident seemed to confirm Eisenhower's earlier prediction that "some day one of these machines is going to be caught, and we're going to have a storm."[28]

Khrushchev at first tried to give the president a face-saving way out of the embarrassment. He stated that he was prepared to accept that Eisenhower knew nothing about the U-2's mission, but he also wanted the president's assurance that similar flights would not be repeated. Eisenhower, however, refused to evade responsibility for the incident. To do so, he believed, would be an admission on his part that he was not fully aware of his nation's military activities, especially one as sensitive as the U-2 flights over Soviet territory.

Turned down by the president, Khrushchev then demanded an apology. Eisenhower angrily refused. He told French President Charles de Gaulle that he was not about to "crawl" on his knees to the Soviet leader. Khrushchev responded by angrily denouncing the president and canceling the invitation he had extended to visit the Soviet Union. Obviously, in the atmosphere of acute superpower hostility produced by the U-2 affair, the Paris summit meeting had little chance of success. On May 19, only two days after the summit began, Eisenhower left Paris. As a result, neither the test ban issue nor the status of Berlin was resolved before Eisenhower left office.

The Congo

In the summer of 1960, the Cold War spread into sub-Saharan Africa. Until then, the region had received little attention from the Eisenhower administration. As in other areas of the world, the anticolonial movement had received virtually no support from the United States. The administration preferred to allow the European imperial powers to govern the pace of African independence.

Nevertheless, the administration was uneasy about the June 30, 1960, decision of the Belgian government to grant independence to the Congo (now Zaire), despite the fact that the Congolese were totally unprepared for self-government. When the Congolese army turned on its white officers and on Belgian settlers, the government of Congolese Prime Minister

Patrice Lumumba was unable to restore order. As a result, Belgian forces intervened in the Congo, an action that stimulated a secessionist movement in its Katanga province. In response, Lumumba appealed to the United Nations for assistance, and in mid-July the world body called for the withdrawal of Belgian troops and agreed to send an international military force to restore order in the country.

To block Soviet involvement in the Congo, the Eisenhower administration supported the UN's actions. However, Lumumba soon soured on the UN military presence in his country, after UN Secretary General Dag Hammarskjold refused to use UN troops to crush the secession movement in Katanga. After his bid for U.S. assistance was rejected, Lumumba turned to the Soviets, who eagerly responded with 100 trucks and 15 air transports, complete with crews and maintenance personnel. Lumumba's willingness to accept Soviet assistance earned him the hostility of the Eisenhower administration. CIA Director Allen Dulles concluded that the Congolese prime minister had been "bought by the communists."[29] In fact, Lumumba was a genuine nationalist, not a communist, and he turned to the Soviets because they alone were willing to help him regain control of his country.

Nevertheless, on August 19, 1960, Dulles sent a cable to CIA Station Chief Lawrence Devlin in which he stated that Lumumba's "removal must be an urgent and prime objective."[30] Soon thereafter, the CIA station in the Congo recruited the Congolese leaders—including Colonel Joseph Mobutu, who would replace Lumumba in September 1960 and rule Zaire into the 1990s—to help overthrow Lumumba. After the Congolese premier was ousted and assassinated on January 17, 1961 (by Katangan authorities, with probable CIA involvement), every U.S. administration that followed Eisenhower's would work closely with the Mobutu regime, some more enthusiastically than others.

The impact of the Congo tragedy and the growing importance of Africa in the Cold War was evident at the fifteenth session of the UN General Assembly that convened in New York in September 1960. At that session, seventeen new nations, all but one of them African and all former colonial territories, were admitted into the world body. The admission of these new states completed the transformation of the UN from an association of predominantly World War II victors to one composed primarily of Third World nations, most of which proclaimed neutrality in the Cold War.

On September 24, in an address before the General Assembly, Khrushchev tried to align the Soviet Union with the Third World by again attacking Western colonialism. He also demanded Hammarskjold's removal from office for allegedly pursuing a colonialist policy in the Congo. Khrushchev suggested that the post of secretary general be abolished and replaced with a collective executive of three representatives— one from the West, one from the socialist bloc, and another from a neutral country. While the Eisenhower administration was able to block implementation of Khrushchev's "troika" solution, the issue revealed that the days of easy U.S. domination of the United Nations had ended.

Laos

Shortly before Eisenhower left office, he faced still another crisis in southeast Asia, this time in Laos. A conflict for control of the Laotian government had developed between three factions: the leftist Pathet Lao, the neutralist government of Prime Minister Souvanna Phouma, with its capital at Vientiane, and a rightist faction led by Prince Boun Oum and Phoumi Nosavan, with headquarters in the royal capital, Luang Prabang. The Eisenhower administration, sided with Boun Oum and Phoumi Nosavan because they seemed to offer the best prospect for saving the country from communism.

The conflict in Laos became a crisis for the Eisenhower administration when, on December 13, 1960 a military coup, conducted by leftist elements cooperating with the Pathet Lao drove Souvanna Phouma from Vientiane. The forces of Boun Oum, who was appointed by the Laotian king to head a new provisional government, soon recaptured Vientiane, but, with Soviet supplies, the Pathet Lao and its allies launched an offensive that threatened to cut Laos in half.

On the last day of 1960, Eisenhower told a meeting of Pentagon and CIA officials, "We cannot let Laos fall to the communists even if we have to fight—with our allies or without them."[31] The group agreed that the Seventh Fleet should be redeployed and readied to back up a plan for American intervention. The plan envisioned U.S. troops holding Vientiane and Luang Prabang in order to free Boun Oum's forces to attack the Pathet Lao in the countryside. Because he was reluctant to commit his successor to the plan, Eisenhower did not implement it before he left the White House. Laos, like the Congo, were problems that the new president would have to face. But the biggest problem Eisenhower would leave his successor was Fidel Castro's Cuba.

The Cuban Revolution

Castro came to power in Cuba on News Year's Day 1959 by overthrowing the government of dictator Fulgencio Batista, who had ruled that island nation since 1934. In return for U.S. support, Batista had permitted U.S. business interests to dominate the Cuban economy, including nearly all of Cuba's oil production, most of its public utilities, half its railways, and 40 percent of its sugar production. Neither Batista nor the Americans did much to alleviate the severe problems that gripped the nation, including high unemployment, illiteracy, and disease. Combined with a poor distribution of wealth (46 percent of Cuba's total land area was held by 1.5 percent of the landowners), these problems, and the refusal of the Battista regime to address them, made Cuba ripe for Castro's revolutionary program.

Soon after taking power, Castro launched a program to drive organized crime from Havana, reduce illiteracy, and improve housing and
medical care for the overwhelming majority of the Cuban population. As
Arbenz had attempted to do in Guatemala, Castro also instituted an
agrarian reform program in Cuba, one aimed at breaking up large estates,
redistributing land to peasant families, and ending foreign domination of
the Cuban economy. Not surprisingly, the agrarian reform program was
opposed by U.S. business interests in Cuba, who pressured the Eisenhower administration to protect their Cuban holdings.

They found a sympathetic ear in the White House. Although Eisenhower promptly recognized Castro's government, he was shocked by its
execution of hundreds of Batista supporters after show trials that made a
mockery of the principles of fair jurisprudence. Mainly for this reason, the
president refused to meet with the Cuban leader when he toured the
United States in April 1959. He also declined to give Cuba economic aid,
which Castro hoped to use to finance his revolutionary program. By the
end of 1959, after the Cuban government took the first steps toward
nationalizing private businesses and foreign holdings in Cuba, Eisenhower
had concluded that Castro was either a communist or was dominated by
the communists.

While Castro was not a communist at this time, the administration
believed that his revolution would undermine U.S. interests not only in
Cuba but throughout Latin America. Soon after Soviet Deputy Premier
Anastas Mikoyan visited Cuba in February 1960, to sign an economic
agreement with the Castro government, the Eisenhower administration
decided to do what it could to overthrow the Cuban leader. On March
17, 1960, the president approved a CIA plan to train Cuban émigrés to
invade their homeland and lead an insurrection against Cuba.

Within days, Castro learned about the presidential decision to overthrow him from spies in the Cuban exile community. Faced with this
U.S.–backed threat, Castro increasingly assumed an anti-American and
pro-Soviet stance. In June 1960, after U.S. and British oil companies
refused to refine Soviet crude oil imported by the Cuban government,
Castro nationalized their refineries. In the previous month, Castro's government established diplomatic relations with the Soviet Union. It also
concluded an economic aid agreement with the Soviet Union and arms
agreements with various East European countries. By the summer of
1960, the Soviet bloc had become Cuba's principal economic and military backer.

The Eisenhower administration responded to Castro's moves by
increasing U.S. pressure on the Cuban economy. In July 1960, with Castro
in the process of confiscating the remaining American investments in Cuba,
Eisenhower cut Cuba's 1960 sugar quota by 700,000 tons. Later that year,
he completely excluded Cuban sugar from the U.S. market for the first
three months of 1961, an action that subsequently would be renewed by
the Kennedy administration. On September 30 the U.S. government

advised American citizens not to travel to Cuba and urged those living in Cuba to send their wives and dependents home. In October, Eisenhower placed an embargo on all American exports to Cuba (save medical and other emergency supplies). The administration also mined the area surrounding the U.S.–held Guantanamo naval base, and declared that the United States would never allow the base to be seized by Cuba.

Castro responded to this increased pressure by completing the nationalization of all remaining U.S.–owned enterprises in Cuba and by moving even closer to the Soviet Union. On September 26, 1960, he made a bitterly anti-American speech before the UN General Assembly that was enthusiastically applauded by Khrushchev. Early in January 1961, after Castro demanded that the staff of the U.S. embassy in Havana be cut to eleven people, the Eisenhower administration formally severed diplomatic relations with Cuba. Shortly before he left the White House, Eisenhower informed the president-elect about the planned invasion of Cuba. He left to Kennedy the decision to implement it.

An Assessment of the Eisenhower Years

To his credit, Eisenhower reopened the dialogue with the Soviet leadership that had been disrupted during the Truman administration. But he did not have much success in improving relations with the Soviet Union, partly because the Red Scare that raged in the United States during his first term made negotiations with the Soviets almost impossible politically. In addition, Dulles and other officials in the U.S. national security establishment opposed a conciliatory policy toward the Soviet Union. Even so, Eisenhower also did not trust the Soviets. His refusal to curb America's reliance on nuclear weapons and his failure to stop U-2 espionage flights over the Soviet Union ultimately doomed an opportunity to conclude a nuclear test ban treaty during his administration.

The growing Soviet-American rivalry in the Third World also worked against a Cold War thaw during the Eisenhower years. In dealing with the prospect of communist expansion into the Third World, both Dulles and the president confused communism with genuine anticolonial movements. The United States often allied itself with existing dictatorships rather than the forces of reform. In contrast to the restraint Eisenhower displayed in dealing with the major communist powers, namely, China and the Soviet Union, the president was often more bellicose than his secretary of state when it came to dealing with Third World insurgencies. More than once, for example in Indochina and in Lebanon, it was Dulles who acted as the restraining influence on the president. Even though U.S. combat troops did not see much action during Eisenhower's presidency, U.S. covert operations in the Third World mushroomed during his tenure.

The Soviets were also responsible for the intensification of the Cold War during the Eisenhower years. Nikita Khrushchev's eagerness to challenge U.S. interests around the world contributed to the spread of the

Cold War in the Middle East, East Asia, Latin America, and even Africa. Khrushchev's aggressiveness was motivated not only by a desire to take advantage of an opportunity to expand Soviet influence but also by the perceived Soviet need to fend off a growing challenge by China for leadership of the communist movement.

Khrushchev's willingness to engage the United States in a nuclear arms race was motivated primarily by his realization that the Soviet Union, despite the continuing development of its nuclear arsenal, was still vulnerable to an American nuclear strike. He undoubtedly believed that the best defense is a good offense and that a forward policy would conceal Soviet nuclear weakness while serving to pressure the West to resolve issues, such as Berlin, to the satisfaction of the Soviet Union. Khrushchev's aggressiveness also made Soviet-American reconciliation impossible during the 1950s.

5

Kennedy and Johnson: Confrontation and Cooperation, 1961–1969

At the beginning of John F. Kennedy's presidency, the Soviets indicated that they were prepared to improve relations with the United States. Khrushchev warmly congratulated the new president on his inauguration day and released two U.S. Air Force officers whose RB-47 reconnaissance plan had been shot down over Soviet territory the preceding July. Kennedy responded to these gestures by removing restrictions on the importation of Soviet crabmeat and by proposing a mutual increase in the number of consulates and scientific and cultural exchanges.

While Kennedy was inclined to improve Soviet-American relations, his ability to do so was restricted by his determination to appear tough toward communism. While campaigning for the presidency, he said: "The enemy is the communist system itself, implacable, insatiable, uneasy in its drive for world domination."[1] While it may be true, as Kennedy intimates have argued, that statements like these were nothing more than campaign rhetoric, they nevertheless precluded the possibility of cultivating public support for a Cold War thaw early in his administration.

Khrushchev's public rhetoric also made Soviet-American reconciliation difficult, if not impossible, early in Kennedy's presidency. On January 6, 1961, the Soviet leader declared his country would support "wars of national liberation" in the underdeveloped world. Khrushchev's declaration, wrote the president's confidante and historian Arthur Schlesinger, Jr., "alarmed Kennedy more than Moscow's amiable signals assuaged him."[2] Although Kennedy was willing to negotiate an end to the Cold War, the Third World challenge which Khrushchev threw at him would have to be dealt with first.

In the opinion of another historian, Bruce Miroff, Kennedy's reaction to Khrushchev's blustering revealed an acute inferiority complex, which the president manifested by a perverse need to prove his leadership capabilities. As a result, rather than ignoring or minimizing Khrushchev's threats, as Eisenhower usually did, Kennedy personalized them and converted them into tests of will, in the process manufacturing crises that need not have been. "There was really nothing in that [Eisenhower] era comparable to the Berlin crisis of 1961 and the Cuban missile crisis of 1962," Miroff observes, both of which represented the closest approaches to a superpower nuclear war during the Cold War.[3]

For whatever reasons, whether they were primarily ideological, political, or psychological—and all were important—in formulating his initial response to the Soviet Union Kennedy chose to emphasize Khrushchev's bellicose actions rather than his friendly gestures. Only after Kennedy had proved to the Soviet leader that he was not soft on communism would diplomacy make any headway during his presidency.

The Bay of Pigs Invasion

Cuba was the scene of Kennedy's first foray into a Third World confrontation with the Soviet Union. Shortly after taking office, he approved an Eisenhower-initiated plan for an invasion of Cuba by 1,400 CIA-trained Cuban exiles. The invasion, which began on April 17, 1961, ended in abject failure after Kennedy at the last hour refused to permit direct U.S. military involvement in the operation. As a result, Castro's forces quickly isolated the invaders' bridgehead and forced them to surrender after only three days of fighting. The surviving invaders, some 1,189 in number, were imprisoned until December 1962, when Kennedy bought their release by providing Cuba with $53 million worth of tractors and other badly needed equipment.

Kennedy was embittered by his humiliation in Cuba. Equally painful for the new president was the realization that, instead of driving the Soviets out of Cuba, the botched operation had drawn Havana and Moscow closer together. On April 16 Castro declared himself a socialist, to ensure a Soviet commitment to defend Cuba. Khrushchev obliged by pledging to give Cuba all necessary assistance. Kennedy responded by warning the Soviets that U.S. "restraint is not inexhaustible."[4] On April 20 he authorized U.S. advisers in Laos, who had been dressing as civilians, to wear military uniforms. On May 15 he announced that he was considering an expansion of U.S. military aid to South Vietnam. On May 25, for the second time since taking office, he asked Congress for a supplemental increase in defense appropriations.

And Kennedy intensified the U.S. effort to overthrow Castro. He approved a CIA-drafted program to undermine the Cuban economy (Operation Mongoose). He also may have known about and even authorized (although there is no concrete proof to support either possibility) several assassination attempts against Castro by the CIA, which acted in consort with the Mafia. In addition, the president adopted the Eisenhower-initiated plans for direct U.S. military action against Cuba, including an invasion. There is much to suggest, writes historian Louise FitzSimons about the Bay of Pigs, "that John F. Kennedy, consciously or unconsciously, spent the rest of . . . his life trying to recover from, and make up for, that initial colossal error."[5]

The Alliance for Progress

Kennedy did not rely solely on U.S. action against Cuba to contain communism in the Western Hemisphere. A little over a month before the Bay of Pigs invasion, on March 13, 1961, he introduced a program called the Alliance for Progress. It was designed to reduce poverty, illiteracy, and disease in the hemisphere, and thereby ameliorate the conditions that encouraged the growth of communism. To help finance the program, the president pledged the United States to provide the Latin American nations (excluding Cuba) with $10 billion over the next ten years.

Formally inaugurated in August 1961, the agenda of the Alliance for Progress included programs for agrarian reform, tax revision, accelerated urban and rural housing development, health and sanitation improvement, and the elimination of illiteracy. The Alliance for Progress also called for national development plans designed to produce fair wages, stable prices, greater integration of the Latin American economies, and a per capita growth rate of 2.5 percent a year. The administration anticipated that the Alliance for Progress would not only prevent the expansion of communism in Latin America, it would also encourage the growth of democracy in a region still dominated by military dictatorships.

While the Alliance for Progress was responsible for some improvement in Latin American social and economic conditions, it did not achieve any of its goals. During the 1960s Latin American economic growth rates averaged only 1.5 percent annually, rather than the 2.5 percent forecast by the administration. Housing, sanitation, and health care improved only marginally, if at all, for the majority of Latin America's poor. There was also no appreciable decrease in adult illiteracy during the decade. The number of unemployed Latin Americans actually rose from 18 million to 25 million, and agricultural production per person declined. Moreover, the distribution of wealth remained grossly inequitable, and most of the region's governments continued to be firmly under military control. In fact, during the Kennedy years, military officers overthrew six popularly elected presidents in Argentina, Peru, Guatemala, Ecuador, the Dominican Republic, and Honduras.

In the opinion of a veteran State Department officer, Thomas Mann, one reason for the failure of the Alliance for Progress was the "illusion of omnipotence" under which he believed the Kennedy administration had worked.[6] The United States had reconstructed Europe; therefore, there was no reason to believe that Latin America could not be reformed. But Latin America was not Europe. Rapid population growth in Latin America (which had one of the fastest rates of increase in the world at 3 percent annually) undercut most of the progress made by the Alliance in reducing poverty and its associated problems. In addition, Latin America lacked the financial and technical expertise, institutionalized political parties, and democratic traditions that characterized most Western European countries. Devastated by World War II, the Western European governments had no alternative but to accept American money and leadership to reconstruct their countries. But the ruling elites in Latin America feared the Alliance for Progress even more than they did communism, for they believed that the U.S.-initiated reform programs posed a greater threat to their hold on power than the communists did.

The United States, however, did not escape its share of the responsibility for the failure of the Alliance for Progress. The Kennedy administration was more than willing to block reforms that threatened U.S. interests in the region. For example, it persuaded the president of Honduras to amend that nation's agrarian law because it had permitted the confiscation of land holdings belonging to the Standard Oil and United Fruit Companies. Also, despite the administration's preference for democratic governments, it soon accepted the necessity of working with military regimes, primarily because they were the strongest barrier to Castro-style revolutions in the region. In other words, the requirements for maintaining U.S. economic and political hegemony in the region took precedence over the social, economic, and political reforms called for in the Alliance for Progress.

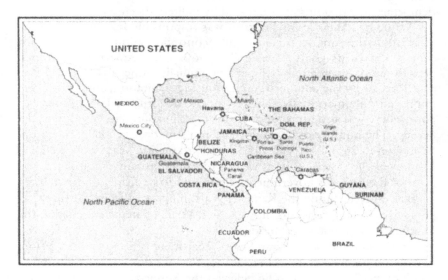

Middle America, 1962

The Vienna Summit and Laos

In the wake of the Bay of Pigs fiasco, Kennedy agreed to meet with Khrushchev, in Vienna, on June 3–4, 1961. According to Arthur Schlesinger, Kennedy "intended to propose a standstill in the Cold War" in which both superpowers would refrain from actions that would "threaten the existing balance of force or endanger world peace."[7] What the president wanted, Khrushchev recalled in his memoirs, was "countries with capitalist systems to remain capitalist, and he wanted us to agree to a guarantee to that effect."[8] Maintaining the status quo, however, was absolutely unacceptable to the leader of a state that preached the inevitability of capitalism's demise.

Nevertheless, at Vienna both Kennedy and Khrushchev agreed to support the status quo in one country, Laos. In so doing, Kennedy rejected Eisenhower's strong suggestion that he send U.S. troops to that country to support the pro-American royalist faction and deny the communist Pathet Lao a victory. While Kennedy sent 500 U.S. marines to neighboring Thailand, he refused to become militarily involved in Laos. He undoubtedly was influenced by the estimate of the Joint Chiefs of Staff that a "victory" in Laos would require 60,000 U.S. troops, a number the president considered excessive and one he realized Congress was not prepared to accept. In addition, U.S. involvement in the Laotian conflict would have risked Chinese intervention. Khrushchev, for his part, saw no good reason for Soviet intervention in Laos. "Why take risks over Laos?" he said to U.S. Ambassador Llewellyn Thompson. "It will fall into our laps like a ripe apple."[9] As a result, the Soviet leader accepted a British proposal for a cease-fire and negotiations in Geneva, in which the Communist, neutralist, and rightist factions would participate.

At the Geneva conference, which began in May 1961 and lasted until June 1962, the conferees agreed that the Pathet Lao would share power in a coalition government headed by the neutralist Premier Souvanna Phouma. The agreement called for the neutralization of Laos and the withdrawal of all foreign troops within seventy-five days. Although the major powers promised to respect Laos's neutrality, by late 1962 both sides were covertly violating the agreement. Nevertheless, the shaky Geneva arrangement held together for the duration of Kennedy's presidency, allowing him to concentrate on more pressing problems, one of which was Berlin.

The Berlin Crisis of 1961

At Vienna, Khrushchev told Kennedy that he wanted his consent to a German peace treaty, one that would finally and formally end World War II, and thereby gain Western recognition for the existing boundaries of Eastern Europe. The peace treaty proposed by Khrushchev at Vienna was essentially the same as the one that Eisenhower had rejected in 1958, primarily because it would have ended the Western military presence in Berlin and turned over control of the access routes to that city to the East

German government. At Vienna, Khrushchev again threatened to sign a
separate peace treaty with East Germany, by the end of 1961, if the Western powers refused to cooperate. Kennedy reacted to Khrushchev by
warning the Soviet leader that, if he carried out his threat, Soviet-American relations would experience "a cold winter."[10]

Khrushchev backed up his Berlin threat with action. On July 8, 1961,
he suspended ongoing reductions in the size of the Soviet army and
ordered a one-third increase in Soviet military spending. To halt the out-
flow of East Germans to the West (estimated at 1,000 people per day by
August), Khrushchev permitted the East German government to begin
erecting the infamous Berlin Wall on August 13, 1961.

Kennedy considered Khrushchev's Berlin challenge not only a threat
to the freedom of West Berlin but also a test of the U.S. commitment to
defend the entire free world. However, unlike Eisenhower's reaction,
Kennedy's initial response was military rather than diplomatic in nature:
1,500 U.S. soldiers were sent down the autobahn in armored vehicles,
and another 150,000 Army reservists were called to active duty. If necessary, Kennedy was prepared to go further. He told Schlesinger that he
believed "that there was one chance out of five for a nuclear exchange."[11]
Fearing a nuclear war over Berlin, many Americans began to build fallout
shelters in their backyards.

Fortunately, the Berlin confrontation abated after Kennedy rejected
advice to knock down the Wall and instead accepted Khrushchev's feelers
for a negotiated settlement of the crisis. Although the Berlin talks, which
began in September, proved inconclusive, they enabled Khrushchev to
drop his deadline for a German peace treaty, thereby permitting the crisis
to fizzle out.

To cover his retreat on Berlin, as well as to respond to Kennedy's
nuclear buildup, on August 30, 1961, Khrushchev announced that he
was resuming Soviet nuclear weapons tests, thereby breaking the thirty-
four-month-old moratorium on superpower testing. In the next sixty
days, the Soviet Union conducted over fifty atmospheric nuclear tests,
including one with a yield of fifty-eight megatons, the most powerful
nuclear device ever detonated. On September 5 Kennedy responded to
Khrushchev's action by ordering the resumption of U.S. nuclear tests.
"What choice did we have?" Kennedy asked UN ambassador Adlai
Stevenson. "We couldn't possibly sit back and do nothing at all." In the
wake of the Bay of Pigs fiasco and the construction of the Berlin Wall,
Kennedy was certain that Khrushchev "wants to give out the feeling that
he has us on the run. . . . Anyway, the decision has been made. I'm not
saying it was the right decision. Who the hell knows?"[12]

A Flexible Response

While Kennedy was changing the U.S. position on nuclear weapons tests,
his advisers were preparing a major revision of U.S. strategic doctrine. In

the late fifties, Kennedy had joined those who considered the Eisenhower administration's massive retaliation strategy a suicidal proposition. Use of U.S. nuclear weapons against the Soviet Union, he predicted, would lead to devastating Soviet nuclear retaliation against the United States. While Kennedy continued to regard nuclear weapons as the primary U.S. deterrent against a Soviet nuclear attack, he did not believe, as Eisenhower had, that they could be used against communist aggression below the nuclear threshold. Their employment in a nonnuclear conflict, he feared, would not only destroy the territory the United States desired to defend but would also risk escalating the conflict to the level of a nuclear exchange between the superpowers.

As a result, Kennedy insisted that the United States must be able to deal with all levels of communist aggression without automatically triggering a nuclear holocaust. This would necessitate, he believed, more emphasis on diplomacy, covert action, antiguerrilla operations, and conventional forces. The "flexible response" strategy that was adopted by the Kennedy administration would enable the United States, in the words of General Maxwell Taylor, chairman of the Joint Chiefs of Staff, to respond "anywhere, at anytime, with weapons and forces appropriate to the situation."[13]

To provide the United States with sufficient conventional forces to deal with nonnuclear aggression, the Kennedy administration doubled the number of ships in the navy and increased the size of the army from eleven to sixteen divisions. In addition, the number of tactical air squadrons were expanded from sixteen in 1961 to twenty-three by the mid-1960s, while airlift capacity expanded by 75 percent.

To deal with communist guerrillas, Kennedy approved the creation of a new counterinsurgency force, whose name, the "Green Berets," was personally selected by the president. By June 1963, some 114,000 U.S. and 7,000 foreign military officers had undergone counterinsurgency training at the Army's Special Forces School at Fort Bragg, North Carolina. In January 1962 Kennedy also created a fifteen-member ad hoc Special Group, chaired by General Taylor, to coordinate U.S. counterinsurgency activities around the globe, but especially in Latin America and Southeast Asia.

Despite the increased reliance on conventional and counterinsurgency forces, however, both the Kennedy administration and that of his successor, Lyndon Johnson, substantially expanded the size of the U.S. nuclear arsenal. By the end of the sixties, the United States had 1,059 ICBMs, 700 submarine-launched ballistic missiles (SLBMs), and over 500 long-range B-52 bombers.

The expansion of the U.S. nuclear arsenal was necessary, argued Robert S. McNamara, Kennedy's defense secretary, to give the United States greater targeting flexibility. McNamara hoped that, by limiting U.S. retaliatory strikes to Soviet military installations, rather than cities (a counterforce strategy), the United States would be able to avoid the type of all-out nuclear war that the massive retaliation strategy would have made all but inevitable. Moreover, McNamara believed, additional nuclear weapons would ensure that the United States would have sufficient nuclear warheads to retaliate effectively after a Soviet first strike.

The Kennedy military buildup ended any possibility of limiting the nuclear arms race with the Soviet Union during his presidency. It made the Soviet military more aware of a missile gap that definitely favored the United States and consequently contributed to the pressure on Khrushchev to increase the size of the Soviet nuclear arsenal.

The buildup of U.S. conventional forces also had mixed results. Though enhancing America's deterrent capability, it added to an escalating military budget, which reached an unprecedented $50 billion by the end of 1963. Moreover, once the administration had the means to intervene in Vietnam, it became more inclined to do so. Thus, the augmentation of U.S. counterinsurgency forces contributed to America's growing involvement in a war that would divide that nation as no conflict had since the Civil War.

The Cuban Missile Crisis

Partly to offset America's nuclear superiority, but primarily to deter another U.S.-backed invasion of Cuba, Khrushchev decided in early 1962 to deploy on that island nation thirty-six medium-range ballistic missiles (with a range of 1,000 nautical miles) and twenty-four intermediate-range ballistic missiles (with a range of 2,200 nautical miles). Since the United States had deployed Jupiter IRBMs in Turkey, the Soviet Union's neighbor, ostensibly for defensive purposes, the Soviet leader had no qualms about trying to do the same thing in Cuba. "It was high time," he recalled thinking in his memoir, "America learned what it feels like to have her own land and her own people threatened."[14]

Deploying Soviet missiles in Cuba also would redress the growing threat to the Soviet homeland that was posed by Kennedy's rapid expansion of the American nuclear arsenal and by McNamara's counterforce strategy. The Soviet Union's sense of vulnerability was undoubtedly aggravated by Deputy Secretary of Defense Roswell Gilpatric's announcement (in October 1961) that the United States was aware that the Soviet ICBM force was much smaller than earlier anticipated.

It is probable that Khrushchev also wanted a dramatic way of achieving a breakthrough on the Berlin problem, and perhaps expected that the successful deployment of missiles in Cuba would do much to neutralize U.S. nuclear superiority, thereby enabling him to increase Soviet pressure on that beleaguered city. In addition, some analysts believe, the successful deployment of Soviet missiles in Cuba would distract attention from Khrushchev's growing domestic problems, primarily the mediocre performance of Soviet agriculture, and solidify the leadership of Soviet Union in the international communist movement, which was being increasingly challenged by the Chinese.

Kennedy, however, refused to allow Khrushchev to redress a strategic balance that was clearly in America's favor. After a U-2 photo-reconnaissance plane first spotted the Soviet missiles in Cuba on October 14, the president decided to force Khrushchev to remove them. It is also quite probable that Kennedy's decision was based on more than strategic considerations. Perhaps because of the humiliation that he had suffered in Cuba, or the criticism he had taken as a result of his inability or unwillingness to do anything about the construction of the Berlin Wall, Kennedy regarded the Cuban missile crisis as a personal test of his leadership ability. He told his brother, Robert Kennedy, that if he did not force the Soviets to remove their missiles from he would be "impeached."[15]

As in the Berlin crisis, Kennedy at first rejected a diplomatic solution to the Cuban missile threat. UN Ambassador Adlai Stevenson suggested that the United States should offer to dismantle its obsolete Jupiter IRBMs in Turkey in exchange for the withdrawal of Soviet missiles from Cuba. But some of Kennedy's advisers, Arthur Schlesinger recalled, "felt strongly that the thought of negotiations at this point would be taken as an admission of the moral weakness of our case and the military weakness of our posture."[16]

At the same time, however, Kennedy refused to approve the opposite approach: direct U.S. military action against the Soviet missile bases in Cuba. Over the objections of the Joint Chiefs of Staff, who wanted to destroy the Soviet missiles with air strikes, Kennedy decided on a naval "quarantine," or blockade, of Cuba followed by an address to the nation on October 22 in which the president called upon Khrushchev "to halt and eliminate this clandestine, reckless and provocative threat to world peace."[17]

Kennedy backed up his words with military action. U.S. forces in Florida began preparations for an invasion of Cuba. More ominously, he ordered the armed forces to prepare for the possibility of nuclear war. As a result, 156 ICBMs were readied for firing and the Strategic Air Command's B-47 and B-52 bombers were placed on alert.

By the time of Kennedy's address to the American people on October 22, forty-two Soviet missiles had arrived in Cuba. Two days later, only nine missiles were in place and fully assembled. Believing that even these were in danger of imminent destruction by U.S. air power, and fearing that the crisis could escalate into an all-out nuclear exchange between the superpowers (one the Soviet Union, given its nuclear inferiority, could not hope to win), Khrushchev backed down on October 28 and agreed to withdraw the Soviet missiles from Cuba. In return, Kennedy publicly promised that the United States would not attempt another invasion of Cuba and—unbeknownst to the American people, the Congress, or the European allies—assured Khrushchev that, once the crisis had ended, he would withdraw the U.S. Jupiters from Turkey. The missiles were removed six months later. The U.S. concessions enabled the Soviet leader to salvage some meager semblance of face.

Kennedy was praised nationwide, even by his Republican critics, for his masterly handling of the Cuban missile crisis, a response Schlesinger characterized as a "combination of toughness and restraint."[18] Yet few discussed what could have happened had he failed. Historian Louise FitzSimons points out what many preferred not to think about: "In the flush of success and relief from danger, Kennedy was determined to force Khrushchev's total capitulation—no matter the cost."[19] During the height of the crisis, the president himself placed the likelihood of disaster at "somewhere between one out of three and even," and lamented that the world's children might not live out their lives.[20]

Ironically, the enhanced short-term prestige that Kennedy experienced in the wake of the Cuban missile crisis only produced greater long-term insecurity for his country. The humiliation Khrushchev suffered at the hands of Kennedy during the missile crisis contributed to his removal from power in October 1964. The new Soviet leadership, headed by Leonid Brezhnev, was determined to avoid a repetition of the humiliation Khrushchev had experienced. Beginning in early 1965, the Kremlin embarked on a massive expansion of the Soviet nuclear arsenal that would enable the Soviet Union to achieve rough nuclear parity with the United States by the end of the decade.

In addition, Kennedy's triumph in the Cuban missile crisis contributed to the development of what historian William J. Medland has called an "arrogance of power," a belief that the United States had the communists on the run. This new attitude helped to explain the growing U.S. involvement in Vietnam.[21]

The Limited Test Ban Treaty

The Cuban missile crisis also had beneficial consequences. The close brush with nuclear war helped to create a climate for productive arms control negotiations, which had not existed since the abortive Paris summit conference of May 1960. Attempting to reduce tensions with the West, Khrushchev, on December 19, 1962, sent Kennedy a personal letter inviting him to intensify the effort to conclude a nuclear test ban treaty. With the humiliation of the Bay of Pigs fiasco erased by his astute performance during the Cuban missile crisis, and sobered by the close superpower approach to nuclear war, Kennedy accepted Khrushchev's invitation.

Six months later, Kennedy delivered the most conciliatory speech on the Soviet Union of his career. In a commencement address at American University on June 10, 1963, he called on Americans to reexamine their attitudes toward the Soviet Union. "In the final analysis, he told his audience, "we all inhabit this small planet. . . . And we are all mortal." [22] Kennedy called upon the American people to support his effort to conclude a nuclear test ban agreement. It would be, he said, an initial step toward preserving the life of the planet. As a sign of good faith in the ultimate success of the test ban talks, Kennedy announced that the United States would not conduct atmospheric nuclear tests as long as the Soviet Union employed similar restraint.

Many considered Kennedy's American University speech the first step toward what would be called détente. But as George F. Kennan, the father of the containment doctrine, remarked, "one speech is not enough" to end the Cold War.[23] Another speech that the president would have delivered on November 22, 1963, had he not been assassinated that day, revealed that Kennedy was still very much a Cold Warrior. In it, he boasted that his administration's "successful defense of freedom," in Berlin, Cuba, Laos, and elsewhere was attributable "not to the words we used, but to the strength we stood ready to use," a reference to his administration's buildup of nuclear and conventional forces. The United States, the president had been prepared to say, must continue its role as the "watchman on the walls of world freedom."[24]

Despite the limited nature of Kennedy's philosophical transformation after the Cuban missile crisis, his American University speech nevertheless had an extremely favorable impact on the Soviet leadership. Khrushchev told Averell Harriman that it was the best speech delivered by a U.S. president since Franklin Roosevelt. In response, on June 20 the Soviets signed a "hot line" agreement, which established a direct teletype link between Moscow and Washington. The agreement was designed to reduce the risks of an accidental nuclear war as well as ease tensions during international crises.

Still, the superpowers were unable to conclude a comprehensive test ban treaty. The major stumbling block was their inability to agree on the number of annual on-site inspections. Khrushchev expressed his willingness to accept three on-site inspections each year, but Kennedy believed that the Senate would not ratify a comprehensive test ban treaty with less than six.

Since the inspection issue was unresolvable, both sides abandoned the goal of a comprehensive agreement. Instead, they accepted a limited agreement that prohibited the testing of nuclear weapons in the atmosphere, in outer space, and beneath the surface of the seas. After promising the Joint Chiefs of Staff that he would pursue a vigorous underground testing program, the Limited Test Ban Treaty was approved by the Senate on September 24, 1963, by a vote of 80 to 14. After the treaty was ratified by both Britain and the Soviet Union, it went into effect on October 11, 1963.

With the ratification of the Limited Test Ban Treaty, the atmospheric testing of nuclear weapons by the superpowers, as well as Britain, officially ended, and the problem of radioactive fallout subsided greatly. However, the Limited Test Ban Treaty in no way ended the nuclear arms race. It simply drove it, quite literally, underground. Between 1945 and

1980 the number of announced U.S. nuclear detonations totaled 638. More than half that number occurred after the Limited Test Ban Treaty was signed.

Nevertheless, by producing even a limited nuclear arms agreement Kennedy helped to institutionalize the collaborative aspects of the Soviet-American relationship. In so doing, one analyst wrote, Kennedy "paved the way for the future integration of arms control considerations into defense policy"—something that Eisenhower could not, or would not, do.[25] Indeed, Kennedy's successors would accept the necessity for strategic arms control largely because of the spadework he did during his short presidency.

The Sino-Soviet Split

The Soviets were willing to work to improve relations with the United States late in Kennedy's presidency because they wanted to reduce the risks of a superpower nuclear war. They also wanted to be free to deal with an increasingly hostile China. Although, in the wake of the Hungarian Revolution, the Soviets and the Chinese had patched up the strains in their relationship caused by Khrushchev's de-Stalinization campaign and promulgation of peaceful coexistence, their relations unraveled again in the late fifties.

The Chinese were upset by the lackluster support they had received from the Soviets during the second Taiwan Strait crisis in 1958, as well as by the Soviet tilt toward India in the Sino-Indian border dispute that flared up the following year. But the Chinese were angered even more by the termination of Soviet nuclear assistance in 1959, a move that convinced Beijing that Moscow could not be trusted. Compounding that outrage was the gradual improvement in Soviet-American relations that followed in the wake of the Cuban missile crisis. By signing the Limited Test Ban Treaty, the Chinese complained, the Soviet leaders had permitted "the imperialists to consolidate their nuclear monopoly and bind the hands of all peace-loving countries subjected to the nuclear threat."[26]

The Soviets, and Khrushchev in particular, were horrified by Mao Zedong's insistence that the Soviet Union must risk nuclear war with the United States to advance the communist cause. This was the primary reason why the Soviets terminated their nuclear assistance program to China in 1959. Said Khrushchev, "Some people [i.e., Mao Zedong] say that it is possible to build a new society on the dead bodies and the ruin of the world. Do these men know that if all the nuclear warheads were touched off, the world would be in such a state that the survivors would envy the dead?"[27]

The Soviet-Chinese rift was brought into the open by Khrushchev at the Twenty-Second Congress of the Soviet Communist Party, which convened in Moscow October 17–31, 1961. In a long address before that body, Khrushchev denounced Albania and its leader Enver Hoxha, who refused to accept de-Stalinization, but everyone knew that the primary target of attack was Mao Zedong. Chinese Premier Zhou Enlai, who was present at the congress, defended Albania, placing heavy stress on the need to preserve the unity of the socialist system. He then threw dirt into Khrushchev's face by laying a wreath on the grave of Stalin, whose body had been removed from the Lenin mausoleum and reburied near the Kremlin wall on Khrushchev's order. Later, in September 1963, the Chinese not only condemned "the errors" of the twenty-second congress, they also accused the Soviets of supporting "antiparty elements in the Chinese Communist Party," that is, those who supported a more pragmatic approach to modernizing China than favored by Mao Zedong.[28]

Kennedy and China

While the Soviets and the Chinese were moving toward an open break, the Kennedy administration pondered its approach to China. According to Arthur Schlesinger, Kennedy considered the state of Sino-American relations "irrational" and "did not exclude the possibility of doing something to change them in the course of his administration."[29] As a first step in this direction, early in his administration the president contemplated relaxing the embargo on U.S. trade with China.

The Chinese appeared to be willing to improve relations with Washington. Early in the Kennedy administration, Wang Kou-chuan, the Chinese ambassador to Poland and China's representative in the Warsaw talks (which since 1958 remained the only official diplomatic contact between the U.S. and Chinese governments), informed U.S. Ambassador to Poland Jacob Beam that the Chinese government was waiting with a "great sense of anticipation" for some new initiatives from the Kennedy administration.[30] Wang also told Beam that, if the United States would terminate its ties with Taiwan, Beijing would make a peaceful settlement of its dispute with Jiang Jeshi.

However, neither Kennedy nor the Congress was willing to abandon Taiwan to improve relations with Beijing. In July 1961 both the Senate and the House of Representatives unanimously passed resolutions that opposed U.S. diplomatic recognition of Communist China and its admission to the United Nations. As a result, the administration dropped the idea of easing the U.S. trade embargo and did not pursue the Chinese peace feeler. In October 1961 it also turned down a bid by Chinese Foreign Minister Chen Yi for talks at the foreign-minister level. Kennedy also supported India in its border dispute with the Chinese by providing the Indians with weapons and transport planes. Moreover, Kennedy vigorously pushed for the completion of the Limited Test Ban Treaty, in the faint hope that it would persuade the Chinese to abandon their nuclear effort.

Kennedy even tried to enlist Khrushchev's support for joint Soviet-American action against China, including a military strike on the Chinese nuclear facilities in Sinkiang. While Khrushchev definitely shared the president's concern about a nuclear-armed China, he could not bring himself to join the world's leading capitalist nation in military action against another communist country, especially one as important in the Marxist movement as China. Khrushchev's unwillingness to cooperate with the United States against China helped to dissuade Kennedy from taking unilateral action, with the result that nothing was done to prevent the Chinese from exploding their first nuclear device on October 16, 1964.

Kennedy and Vietnam

During Kennedy's presidency, the U.S. role in the Vietnam conflict also intensified. Ironically, as a congressman in the early 1950s Kennedy had opposed U.S. intervention in Vietnam. In April 1954, when President Eisenhower was considering U.S. military intervention to save the French garrison at Dien Bien Phu, then Senator Kennedy said: "To pour money, materiel, and men into the jungles of Indochina without at least a remote prospect of victory would be dangerously futile and self-destructive."[31] However, by the time Kennedy entered the White House, he unequivocally embraced Eisenhower's domino theory. He now believed that a communist victory in Vietnam would not only expand China's influence in Southeast Asia but also demonstrate the efficacy of Mao's guerrilla warfare strategy, which the new president had studied intently.

Kennedy regarded the counterinsurgency program his administration adopted as the best way to prevent the communist conquest of South Vietnam. By the time of his death in November 1963, the number of U.S. military advisers in South Vietnam had increased from approximately 700 to 16,700. Kennedy also permitted U.S. military advisers to participate in combat and agreed to assist covert raids by South Vietnamese forces against North Vietnam. Finally, he approved a CIA-sponsored coup against President Diem by the South Vietnamese generals, which resulted not only in Diem's overthrow but also his murder only one month before Kennedy's assassination. As a result of Kennedy's policies, his successor, Lyndon Johnson, would be left with a U.S. commitment to South Vietnam much deeper than the one Eisenhower had left to Kennedy in 1961.

What factors account for the transformation in Kennedy's attitude toward Vietnam? Perhaps the most important was his fear that without greater U.S. military involvement South Vietnam would collapse during his tenure in the White House. Despite considerable U.S. economic and military aid to South Vietnam during the Eisenhower administration, by

1961 the Vietcong had gained control of about 80 percent of the country's villages. They had done so by empowering the peasants to seize and redistribute land owned by their landlords. Kennedy apparently believed he could not allow a communist victory in Vietnam, particularly after Republican critics began charging that his mishandling of the Bay of Pigs invasion, acquiescence to the construction of the Berlin Wall, and acceptance of a neutralized Laos demonstrated that he was soft on communism.

Moreover, unlike landlocked Laos, South Vietnam was much more accessible to U.S. naval air power and thus a better area in which to deploy the president's new counterinsurgency forces. Kennedy was able to persuade the American people, Congress, and the news media that the Green Berets had the "right stuff" for the Vietnam conflict.

According to *The Pentagon Papers* (a Defense Department history of U.S. involvement in the Vietnam War that was leaked to and published by the *New York Times* in 1971), Kennedy also was prepared to commit U.S. ground combat forces to Vietnam. But Diem turned down the president's offer because he feared that a larger U.S. military presence in his country would deprive him of what little independence he still retained. Only after the South Vietnamese military situation sharply deteriorated did Diem, in October 1961, feel compelled to request U.S. combat troops.[32]

By then, however, Kennedy had changed his mind about the wisdom of committing U.S. combat forces. The Berlin crisis had persuaded him that the United States did not have sufficient ground forces to defend Western Europe, let alone South Vietnam. As a result, Kennedy decided that the bulk of the ground fighting would have to be done by the South Vietnamese themselves, supported wherever possible by the Green Berets.

Some observers argue that, had Kennedy lived, he would have withdrawn even the Green Berets from Vietnam during his second term. In this vein, friend and journalist Charles Bartlett reported that the president had said to him, "We don't have a prayer of staying in Vietnam. . . . But I can't give up a piece of territory like that to the Communists and then get the American people to reelect me."[33] In early October 1963, as a way of signaling his displeasure with Diem, whose refusal to make meaningful reforms contributed to the South Vietnamese president's rapidly declining popularity, Kennedy announced publicly that the 1,000 U.S. advisers would be withdrawn by the end of that year. He also said that all U.S. advisers would be out of the country by the end of 1965. However, Kennedy conditioned his promise to withdraw U.S. advisors on the capability of the South Vietnamese to fight the communists on their own.

Others argue that Kennedy was not prepared to withdraw from Vietnam, even if he had been safely reelected. "I had hundreds of talks with John F. Kennedy about Vietnam," Secretary of State Dean Rusk said, "and never once did he say anything of this sort."[34] Moreover, as a condition for obtaining the South Vietnamese army's participation in the coup that overthrew Diem, Kennedy had made a commitment to assist the new military regime. He would have found it extremely difficult to break this commitment without damaging his newly won prestige following the Cuban missile crisis.

While of course it is impossible to state with any certainty what Kennedy would have done in his second term, nothing he did during his abbreviated presidency prevented his successor, Lyndon Johnson, from expanding America's involvement in Vietnam. Indeed, if anything, Kennedy's counterinsurgency program, flexible response strategy, and military buildup gave Johnson the means to fight a much larger war in South Vietnam.

Kennedy and Africa

During the presidential campaign of 1960, Kennedy criticized the Eisenhower administration for refusing to support the growing anticolonial movement in Africa and for its hostility toward African neutralism. Mali's Foreign Minister Jean-Marie Kone told Kennedy that "Americans tend to see communists everywhere" and judged African nations solely on their commitment to anticommunism.[35]

Despite Kennedy's campaign pledges to keep the Cold War out of Africa, encourage African nationalism, and tolerate "genuine" African neutralism, the substance of America's African policy changed little during his presidency. As in Vietnam, his desire to contain the spread of communism took precedence over his professed sensitivity for African nationalism and neutralism. Nevertheless, while Kennedy intended to fight communism in Africa, he was unwilling to make it a major theater of the Cold War. He thought the West could win the "struggle" for Africa simply by denying Khrushchev a victory. The goal should not be "winning the African states to capitalism or military alliance," he said, but merely "to prevent the dominance of the continent by the Communist bloc."[36]

Fortunately for Kennedy, Khrushchev also was unwilling to make Africa a major theater of the Cold War. By the 1960s the Soviets had gained some influence in Mali, as well as Ghana and Guinea, and they had tried to exploit the chaos in the Congo in the wake of its independence from Belgium. However, the Soviets did not make Africa a major priority in their foreign policy until the mid-1960s, when China began to compete with them for the allegiance of the African states.

Even though Soviet influence in Africa was limited, the Kennedy administration tried to woo pro-Soviet African "neutralists" such as Ghana's Kwame Nkrumah. Kennedy agreed to support a $40 million loan to help finance construction of a Ghanaian hydroelectric-aluminum project on the Volta River, and he continued to support the project even after Nkrumah visited a number of communist capitals, including Beijing, bringing into question his professed neutrality in the Cold War. However, Kennedy agreed to release the funds only after Nkrumah pledged to support political freedom and private enterprise in his country and promised never to expropriate U.S. investments. Nkrumah repaid Kennedy for his support of the Volta dam project by refusing to permit Soviet aircraft to refuel in Ghana during the Cuban missile crisis.

African nationalists like Nkrumah were aggravated by the fact that the United States, under Kennedy, continued to defer to its European allies on African colonial matters. To be sure, Kennedy accepted the need for U.S. involvement in the Congo to nip the growth of Soviet influence in the region. However, while posing as a friend of African nationalism, he refused to commit U.S. power to halt an attempt by Moise Tshombe, who was supported by Belgium, to establish an independent state in the Congo's Katanga province. Memories of the Bay of Pigs, as well as expected opposition from Britain and France, Belgium's allies, contributed to Kennedy's decision to encourage the UN to take the lead in subduing the rebellious province. With the assistance of U.S. aircraft and supplies, the UN forces succeeded in crushing the Katangan independence movement in December 1962.

Kennedy also pressured Portugal to accept the independence of Angola, a Portuguese colony in West Africa. In March 1961 the United States endorsed a UN resolution calling for self-determination in Angola. The administration also restricted U.S. arms transfers to Portugal, after determining that napalm and other U.S.-made weapons were being used against the Angolan rebels. But Kennedy refused to break with Portugal over Angola, not only because the Portuguese were NATO allies but also because he was unwilling to jeopardize the U.S. lease of military bases on Portugal's Azores Islands. Despite the complaint of Kennedy's ambassador to India, John Kenneth Galbraith, that "we are trading in our African policy for a few acres of asphalt in the Atlantic," the United States abstained on two UN resolutions involving Portugal.[37] Not surprisingly, the Portuguese repaid the favor by renewing the U.S. lease of the Azores bases. The Angolan independence leader, Holden Roberto, accused the president of abandoning the Angolan nationalists in their hour of need.

The Kennedy administration also did little to end white rule in South Africa. The United States engaged in a symbolic protest of South Africa's apartheid (segregation) policy, but it refused to endorse economic sanctions, which eventually (in the 1990s) would contribute to apartheid's demise and the creation of a black majority government. Kennedy's hands-off policy toward South Africa was motivated not only by a desire to ensure that the United States remained that country's largest trading partner but also by the fact that the United States was dependent on valuable South African minerals, including diamonds, gold, and manganese. In addition Secretary of State Rusk had persuaded the president that "excessive pressure" on South Africa might lead to racial war and possible "communist infiltration" in that country.[38]

Apparently, only the pressure of U.S. civil rights leaders and African nationalists moved Kennedy to impose a unilateral arms embargo on South Africa, effective January 1, 1964. But the embargo was undermined by permitting the South Africans to continue to purchase spare military parts from the United States. As a result, Kennedy's largely symbolic gesture had no effect on South Africa's racial policies.

In the end, Kennedy's policies toward Angola and South Africa displayed the wide disparity that existed between his words and his performance on sub-Saharan Africa. Although he realized that the decolonization of Africa required a new U.S. diplomacy more sensitive to African nationalism and neutralism, he was unwilling to jeopardize America's preeminent relationship with its European allies, one of which (Portugal) still retained African colonies. Kennedy no doubt took comfort from the fact that he did not "lose" Africa to communism during his short tenure in office. This, obviously, was more important to him than African nationalism or neutralism.

The Peace Corps

Although Kennedy's ventures into the Third World were motivated primarily by his anticommunist impulse, they also possessed a humanitarian aspect. In 1961 Kennedy inaugurated a new program, the Peace Corps, by sending 500 young Americans to teach in the schools and work in the fields of eight developing countries. By 1963 there were 7,000 Peace Corps volunteers working in forty-four countries. Three years later at the high point of the program, over 15,000 volunteers would be working overseas.

The Peace Corps was one of Kennedy's most significant legacies. By the mid-1980s more than 100,000 Americans had served overseas with the Peace Corps. Although the image of the Corps would be tarnished, unjustifiably, by the military actions, both covert and overt, of the United States elsewhere in the Third World, the work of its volunteers would be recognized as well. "What a different world it would have been," historian Richard Walton notes, "if the John Kennedy who sent idealistic young volunteers to the villages of Africa, Asia, and Latin America had prevailed over the John Kennedy who sent young soldiers to the jungles of South Vietnam."[39]

The Johnson Doctrine

As a politician in Texas and in the U.S. Congress, both as a representative and as a senator, Lyndon Baines Johnson had built a reputation as a wheeler-dealer; he was a man who got things done. And so he was in the White House as well. In terms of the quantity of domestic legislation passed, no president has equaled Johnson, with the exception of Franklin D. Roosevelt. But while Johnson was a master of domestic politics, he knew little about the world outside the United States. "Foreigners," he once remarked, only half-jokingly, "are not like the folks I am used to." Even though Johnson's knowledge of foreign affairs was extremely shallow, he nevertheless was as determined as his slain predecessor to contain world communism.[40]

This was particularly true with respect to Latin America, which the Texan considered to be America's back yard. Johnson's Latin America policy, like Kennedy's, was dominated by the fear of communist expansion. Because Cuba was regarded as the source of the contagion, the Johnson administration endeavored to intensify Cuba's hemispheric isolation, and it was largely successful in doing so. In mid-1964, after an investigating committee of the Organization of American States (OAS) determined that Cuba had sent arms to Venezuelan terrorists, the hemisphere's foreign ministers voted 15 to 4 to sever all diplomatic ties and suspend trade and sea transportation with that nation. By the end of the year, all OAS members except Mexico had complied.

Fear of communism was also a primary factor in Johnson's policy toward Panama, where nationalist unrest erupted into anti-U.S. riots in January 1964. The trouble began after high school students in the U.S.-controlled Canal Zone raised the Panamanian flag in violation of a Canal Zone law. The incidents ignited four days of rioting during which four U.S. soldiers and twenty-four Panamanians were killed. In his memoir, Johnson recalled that the violence, rather than being the product of frustrated Panamanian nationalists, who sought the abrogation of a 1903 treaty granting the United States perpetual sovereignty over the Canal Zone, was fomented by "Castro, working closely with the Panamanian Communist party, [which] had been sending guns, money, and agents into Panama."[41] In making this statement, Johnson ignored a CIA report that concluded that there were only "some 100 Cuban-trained, Panamanian would-be revolutionaries."[42] This implied that the Cubans were not involved in the unrest.

While Canal Zone police were able to restore order, the problem of sovereignty over the canal remained. In an attempt to resolve it, in December 1964 Johnson, acting on the advice of a presidential review committee, ordered the State Department to negotiate a new agreement to replace the 1903 treaty. By June 1967 U.S. and Panamanian negotiators were able to produce three new agreements. One outlined arrangements for a new sea-level channel. Another provided for the defense and neutrality of the existing canal. The third explicitly recognized Panamanian sovereignty over the Canal Zone and its integration with Panama. In return for these concessions, the Panamanian negotiators agreed that the canal would continue to be operated by a commission composed of five Americans and four Panamanians. In addition, the Panamanians agreed to permit the United States to retain its military bases in the Canal Zone until 2024, and possibly longer if the leases were renewed.

These concessions to the United States, however, were unacceptable to the Panamanian National Assembly, which demanded that they be revised. Johnson refused to make further concessions. His resistance may have been influenced by a remark by the U.S. military commander in the zone, General Robert W. Porter, who argued that more, not less, U.S. bases were needed at this "most critical period in the fight against communism in Latin America."[43] As a result, it was not until 1978 that the United States and Panama agreed to a treaty that restored Panamanian sovereignty over the Canal Zone.

The riots in Panama, combined with disappointing progress in solving Latin America's indigenous problems, contributed to growing cynicism in the United States toward the Alliance for Progress. Not only were the economic growth rates of the Latin Americans lower than those that had been projected by the Alliance, the overthrow of seven constitutional governments in the region between 1961 and January 1964 indicated that democracy was not taking root. As a result, Johnson and the Congress cut funding for the Alliance by nearly 40 percent over the next two years.

In March 1964 Thomas C. Mann, whom Johnson had appointed the assistant secretary of state for inter-American affairs, informed U.S. ambassadors to Latin America that, rather than promoting social reform in the region, the Johnson administration would emphasize protecting nearly $10 billion in U.S. private investment in the area. The absence of strong democratic governments in the region compelled the Johnson administration to rely on indigenous military elites to protect these interests. As a result, while Alliance for Progress funding decreased, U.S. military assistance to Latin American governments increased during the Johnson years.

The support the United States gave the Latin American military establishments, the Johnson administration hoped, would preclude the necessity for overt intervention in the internal affairs of the region. That prospect was shattered in April 1965 when Johnson sent 22,000 U.S. troops into the Dominican Republic ostensibly to prevent the overthrow of that country's government by pro-Castro rebels.

Historians have generally placed the responsibility for the civil war that erupted in the Dominican Republic that spring on that nation's ruling military junta, particularly the junta's decision to postpone elections that had been scheduled during the previous year. The junta, which had come to power in 1963 by overthrowing the elected government of Juan Bosch, feared that elections would restore Bosch to power. Violence, in turn, erupted when pro-Bosch elements of the Dominican army rebelled against the junta.

Johnson boasted that his decision to intervene in the Dominican Republic prevented a communist takeover of the country. While that assessment is debatable, what is less controversial is that his decision to send U.S. troops into the Dominican Republic—without the consent of either the OAS or the U.S. Congress, let alone the Dominican government—was a blatant violation of the three-decade-old Good Neighbor policy of avoiding U.S. military intervention in Latin America.

Johnson's action revived Latin American fears of the Big Stick policy first employed by Theodore Roosevelt. It triggered anti-American demonstrations throughout the hemisphere. In response, Johnson felt compelled to seek a face-saving way out the crisis by turning to the OAS. Fortunately for the president, the OAS obliged by creating a multinational military force to replace the U.S. troops in the country. This enabled Johnson to withdraw all U.S. forces by September 1966. By then, Dominican voters had elected a right-of-center politician, Joacquin Balaguer, as the nation's new president.

While the election of Balaguer represented a return to civilian government in the Dominican Republic, the Johnson administration did little to encourage the growth of democracy elsewhere in Latin America. In fact, in 1964 the administration offered to put a U.S. naval force at the disposal of the Brazilian military to assist them in overthrowing that country's civilian president, Joao Goulart, whose leftist policies were regarded as a threat to U.S. interests. As events turned out, the U.S. Navy was not needed, and the Johnson administration promptly recognized the new military government of General Castelo Branco.

In Chile, during the same year, the Johnson administration also helped to elect an anticommunist president, Eduardo Frei, by covertly spending at least $3 million on his campaign. Besides the successful outcomes in Chile and Brazil, the administration took comfort from the murder of Castro's revolutionary lieutenant Ché Guevera, by the Bolivian army in 1967. Thus, while the bright promise of the Alliance for Progress faded during his presidency, Johnson could nevertheless boast that he left office without any further expansion of communism in the region.

Johnson and the Escalation in Vietnam

Johnson was equally determined to prevent the expansion of communism in Southeast Asia, but the price the United States had to pay in lives and money to do so would be much higher than in Latin America. Between November 1963 and July 1965, Johnson transformed Kennedy's program of limited U.S. assistance to South Vietnam into an open-ended commitment to defend that country. By 1968 the United States would have over 500,000 troops in Vietnam.

Johnson believed, probably correctly, that South Vietnam would collapse if the United States did not expand its participation in the war. Remembering the conservative backlash against the Truman administration after the communist takeover of China, Johnson believed he could not abandon South Vietnam and remain in the White House. Shortly after assuming the presidency, Johnson said privately, "I am not going to lose Vietnam. I am not going to be the president who saw Southeast Asia go the way China went."[44] If the United States pulled out of Vietnam, Johnson warned on one occasion, "it might as well give up everywhere else—pull out of Berlin, Japan, South America."[45]

Taking advantage of a dubious North Vietnamese torpedo boat attack on two U.S. destroyers (the U.S. S. *Maddox* and the U.S.S. *Turner Joy*) in the Gulf of Tonkin during August 1964, Johnson gained congressional approval for a resolution authorizing him "to take all necessary measures to repel any armed attack against the forces of the United States and to prevent further aggression" against South Vietnam and any member of the Southeast Treaty Organization.[46] The resolution, which was approved on August 7, passed in the House 416 to 0 and in the Senate by an 81 to 2 margin. It was as close as the legislature would come to a declaration of war on North Vietnam.

With a presidential election approaching in November, Johnson did not order retaliation after the Vietcong attacked the U.S. air base at Bien Hoa, ten miles from Saigon, on November 1, 1964. Five Americans were killed in that attack. Portraying his Republican opponent, Senator Barry Goldwater, as a warmonger, Johnson won a landslide election victory. However, on February 7, 1965, one day after the Vietcong attacked a U.S. Army barracks in Pleiku in the Central Highlands, killing nine Americans, Johnson initiated a sustained bombing campaign against North Vietnam (Operation Rolling Thunder).

The expanded air war provided the pretext for introducing the first U.S ground combat forces into Vietnam. Anticipating more Vietcong attacks on U.S. air bases, General William Westmoreland, the commander in chief of U.S. forces in South Vietnam, in late February urgently requested two Marine landing teams to protect the air base at Danang. Johnson agreed, and the troops arrived in March 1965.

By then it was apparent that the limited bombing campaign undertaken in February would not produce immediate results. With the Vietcong overrunning one provincial capital after another, it was obvious that South Vietnam was on the verge of military collapse. Johnson concluded that there was no alternative but to introduce substantial U.S. ground forces into the conflict. In July 1965 he approved the immediate deployment of 50,000 U.S. troops to South Vietnam. He privately agreed to commit another 50,000 before the end of the year as well as additional forces later if they were needed. The president also authorized Westmoreland to employ U.S. troops in offensive, as well as defensive, operations in South Vietnam. In effect, Johnson cleared the way for the United States to assume the main burden of fighting the Vietcong.

Although Johnson consulted with congressional leaders before he committed combat units to Vietnam, he did not request another congressional resolution authorizing him to do so. He felt that the Gulf of Tonkin Resolution already provided sufficient authorization. Moreover, he did not want to put the country on a war footing, because he feared a public backlash against U.S. involvement in the conflict; he also wanted to maintain congressional and public support for his Great Society reform program, which he feared might be set aside if the war were given priority status. Johnson believed that he could wage war and implement a major reform program simultaneously, something no other president had ever attempted.

Ultimately, Johnson's decision to expand the U.S. military commitment in Vietnam was unsuccessful. Public opposition to U.S. participation in the war would force him to withdraw from the presidential campaign of 1968. The Republican victory in the election that November would mean the end of Johnson's Great Society program as well as the inauguration of a new Vietnam policy.

A Flawed Strategy

One reason for the failure of Johnson's Vietnam policy was the inherent unworkability of the U.S. military strategy. The gradual escalation of the U.S. bombing campaign allowed the North Vietnamese sufficient time to disperse their population and resources and to develop an air defense system that would destroy a large number of U.S. aircraft. Moreover, the U.S. Army never developed a consistent strategy for stopping the infiltration of regular North Vietnamese units and supplies into the South. Instead, General Westmoreland's search-and-destroy strategy was designed primarily to protect the cities of South Vietnam while killing as many Vietcong as possible. Westmoreland grossly miscalculated North Vietnam's willingness to suffer huge losses in manpower as well as its capacity to replace those losses. An estimated 200,000 North Vietnamese males reached draft age each year, far more than the U.S. forces could kill.

North Vietnam was also able to sustain its war effort by drawing on both Soviet and Chinese military and economic assistance. With the Sino-Soviet split deeper than ever, even after Khrushchev's demise, both communist powers tried to outdo each other in helping North Vietnam. Their combined assistance between 1965 and 1968 exceeded $2 billion, an amount that more than offset the losses North Vietnam suffered from U.S. bombing. In addition, between 1962 and 1968 approximately 300,000 Chinese soldiers went to North Vietnam, 4,000 of whom were killed. Though not participating in ground combat, they helped operate antiaircraft weapons and communications facilities.

Without question, the presence of the Chinese military in North Vietnam was largely intended to deter a U.S. invasion, and, clearly, it was successful in doing so. Fearing that an expansion of the ground war into North Vietnam would again bring Chinese soldiers into conflict with U.S. troops, as had happened in the Korean War, the administration refrained from taking that step. Unwilling to fight an all-out war with North Vietnam, Johnson ensured that the conflict would become a war of attrition. In such a war the communists were bound to win because they were willing to accept much higher casualties than were the American people.

A Failure of Diplomacy

Although Johnson pursued a negotiated settlement of the Vietnam conflict, there never was much chance that diplomacy would succeed in ending the war during his presidency, primarily because the peace terms offered by the two sides were too far apart. Initially, the North Vietnamese demanded a cease-fire as a precondition for beginning negotiations and an American pledge that all U.S. forces would ultimately be withdrawn from Vietnam. They also insisted that the "puppet" Saigon regime be replaced by a government in which the National Liberation Front (a coalition of communist and noncommunist opponents of the South Vietnamese government) would play a prominent role. The United States demanded the complete withdrawal of North Vietnamese troops from the South and the exclusion of the Vietcong from any political settlement of the war. In effect, the Johnson administration was resolved to maintain South Vietnam as an independent, noncommunist state, while North Vietnam was determined to reunify the country under a communist government. While the Johnson administration periodically halted the bombing of North Vietnam during the war, in the hope of bringing the North Vietnamese to the negotiating table, its refusal to abandon South Vietnam to the communists made a negotiated settlement of the conflict impossible during the Johnson years.

Johnson did not attempt to persuade or pressure the Chinese to end their support for North Vietnam. Both the president and the American public as a whole continued to regard China as an aggressive and expansionist power. In May 1965 Johnson declared: "Over this war—and all Asia—is another reality: the deepening shadow of Communist China. . . ."[47]

Not everyone, however, accepted the view that China was an expansionist power. During hearings conducted before the Senate Foreign Relations Committee in 1966, a number of scholars argued that the U.S. government had grossly misinterpreted Chinese foreign policy. These scholars viewed China's foreign policy as essentially defensive in nature, rather than ruthlessly imperialistic. They argued that, even though Beijing sympathized with the goal of world revolution and supplied limited assistance to scattered guerrilla groups around the globe, there was little real evidence to show that the Chinese were trying to conquer Asia. However, this interpretation of Chinese motives would not be generally accepted until Johnson's successor, President Richard Nixon, made his unprecedented trip to Beijing in 1971.

In 1966, however, the initiation of the so-called Cultural Revolution in China by Mao Zedong made it virtually impossible for Americans to accept the scholars' view of a benign Chinese foreign policy. Lasting a full decade, the Cultural Revolution was a massive political upheaval instigated and manipulated by an aging Mao Zedong in an ultimately successful attempt to maintain his preeminent position of power. Backed by students, peasants, and workers, many of whom were organized as "Red Guards," Mao purged tens of thousands of bureaucrats and technical experts whom he accused of sabotaging the revolution. Millions of other Chinese lost their jobs and perhaps another half million their lives during the persecution.

Besides aggravating anti-Americanism in China, the Cultural Revolution raised Chinese animosity toward the Soviet Union to new heights. Fistfights broke out between Chinese and Soviet civilians in Moscow and Beijing. In 1969 military combat would erupt between the ground forces of the two nations along China's Manchurian border with Soviet Siberia.

Against this backdrop of growing Sino-Soviet hostility, on October 7, 1966, Johnson called for a new U.S. approach to the Soviet Union, which he characterized as "a shift from the narrow concept of coexistence to the broader vision of a peaceful engagement." Toward this goal, Johnson approved a number of unilateral U.S. steps, including reducing export controls on trade with the Soviet bloc, permitting the Export-Import Bank to extend credits to the Soviet Union, Poland, Hungary, Bulgaria, and Czechoslovakia, negotiating a civil air agreement with the Soviet Union, and pressing for early congressional action on a U.S.-Soviet consular agreement. Johnson also proposed mutual NATO and Warsaw Pact troop reductions and called for "measures to remove territorial and border disputes as a source of friction in Europe."[48]

But the Soviets found it impossible to publicly endorse détente with the United States at a time when the Americans were intensifying their war with North Vietnam. On October 15, 1966, the Soviet government declared that "the piratical bombing attacks against a socialist country, the Democratic Republic of Vietnam, must be halted and the aggression against the Vietnamese people stopped" if the United States wanted improved relations with the Soviet Union.[49]

By early 1967, however, the Soviets had reversed themselves and were willing to support a negotiated settlement of the war. The growing Chinese hostility toward the Soviet Union, which the Cultural Revolution had intensified, probably convinced the Soviets that they had nothing to lose and everything to gain by trying to end the war in Vietnam. Negotiations over Vietnam would improve relations with the United States at a time when Sino-Soviet relations were deteriorating. Furthermore, the Soviets might be able to reinforce their influence with the North Vietnamese at China's expense, especially if they succeeded in getting the United States to agree to a military withdrawal from Vietnam.

Accordingly, the Soviets agreed to cooperate with a peace initiative sponsored by British Prime Minister Harold Wilson in early 1967. Wilson persuaded Soviet Premier Alexei Kosygin to try to bring the North Vietnamese to the negotiating table on the basis of a two-track proposal (code-named Marigold) that was unveiled by the United States in late 1966. It called for the United States to stop the air strikes against North Vietnam in return for a private assurance from the North Vietnamese that they would stop infiltrating key areas of South Vietnam. If Hanoi complied, the United States would freeze its combat forces at existing levels and peace talks would begin.

But by the time Kosygin had agreed to support Wilson's initiative, the Johnson administration had soured on Marigold. The Americans were

angered by continued North Vietnamese infiltration during a U.S. bombing halt that coincided with the Vietnamese Tet holiday. Therefore, Johnson now insisted that Hanoi must stop its infiltration before he would
end the bombing. Wilson later lamented the loss of a "historic opportunity" to end the war.[50] Still, while the Wilson-Kosygin initiative was han-
dled badly by the Johnson administration, there is little reason to assume
that even the most skillful third-party diplomacy would have achieved a
breakthrough in the stalemate in the absence of concessions neither side
was prepared to make.

Loss of Popular Support

With no prospect of either a military or diplomatic end to the war, the
carnage inevitably grew. By late 1967 the number of U.S. military personnel killed in action reached 13,500. Many Americans were wondering if
the war was worth the mounting deaths that were so vividly displayed on
the nightly news. Slowly, American public opinion turned against the
administration. College students in particular became bitter opponents of
the war. But opposition to the conflict also increased in Congress, with
Senators William Fulbright (Dem.–Ark.) and Wayne Morse (Rep.–Ore.)
leading the attack, bringing to a standstill legislative progress on Johnson's cherished Great Society program. By 1967 growing demonstrations
against the war and vicious personal criticism of the president had made
Johnson a virtual prisoner in the White House.

The increasing unpopularity of the war, however, did not sway Johnson from his goal of preserving a noncommunist South Vietnam. For the
president in 1967, there was no acceptable alternative but a continuation
of the war. Accordingly, in August 1967 he approved General Westmoreland's request for an additional 45,000–50,000 troops, but he imposed
a new ceiling of 525,000 U.S. military personnel, a level that was not
surpassed for the remainder of the war. In November 1967 Westmoreland assured Johnson that the United States was "turning the corner" in
Vietnam.[51]

Then, much to the surprise of U.S. intelligence, the supposedly
nearly beaten North Vietnamese and their Vietcong allies launched a
major offensive against the cities of South Vietnam in February 1968.
Coinciding with the Vietnamese Tet holiday, the communist forces
attacked more than 100 towns and cities, including Saigon, where the
grounds of the U.S. Embassy were penetrated, and Hué, the ancient capital of Vietnam, which the communists held for more than a month
before they were finally driven out.

While American and South Vietnamese forces were able to repel the
communist onslaught, and inflict enormous losses on the enemy in the
process, they also suffered heavy casualties. The Tet offensive was a significant military victory for the United States, but it was also a stunning psychological defeat. To most Americans, who had been subjected to repeated

administration claims that the war was being won, it seemed incredible that the communists could mount such an impressive offensive. After Tet, with no end to the war in sight, a Gallup poll in March 1968 reported that a clear majority of "Middle America" had turned against the administration. The same poll showed that Johnson's approval rating had reached a new low of 30 percent.

General Westmoreland seemed oblivious to the growing hostility of the American people and Congress toward the war. He insisted that the communists had been dealt a crippling blow during Tet and that the war could be won by launching new ground offensives against their bases in Laos, Cambodia, and North Vietnam, and by intensifying and expanding the bombing campaign, especially around Hanoi and Haiphong. To implement this strategy, Westmoreland requested an additional 206,000 troops.

Johnson's advisers, particularly Clark Clifford (who had replaced McNamara as secretary of defense after the latter had become disillusioned with the war and resigned), realized that Westmoreland's request marked a watershed in the administration's Vietnam policy. Approving it would have required declaring a state of national emergency, calling up the National Guard and Army reserve forces, and increasing the defense budget by billions of dollars, all at a time when the economy was already stressed by growing war-stimulated inflation. Moreover, Clifford impressed upon the president that there was no reason to believe that additional troops would bring the United States any closer to ending the conflict. Johnson accepted Clifford's advice. He informed the defense secretary that he was prepared to send additional troops to Vietnam if they were required to hold the line, but he would not expand the U.S. commitment to the war.

Johnson's End Game

While the Tet offensive marked a watershed in Johnson's Vietnam policy, the New Hampshire presidential primary on March 13, 1968, proved to be a turning point in his presidency. Senator Eugene McCarthy (Dem.–Wis.), an unabashed peace candidate, startled the nation by winning 42.4 percent of the Democratic vote. While Johnson received 49.5 percent of the vote, even though he was not a declared candidate, McCarthy's strong showing in the New Hampshire primary dramatized the president's political vulnerability. As a result, the president's political archrival, Robert Kennedy, decided to challenge him for their party's presidential nomination.

The New Hampshire primary also persuaded Johnson to alter the administration's war strategy. On March 23 he announced that General Westmoreland would become the Army's new chief of staff. While touted as a promotion for Westmoreland, knowledgeable sources said that the general had been kicked upstairs. The change of command in Vietnam was a prelude to a change in the administration's strategy. On

March 31, 1968, Johnson told a nationwide television audience that he was freezing the U.S. troop level in South Vietnam and ordering a partial suspension of the bombing against North Vietnam, all in the hope of getting peace talks started. He concluded his address with a stunning announcement that he would not be a candidate for his party's presidential nomination.

Much to Johnson's surprise, the North Vietnamese accepted his offer to begin peace negotiations, and formal talks began in Paris on May 13, 1968. But they were soon deadlocked. While Johnson had changed the administration's military strategy, he had not abandoned his goal of preserving a noncommunist government in South Vietnam. At the same time, the North Vietnamese had not abandoned their goal of reunifying Vietnam under Hanoi's leadership. They had agreed to participate in the Paris talks primarily to get the bombing stopped, split the Americans from the South Vietnamese, who opposed peace talks, and intensify antiwar pressures in the United States. The North Vietnamese demanded the "unconditional cessation of U.S. bombing raids and all other acts of war."[52] But the Johnson administration refused to stop the bombing until Hanoi agreed to deescalate its effort to defeat South Vietnam. It was a condition the North Vietnamese would not accept. As a result, the Paris talks dragged on inconclusively throughout the remainder of Johnson's term in office.

In the meantime, the administration intensified both the air and ground war in South Vietnam. The number of B-52 bombing missions tripled in 1968. In March and April of that year, the United States and South Vietnam conducted the largest search-and-destroy mission of the war, sending more than 100,000 troops against Vietcong forces surrounding Saigon. The United States also pressed the South Vietnamese to do more of the fighting, through a policy called "Vietnamization." The South Vietnamese force level was increased from 685,000 to 850,000 troops. Nevertheless, U.S. officials admitted that the South Vietnamese were nowhere near being prepared to defend themselves. "Worst of all," Defense Secretary Clifford observed after a trip to Saigon, "the South Vietnamese leaders seemed content to have it that way."[53]

On the home front, in the meantime, support for the war continued to erode—a process that was exacerbated by increasing domestic turmoil that was aggravated by two major political murders. On April 4, 1968, the civil rights leader Martin Luther King, Jr., was shot to death, triggering riots in the nation's ghettos. Two months later, on June 6, Robert Kennedy was shot and killed by an assailant. His death also traumatized the nation and hurt particularly the liberal, antiwar wing of the Democratic Party, which had hoped Kennedy's election to the presidency would bring an end to the conflict in Vietnam. As it was, the Democratic National Convention in Chicago that August reflected in microcosm the divisiveness produced by the war throughout the nation. The convention was disrupted by clashes between antiwar radicals and the city's police.

The conflict outside the convention hall and clashes between liberals and conservatives inside did much to diminish the prestige of the Democratic Party and its presidential nominee, Vice President Hubert Humphrey.

To assist Humphrey's campaign, President Johnson belatedly (in early November) announced a complete halt in the bombing of North Vietnam. Four days later, he announced that in return for this concession the North Vietnamese had agreed to resume the Paris peace talks in January, with, for the first time, representatives of South Vietnam and the Vietcong at the negotiating table. Johnson's last-minute gambit, however, failed to prevent the Republican candidate, Richard M. Nixon, from winning a narrow victory in the presidential election.

Strangely enough, while Johnson lost the presidency because of his war policy, he won his personal battle to leave the White House with the U.S. commitment to a noncommunist Vietnam intact. But the price the United States paid for this "victory" was dear in deed. There would be four more years of fighting, and thousands more American casualties, before U.S. participation in the war finally ended.

Stillborn Détente

While the Vietnam War complicated Soviet-American relations during the Johnson years, both superpowers nevertheless attempted to narrow the gap that separated them. The Johnson administration was interested in improving relations with the Soviet Union because it wanted Soviet assistance in getting the North Vietnamese to the negotiating table. On the other hand, the Soviets hoped improved relations with the United States would enable them to acquire badly needed Western technology. In addition, both sides were bothered—perhaps the Soviets, by now, even more than the Americans—by the growing Chinese nuclear threat, which appeared more ominous after the explosion of the first Chinese hydrogen bomb in June 1967 and in light of the apparent irrationality that characterized Chinese behavior during their Cultural Revolution.

At the same time, Americans were anxious about the growth of the Soviet nuclear arsenal (by 1969 the Soviets would acquire approximate parity with the United States in the number of strategic nuclear weapons) and eager to begin negotiations that would place a ceiling on the size of the superpower nuclear weapons stores.

Both the Soviet Union and the United States also were eager to halt the spread of nuclear weapons to nonnuclear-weapon states. To this end, the United States and the Soviet Union (as well as the other nuclear powers, Britain, France, and China) signed a protocol to the 1967 Treaty of Tlatelolco in which they promised to respect the denuclearization of Latin America and to refrain from using, or threatening to use, nuclear weapons against any of the treaty's contracting parties. The treaty, which went into effect in 1968, was soon signed by every Latin American state except Guyana and Cuba.

Shortly before the signing of the Treaty of Tlatelolco, the superpowers also concluded negotiations on the Outer Space Treaty, which prohibited the installation of military bases and fortifications, the testing of weapons, and the conduct of military maneuvers on the moon and other celestial bodies. The treaty also prohibited the placing of weapons of mass destruction into orbit around the earth or stationing them in outer space or on celestial bodies. It was approved by the Senate by an 88–0 vote in April 1967 and went into effect the following October.

Perhaps the most significant arms control agreement concluded during the Johnson years, however, was the Nuclear Nonproliferation Treaty (NPT). It banned the transfer of nuclear weapons or nuclear explosive devices to nonweapon states or their acquisition by such states. In return for this concession, the nuclear-weapon states promised to provide nonmilitary nuclear assistance to nonweapon states that ratified the treaty. To ensure that ostensibly civilian nuclear assistance would not be diverted to military purposes, the treaty required the nonweapon states to subject their nuclear facilities to periodic inspections by the International Atomic Energy Agency (IAEA). The nuclear-weapon powers also promised to engage in serious negotiations to reduce the size of their respective nuclear arsenals and to participate in review conferences every five years to monitor compliance with the treaty.

The NPT was signed in Washington, Moscow, and London on July 1, 1968. The Senate approved ratification of the treaty on March 16, 1969, by a vote of 83 to 15. It was also ratified by Britain and the Soviet Union. By the time the treaty went into effect on March 5, 1970, ninety-seven states had signed it and forty-seven states had ratified it. By 1975, the date of the first treaty review conference, there were 111 signatories, including 96 full parties. Although France refused to ratify the treaty, it did declare that it would abide by the treaty's provisions. The Chinese, on the other hand, not only refused to ratify the treaty, they declared that further nuclear weapons proliferation among the "revolutionary" states would be a positive development because, they believed, it would contribute to the breakup of the "Soviet-American nuclear monopoly."[54]

The successful negotiation of the Nuclear Nonproliferation Treaty produced an atmosphere that was conducive to further U.S.-Soviet arms control discussions. New technologies were coming on line that both sides knew could promote a costlier arms race. The Soviets were deploying an antiballistic missile (ABM) defense system, and the United States was preparing to do so. In addition, both sides were developing a new generation of offensive missiles called MIRVs, or multiple independently targeted reentry vehicles. The first American MIRV missiles could carry three warheads, each of which could be guided to a separate target.

While the Johnson administration was determined to deploy MIRVs, it hoped it could persuade the Soviets to accept an ABM ban. It had concluded that any ABM system would be obsolete by the time it was deployed, since the other side would inevitably overwhelm it with MIRVs.

Without an ABM ban, each side would spend billions on these systems and gain nothing.

The Soviets, initially, were not willing to curb their ABM program. At a hastily arranged summit conference at Glassboro, New Jersey, on June 23 and 25, 1967, Johnson and McNamara tried in vain to persuade Soviet Premier Alexei Kosygin that an ABM race would be the height of folly. Kosygin insisted that the Soviet ABM system was purely defensive in nature and was no threat to the United States. He also did not accept the American argument that ABMs were inherently destabilizing. "You don't understand," McNamara told Kosygin. "Whatever you do, we will maintain our deterrent and build more missiles." Kosygin became upset and pounded the table, saying, "Defense is moral, offense is immoral."[55] Bowing to the inevitable, the Johnson administration felt it had no choice but to go ahead with the construction of an American ABM system, called Sentinel.

In spite of the superpowers' inability to ban ABMs, the Johnson administration attempted to restrict the growth of offensive strategic nuclear weapons. While the Soviets expressed a willingness to participate in strategic arms limitations talks (SALT) as early as February 1967, the new negotiations languished until very late in Johnson's presidency. The delay was partly the result of Soviet reluctance to negotiate with the United States at a time when the Johnson administration was still trying to bomb North Vietnam into submission. In addition, the Soviets were reluctant to restrict their strategic programs until they reached approximate nuclear parity with the United States, a goal they achieved in 1969.

Yet Johnson did not give up on SALT. He saw the talks as a way of diverting public attention from the war in Vietnam and, after his decision not to seek another term in office, a way to cap his presidency. His decision to restrict the bombing of North Vietnam and the willingness of the North Vietnamese to begin peace talks in Paris no doubt made it easier for the Soviets to participate in SALT. But probably a more significant reason for the changed Soviet attitude was the continued buildup of the Soviet strategic arsenal. Possessing 800 ICBMs and 130 SLBMs by 1968, the Soviets felt that they could now deal with the United States from a position of strength. As a result, on August 19, 1968 Soviet Ambassador Anatoly Dobrynin informed the administration that his government was ready to begin the strategic arms talks. Both sides agreed that the talks would open with a summit meeting attended by Johnson and Kosygin on September 30.

Johnson, however, was not fated to end his presidency with a SALT triumph. On August 20 Soviet tanks and troops stormed into Czechoslovakia as part of a successful move to overthrow the government of Alexander Dubçek, whose reforms the Soviets had come to consider anti-socialist. In the wake of the Soviet invasion of Czechoslovakia, Johnson was compelled to cancel the September 30 summit.

The Kennedy-Johnson Legacy

The Kennedy-Johnson years marked a watershed in the history of the
Cold War. The United States and the Soviet Union made their closest
approach to a nuclear war, in the Cuban missile crisis, during Kennedy's
presidency. The deterioration of the Cold War relationship early in
Kennedy's presidency was due primarily to the inability of the two sides to
resolve the Berlin problem and to Khrushchev's attempt to challenge
growing U.S. nuclear superiority, and preclude a U.S. invasion of Cuba
by deploying intermediate-range ballistic missiles in that island nation.

The personality conflict between Kennedy and Khrushchev also was
an important factor in the deterioration of Soviet-American relations.
Intelligent but brash, the young American president entered office determined to reverse the stagnation of the Eisenhower years. Kennedy's
approval of the ill-conceived Bay of Pigs invasion was not only personally
humiliating but also encouraged the already overconfident Khrushchev to
challenge the young president in Berlin, Cuba, Vietnam, and the Congo.
Their conflicting personalities also exacerbated the Cuban missile crisis
which almost produced a nuclear conflagration .

During the Kennedy-Johnson years, the U.S. containment strategy
experienced its first significant failures in the Third World. Kennedy failed
to reverse the communist takeover of Cuba, and Johnson was unable to
defeat the communist insurgency in Vietnam. The failure in Vietnam, in
particular, would contribute to the future unwillingness of the American
people and the Congress to use military force to check or reverse communist insurgencies.

The Kennedy-Johnson years also witnessed the beginning of détente.
In the wake of the almost catastrophic Cuban missile crisis, the United
States and the Soviet Union signed the first significant nuclear arms control agreements: the Limited Test Ban Treaty and the Nuclear Nonproliferation Treaty. Only the Soviet military intervention in Czechoslovakia
prevented Johnson from beginning strategic arms limitation talks before
he left office in January 1968. The accolades for détente, which Johnson
so greatly desired, would be garnered by his successor, Richard Nixon.

6

Nixon, Ford, and Détente, 1969–1977

The Revival of Détente

In his inaugural address on January 20, 1969, Richard Nixon declared that the United States was prepared to enter "an era of negotiation" with the communist world.[1] Considering his background as an ardent Cold Warrior, many were surprised by Nixon's apparent eagerness to bury the hatchet with the communist world, but beneath the veneer of anticommunism was a core of realistic pragmatism. What mattered most to Nixon was the advancement of U.S. interests. If cooperation with a communist state served that purpose, he was prepared to modify his Cold War reputation.

Nixon had a number of specific reasons for wanting to improve America's relationship with the Soviet Union and China. One was a desire to extricate the United States from the Vietnam conflict without suffering a humiliating defeat. He believed this could be achieved by isolating North Vietnam from its two main sources of supply and support, the Soviet Union and China.

Nixon also hoped that détente between the superpowers would facilitate the conclusion of a SALT agreement that would place a cap on an alarming Soviet nuclear buildup. Between 1967 and 1969 the size of the Soviet nuclear arsenal had increased from 570 to 1,050 ICBMs, giving the Soviets parity with the United States in numbers of that weapon system. With Congress reluctant to authorize additional defense spending, Nixon surmised that SALT was the only feasible way to restrain the Soviet strategic buildup. In addition, the prospect that the Soviets would build a nationwide ABM system made SALT an urgent necessity for the new president.

Auspiciously, the Soviet Union seemed to be even more eager than Nixon to improve superpower relations. Within hours of Nixon's inaugural address, the Soviets invited him to resume SALT soon. They were eager to preserve their about-to-be acquired nuclear weapons parity with the United States, and they saw SALT as the only way to halt or restrain the deployment of new U.S. multiple-warhead missiles (MIRVs), at least until they had time to deploy their own.

Economic factors were also important in the Soviet desire to pursue détente with the United States. The inability of the Soviet Union's collectivized farms to feed its people was increasingly apparent, as was the declining rate of Soviet industrial growth. Indeed, the relative backwardness of Soviet technology was demonstrated in the way the Soviet space achievements of the late 1950s and early 1960s gave way to repeated failures late in the decade. The Soviet leadership realized that a relaxation of tensions with the United States was the prerequisite for obtaining badly needed Western economic and technical assistance.

Eastern Europe was another concern of the Soviets. Even after Warsaw Pact forces had brought Czechoslovakia back into the hard-line communist fold, the Soviets were uneasy about the potential for unrest in the other satellite states.

The problems with their European satellites were only compounded by the Soviet Union's deteriorating relationship with China. In March 1969, after several exchanges of gunfire between Soviet and Chinese troops on the Ussuri River, which separates Chinese Manchuria and Soviet Siberia, the prospect of a Sino-Soviet war did not seem out of the question, particularly after the Soviets massed forty divisions on the frontier facing China. The Soviets apparently were prepared to reduce tensions with the United States and its European allies if only to free themselves to deal with the seemingly unreasonable Chinese.

Henry Kissinger

While Nixon was the source of power behind the new approach to the Soviet Union, Henry Kissinger was its intellectual architect. A Harvard professor before he joined the administration as national security adviser, and later (beginning in 1973) serving as secretary of state, Kissinger had criticized the traditional U.S. approach to the communist world, with its heavy emphasis on military rather than diplomatic solutions to the problems of the Cold War. He believed that the United States had to rely on both diplomacy and military power if it was to advance its national interests effectively in an increasingly complicated international arena.

Kissinger's primary goal was the creation of a new framework of international relations in which the Soviet Union could participate as a nonrevolutionary power and thereby make possible a resolution of the issues that had perpetuated the Cold War. To this end, Kissinger sought to enmesh the Soviet Union in a web of mutually beneficial relationships with the United States, in the hope that they would induce the Soviets to abandon, or at least restrain, their aggressive behavior. Kissinger was under no illusion that this would happen over night. At times, he believed, it would be necessary for the United States to apply the required restraint on Soviet international behavior. In effect, Kissinger believed the administration should use a carrot-and-stick approach: rewarding the Soviets when they cooperated with the United States, checking them when they did not.

Like the president, Kissinger championed SALT. He believed that some limitation on the nuclear arms race was necessary to provide both sides with the required degree of security to make the accommodations necessary to build the new cooperative relationship he envisioned. While Kissinger was willing to engage in SALT, equally important to him were Indochina, the Middle East, and the Berlin problem. In a controversial policy called "linkage," Kissinger endeavored to connect progress in SALT to the willingness of the Soviets to cooperate on these issues.

The Soviets deeply resented Kissinger's linkage strategy. To them, it implied that the Soviet Union needed a SALT agreement more than the United States. They were also unwilling to restrain themselves in assisting revolutionary forces around the world. As a result, Soviet-American détente was not only slow to blossom, as events were to demonstrate, but its roots were not very deep.

The Nixon Doctrine and SALT

Before engaging the Soviets in SALT, Kissinger had insisted that a review of U.S. strategic doctrine was necessary. In July 1969, after the review was completed, the Nixon Doctrine was unveiled by the president during a visit to Guam in July 1969. The Nixon Doctrine resembled the Kennedy-Johnson flexible response strategy in insisting that the United States must be able to deter communist aggression with both conventional and nuclear forces. However, instead of the two-and-a-half-war capability (the ability to fight major conflicts in Europe and Asia simultaneously as well as a limited war elsewhere) called for in the Kennedy-Johnson strategy, the Nixon administration adopted a one-and-a-half-war posture (which called for sufficient forces to fight one major war in a single theater simultaneously with a limited war elsewhere). In effect, the Nixon Doctrine implied that the United States no longer considered China a threat to U.S. interests.

The Nixon Doctrine also resembled the Eisenhower strategy. It called on America's allies to assume the primary burden of engaging an aggressor in ground combat. The United States would confine its role to one of providing supplementary conventional and, if needed, nuclear assistance. Partly as a result of the Nixon Doctrine, and partly due to the administration's impending decision to withdraw U.S. ground forces from Vietnam, the size of U.S. conventional forces would diminish appreciably during the Nixon-Ford years. Between 1969 and 1975 air force squadrons declined from 169 to 110, army and marine divisions from 23 to 16, and navy combat ships from 976 to 495.

Nixon called the nuclear component of his strategic doctrine "sufficiency." It reflected the assumption that it would be prohibitively and unnecessarily costly to maintain U.S. nuclear superiority in numbers of strategic missiles. "Sufficiency" called for enough nuclear force to inflict an unacceptable level damage on a potential aggressor.

Like Kennedy and Johnson, Nixon emphasized the development of counterforce weapons with the ability to destroy "hardened" (reinforced) Soviet ICBM silos. Counterforce weapons were seen not only as a better alternative to a suicidal massive retaliation against Soviet cities but also as the only feasible way the United States could maintain a lead over the Soviet Union in numbers of warheads, at a time that it was conceding to the Soviets numerical superiority in numbers of launch vehicles. Accordingly, in late 1971 the administration accelerated the development of the highly counterforce-capable B-1 bomber and the Trident submarine.

The Nixon administration also decided to proceed with the development of an American ABM, which was renamed Safeguard. It was needed, the administration argued, to protect Minuteman silos against a Soviet nuclear attack and to give the United States protection against an accidental launch or an attack by a future nuclear power. The administration also hoped to use Safeguard as a bargaining chip to win Soviet concessions in SALT.

Over the objections of critics who argued that Safeguard would be unworkable and a waste of money, the program was approved on August 6, 1970, by the narrowest of margins. A 50–50 tie vote in the Senate was broken by the vote of Vice President Spiro Agnew. In the end, however, only one Safeguard site was built, instead of the twelve originally envisioned, and even that one was shut down in 1975 after Nixon's successor, Gerald Ford, accepted the critics' argument that Safeguard could not avoid being overwhelmed by Soviet MIRVs.

With its military review complete, the administration finally agreed to begin SALT in November 1969, but the talks, which were held in Helsinki, Finland, quickly bogged down. The largest obstacle to progress involved whether both offensive and defensive weapons should be included in a treaty. The Soviets wanted an agreement limiting only defensive weapons, so that they could restrict deployment of the American ABM system while being free to develop their own MIRV program. On the other hand, the United States wanted to limit both offensive and defensive weapons systems so as to block development of a Soviet MIRV capability, which, when combined with Soviet quantitative superiority in missiles, would give the Soviets an enormous lead in number of warheads. A breakthrough in the talks would not occur for eighteen months, in May 1971, when the Soviets finally agreed to participate in talks that would eventually produce limits on both offensive as well as defensive nuclear weapons systems.

Ostpolitik *and Berlin*

While the Nixon administration preferred to go slowly in promoting Soviet-American détente, primarily to give linkage time to develop, America's West European allies were eager to improve relations with the Soviets quickly in order to reduce tensions in Europe and open up the Eastern bloc to Western trade, ideas, and travelers.

Under the leadership of Chancellor Willy Brandt, Bonn took the lead in normalizing Western relations with the Soviet bloc. In 1967 West Germany established diplomatic relations with Romania and in the following year with Yugoslavia. In December 1970 West Germany's relations with Poland were normalized on the basis of a treaty that recognized existing frontiers, including Poland's western border, the Oder-Neisse line. By 1974 West Germany had also established diplomatic relations with Czechoslavakia, Bulgaria, and Hungary.

Brandt also took the lead in attempting to resolve the Berlin problem. In a West German–Soviet Treaty signed in August 1970, both parties renounced the use of force and recognized the existing frontiers of Europe. The Soviets also affirmed Germany's right to reunify through peaceful means.

As a step in that direction, Brandt defined a new West German relationship with East Germany. Shortly after becoming chancellor in October 1969, he indicated that the German Democratic Republic was to be considered a separate state within a single German nation. On December 21, 1973, West and East Germany signed a treaty reaffirming the inviolability of their common frontier.

Brandt's *Ostpolitik* alarmed the Nixon administration. Kissinger insisted that in pursuing détente the allies should follow the lead of the United States. The administration not only wanted to link progress in détente to Soviet concessions not only on issues that were purely European in nature, such as Berlin and conventional force reductions, but also on issues that were of particular importance to the United States, such as SALT and the Vietnam War. Moreover, Kissinger feared that Brandt would make concessions to Moscow that could weaken NATO. In attempt to gain control of Brandt's *Ostpolitik*, Kissinger pressed for a four-power settlement in Berlin as a condition for final Western approval of the Soviet–West German treaty.

While the Soviets undoubtedly intended to use détente to divide NATO, as Kissinger had feared, this was only one of their objectives. They also wanted to freeze the status quo in Central Europe to cement their hold on Eastern Europe and to free themselves to deal with the Chinese, if that proved necessary. Moreover, the Soviets realized that to promote détente they had to resolve the German issue. A Berlin agreement would improve the chances for success with SALT and thus the prospects for obtaining badly needed Western economic aid. As a result, the Soviets agreed to participate in four-power talks on Berlin, which began at the ambassadorial level on March 26, 1970.

The China Card

While the Nixon administration was engaging the Soviets in SALT and the Berlin talks, as well as a variety of other linkage-related issues, the administration was also taking the first step toward improving U.S. relations with China. The initiative for the new China policy was Nixon's. In an article in the October 1967 issue of *Foreign Affairs,* Nixon wrote that "any American policy must come urgently to grips with the reality of China. There is no place on this small planet for a billion of its potentially most able people to live in angry isolation."[2] Nixon came to see that Sino-American rapprochement could not only add leverage to America's Soviet policy but perhaps also facilitate an honorable U.S. military withdrawal from the Vietnam conflict.

The Chinese leadership was also becoming amenable to the idea of improving Sino-American relations. The Chinese were alarmed both by the Soviet invasion of Czechoslovakia in August 1968 and the so-called Brezhnev Doctrine by which the Soviets attempted to justify it. Brezhnev proclaimed the right of the Soviet Union to intervene to uphold socialism in neighboring states, which, the Chinese feared, included their own country. Indeed, the Ussuri River conflict in March 1969 can be seen as an attempt by the Chinese to demonstrate to the Soviets that, unlike the Czechoslovaks, China would resist a Soviet invasion of its territory.

In so resisting, the Chinese received crucial support from the new administration. By mid-1969 Kissinger and the president had arrived at the "revolutionary thesis" that U.S. interests would not be served if the Soviet Union militarily "smashed" China. In early October 1969, without public notice, Nixon placed the Strategic Air Command on the highest level of nuclear alert, no doubt to impress the Soviets with the administration's determination to deter a Soviet nuclear strike on China. Earlier Nixon had declared that the United States "shall provide a shield if a nuclear power threatens the freedom of a nation allied with us or of a nation whose survival we consider vital to our security."[3]

The Soviets obviously got the president's message. On October 20, 1969, they sent Nixon an aide-mémoir which warned that any attempt by the United States to take advantage of the Sino-Soviet dispute would impair U.S.–Soviet relations. Perhaps not coincidentally, on the same day Soviet and Chinese representatives began negotiations that eventually ended the Ussuri River crisis.

While the Soviets were easing the pressure on China's northern frontier, the Nixon administration took the first steps toward reducing the U.S. military presence on China's southern periphery, that is, in Vietnam.

In July 1969 Nixon announced a reduction in the authorized U.S. troop ceiling from 549,500 to 484,000 by December 15, 1969, in effect beginning the long withdrawal of U.S. ground forces from Vietnam. Nixon also permitted American scholars, journalists, and students to travel to China, suspended U.S. naval patrols in the Taiwan Strait, and rescinded the $100 ceiling on the purchase of Chinese goods by Americans.

In this atmosphere of relaxing Sino-American relations, the Warsaw talks resumed in January 1970. At a second meeting in February, the Chinese announced that the U.S. delegation would be welcome in Beijing. However, a third Warsaw meeting, scheduled for May, was canceled by the Chinese after U.S. ground forces invaded Cambodia in an attempt to destroy Vietcong staging bases in that country.

Nevertheless, the Nixon administration accelerated its effort to improve U.S. relations with China. In the fall of 1970, the administration opened secret diplomatic channels to China through Romania and Pakistan. The Chinese responded, in March 1971, by extending an invitation for a U.S. envoy to come to Beijing. As a result, Kissinger secretly visited the Chinese capital from July 9 to 11, 1971. There, he and Zhou Enlai agreed in principle that Taiwan should be considered a part of China and that the political future of the island should be settled peacefully by the Chinese themselves. The two men also agreed that the political future of South Vietnam would have to be settled by the Vietnamese without outside intervention. Zhou then extended an invitation to Nixon to visit China, which the president promptly accepted.

Nixon responded with additional concessions of his own. He lifted the embargo on trade with China, ordered a halt to spy flights over Chinese territory, and reversed a decision to station nuclear weapons near the mainland. The Nixon administration also reversed the long-standing U.S. policy of opposing China's membership in the United Nations, while insisting that some way be found to keep Taiwan in the world body. While this action would strain the U.S.–Taiwanese relationship, it also demonstrated that the goal of normalizing U.S. relations with China had become the more important priority.

The Soviet-American Thaw, 1971

The Soviet government was not pleased with the news of Kissinger's secret trip to Beijing and the subsequent announcement, in July 1971, that Nixon would pay an official visit to China in 1972. Still, as Nixon and Kissinger had correctly predicted, the opening to China spurred the Soviets to assume a more accommodating attitude toward the United States.

In May 1971 a breakthrough occurred in SALT. Both sides agreed that the treaty would focus on defensive weapons, while a separate interim agreement would place a ceiling on the numbers of offensive missiles, or, ICBMs. The SALT breakthrough came on the heels of other arms control agreements: the Joint Space Mission Agreement (October 1970) and a treaty signed in February 1971 prohibiting the emplacement of nuclear weapons on seabeds or ocean floors. In September 1971 the superpowers also concluded the Agreement on Measures to Reduce the Risk of Accidental Outbreak of Nuclear War.

In May 1971 the superpowers also broke the deadlock that had blocked progress on a European security conference. The United States agreed to participate in the conference in exchange for a commitment from the Soviet Union to participate in mutual and balanced (conventional) force reduction talks (styled MBFR), which began in 1972.

The superpowers approved the Quadripartite Treaty on Berlin in August 1971. By the terms of the treaty, the Soviets—for the first time—guaranteed unimpeded road and rail access from West Germany to West Berlin and accepted the right of West Berliners to visit East Germany and East Berlin for thirty days each year. The Soviets also recognized the right of West Berliners to travel on West German passports as well as Bonn's right to represent West Berlin in international bodies.

The superpowers also made significant progress in promoting trade. In May 1971, as a part of the SALT breakthrough negotiated that month, the United States secretly agreed to sell the Soviets $136 million worth of grain. In February 1972, after discussions with the State Department, the Soviet government agreed to reopen Lend-Lease settlement talks as part of a larger trade agreement. In return, the Nixon administration announced that it would attempt to obtain congressional authorization to reduce restrictions on U.S. exports to the Soviet Union as well as grant the Soviet Union most-favored-nation status, by imposing America's lowest tariff rate.

Not to be outdone by the approaching Sino-American summit, the Soviets invited Nixon to meet with Brezhnev in Moscow. Nixon had requested a summit in mid-1970, but the Soviets had been reluctant to participate in one so soon after the U.S. incursion in Cambodia. Other problems—the election of a Marxist, Salvador Allende, as president of Chile, the Syrian invasion of Jordan, and the U.S. discovery of a Soviet submarine base in Cienfuegos, Cuba—blocked a summit meeting the following year. Only after the United States had agreed to conclude the Berlin talks, in what amounted to a form of reverse linkage, did the Soviets finally agree to participate in a summit. On October 14, it was announced that the Moscow summit would be held in May 1972.

The Indian-Pakistani War, 1971

The Moscow summit was nearly disrupted by a war between India and Pakistan. The crisis began when Pakistani East Bengal, which was separated from western Pakistan by 1,000 miles of hostile Indian territory, arose in full revolt against the central authorities in Islamabad. War between Pakistan and India broke out after the Indians intervened to help the East Bengalis win their independence.

The outbreak of this conflict was undoubtedly encouraged by the Soviets. In an attempt to humiliate the Chinese, who had befriended Pakistan, the Soviet Union signed a treaty of friendship with India on August 9, 1971. It provided for mutual consultation and military assistance should either party be threatened by a third country. Needless to say, the timing of the treaty, shortly after the announcement that President Nixon would be making a visit to China, was not entirely coincidental.

Before signing the friendship treaty with the Soviet Union, India's perennial hostility toward Pakistan had been restrained by the fear of China, which had befriended the Pakistanis. Now the Indians, with the encouragement of Moscow, stepped up their assistance to the East Bengal rebels, thereby challenging not only Pakistan but China as well. On November 21, 1971, India's military confrontation with Pakistan turned into open warfare.

As the Indian forces overran East Bengal, the Nixon administration warned the Soviets, on December 10, that the United States was prepared to use force against India if the Indians attacked Pakistan. To reinforce his warning, the president that day ordered a U.S. naval task force into the Bay of Bengal. Simultaneously, the Chinese began to mass troops on the frontiers of Sikkim and Bhutan, two Indian protectorates.

The Soviets responded to the Sino-American moves by sending their own naval units into the Indian Ocean and by issuing thinly veiled nuclear threats against the Chinese. However, the Soviets apparently did not want the crisis to escalate into a superpower confrontation or disrupt their effort to build détente with the West. Consequently, on December 14 they pressured the Indians to conclude their military operations in East Bengal quickly and refrain from attacking Pakistan. On December 16, with the fall of Dacca, capital of East Bengal, the Indians declared a cease-fire.

While the United States succeeded in defending the territorial integrity of western Pakistan, it did not prevent East Bengal from proclaiming its independence (as Bangladesh). In effect, an ally of the United States and a friend of China was defeated. In response, Pakistan withdrew from the SEATO alliance in 1972. As another negative consequence, the appearance of a U.S. nuclear-armed naval force off India's coast was instrumental in Indian's decision to explode a nuclear device in 1974.

Nixon's Trip to China

On July 15, 1971, Nixon announced to a startled world that he would be traveling to China before May 1972. He also issued orders to reduce the 9,000-troop U.S. garrison on Taiwan. The previous August, Secretary of State William Rogers had announced that the United States would no longer oppose Beijing's admission into the United Nations, as long as Taiwan was permitted to retain a seat in the world body. However, despite intensive last-minute lobbying by UN Ambassador George Bush to keep Taiwan in the United Nations, on October 25, 1972, the General

Assembly voted 76 to 35 to expel Taiwan from the world body and award China's seat to Beijing.

Nixon's trip to China, from February 21 to 28, 1972, was nonetheless a major diplomatic success. To Kissinger's surprise and delight, he and Nixon were invited to meet Mao Zedong immediately after their arrival in the Chinese capital. Unable to reach complete agreement on the Taiwan issue, both sides signed a joint communiqué in Shanghai in which each stated its position on the issue. The Chinese insisted that Taiwan was a part of China and "the crucial question obstructing the normalization of relations between China and the United States." The American side acknowledged that there was "but one China and that Taiwan (was) a part of China." However, the Americans also insisted on "a peaceful settlement of the Taiwan question by the Chinese themselves." In addition, the Americans pledged "the ultimate withdrawal of all U.S. forces and military installations from Taiwan" and a gradual reduction of U.S. forces "as the tension in the area diminished." The implication of this pledge was that the United States would gradually withdraw from Vietnam as the war drew to a close but would pull out completely only after Beijing had formally renounced force as a way of "liberating" Taiwan.[4] While the U.S. commitments in the Shanghai Communiqué represented substantial concessions to the Chinese, they also benefited the United States, as Kissinger had intended—by giving the Chinese a stake in ending the Vietnamese War.

In addition to the Shanghai Communiqué, the Americans and Chinese concluded agreements on travel, tourism, and trade. They also agreed that a senior U.S. representative would be stationed in Beijing. A year later, official liaison offices, which were embassies in all but name and protocol, were established in Washington and Beijing.

At the final banquet, Nixon proclaimed that his visit to China had been "a week that [had] changed the world."[5] In many ways it had. In Moscow, however, the reaction was one of sullen anger and suspicion. In Tokyo, which was not consulted about the president's trip prior to its announcement, the government of Eisaku Sato fell. On Taiwan, Jiang Jeshi declared that the United States could no longer be trusted as an ally. Clearly, China had become a major factor in the conduct of U.S. diplomacy.

A New Vietnam Strategy

Shortly after entering the White House, Nixon assigned Kissinger and the National Security Council, which Kissinger chaired, the task of formulating a strategy that would permit the United States to end its participation in the Vietnam conflict "with honor." Ironically, during the 1960s, Kissinger had been a frequent critic of U.S. intervention in Vietnam. He regarded Kennedy's commitment of 16,000 military advisors to South Vietnam as a mistake, considering that the French could not defeat the Vietminh with 200,000 troops, and he regarded Johnson's decision to expand the U.S. commitment to South Vietnam to 500,000 men and women a national tragedy. Nevertheless, Kissinger believed that the United States could not pull out of Vietnam precipitously without destroying its ability to maintain the global balance of power elsewhere.

At the same time, however, Kissinger realized that the American people and Congress would not permit an indefinite continuation of U.S. involvement in the conflict. He decided, with Nixon's support, that U.S. troops would have to be gradually withdrawn from South Vietnam and the responsibility for defending the country turned over to the South Vietnamese themselves, a process called Vietnamization. In 1969, 65,000 U.S. troops were withdrawn from South Vietnam, 50,000 in the following year, and 250,000 in 1971. By mid-August 1972 the last U.S. ground combat units would leave Vietnam.

Kissinger, shortly before being appointed Nixon's national security adviser, laid out a two-track approach for the Vietnam peace negotiations. One track consisted of negotiations between the United States and North Vietnam. Its objective was a military settlement of the war that would permit the withdrawal of U.S. forces from Vietnam. The other track consisted of negotiations between the Saigon government and the National Liberation Front to determine the political future of South Vietnam. After agreements were reached on both tracks, an international conference would be convened to work out guarantees and safeguards. Kissinger added that "once North Vietnamese forces and pressures are removed, the United States has no obligation to maintain a government in Saigon by force."[6]

Despite the withdrawal of U.S. troops, Nixon had no intention of abandoning South Vietnam. He wanted a peace that would last, one that would justify the sacrifices made by the Americans who had died in Vietnam. As a result, the president was more concerned about South Vietnam's ultimate survival than Kissinger and insisted on reinforcing the South Vietnamese army before a peace agreement was signed. In 1969 alone, the United States shipped $1 billion in weapons and materiel to the South Vietnamese.

To cover the U.S. retreat, while allowing time for the South Vietnamese army to be reinforced, the administration intensified the air war over South Vietnam and, without publicizing it began bombing Vietcong bases in neighboring Cambodia in March 1969. Nixon saw the intensified air war primarily as a way to weaken North Vietnam and improve Saigon's chances of surviving after the U.S. withdrawal, but Kissinger saw it primarily as means of forcing the North Vietnamese to accept his two-track strategy. Already, at this early date, the president and his national security advisor were embarked on a collision course over Vietnam.

The Paris Peace Talks

It soon became obvious, after the Paris peace talks resumed at the end of January 1969, that Hanoi would not accept Kissinger's double-track formula for ending the war. Instead, the North Vietnamese pursued a single-track negotiation, maintaining that the military and political elements of a settlement were inseparable. Consequently, the North Vietnamese rejected Kissinger's proposal for a mutual withdrawal of troops and instead insisted on a unilateral U.S. pullout. They also refused to accept the continuation of the regime of South Vietnamese President Nguyen Van Thieu, insisting that it must be replaced by the Provisional Revolutionary Government (PRG), the new name of the National Liberation Front. Only then, apparently, would the North Vietnamese accept a negotiated settlement of the war.

Thus, instead of spurring negotiations, Nixon's decision to begin the unilateral withdrawal of U.S. troops only encouraged the North Vietnamese to believe that their conquest of South Vietnam was inevitable. Moreover, as more U.S. troops departed from Vietnam without any progress in the negotiations, the less incentive Hanoi had to reach any agreement at all. Just as the Johnson administration had given up a bargaining chip by halting the bombing of North Vietnam in 1968, the Nixon administration's decision to withdraw its troops unilaterally from South Vietnam further reduced U.S. leverage over the North Vietnamese.

As the Paris talks dragged on without any end in sight, the American antiwar movement revived. On October 15, 1969, demonstrations began all over the nation, with protesters demanding a moratorium in the war. In a nationwide address in early November, Nixon responded by asking the "great silent majority" of the American people for their support and patience. The favorable public reaction to the speech gave Kissinger additional time to negotiate with Le Duc Tho, North Vietnam's new chief negotiator. Despite four trips to Paris between February and April 1970, the deadlock remained unbroken.

Cambodia

In the spring of 1970, the Paris peace talks were eclipsed by events in Cambodia. In March Cambodia's neutralist ruler, Prince Norodom Sihanouk, was overthrown by Lon Nol, a right-wing officer who promptly launched a campaign to clear his country of communists. By mid-April, however, the Cambodian communists (known as the Khmer Rouge), supported by North Vietnam, had surrounded the capital, Phnom Penh, and were threatening to oust Lon Nol. In desperation, Lon Nol appealed for U.S. military assistance. An alarmed Nixon feared that a communist victory in Cambodia would undermine the ability of a non-communist South Vietnam to survive the planned U.S. military withdrawal. Moreover, both he and Kissinger worried that refusing to help Lon Nol would destroy the credibility of the U.S. guaranty to other client states as well. Consequently, on April 30, 1970, Nixon announced that he was sending U.S. troops into Cambodia to destroy Vietcong sanctuaries in that country. The president told a nationwide audience that "if, when the chips are down, the world's most powerful nation acts like a pitiful, helpless giant, the forces of totalitarianism and anarchy will then threaten free nations and free institutions throughout the world. . . . "[7]

The U.S. incursion into Cambodia touched off the most massive antiwar demonstrations of the Vietnam era. Hundreds of university campuses were in upheaval. At Kent State University in Ohio, four students were killed when National Guardsmen opened fire on student demonstrators. Far from shortening the war, the U.S. invasion widened it. By the time U.S. troops left Cambodia in July 1970, half that country was in communist hands. In 1975, when South Vietnam collapsed, the Khmer Rouge would complete the conquest of Cambodia and kill 1 million of the country's 6 million people before it was toppled by an invading Vietnamese army in 1978.

Laos

By the end of 1970, Kissinger had concluded that, short of dumping Thieu, a cease-fire in place was the only way to break the stalemate in the Paris peace talks. He believed that, by allowing the communist forces to hold the territory they controlled in South Vietnam, a cease-fire in place offered Hanoi a reasonable prospect of ultimate victory, which he believed was a prerequisite to getting them to sign a peace settlement.

Kissinger secretly offered the cease-fire-in-place proposal to North Vietnam in September 1970. But the North Vietnamese refused to embrace it until the United States accepted their four-point program, which required the immediate ouster of the Thieu government and its replacement by a coalition government dominated by the PRG. Hanoi refused to consider a cease-fire in place because its hold on South Vietnam was not sufficiently strong in 1970 to warrant its acceptance. For the remainder of the war Hanoi would concentrate on developing and strengthening the communist infrastructure in South Vietnam to ensure that, when it came time to accept a cease-fire in place, the communists would control the country.

The North Vietnamese also intensified their effort to funnel troops and supplies down the Ho Chi Minh Trail, which ran through Laos and into South Vietnam. In an attempt to disrupt it, in early 1971 Nixon approved a plan to permit the South Vietnamese army to cross the border into Laos. After the Cambodian experience, Nixon was not prepared to employ U.S. troops for the operation, but he did agree to give air support to the 20,000 South Vietnamese troops who entered Laos in February. Nevertheless, the South Vietnamese were beaten back by North Vietnamese forces and withdrew two months later.

After the collapse of the Laotian operation, Kissinger again took the diplomatic initiative. He persuaded the president to offer two additional concessions to the North Vietnamese. The first was a pledge to withdraw all remaining U.S. forces within six months after the signing of the agreement; the second was a promise that Thieu would resign one month before elections were held in South Vietnam. Six times during 1971 Kissinger went to Paris to try to reach agreement with Le Duc Tho. And six times Le Duc Tho insisted on Thieu's immediate removal as well as a date for total U.S. withdrawal.

Kissinger finally realized that Hanoi would not compromise and would not sign a peace agreement unless the United States agreed to remove Thieu. Only then would the North Vietnamese permit the United States to withdraw "with honor" from Vietnam. Accordingly, by late 1971 Kissinger had concluded that the only way Hanoi could be made to accept a negotiated settlement was to isolate North Vietnam from its main sources of supply, the Soviet Union and China. This, he believed, could be achieved by promoting détente with both communist powers.

Triangular Diplomacy

As Kissinger had hoped, as Sino-American relations gradually warmed, the Chinese became increasingly willing to help the United States extricate itself from Vietnam. The Chinese were motivated not only by a desire to ensure continued U.S. support against the Soviet Union but also by the hope of keeping Vietnam divided and therefore more malleable to Chinese wishes. The last thing the Chinese wanted was a unified and highly militarized Soviet client on their southern frontier.

As a result, while the Chinese strongly criticized Nixon's expansion of the war to Cambodia and Laos, they did nothing to counter it. In fact, in November 1971 Mao Zedong personally berated the North Vietnamese prime minister, Pham Dong, for refusing to compromise with the Americans. He also summarily rejected a North Vietnamese request to cancel Nixon's visit to China. The culmination of that trip, the Shanghai Communiqué, made no mention whatever of Vietnam. The Chinese, in the meantime, curtailed supplies to the North Vietnamese by denying the Soviets transit rights across China.

Surprisingly to Kissinger, the Soviets were not as cooperative as the Chinese, at least not initially. He had thought that the Soviets would be willing to assist the United States withdrawal from Vietnam to secure a SALT agreement, access to Western trade and economic assistance, and other benefits of détente. But Soviet assistance to North Vietnam actually increased during Nixon's first years in office. The Soviets not only were eager to create a strong client state on China's southern flank, they wanted to keep the United States tied down in Vietnam as long as possible to prevent the transfer of U.S. resources to other areas where Soviet interests were more extensive, such as Europe and the Middle East.

The unwillingness of the Soviets to help the United States reach a settlement of the war angered Nixon. "If the Soviet Union will not help us get peace," he told Soviet Ambassador Anatoly Dobrynin, "then we will have to pursue our own methods for bringing the war to an end."[8]

To drive this point home, the United States procrastinated on all the negotiations in which the Soviet Union was interested: SALT, the Middle East, and expanded economic relations.

It was not until 1971 that the Soviet Union's Vietnam policy began to respond to U.S. pressure. The shift occurred not only because the Soviets wished to break the logjam on Berlin and SALT but also because the United States was making concessions the Soviets believed the North Vietnamese could and should accept. Especially appealing to the Soviets was the U.S. cease-fire-in-place proposal, primarily because it gave the North Vietnamese the prospect of controlling a substantial portion of South Vietnam after the Americans withdrew.

The scenario the Soviets envisioned for the war's conclusion involved three phases. First, North Vietnam would have to mount a major offensive to inject its forces into South Vietnam. Second, once it had substantial forces in South Vietnam, Hanoi would negotiate a settlement that would allow the Americans to withdraw. Finally, once U.S. withdrawal was complete, Moscow would support the resumption of Hanoi's conquest of South Vietnam. The Soviets concluded that they could support the Kissinger plan for ending the war, with the important exception of its ultimate outcome, the final defeat of South Vietnam.

The North Vietnamese Offensive, Spring 1972

In preparation for Hanoi's offensive, the Soviet Union began sending the North Vietnamese large quantities of military equipment in August 1971. The North Vietnamese undoubtedly resented the subordination of their military strategy to the requirements of the Soviet Union's détente diplomacy, but because of their dependence on Soviet military aid, they had no choice but to tolerate Soviet interference in their war plan.

In March 1972 the North Vietnamese launched their offensive. Spear-headed by Soviet-made tanks, 120,000 North Vietnamese troops struck into South Vietnam across the demilitarized zone, in the Central Highlands, and in the area northwest of Saigon. Achieving an almost complete surprise, they routed the defending ARVN forces and quickly advanced toward the towns of Quang Tri in the north, Kontum in the Central Highlands, and An Loc, just sixty miles north of Saigon. Thieu was forced to commit most of his reserves to defend the threatened towns, thus freeing the Vietcong to mount an offensive in the Mekong Delta and in the heavily populated regions around Saigon.

Although stunned by the magnitude of the North Vietnamese invasion, Nixon refused to permit South Vietnam to fall. However, with only 95,000 U.S. soldiers remaining in South Vietnam (of which only 6,000 were combat troops) and with the commitment of additional ground forces politically impossible, Nixon turned to air power to crush the North Vietnamese offensive. He approved massive B-52 bomber strikes on North Vietnam, including attacks on fuel depots in the Hanoi-Haiphong area.

Simultaneously, Kissinger secretly traveled to Moscow to meet with Brezhnev on April 20–21. He warned the Soviet leader that a continuation of the war could severely damage détente and have grave consequences for North Vietnam. However, as a carrot to accompany this stick, Kissinger made explicit, for the first time, America's willingness to permit North Vietnamese forces to remain in South Vietnam after a cease-fire was arranged. Brezhnev, who denied Soviet complicity in the North Vietnamese offensive, assured Kissinger that he did not want anything to stand in the way of the impending Moscow summit.

To Le Duc Tho in Paris Kissinger repeated the cease-fire-in-place offer on May 1, as well as the threat to intensify the U.S. air war, but the North Vietnamese were too intoxicated with the success of their offensive to consider a cease-fire in place. On May 3 the northernmost province of South Vietnam, including the city of Quang Tri, fell to the North Vietnamese. Still confident of victory, Hanoi flatly rejected Kissinger's cease-fire offer.

Prompted in part by General Creighton Abrams's warning that South Vietnam was on the verge of military collapse, Nixon approved the most drastic escalation of the war since 1968. On May 8 he announced that the Navy was mining Haiphong harbor and would blockade North Vietnam's coast. He also said that he had approved a resumption of the massive, sustained bombing offensive against the North, which President Johnson had suspended shortly before leaving office. Nixon accepted the possibility that the moves he had ordered could provoke the Soviets into canceling the Moscow summit, but he was willing to assume that risk rather than go to Moscow while a major U.S. client was collapsing.

As Kissinger had hoped, the Soviets' desire to obtain the benefits of détente superseded their desire to help Hanoi, and they did not cancel the Moscow summit. Furthermore, while the Soviets continued to provide military assistance to the North Vietnamese, they privately urged Hanoi to accommodate the United States in their obvious desire to get out of Vietnam. The Chinese, for their part, issued perfunctory protests against Nixon's escalation of the war but also quietly exerted pressure on the North Vietnamese to settle with the United States.

As the Nixon administration had expected, the U.S. mining and blockade of North Vietnam's coast assured that the capture of Quang Tri would mark the high-water mark of the communist spring offensive, not the beginning of South Vietnam's collapse. Hanoi needed long supply lines to keep its offensive rolling, and the mining of its harbors guaranteed that it would not be getting those supplies as quickly as they were needed. The Chinese, who did not want to strain their relationship with the United States, did not allow Moscow to use either the Chinese rail system or any ports in southern China to get supplies around the U.S. blockade. As a result, during the next month, South Vietnamese forces were able to check the North Vietnamese advance. With the military situation in Vietnam stabilized, Nixon was able to attend the Moscow summit in late May.

The Moscow Summit, May 1972

In Moscow, on May 26, 1972, Nixon and Brezhnev signed two historic arms control documents. The first was the ABM Treaty. It established a ceiling of 100 ABM launchers for each of the two ABM sites that each country was permitted. The United States already had a protected ICBM field in North Dakota and therefore was permitted to build an additional ABM site around Washington. The Soviet Union, which already had an ABM site around Moscow, was permitted to add another one around an ICBM field. The treaty also prohibited the construction of ABM-related radars outside these two permissible sites.

In effect, the ABM Treaty, by ruling out the possibility of nationwide ABM defenses for each side, preserved the retaliatory capability of both powers. In addition, the treaty prohibited the development and deployment of space-based ABM weapons. The interpretation of this provision would become a major point of Soviet-American disagreement during the administration of President Ronald Reagan. The ABM Treaty would be monitored by national means of verification, that is, primarily reconnaissance satellites and electronic eaves-dropping equipment, thus the agreement bypassed the old obstacle of on-site inspection.

The treaty also provided for a Standing Consultative Commission, whose function was to establish procedures for implementing the treaty, for dealing with suspected violations of the treaty, and for discussing additional measures to limit strategic weapons. The Standing Consultative Commission would meet at least twice a year, and at any time a party to the treaty requested its convocation.

The second document signed at the Moscow summit was the Interim Agreement. It limited for five years the numbers of ICBMs and SLBMs to those deployed in 1972 or under construction. At that time, the Soviet Union had a total of 2,328 missiles: 1,618 land-based ICBMs and 710 on submarines. The United States had a total of 1,710 missiles: 1,054 land-based ICBMs and 656 on submarines. The United States accepted Soviet numerical superiority in these weapons as compensation for its lead in MIRVs.

During the Moscow summit, both sides supplemented the SALT agreements with a number of other accords. One was the Basic Principles of Relations. In this agreement, both sides agreed that their differences in ideology and social systems would not be permitted to jeopardize détente. They also pledged "their utmost to avoid military confrontations and to prevent the outbreak of nuclear war."[9] In addition, the parties agreed to continue their efforts to limit other armaments and to expand commercial, economic, environmental, scientific, technological, and cultural ties.

The Moscow summit marked the high point of détente as well as the post–World War II effort to control the nuclear arms race. "Never before," Kissinger said, "have the two world's most powerful nations . . . placed their central armaments under formally agreed limitation and restraint."[10]

Kissinger's elation was not universally shared. Liberals objected that the agreements did nothing to prevent qualitative improvements in strategic weaponry, such as the B-1 bomber and the Trident submarine. Nor did SALT I do anything to prevent the enormous expansion of warheads that resulted from the unrestricted MIRV programs both nations were pursuing. Conservatives, on the other hand, believed the agreements did too much. The Interim Agreement, they pointed out, awarded the Soviets a significant measure of ascendancy over the United States both in overall numbers of offensive missiles and in combined throwweight (payload capacity) of its ICBM launchers. Conservatives believed that, in effect, the SALT agreements reduced the United States to a second-rate status in the nuclear equation, and thereby made America and its allies vulnerable to Soviet nuclear blackmail. To win conservative support for the agreements, the administration accepted an amendment to the Interim Agreement that was drawn up by Senator Henry "Scoop" Jackson (Dem.–Wash.). It provided that future strategic arms limitation agreements would be based on the principle of equal strategic forces.

The Senate ratified the ABM Treaty on August 3 by a vote of 88 to 2. The Interim Agreement, because it was not in treaty form, had to be approved by both houses of Congress. It passed in the Senate on September 14 by a vote of 88 to 2 and in the House by 329 to 7. Both the ABM Treaty and the Interim Agreement became effective in October 1972.

In the wake of the Moscow summit, during the summer and autumn of 1972, a number of advances also took place in U.S.–Soviet economic relations. First, several U.S. businesses signed contracts with the Soviet government. Second, the Soviet Union agreed to buy $750 million worth of U.S. grain, with $500 million of that amount purchased with credits provided by the U.S. Commodity Credit Corporation. This agreement was augmented by a U.S.–Soviet maritime agreement, which established premium rates for American vessels carrying grain to Soviet ports and substantially increased the number of ports in each country open to ships of the other. Finally, in October, both countries signed a comprehensive trade agreement in which the Soviets agreed to repay $722 million in World War II Lend-Lease debts in exchange for an administration promise that it would grant the Soviet Union most-favored-nation trading status, subject to the approval of the Congress.

The Vietnam Endgame

During the Moscow summit, both Nixon and Brezhnev agreed that they would not permit the conflict in Vietnam to impede the development of détente. However, Brezhnev flatly rejected Nixon's request to stop Soviet arms shipments to North Vietnam. Nevertheless, in mid-June 1972, Soviet President Nikolai Podgorny visited Hanoi to convey Washington's latest negotiating position.

In light of the bombing that North Vietnamese endured during the late spring and summer of 1972 and the withdrawal of the last U.S. combat troops from Vietnam on August 12, Hanoi was finally ready to give the United States a face-saving way out of the war. By late summer, and for the first time since the war began, the PRG had achieved the extent and depth of political control in the South Vietnamese countryside that would permit Hanoi's acceptance of a cease-fire in place.

By the end of September, both Washington and Hanoi were pushing to reach an agreement before the approaching U.S. presidential election. The North Vietnamese believed that Nixon, to get a peace settlement, would be more willing to compromise before the election than after it— an impression Kissinger did nothing to dispel.

By October 11, after three weeks of intensive negotiations, Kissinger and Le Duc Tho had hammered out the fundamentals of an agreement. Within sixty days after a cease-fire, the United States would withdraw its remaining (noncombat) troops, and North Vietnam would return American POWs. A political settlement would then be arranged by a tripartite National Council of Reconciliation and Concord (composed of representatives of the Saigon government, the Vietcong, and neutralists). It would administer elections and assume responsibility for implementing the agreement. Only a couple of issues remained to be resolved, the most perplexing of which was the future status of the demilitarized zone. But Kissinger and Tho, eager to wrap up the negotiations as quickly as possible, agreed that these items could be left until later and that, after consulting with Nixon and Thieu, Kissinger would proceed on to Hanoi to initial the treaty on October 22.

In his haste to get an agreement, Kissinger badly miscalculated Thieu's willingness to do what the United States desired. He also underestimated the depth of Nixon's support for the South Vietnamese president. Thieu refused to turn the fate of South Vietnam over to the proposed electoral committee, and he insisted that he would never accept an agreement that awarded sovereignty to the PRG and permitted North Vietnamese troops to remain in the South. Instead, Thieu demanded wholesale changes in the agreement, including the establishment of the demilitarized zone as a boundary between two sovereign Vietnamese states. He obviously hoped his conditions would wreck the agreement, ensure the continuation of the war, and thereby preclude America's complete withdrawal from Vietnam.

After spending five days in Saigon trying unsuccessfully to convince Thieu to accept the agreement, Kissinger urged Nixon to go ahead without out Saigon's approval. But Nixon refused to abandon Thieu. He did not want to be accused of having "flushed Thieu down the election drain," as one presidential assistant put it, in order to win reelection. In addition, Nixon not only shared some of Thieu's reservations about the draft agreement, he was confident that he would win the presidential election without its completion. After the election, he believed, he would be in a better position to demand that North Vietnam meet U.S. demands or, as he said, "face the consequences of what we could do to them."[11] In addition, while Nixon was not prepared to let Thieu block an agreement indefinitely, a brief delay would provide time to give South Vietnam additional assistance and weaken Hanoi's ability to threaten the peace.

As a result of these considerations, Nixon partially turned down Kissinger's October 23 request that, as a sign of U.S. sincerity, he suspend bombing of North Vietnam and all air support to the South Vietnamese army. While the president agreed to suspend the bombing of the North, he refused to stop air support for the South Vietnamese. Instead, Nixon ordered Kissinger to inform Hanoi that the United States would need more time to win Thieu's acquiescence to the agreement. Over the next few weeks, the United States began the delivery to South Vietnam of more than $1 billion worth of military hardware, which would leave Thieu with the fourth largest air force in the world. Nixon also gave Thieu "absolute assurances" that, if the North Vietnamese violated the peace agreement, he would order "swift and severe retaliatory action." Nixon ordered the Joint Chiefs of Staff to begin immediate planning for such a contingency.[12]

In spite of Nixon's actions in helping Thieu sabotage an early peace settlement, Kissinger stated publicly on October 31 that "peace is at hand."[13] But the additional demands he made upon North Vietnam, when the talks resumed in early November, raised further obstacles to a quick agreement. Kissinger asked Le Duc Tho to accept at least a token withdrawal of North Vietnamese troops from the South. He also requested changes in the text of the peace agreement that would have weakened the political status of the Vietcong, restricted the powers of the tripartite commission, and established the demilitarized zone as a virtual boundary between two sovereign Vietnamese states. After Nixon's landslide victory over George McGovern in the November election, Kissinger warned the North Vietnamese that the president would not hesitate to "take whatever action he considers necessary to protect U.S. interests."[14]

Certain that they had been betrayed, and refusing to give way in the face of threats, the North Vietnamese angrily rejected Kissinger's proposals. They then raised numerous counter demands of their own, including an old one, that Thieu must be removed from power as a part of the final agreement.

By this time, Kissinger's patience with the North Vietnamese was wearing very thin. Conveniently forgetting the U.S. role in the breakdown of the talks, he complained bitterly that Hanoi has "goaded us beyond endurance."[15] He also informed Nixon that the North Vietnamese were deliberately stalling in order to force a break between the United States and Thieu. Frustrated and impatient for results, Nixon and Kissinger decided to break off the talks and turn again to air power in another attempt to make Hanoi more malleable to U.S. demands.

On December 14, one day after Le Duc Tho returned to Hanoi for consultations, Nixon and Kissinger sent a cable to the North Vietnamese government warning that grave consequences would follow if they did not resume "serious" negotiations within seventy-two hours. On December 18, one day after the U.S. ultimatum expired, Nixon gave the order to execute Linebacker-2, an intensified bombing campaign of North Vietnam. He made absolutely clear to the U.S. military that he wanted them to inflict the maximum amount of damage possible on North Vietnam. "I don't want any more of this crap about the fact that we couldn't hit this target or that one," he lectured Admiral Thomas Moorer, chairman of the Joint Chiefs of Staff. "This is your chance to use military power to win this war and if you don't, I'll consider you responsible." [16]

Over the next twelve days, the United States unleashed the most intensive, and devastating attacks of the war on North Vietnam. Some 36,000 tons of bombs were dropped, more than the entire number dropped from 1969 and 1971. As a result, much of the vital military supplies that Hanoi had husbanded since the U.S. naval blockade began the previous May were destroyed. Nixon and Kissinger claimed later that this Christmas bombing campaign compelled the North Vietnamese to accept a settlement satisfactory to the United States. At the same time, the public uproar in the United States created by the bombing campaign, along with hostile pressure from China and the Soviet Union, compelled the administration to finally sign the peace agreement. In the wake of the bombing campaign, Nixon's popular approval rating plummeted to 39 percent. On January 2 and 4, 1973, the House and Senate Democratic caucuses voted by large margins to cut off all funding for the war as soon as U.S. troop withdrawal was completed and the repatriation of prisoners of war could be arranged.

The Paris Peace Settlement, January 1973

Nixon had indicated to the North Vietnamese that he would stop the bombing if they agreed to resume the peace talks. Hanoi consented, and the negotiations resumed in Paris on January 8, 1973. After six days of marathon sessions, marked by compromise on both sides, Kissinger and Le Duc Tho resolved their remaining differences.

The changes from the October agreement were largely cosmetic, enabling each side to claim that nothing had been given up. Most important, the bombing did not produce a settlement very different from the one the United States had rejected earlier. On the major sticking point, the demilitarized zone, the North Vietnamese agreed to refer to it in the treaty, but the United States accepted its description as a "provisional and not a political and territorial boundary," thereby preserving the substance of Hanoi's position. [17]

The major provisions of the Paris agreement were these: (1) the United States would withdraw all of its military forces from South Vietnam and cease all air attacks on the North, (2) the United States implicitly recognized Hanoi's right to maintain close to a quarter of a million troops in the South, (3) an international Control Commission, which included members from communist Poland and Hungary, would be created to enforce the agreement, and (4) the United States promised to "contribute to the postwar reconstruction in North Vietnam without any political conditions." A sum of $3.25 billion was proposed, though Kissinger pointed out that appropriations could only be made if Congress agreed. Also kept secret from the North Vietnamese, as well as the American people, was Nixon's promise of November 14, 1972, to Thieu that the United States would "meet all contingencies in case the agreement is grossly violated."[18]

Because the Paris agreement took all the U.S. military pressure off the North Vietnamese while permitting them to leave their forces in South Vietnam, it was a disaster for the Saigon government. Not surprisingly, Thieu at first refused to sign it. This time, however, Nixon compelled him to accept it, but only after promising him again, on January 5, 1973, that, if he did, the United States would "respond with full force" if North Vietnam violated the agreement.[19] At the same time, Nixon made clear that, if Thieu continued to resist, he would cut off further U.S. assistance to Saigon and would sign the treaty without him. After stalling for several more days, Thieu buckled under and dropped his opposition to the Paris accord.

The Paris agreement, which finally was signed on January 27, 1973, seven days after Nixon's inauguration, did not end the conflict in Vietnam. It simply permitted the United States to withdraw without an immediate loss of face. North Vietnam remained as determined as ever to conquer the South and hence had no intention of observing the accords. For the North Vietnamese, Nixon's "peace with honor" represented just another phase in their thirty-year struggle to control Vietnam.

The Washington Summit, June 1973

In the wake of the Paris peace accord, the first half of 1973 marked the high-water mark of the Nixon-Brezhnev détente. The two leaders held another summit, in Washington, in June. They signed four executive agreements dealing with oceanography, transportation, agricultural research, and cultural exchange. They also signed a declaration of principles aimed at accelerating the SALT II negotiations, which had stalled in Geneva. Additionally, the two leaders agreed to increase their cooperation on nuclear energy research. Other agreements involved the expansion of airline service and the establishment of a Soviet trade mission in Washington. While the Washington accords were not as significant as the agreements signed at the Moscow summit the previous year, they nevertheless provided evidence of the common Soviet-American desire to maintain the momentum of détente.

Perhaps the most significant accord signed at the Washington summit was the Agreement on the Prevention of Nuclear War. It bound the two parties to act "in such a manner as to prevent the development of situations capable of causing a dangerous exacerbation of their relations." The agreement obliged the superpowers to begin "urgent consultations" whenever relations between them or between either of them and another country appeared to involve the risk of nuclear conflict.[20]

The Yom Kippur War, October 1973

In all probability, the Soviets knew as early as the Washington summit, when they were signing the Agreement on the Prevention of Nuclear War, that Egypt was planning to attack the military positions the Israelis had established on the Sinai Peninsula during the 1967 war, although the Soviets probably did not know the date the attack would begin. The Soviets did not share this information with the United States. Furthermore, the Soviet Union continued to supply weapons to Egypt, apparently in violation of their pledge in the Agreement on the Prevention of Nuclear War "to refrain from the threat or use of force" against either "the other party" or "the allies of the other party."

The Soviets were aware, in March 1973, three months before the Agreement on the Prevention of Nuclear War was signed, that Nixon had promised Israeli Prime Minister Golda Meir forty-eight U.S. Phantom jets, which would be delivered over a four-year period. This U.S. action convinced Egyptian President Anwar Sadat that only another war could regain the territories lost by the Arabs in the 1967 conflict. As a result, Sadat developed a common strategy with President Hafaz Assad of Syria, who promised to attack the Golan Heights while Egyptian troops struck at Israeli positions on the Suez Canal. Saudi Arabia's King Faisal pledged to use his country's vast oil supplies as a weapon against Israel's friends.

The Arab attack began on October 6, 1973, on the Jewish holy day of Yom Kippur. Nixon and Kissinger were angered by the duplicity of the Soviet leaders, who had not only refused to warn them about the Arab attack but actively conspired with the Arabs, in clear violation of the Agreement on the Prevention of Nuclear War. Responding to desperate pleas for help from the Israeli government, which was in a near panic because of early Arab military successes, the Nixon administration mounted a massive airlift of U.S. planes and materiel to Israel. With U.S. assistance the Israelis were able to take the offensive against the Arabs. They pushed the Syrians out of the Golan Heights and advanced toward Damascus. They also crossed the Suez Canal and encircled the Egyptian Third Army, with 100,000 troops, on October 23.

The crisis swelled into a superpower confrontation the next day when the Soviets threatened to intervene with troops to prevent another Arab humiliation. In response, the following day, President Nixon, at the urging of Kissinger, placed U.S. strategic forces on an intermediate defense condition (DEFCON) level. In so doing, both sides ignored their mutual pledge contained in the Agreement on the Prevention of Nuclear War not to take action that would endanger the superpower peace. While Brezhnev immediately accused the United States of threatening nuclear war, he nevertheless was eager to reduce the risk of superpower confrontation. Consequently, the Soviets supported a UN cease-fire resolution, which finally ended the fighting and, in turn, enabled the United States to cancel its military alert on October 31.

After the cease-fire went into effect, Kissinger engaged in extensive shuttle diplomacy between the Arab capitals and Israel. By January 1974 he was able to negotiate a partial Israeli withdrawal from the Suez Canal and, during the following year, from Syrian territory as well. While the Soviets deplored their exclusion from Kissinger's talks, they did not interfere, since the agreements benefited their Arab clients by restoring peace.

Nevertheless, the Yom Kippur War and its diplomatic aftermath were major setbacks for the Soviet Union. Not only were the Soviets unable to prevent another Arab defeat at the hands of the Israelis, they had to watch their Arab clients (Egypt in particular) turn to the United States to win back some of their lost territories. Through Kissinger's diplomatic efforts, Egypt not only received back its territory, but 200 American observers were also sent to monitor the Egyptian-Israeli cease-fire line. In addition, Kissinger promised $700 million in annual economic aid from the United States, which reduced Egypt's dependence on the Soviet Union.

Despite the ability of the Soviet Union and the United States to defuse the superpower crisis caused by the Yom Kippur War, the duplicity practiced by both Moscow and Washington before, during, and after that conflict raised serious doubts on both sides of the Iron Curtain about the superpowers' ability to cooperate on any issue, let alone one as complicated and emotional as the Middle Eastern crisis. Their inability to agree on an approach for solving the core problem in the Middle East, the conflict between the Israelis and the Palestinians, ensured that that region would remain a major area of Cold War tension.

The Demise of the Soviet-American Trade Agreement

Détente was weakened not only by the superpower confrontation during the Yom Kippur War but by rising opposition within the United States to the developing Soviet-American trade relationship. As early as September 1972, the Nixon administration realized that gaining Senate ratification of the new Soviet trade treaty, which was signed by both parties the following month, would not be an easy task. In August of that year, the Soviet government had clamped a tax on Soviet citizens wishing to emigrate from the Soviet Union. The tax, which was as high as $30,000 per person, was designed to discourage the emigration of Soviet Jews to Israel.

Taking advantage of the Soviet action, Senator Henry Jackson jumped at the chance to embarrass the Nixon administration and enhance his own presidential ambitions. Declaring that "the time has come to place our highest human values ahead of the trade dollar," Jackson in

October 1973 tacked an amendment onto the administration's trade bill that prohibited most-favored-nation status to any "nonmarket economy country" that limited the right of emigration, a very thinly disguised reference to the Soviet Union.[21] A similar amendment, introduced in the House of Representatives by Congressman Charles A. Vanik (Dem.–Ohio) passed by a 319 to 80 vote in December 1973. The Jackson-Vanik Amendment represented a significant defeat for Nixon, who had promised the Soviet leaders that most-favored-nation status would be granted without linkage to the emigration issue.

The administration reacted with indignation to congressional tampering with its trade bill. Kissinger warned that the Jackson-Vanik Amendment would not only set back the fight for freer emigration from the Soviet Union but could jeopardize the whole process of détente. Rather than attempt to pin down the Soviets to public assurances that would publicly embarrass them, Kissinger preferred to hold the Soviets to private assurances that they would not harass Soviet Jews who wished to leave the Soviet Union.

Kissinger's warning proved to be prophetic. Nixon's successor, President Gerald Ford, signed a final version of the trade bill on January 3, 1975, granting the Soviet Union most-favored-nation status contingent on the increased emigration of Soviet Jews. The Soviet government responded by informing the administration that it would not implement the 1972 trade agreement, nor would it pay its Lend-Lease debt. While both sides announced that the cancellation of the trade pact would not interfere with the further development of U.S.–Soviet relations, its demise nevertheless was the beginning of the end of détente during the Brezhnev years.

The 1974 Moscow Summit, Watergate, and Vladivostok

While détente was strained during the Yom Kippur War, its decline did not become evident until Nixon's second visit to Moscow, in June 1974. Both sides still believed that it was necessary to maintain the guise of good relations, even though concrete progress on limiting strategic weapons was proving impossible to achieve.

Two nuclear arms control agreements were signed at Moscow. The first reduced the number of ABM sites that each country could maintain to one, instead of the two permitted by the 1972 ABM Treaty. The second agreement, the Threshold Test Ban Treaty (TTBT), prohibited underground nuclear tests above a level of 150 kilotons. An accompanying agreement, the Peaceful Nuclear Explosions Treaty, was signed two years later. It established a 150-kiloton threshold for nonmilitary underground nuclear explosions.

The inability of Kissinger to produce a "conceptual breakthrough" on SALT II at Moscow was undoubtedly affected by the administration's increasing preoccupation with the Watergate scandal. Kissinger privately expressed his fear that the Soviets were reluctant to conclude a new SALT agreement with a president who appeared to be on his way out of office. Not until after Nixon resigned the presidency, on August 9, following the initiation of impeachment proceedings by the House of Representatives, did the Soviets indicate their eagerness to work with his successor, Gerald Ford.

In late November 1974 Ford and Brezhnev met in Vladivostok. The two leaders agreed to limit the numbers of all strategic offensive nuclear weapons and delivery vehicles (including MIRVs) through 1975. The Vladivostok Accord stated that the future conduct of SALT would be based on these principles: (1) an overall ceiling of 2,400 delivery vehicles for both sides, (2) a ceiling of 1,320 MIRVs, (3) the inclusion of bomber-launched and land-mobile missiles in the overall total, (4) the limitation of Soviet heavy missiles at 313 deployments, with no new silo constructions permitted, (5) after the conclusion of an agreement, further negotiations beginning no later than 1980–1981 on the issues of additional limitations and possible strategic force reductions to take effect after 1985, and (6) resumption of negotiations for an agreement based on these principles in Geneva in January 1975. Kissinger hailed the agreement as a "breakthrough" that would "mean that a cap has been put on the arms race for ten years"[22]

Conservatives, however, considered the Vladivostok Accord fatally flawed. They pointed out that, while the accord embodied the principle of equality in numbers of strategic delivery systems, it made no provision for equality of throw-weight or for equality of warhead numbers. Conservatives feared that the Soviets would eventually convert their three-to-one advantage in throw-weight, which was left unaffected by the agreement, into a first-strike capability. Liberals, on the other hand, asserted that the key flaw in the Vladivostok Accord was the height of the proposed ceilings. The United States would actually have to build more strategic weapons to reach them.

Despite the Vladivostok agreements, the SALT II negotiators made little headway for the remainder of the Ford administration. Like the MBFR talks, which were tied up by East-West disagreement over the size of conventional force reductions, SALT II remained hopelessly deadlocked.

The Fall of Indochina, 1975

Even more depressing to the administration than the arms control deadlock was the continuation of the conflict in Vietnam. Neither the North nor the South Vietnamese ever had any intention of abiding by the Paris accords. The North Vietnamese considered the Paris agreements a peace settlement with the United States, not the Thieu government. Hanoi still sought unification of the country on its own terms, which did not include a provision for an independent South Vietnam. Within one year of the Paris accords, the North had introduced an additional 100,000 to

120,000 regular troops into the South and increased its tanks and artillery strength by four times.

Thieu thought he would continue to receive U.S. support, as Nixon had promised. But Nixon's promises to Thieu were kept secret from the Congress and the American people, who were led to believe that the Paris accords meant that the war, or at least U.S. participation in the conflict, was over. Neither was prepared to countenance U.S. reentry into the conflict, and Nixon, who was crippled politically by the Watergate scandal, was in no position to resist their will.

Indeed, Congress took several steps to ensure that U.S. reentry into the conflict would be impossible. In June 1973 the Congress denied further funding to support U.S. combat activities, or aerial reconnaissance, in or over Cambodia, Laos, North Vietnam, and South Vietnam after August 15, 1973. With the bombing option removed, the Nixon administration lost its only means of enforcing the Paris agreement.

In addition, on November 7, 1973, both houses of Congress overrode Nixon's veto and passed the War Powers Act. It required the president to consult Congress before committing U.S. forces to combat. If an emergency required the president to act without getting prior approval from Congress, he had to report to Senate and House within forty-eight hours of the deployment of soldiers. After that, he had sixty days to use the troops without gaining the consent of Congress. If both houses approved, the president could continue to deploy the troops. If not, he was required to terminate hostilities and remove the troops within ninety days of their injection into combat.

In addition to depriving the administration of its "stick" in enforcing the Paris agreement, the Congress also removed from the North Vietnamese the economic incentive for abiding by it. By July 1973 it was clear that there was no congressional support for the economic assistance program that Kissinger had promised the North Vietnamese. However, the Congress also drastically cut back aid to South Vietnam. In 1972 it had approved $2 billion in assistance to that country, but by 1975 it was considering a final grant of $600 million. By then, U.S. economic assistance to Cambodia had been cut off altogether.

Kissinger was vitriolic in his denunciation of Congress's actions. He argued that the Congress was primarily responsible for the U.S. failure to save South Vietnam. Yet, as historian P. Edward Haley points out, Kissinger's criticism was disingenuous and contradictory. The administration kept secret its promises to Thieu because it knew that the Congress would reject them. Yet it acted as if Congress should have upheld them.[23]

The end of U.S. military and economic support directly contributed to the collapse of South Vietnam. What surprised most people, however, was the speed with which it occurred. In mid-March 1975 the North Vietnamese launched an offensive against Ban Me Thuot, a provincial capital in the Central Highlands. In response, Thieu ordered a strategic retreat of the South Vietnamese army to the more defensible Mekong

River Delta. But once started, the retreat turned into a panic-driven rout. Apparently, South Vietnam's soldiers no longer believed (if they ever had) that they could win the war, and they clearly no longer wanted to be a part of it.

On April 10, 1975, in a last-ditch bid to save the Saigon regime, President Ford requested congressional authorization to send South Vietnam and Cambodia $722 million in emergency military assistance and $250 million in economic and humanitarian aid. Congress rejected the request. On April 30, with Saigon surrounded by communist forces, Thieu resigned. His successor, General Duong Van Minh, almost immediately surrendered, but not before the United States was able to evacuate 150,000 South Vietnamese. The next year, North and South Vietnam were reunited. The Ford administration responded by freezing South Vietnam's assets, refusing to recognize its reunification with North Vietnam, and imposing an embargo on U.S. trade, loans, and travel to Vietnam.

Both Cambodia and Laos also fell to communist forces. In Laos, the communist Pathet Lao came to power August 22, 1975. In Cambodia, the Khmer Rouge captured Phnom Penh on April 16, 1975. The communists then began a systematic massacre of nearly 15 percent of the country's population before they themselves were ousted from power by the Vietnamese army in 1978.

On May 12, only thirteen days after the fall of Saigon, Ford and Kissinger found a way to strike back at the communists, without violating congressional restrictions on the use of force. An American cargo ship, the *Mayaguez,* with its crew of thirty-nine men, was seized by the Khmer Rouge after it had strayed too close to the Cambodian coast. In the wake of the Vietnam debacle, Ford's use of the Marines to free the crew proved to be enormously popular with the American people. However, forty-one U.S. Marines were killed in the operation.

The successful release of the *Mayaguez* 's crew brought only temporary relief from the enormity of the humiliation suffered by the United States in Indochina. Fifty thousand Americans had lost their lives in Indochina, billions of dollars had been spent, and the American people had not been so divided since the Civil War, all in a vain effort to halt the spread of communism in this region of the world. Indeed, Vietnam was the most tragic defeat for the containment strategy since its inception. Needless to say, the Soviet Union, which assisted the North Vietnamese and congratulated them on their victory, received a large portion of the odium for the collapse of South Vietnam. Soviet involvement in South Vietnam's demise would add another nail in détente's coffin.

Angola

Kissinger believed—and it is hard to discount his belief—that Soviet "adventurism" was encouraged by the inability of the United States to save South Vietnam. "From America's failure," he wrote, "Moscow drew the conclusion—which the advocates of the Domino Theory had so feared—that the historical correlation of forces had shifted in its favor. As a result, it tried to expand into Yemen, Angola, Ethiopia, and ultimately Afghanistan."[24]

In Angola, which had just gained its independence from Portugal in 1975, the opportunity for Soviet intervention occurred as a result of a civil war between three rival factions that were contending for control of the country. The Soviets supported the Marxist faction, the Popular Movement for the Liberation of Angola (MPLA). Another party to the conflict, the National Front for the Liberation of Angola (FNLA), was supported initially by the Chinese. The third faction, the National Union for the Total Independence of Angola (UNITA), was supported by South Africa.

Kissinger feared that an MPLA victory in Angola could provide the Soviet Union with a springboard for the expansion of its influence throughout sub-Saharan Africa. Calculating that Congress's memory of U.S. intervention in Indochina would probably deter the United States from direct involvement in Angola, Kissinger developed an indirect approach in an attempt to prevent an MPLA victory. On the one hand, he tried to apply to Angola the leverage of linkage. He told the Soviets that the conclusion of a SALT II agreement, as well as U.S. trade concessions, would be jeopardized by Soviet intervention in Angola. However, in the wake of the Jackson-Vanik Amendment, the Soviet leadership was no longer as eager as it had been for trade with the United States. Moreover, the Soviets realized that Ford wanted a SALT II agreement at least as much as they did to improve his prospects in the 1976 presidential election. Consequently, the Soviets felt they could afford to ignore Kissinger's attempt to link Angola to SALT. In addition, because of the restrictions that the Congress had placed on the executive branch's ability to conduct foreign policy, the Soviets were not intimidated by the prospect of U.S. intervention in Angola.

In the wake of the Vietnam experience, Congress in 1975 also acted to reduce the executive branch's ability to conduct covert actions. Two congressional intelligence committees—the Senate committee was chaired by Frank Church (Dem.–Ida.) and the House committee by Otis Pike (Dem.–N.Y.) examined twenty-five years of covert operations by the Central Intelligence Agency. On the basis of the evidence presented to his committee, Senator Church concluded that the CIA was a "rogue elephant" that not only had tried to operate without congressional oversight but had engaged in illegal domestic surveillance as well.[25] The revelations of the intelligence committees damaged the reputation of the CIA, and limited Kissinger's freedom of action by asserting that Congress had the right to set the boundaries of the nation's foreign policy. Needless to say, all of this only encouraged the Soviets to believe that they would have a free hand in Angola.

Blocked by Congress from playing a direct role in the Angolan conflict, Kissinger tried to enlist the support of China against the Soviets by giving U.S. support to the Chinese-backed FLNA. By this time, however, the Chinese had tired of being played off against the Soviets for the benefit of the United States. During 1973 Mao Zedong had personally led an effort to deepen the new Sino-American relationship to counter the influence of the Soviet Union. In a meeting with Kissinger in November 1973, Mao said that China would normalize relations with the United States whenever Washington wished and that Taiwan would not be an obstacle to improved Sino-American relations. However, for whatever reasons (Kissinger suggested the administration's preoccupation with the Watergate scandal), the United States failed to take up Mao's offer. As a result, Mao's pro-American policy was eclipsed by that of his chief rival, Vice Premier Deng Xiaoping, who criticized Kissinger for dragging his feet on normalizing relations with China while the United States assiduously promoted détente with the Soviet Union.

In early April 1974, Deng set forth a new Chinese foreign policy. It was based on a so-called three-worlds concept. As Deng described it, the United States and the Soviet Union occupied the first world; the developed nations of Europe and Asia represented the second world; and the developing nations of Asia (including China), Africa, and Latin America composed the third world. Deng said that China would follow a policy independent of both superpowers and antagonistic toward neither.

Acting under Deng's influence, the Chinese indicated their desire to reconsider Moscow's earlier offer of a nonaggression pact, contingent on Soviet willingness to make certain concessions on China's border claims and to withdraw substantial numbers of troops from the border area. Rather than challenging the Soviets in Angola by increasing their support for the FLNA, the Chinese gradually withdrew from the conflict. As a result of Deng's policy, China now would attempt to gain concessions from both superpowers, in effect, engaging in its own brand of Kissinger's triangular diplomacy.

To prevent the Chinese from moving closer to Moscow, Kissinger was prepared to offer China unspecified concessions on the Taiwan issue. However, the Chinese, who gave him a decidedly cool reception when he visited Beijing in November 1975, refused to take the bait. Not only did Mao Zedong not receive Kissinger, the secretary of state's meeting with Zhou Enlai, who had entered the hospital for treatment of the illness (cancer) that would take his life in January 1976, was terminated after only half an hour.

Faced with the failure of his gambit to draw Beijing into a proxy conflict with Moscow in Angola, Kissinger injected the United States into the Angolan conflict by giving the FLNA covert support. He hoped that, at the very least, U.S. aid could produce a stalemate in Angola that would prevent the MPLA from dominating the country. But, in a stunning move, the Soviet Union countered Kissinger's effort to help the FLNA by enlisting the support of Cuba, which provided the MPLA with weapons and, eventually, 11,000 combat troops. With Cuban assistance, the forces of the MPLA crushed the FLNA in a major battle outside the capital of Luanda.

Kissinger, in deepening frustration, pleaded with the Congress to match the aid provided by the Soviet Union and Cuba, but the Congress flatly turned him down. Senators Dick Clark (Dem.–Iowa) and John Tunney (Dem.–Calif.) led the opposition to CIA action in West Africa. They attached an amendment to a foreign aid appropriation bill passed by the Senate that effectively banned covert activities in Angola. The House also voted 323 to 29 to stop further covert aid to the rebels in Africa. President Ford responded by accusing the legislative body of "having lost its guts."[26]

Finally, in February 1976, the Organization for African Unity (OAU) placed its official approval on the Soviet-backed MPLA as the official government of Angola. While this did not end the civil war in that country, the establishment of a strong Soviet position in southern Africa represented another stinging defeat for Kissinger's diplomacy, and another blow to Soviet-American détente.

Cuba and Chile

While Nixon and Kissinger were pursuing détente with the Soviet Union and China, both were nevertheless concerned about the possibility of further communist expansion in the Western hemisphere. Of particular concern to Nixon were Cuba and Chile.

In September 1971 the administration learned that the Soviets were constructing a nuclear submarine base in Cienfuegos, Cuba. The administration responded by warning the Soviets that the base violated the understanding reached by Kennedy and Khrushchev, during the Cuban missile crisis in 1962, that the Soviet Union would not deploy nuclear weapons in Cuba. The Soviets assured the Americans that they had no intention of constructing a submarine base in Cuba, and within two weeks, construction slowed down and soon stopped completely.

In Chile, the Nixon administration was concerned about the prospect that socialist Salvador Allende would become the first elected Marxist leader of a hemispheric country. Kissinger remarked: "I don't see why we need to stand by and watch a country go communist due to the irresponsibility of its own people."[27] On September 15, 1970, Nixon ordered the CIA to help organize a military coup d'état in the event that it was not possible to prevent Allende's accession to the presidency. Nixon also cut U.S. aid programs to Chile to, as the president put it, "squeeze" the country's economy until it "screamed."[28]

After Allende assumed the presidency, the so-called Forty Committee, which was made up of the administration's top national security officials, including Kissinger, and was responsible for supervising covert operations within the Nixon administration, authorized over $7 million in covert support to the anti-Allende forces in Chile. The U.S. pressure soon produced the proper conditions for a coup. Chile's economy collapsed, opposition to Allende grew, and in September 1973 the military overthrew Allende (who was murdered) and replaced him with a right-wing dictatorship headed by General Augusto Pinochet.

With the exception of Cuba and Chile, Nixon and Kissinger showed little interest in Latin America. When Nixon did address the indigenous problems of Latin America, he criticized the Alliance for Progress and suggested that it was unwise to attempt to make the Latin American nations mirror images of the United States. At the same time, however, the United States was still not prepared to let Latin American nations emulate the Soviet model, as the overthrow of Allende so obviously demonstrated.

The Helsinki Final Act, 1975

The decline of détente was not an even process. During the summer of 1975, two events served to lessen the negative impact on Soviet-American relations caused by the communist victory in Indochina. The first was the joint U.S.–Soviet *Apollo-Soyuz* space mission. It was not only a significant scientific and technological achievement but also an impressive demonstration of superpower cooperation in a field in which they had competed fiercely.

The second and more important event was the signing of the Helsinki "Final Act" on August 15, 1975. The Helsinki agreement represented the high point of European détente and the culmination of the two-year-old Conference on Security and Cooperation in Europe. The Final Act, which was signed by thirty-five European states (as well as Canada and the United States) consisted of four sections, called "baskets." The first basket included general declarations on such topics as European security and human rights. The second called for increased East-West cooperation in economics, science, technology and the environment. The third basket set forth principles on the international movement of people and ideas, and the fourth basket arranged for follow-up meetings to discuss compliance with, and modifications to, the agreements.

The Final Act seemed to give something of value to both sides. The Soviets gained Western recognition of Europe's existing boundaries (although, under pressure from Kissinger, the Soviets agreed that borders could be modified by peaceful means). The West, in turn, gained a Soviet-bloc promise to respect the free movement of people and ideas across the East-West frontier and to permit greater cultural and educational exchanges between the two sides of the Iron Curtain. The signatories also promised to resolve international disputes by peaceable means and to refrain from interfering in the internal affairs of other signatory states. The Helsinki accord also contained a number of confidence-building measures, such as notification of military maneuvers involving more than 25,000 troops, that were designed to reduce military tensions on the continent. Finally, the Helsinki accord called for periodic reviews to discuss how well the agreements were being implemented.

The Final Act proved to be the closest thing to a peace treaty ending World War II, as well as the Cold War in Europe, that was possible while Germany was still divided. Its critics felt that the West had given the Soviets too much, namely, recognition of the status quo in Eastern Europe, in exchange for too little, that is, promises to respect human rights that almost nobody expected the Soviets to keep. Conservatives were particularly upset by the statement of Helmut Sonnenfeldt, State Department advisor on communist affairs, that it was in the long-term interest of the United States to encourage East European states to develop "a more natural and organic" relationship with the Soviet Union. The so-called Sonnenfeldt Doctrine seemed to indicate that the continuation of communist governments in Eastern Europe was vital to the stability of the continent, and thus opened the Ford administration to the charge that Helsinki was a replay of Franklin Roosevelt's "sellout" at the Yalta conference.

At Helsinki, however, the West gave the Soviets no more than they had already possessed since 1945, that is, control over Eastern Europe. Moreover, while the Soviets and their satellites did not implement the human rights provisions of the Helsinki accord, the fact that they had signed a document recognizing them established another standard by which communism could be judged, and ultimately undermined. Also important, symbolically, was the Eastern bloc's recognition that the United States could not be excluded from the affairs of Europe.

However, as 1975 progressed and the Soviet government continued to arrest dissidents in violation of the Helsinki accord, the critics' accusations gained credibility. Indeed, the human rights issue may have contributed to Ford's defeat in the 1976 election. During his debate with the Democratic presidential candidate, Governor Jimmy Carter of Georgia, Ford awkwardly denied that Eastern Europe was under the domination of the Soviet Union. This weak rationalization of the Helsinki agreement offended large numbers of East European ethnic-Americans and in the opinion of some political observers, eventually cost Ford the presidential election. By that time, détente had become a dirty word.

The Debate over Détente

The events of 1975–1976 intensified the debate over the nature and purpose of détente. Its conservative critics argued that détente was a one-way street, with the Soviet Union giving little in return for the benefits it had received. What caused conservatives the most consternation was their belief that by subsidizing the Soviet economy the administration was helping the Soviet Union augment the size and quality of its military establishment. Ronald Reagan, during his unsuccessful campaign for the 1976 Republican presidential nomination, charged that under Ford "this nation has become Number Two in a world where it is dangerous—if not fatal—to be second."[29]

Liberals, on the other hand, were angered by the administration's ambivalent reaction to the continued violation of human rights in the Soviet bloc. At Kissinger's behest, President Ford refused to receive at the White House Alexander Solzhenitsyn, a prominent Soviet writer and dissident who was expelled from the Soviet Union in 1974 for "anti-Soviet" activities. Kissinger said that Solzhenitsyn's hostility to the Soviet leadership and détente would make "the symbolic effect" of a meeting with the president "disadvantageous" from "a foreign policy aspect."[30] Conservative critics of détente considered the administration's handling of Solzhenitsyn another example of how it was "appeasing" the Soviet Union.

The Soviets, for their part, never intended to abandon their effort to promote revolutionary activity in the Third World, despite Kissinger's hopes that they would in return for the benefits of détente with the West. In the eyes of the Soviets, détente was a necessary accommodation by the West to a "correlation of forces" that the Soviets viewed as increasingly favorable to the communist movement. They were encouraged in this assessment by their ability to achieve nuclear parity with the United States and by the increasing difficulty of the United States in maintaining its position in the Third World, as the communist victories in Indochina and Angola seemed to demonstrate. Needless to say, this new Soviet assertiveness fueled the suspicions of Western critics of détente, who thought that any agreement with the Soviets would be worth little more than the paper on which it was written.

Kissinger rejected the charge that détente was just another form of appeasement. The administration, he asserted, had repeatedly resisted Soviet "adventurism" in Cuba, the Middle East, and Angola. The Soviet intervention in Angola had been successful, Kissinger charged, because Congress had denied the administration both the carrot and the stick by which it expected to restrain Soviet behavior in the Third World. The Jackson-Vanik Amendment had killed the prospect of expanded Soviet American trade. And the Clark and Tunney Amendments had denied the administration the funds to finance covert operations against the Marxist forces in Angola.

Kissinger also discounted the criticism that the benefits of détente were one-sided in favor of the Soviet Union. The United States had gained much from the Cold War thaw, he asserted, including the SALT agreements, a Berlin treaty, and the Soviet Union as a market for U.S. farmers. In his memoir, Kissinger warned against the kind of "simplistic and essentially militaristic" approach to the Soviet Union that conservative critics of détente seemed to favor. "American policy," he insisted, "must embrace both deterrence and coexistence, both containment and an effort to relax tensions."[31]

Nevertheless, by the early spring of 1976 détente lay in shambles. Ford's solution to the problem was to reduce Kissinger's visibility, by stripping him of his position as national security assistant, while retaining the substance of his policies. Kissinger remained secretary of state until Ford left office in January 1977, but he no longer had the authority he once enjoyed. With détente being undermined by both the Soviets and its U.S. critics, Ford found it politically impossible to create the type of understanding with the Soviets he once thought was possible. As a result, the effort to revive détente would fall to Ford's successor, President Jimmy Carter.

7

Carter and the Decline of Détente, 1977–1981

Conflicting Views of the Soviet Union

When Jimmy Carter entered the White House in January 1977, he knew little about foreign affairs. He had been a nuclear engineer, a successful businessman, and governor of Georgia. His only significant experience with international relations came from serving on the Trilateral Commission, an organization committed to redirecting the emphasis of America's foreign policy away from the communist world to Western Europe and Japan. After his election to the presidency in November 1976, Carter gave positions in his administration to many of the commissions's members. Zbigniew Brzezinski, a Polish-born professor of political science and director of the Trilateral Commission, became national security adviser. Cyrus Vance, a Wall Street lawyer when he was not serving in government, was named secretary of state, and Harold Brown was appointed secretary of defense. Both had served on the commission.

Unlike Richard Nixon and Gerald Ford, both of whom relied heavily on Henry Kissinger, Carter did not permit one individual to oversee the nation's foreign policy. Instead, from the beginning, the new president intended to rely on advice from both Vance and Brzezinski, but he, himself, intended to direct the administration's foreign policy. According to Carter's aide, Hamilton Jordan, "Zbig would be the thinker, Cy would be the doer, and Jimmy Carter would be the decider."[1]

While Vance and Brzezinski initially believed that they could work together, and actually did during the administration's first year, their differing philosophies of international relations, and particularly the different

ways they thought about the Soviet Union, inevitably brought them into
conflict. For a president who felt confident directing the nation's diplomacy, such as Franklin Roosevelt, conflicting advisers often served as cata-
lysts for effective decision-making. But for a president as diplomatically
inexperienced as Carter, relying on the conflicting advice of Vance and
Brzezinski often led to confusion and vacillation in the conduct of the
nation's foreign policy. Ultimately, by the end of Carter's presidency the
infighting would produce almost a total transformation of the president's
initial Soviet policy.

Vance believed in a diplomatic approach to the Soviets. Ever the
pragmatist, he believed that the Soviet Union and the United States had
mutual interests, such as arms control, that transcended their ideological
rivalry. While Vance admitted that the Soviet Union was engaged in a policy of "unceasing probing for advantage in furthering its national interest," he believed that, if the United States acted with "patience and
persistence" to check these probes, it would be possible to reach mutually
advantageous agreements with the Soviet Union, particularly in the area
of arms control.[2]

While Vance's views were preeminent early in Carter's presidency,
they were increasingly challenged by those of Brzezinski. The national
security adviser believed that expansion was the primary motive behind
Soviet foreign policy and that U.S. military power, rather than diplomacy,
was the most effective way of checking it. Where Vance looked for areas
of cooperation with the Soviet Union, Brzezinski concentrated on the
competitive aspects of the Soviet-American relationship, particularly in
the Third World, which he considered the key arena of East-West competition. Where Vance emphasized local factors as the causes of Third World
instability, Brzezinski blamed the meddling of the Soviet Union. The primary way to deal with Third World unrest, Brzezinski believed, was to
respond forcefully to Soviet intervention in the developing nations. For
Brzezinski, this response included not only the use of, or the threat of
using, U.S. conventional power but also the linkage of Soviet actions in
the Third World with other issues, particularly economic relations and
SALT.

Vance rejected linkage. He believed that certain issues, such as SALT,
were too important to U.S. interests to be tied to the Third World, or to
other superpower issues. But to Brzezinski, SALT was simply another
means of restricting the expansion of Soviet military power. Vance came
to resent Brzezinski's Cold Warrior approach to the world, and especially
his successful effort to become the administration's foreign policy
spokesperson. When it became clear, in the wake of the Soviet invasion of
Afghanistan in 1979, that Brzezinski's views had become the president's,
Vance resigned.

While Carter eventually adopted Brzezinski's confrontational approach
to the Soviet Union, he did so only very reluctantly, and never completely.
Carter, Brzezinski wrote, wanted to be remembered primarily as a great

peacemaker, with Woodrow Wilson as his model. But Brzezinski cautioned Carter: "You first have to be a Truman before you are a Wilson."[3]

At heart, however, Carter was a devout, born again Baptist, who was more comfortable with the moralistic idealism of Woodrow Wilson than he was the realpolitik of Truman—or Brzezinski. Like Wilson, Carter insisted that America must be a beacon to the world, illuminating and fostering the great ideals of freedom, democracy, and human rights.

Carter believed that those principles had been sacrificed because of the realpolitik practiced by Nixon and Kissinger. In the name of creating an enduring balance of power, they had employed such unsavory tactics as secret diplomacy, back channels, and covert support for repressive, right-wing dictatorships. As a result, in Carter's estimation America's ideals had been tarnished. To refurbish them, he insisted that the promotion of human rights must be the centerpiece of his administration's foreign policy. "We can never be indifferent to the fate of freedom elsewhere," Carter declared in his inaugural address. "Our commitment to human rights must be absolute."[4]

Carter, again like Woodrow Wilson, wanted to create a new international order based on a community of interests rather than on a balance of power. Neither the United States nor the Soviet Union, Carter believed, could control the world's destiny. Rather than trying to compete with the Soviets in trying to run the world, Carter wanted to enlist the support of the Soviet Union in alleviating such global problems as the proliferation of nuclear weapons, ecological pollution, and poverty. Some give Carter credit for being the first—almost a decade before Mikhail Gorbachev assumed power in the Soviet Union—to envision a post–Cold War international environment.

Carter was not naive about the Soviet Union's record of oppression, the nature of its nuclear threat, or its potential for challenging America's global interests. But he believed he could draw the Soviet Union into a more cooperative relationship by downplaying the ideological differences that divided the two countries, and instead concentrating on problems that both powers had a mutual interest in solving, such as the nuclear arms race. Clearly, SALT II would be the centerpiece of Carter's effort to revive Soviet-American détente.

SALT II Stalemate

The Soviets also were eager to get on with SALT. Even before Carter took office, Brezhnev wrote to him recommending an early conclusion of a SALT II treaty. Brezhnev wanted the treaty to be based on the Vladivostok Accord, which he and Ford had signed in November 1974. Once a SALT II Treaty was in place, Brezhnev suggested, then—and only then—could talks on a SALT III treaty incorporating reductions in the numbers of launchers begin, perhaps as early as the fall of 1977, just as the SALT I Interim Agreement would be expiring. During the presidential campaign,

Carter told Brezhnev that, if elected, he would move quickly to negotiate a SALT II treaty based on the Vladivostok Accord, provided the unresolved status of the Soviet Backfire bomber and cruise missiles could be settled, and then move on to deep cuts in SALT III.

However, shortly after Carter's inauguration, Senator Henry Jackson sent the president a memorandum that opposed the Vladivostok Accord. Jackson insisted that deep cuts in the Soviet Union's ICBM and IRBM arsenals must be a part of the SALT II treaty, not SALT III. The limits set by the Vladivostok Accord, Jackson argued, were too high. When Soviet missiles were armed with multiple warheads, by the 1980s, America's Minuteman ICBMs would become vulnerable to a Soviet first-strike. Jackson also felt that the Vladivostok Accord placed too many restrictions on the U.S. cruise missile program and not enough on the Soviet Backfire bomber.

Carter recognized the significance of the Jackson memorandum. "Jackson," Vance explained, "would be a major asset in a future ratification debate if he supported the treaty, and a formidable opponent if he opposed it."[5] Largely because of Jackson's opposition, the Senate confirmed Paul Warnke as the administration's chief SALT negotiator but only by a slim margin. The administration could not help but realize that the favorable vote for Warnke was short of the two-thirds majority required for ratification of a SALT II treaty.

Prompted by his fear of Jackson's ability to block ratification of a SALT II treaty, Carter tried to win the senator over by making Jackson's proposal for deep cuts the administration's initial SALT proposal. But Vance felt that it was a mistake to abandon the Vladivostok framework. He believed it "offered the best prospect for a rapid conclusion of a SALT II treaty."[6] The Soviets, he pointed out, were not prepared to accept deep cuts in their arsenal in SALT II, and consequently he believed they should be left for SALT III. Carter, however, felt that he could overcome Soviet objections to deep cuts by communicating directly with Brezhnev and by cutting the number of B-1 bombers that would initially be built from eight to five and delaying for one year the development of a new ICBM, the MX missile. Brezhnev was not impressed by Carter's concessions and he refused to abandon the Vladivostok Accord.

Prompted by Brezhnev's negative response, Carter decided to compromise. He instructed Vance to offer the Soviets two proposals when he met with Soviet Foreign Minister Andrei Gromyko on March 28, 1977. The first, called the comprehensive plan, was preferred by the president. It included a proposal for deep reductions in the Vladivostok ceilings, from 2,400 to 1,800 launchers and from 1,320 MIRVed ICBMs and SLBMs to between 1,200 and 1,000. The comprehensive plan also called for the number of Soviet heavy missiles to be reduced from the Vladivostok ceiling of 313 to 150. The comprehensive plan also offered to exempt the Soviet Backfire bomber from the strategic weapons limitations if the Soviets agreed to a number of measures that would limit the Backfire's range. The second plan that Vance took with him to Moscow was sometimes called the deferral plan. It was simply the Vladivostok Accord without any references to the Backfire or the cruise missile.

The Soviets were not interested in either U.S. plan. Brezhnev warned that, if the United States persisted in seeking deep cuts in Soviet nuclear forces, especially heavy missiles, the Soviet Union would have the right to demand the removal of U.S. bases in Western Europe and the liquidation of submarines belonging to NATO, medium-range bombers, and other vehicles capable of delivering nuclear weapons to Soviet targets. He also reminded Vance that he had agreed to exclude these systems from SALT in exchange for Kissinger's agreement to leave intact the Soviet heavy ICBM force.

As for the second U.S. option, the deferral plan, Brezhnev was as adamantly negative about it as he had been about a similar proposal from Kissinger that he rejected a year earlier. The Soviet leader wanted the cruise missile to be included in the SALT limitations but not the Backfire bomber, which he insisted again was not a strategic weapon. As a result, SALT was stalemated even before serious negotiations between the Soviets and the new American administration could begin.

The Soviets did agree to a number of other administration arms control proposals. As a result, working groups were set up to study proposals for a comprehensive nuclear test ban, additional limitations on nuclear proliferation, prior notification of missile tests, the demilitarization of the Indian Ocean, curbs on civil defense programs as well as chemical, conventional, radiological, and antisatellite weapons, and limitations on conventional arms transfers to Third World countries.

Nevertheless, the stillbirth of the comprehensive plan was a major disappointment for the Carter administration and the first significant indication that the revival of détente would not be easy. It also produced the first serious split in the Carter administration, with Brzezinski and Vance blaming each other for the negative Soviet reaction, and created the damaging impression that the administration did not know what it was doing.

By the time Vance and Gromyko met again in Geneva on May 18, however, the acrimonious atmosphere produced by the failure of their March meeting had largely dissipated. After three days of talks, Vance announced that they had agreed to a new framework for the negotiations. It consisted of three "tiers," or parts, which combined some of the elements of the Vladivostok Accord with those of the March comprehensive proposal.

The first tier consisted of a treaty lasting until the end of 1985 that would be based on the launcher and MIRV ceilings of the Vladivostok Accord. The second tier included a three-year protocol to the treaty that would place limitations on particular weapon systems (such as cruise missiles and mobile ICBMs), missile modernization, and new types of missiles. The third tier consisted of a joint statement of principles to establish a framework for future negotiations leading to a SALT III agreement.

With the negotiating framework in place, the Soviet and American delegations began work in Geneva on the details of the new package. Numerous difficulties had to be overcome, and two years of difficult and complicated negotiations would take place before a final agreement would be concluded. The delay gave the hard-line opponents of SALT II the time they needed to marshal their resources and public opinion against the treaty.

Human Rights

The hostility of the Soviets to the administration's initial SALT proposals was undoubtedly reinforced by the president's decision to make the promotion of human rights on a global basis a major goal of his administration. In mid-February 1977 Carter assured the prominent Soviet dissident and physicist (and father of the Soviet hydrogen bomb) Andrei Sakharov that the United States would not ignore human rights in the Soviet Union. In March, only days before Vance arrived in Moscow with the administration's deep-cuts proposal for SALT, Carter requested substantial increases in funding for Radio Free Europe and Radio Liberty, and augmented broadcasts to the Soviet Union by the Voice of America.

Carter did not want to incite tension with the Soviet Union, but he preferred to disregard the possibility—indeed, the probability—that Soviet leaders would regard his human rights campaign not only as inconsistent with détente but also threatening to their hold on Eastern Europe, if not the Soviet Union itself. In a letter to Carter in late February, Brezhnev complained about U.S. "interference" in the Soviet Union's internal affairs. The Soviets also reacted by launching an accelerated program of repression. In March 1977 the Soviets arrested six prominent Jewish dissidents, including Alexander Ginzburg, Yuri Orlov, and Anatoly Shcharansky, accusing them of working for the CIA. Nevertheless, Carter, urged on by Sakharov, persisted in his condemnation of Soviet human rights violations. At the Belgrade meetings of the Conference on Security and Cooperation in Europe, which began in November 1977, the United States again accused the Soviet Union and its Eastern European satellites of abusing human rights.

For the rest of Carter's presidency, the human rights issue would aggravate the Soviets and thereby impair the revival of détente. At Carter's only summit meeting with Brezhnev, in Vienna in June 1979, the Soviet leader said to him, "Human rights is a sensitive subject for us and is not a legitimate ground for discussion between you and me." Carter responded: "The subject of human rights is very important to us in shaping our attitude toward your country. You voluntarily signed the Helsinki Accords, which made this issue a proper item of state-to-state relations."[7] Obviously, Carter's human rights policy would make superpower cooperation on other issues more difficult to achieve.

African Crises

Soviet leaders also contributed to the difficulty of reviving détente during the Carter years. Like Carter, they believed that they, too, had a responsibility to advance their ideology on a global basis, particularly in the less developed regions of the world.

In November 1977 the Soviets began to airlift arms and Cuban troops into Ethiopia to aid that country in its attempt to repel an invasion of its Ogaden province by the army of neighboring Somalia. Although drought-stricken and lacking significant natural resources, Ethiopia and Somalia were strategically located on the Horn of Africa, the eastern corner of the continent that flanks the approaches to the oil of the Persian Gulf via the Red Sea. Their strategic location and the fact that the Ethiopians and Somalis were clients respectively of the Soviet Union and the United States created the conditions for yet another Cold War confrontation in the Third World, particularly after the Somalis requested U.S. help to stem the Cuban- and Soviet-supported Ethiopian counteroffensive.

The Somali request widened the split between Brzezinski and Vance. Brzezinski wanted Carter to dispatch an aircraft carrier to the Somali coast as a sign of American determination to check Soviet expansion into the Horn of Africa. He warned the President that a failure to make a forceful response could jeopardize not only Western interests in Africa and southwestern Asia but also the SALT II Treaty, particularly if the Soviet-backed Ethiopian counteroffensive against Somalia coincided with the signing of the treaty. Vance, on the other hand, argued that the African situation should be dealt with in the local context, and not primarily as an aspect of the East-West conflict. In other words, the Ethiopians, albeit with Soviet and Cuban support, were defending their Ogaden province against Somali aggression.

Vance also argued against linking SALT to Soviet actions in Africa. To do so, he said, would be tantamount to "shooting ourselves in the foot" since the United States had as much to gain from strategic arms control as the Soviet Union.[8] Rather than resorting to force, Vance recommended a diplomatic solution to the crisis. He preferred to believe Soviet assurances that their forces would only be used to help the Ethiopians expel the Somali invaders from the Ogaden, not to invade Somalia itself. With Defense Secretary Brown's support, Vance was able to persuade Carter to seek a diplomatic solution to the crisis and not to commit the aircraft carrier. In the end, as Vance predicted, the Ethiopian crisis wound down without the necessity of a U.S. military reaction. On March 14, 1978, the Somalis completed their withdrawal from the Ogaden, and the Soviets and Cubans refrained from invading Somalia, just as they had assured Vance they would do at the beginning of the crisis.

Nevertheless, Brzezinski felt that Carter's decision to reject a show of U.S. power during the crisis was a mistake the president would live to regret. "Had we conveyed our determination sooner," Brzezinski recalled in his memoirs, "perhaps . . . we might have avoided the later chain of events which ended with the Soviet invasion of Afghanistan and the suspension of SALT."[9] However, Brzezinski did not explain how an American aircraft alone would have changed the outcome of the crisis. As subsequent events would demonstrate, though Brzezinski had lost only a battle, he would eventually win the war with Vance for preeminent influence over Carter.

In the wake of the Ethiopian-Somali crisis, the president became increasingly skeptical about the willingness of the Soviet Union to cooperate with the United States in ending the Cold War. As a consequence, he decided to become more active in confronting the Soviets in Africa. On May 27, 1978, in a White House meeting with Soviet Foreign Minister Gromyko, Carter accused the Soviet Union of supporting an incursion into Zaire by Angolan-based exiles from Zaire's Shaba (Katanga) province. Although Gromyko promptly denied Soviet involvement, Carter decided to support the pro-Western government of Colonel Joseph Mobutu in resisting the invasion. He ordered U.S. transport planes to assist in an airdrop of French, Belgian, Moroccan, Senegalese, and other African troops into Zaire. The administration also placed units of the 82nd U.S. Airborne Division on alert, but before it was needed, the Katangan exiles were driven back into Angola.

As a result of the crisis in Zaire, the primary focus of the Carter administration's African policy, which initially had tried to emphasize the promotion of racial justice and majority rule in southern Africa—and, in fact, was particularly successful in doing so in Rhodesia (Zimbabwe)—eventually shifted to containing the influence of the Soviet Union in the continent as a whole.

Latin America

Initially, the Carter administration did not believe that the Soviet Union had much opportunity to expand its influence in the Western Hemisphere. Consequently, it believed that it could make the region a centerpiece of its human rights policy and reverse the traditional U.S. strategy of supporting oppressive, but anticommunist, dictatorships. The military dictatorships of Argentina, Brazil, and Chile, which had notorious human rights records, were singled out for administration pressure, but the pressure was not evenly or consistently applied.

Concerning Argentina, the administration reduced economic assistance, halted the commercial sale of conventional weapons, blocked loans through the Inter-American Development Bank, and held up an Export-Import Bank credit for the purchase of generator turbines. The administration reduced this pressure after the military dictatorship promised a return to civilian government in 1979 (a promise it did not keep).

U.S. relations with Brazil remained strained throughout the Carter administration, in spite of the president's decision to praise any positive human rights actions by the military dictatorship, rather than harp on its violations. Nevertheless, Brazil would refrain from joining the U.S.-initiated grain embargo against the Soviet Union in the aftermath of the 1979 Soviet invasion of Afghanistan.

In the case of Chile, the administration did not even attempt to improve relations with the military regime of General Augusto Pinochet, whom Carter had condemned for overthrowing the duly elected Salvador Allende in 1973. If anything, U.S.–Chilean relations went from bad to worse when Chile refused to deliver for trial in the United States three Chileans accused of the murder in Washington of Orlando Letelier, an opponent of the Pinochet regime living in exile.

In addition to promoting human rights, the Carter administration attempted to repair Latin America's image of the United States by resolving the long-festering dispute over the Panama Canal. On September 7, 1977, Panama and the United States signed two treaties designed to achieve that objective. The first treaty provided for the transfer of sovereignty over the canal to Panama on December 31, 1999. It stipulated that, until then, the canal would be operated jointly by Panama and the United States. It required the United States to give Panama payments of $10 million per year, plus as much as an additional $10 million from surplus operating revenues. The second treaty granted the United States an indefinite right to defend the neutrality of the canal but, to meet the demand of the Panamanians, stipulated that that right applied only against external threats.

On April 18, 1978, the first Panama Canal Treaty was approved by the Senate 68 to 32, just a single vote more than necessary. But the administration's Panamanian triumph proved to be a Pyrrhic victory. In winning support for the treaties, the administration expended the scarce political capital that it would need when it came time to ratify a SALT II treaty. Ronald Reagan, Carter's most likely challenger in 1980, accused the administration and its supporters in the Congress (both Republicans and Democrats) of acting like Santa Claus in "giving away" the canal. As a consequence, many Republican senators who had voted for the Panama treaties believed they could not afford to support the SALT II Treaty and still remain aligned with their party.

In addition to resolving the Panama dispute, the Carter administration tried to improve U.S. relations with Castro's Cuba. In March 1977, after Carter removed restrictions on Americans traveling to Cuba, the two countries began discussions on the location of their common maritime boundary. In April, they signed a fisheries' agreement. The following month, they agreed to open "interest sections" in third-country embassies in each capital.

But the effort to improve U.S. relations with Cuba was short-lived. In November 1977 Brzezinski claimed that the Cubans had dramatically built up their forces in Angola, before they actually had done so. Nevertheless, Brzezinski's attack was instrumental in persuading the Cubans that they had nothing to lose, in the way of better relations with the United States, by sending additional Cuban troops to Africa.

The Failure of U.S.–Vietnamese Rapprochement

Cuba was not the only communist country with which the Carter administration failed to normalize U.S. relations. Another was Vietnam. The administration had hoped that the establishment of normal diplomatic relations with Hanoi would not only help to heal the wounds of an unfortunate war but also keep Vietnam out of the Soviet camp. To this end, the administration eased travel restrictions to Vietnam and, while it maintained the trade embargo with Vietnam, it permitted the transfer of $5 million in private humanitarian assistance to the Vietnamese. In addition, the United States dropped its veto of Vietnam's admission to the United Nations and supported the opening of talks between the Vietnamese and officials of the International Monetary Fund and the World Bank in December 1976 and January 1977.

Hanoi reciprocated by permitting a delegation of Americans, headed by Leonard Woodcock, former head of the United Auto Workers, to visit Vietnam to investigate the whereabouts of Americans missing in action during the war. The Woodcock commission secured the return of the bodies of eleven Americans killed in the war but concluded that there were no remaining U.S. prisoners of war in Vietnam. The commission also reported that the Vietnamese government was ready to move quickly toward normalizing its relationship with the United States.

Normalization talks began in Paris in May 1977, but they were quickly stymied by a Vietnamese effort to obtain $3.25 billion in U.S. economic assistance that had been promised secretly, but ambiguously, by President Nixon in 1973. (On May 19, 1977, the Vietnamese released the text of Nixon's secret letter to Premier Pham Van Dong, dated February 1, 1973, in which the president had promised aid "without any preconditions."[10]) The Carter administration maintained that, even if Nixon's promise had been made, any obligation to implement it had been nullified by the North Vietnamese conquest of South Vietnam. Moreover, the Vietnamese demand for U.S. reparations triggered an explosion of anger in Congress. By a vote of 266 to 131 the House of Representatives voted to forbid the State Department to negotiate "reparations, aid, or any other form of payment" to Vietnam.[11]

By 1978 Hanoi was ready to drop its demand for reparations, but by then the effort to normalize U.S.–Vietnamese relations was eclipsed by the outbreak of a conflict between Vietnam and Cambodia, which soon escalated into another superpower confrontation. The war began because of a Vietnamese incursion into Cambodian territory in April 1977, followed by another Vietnamese attack in December of that year. The Vietnamese aggression was triggered by an unresolved border dispute between the two countries. Eager to block the establishment of Vietnamese hegemony over Indochina, China reacted by providing diplomatic support to Cambodia. In response, Vietnam turned to the Soviets, who were more than willing to help the Vietnamese generate pressure on China's southern periphery. Accordingly, the Soviets agreed to provide the Vietnamese with badly needed economic assistance.

Had the standards of human rights alone prevailed, the United States should have supported Vietnam; the Cambodian Khmer Rouge under Pol Pot had murdered 1 million of its own people. However, Brzezinski was able to persuade Carter that the maintenance of a balance of power between China and the Soviet Union required the United States to ignore Pol Pot's massacre of the Cambodian people and side with his government against the Vietnamese. In addition, Brzezinski was successful in persuading Carter to play the "China card" by taking the final step towards normalizing Sino-American relations.

The Sino-American Entente

By the spring of 1978, the Chinese were more than willing to normalize relations with the United States. They were eager to enlist U.S. power as a counterweight to the Soviet Union's growing influence in Southeast Asia. By the end of that year, Deng Xiaoping, the ardent opponent of Soviet-American détente, had emerged triumphant from the power struggle that ensued in the wake of Mao Zedong's death (in 1976). Deng had charged that U.S. trade and technological assistance to the Soviet Union was tantamount to "feeding chocolates to the Polar Bear."[12] Instead of promoting détente with the Soviet Union, Deng wanted the United States to enter a collaborative relationship with China designed to block the establishment of Soviet "hegemony" in East Asia.

While Deng was eager to improve relations with the United States, he was insistent that the United States must first withdraw diplomatic recognition from Taiwan, terminate the U.S.–Taiwanese mutual defense treaty, and remove all U.S. troops from that island. While Vance felt no emotional commitment to Taiwan, he feared that too swift a rapprochement with Beijing would aggravate Moscow and jeopardize SALT. Brzezinski, not surprisingly, was more than happy to agitate Moscow. He believed that a closer Sino-American relationship would not only make the Soviets behave better in Africa, Asia, and elsewhere but would also ensure that SALT II would be concluded on terms favorable to the United States. As a consequence, Brzezinski insisted that America's ties to Taiwan should not be permitted to block a U.S. move toward China, which he believed was vital to the maintenance of the global balance of power.

Brzezinski's views, again, were accepted by the president. Over the objections of Vance, who believed that the national security adviser should not play a diplomatic role, Carter dispatched Brzezinski to Beijing in May 1978. Vance feared that Brzezinski's trip would raise doubts as to who spoke for the United States and also aggravate Soviet-American relations at a time when they were particularly strained as a result of increased Soviet military pressure on China's northern frontier. On May 9, just two weeks before Brzezinski was to arrive in Beijing, the Soviets precipitated the largest military clash on the Sino-Soviet border since 1969 by conducting a brief military intrusion across the Ussuri River. A few days later,

Moscow declared that a "mistake" had been made but offered no apology to the Chinese.[13]

Brzezinski, not surprisingly, was exhilarated by his talks with the Chinese leadership. "We have been allies before," he told Chinese Foreign Minister Huang Hua. "We should cooperate again in the face of a common threat, . . . the emergence of the Soviet Union as a global power."[14] Spurred by Brzezinski's visit, the Chinese and Americans worked out a compromise on the Taiwan issue during the summer and fall of 1978. The United States reaffirmed its adherence to the 1972 Shanghai Communiqué, the essence of which was that there was but one China that included Taiwan. In addition, the United States agreed to recognize the Peoples' Republic as the sole government of China. The United States also agreed to terminate its diplomatic relations with Taiwan as well as their mutual defense treaty (one year after notifying the Taiwanese).

While the Carter administration agreed to withdraw the last U.S. troops and all U.S. officials from Taiwan, the Chinese were informed that the United States would continue to sell Taiwan defensive military weapons and would maintain trade and cultural relations with the Taiwanese. The Chinese promised not to contradict the stated U.S. expectation that the ultimate status of Taiwan would be resolved by peaceful means, yet they refused to give an explicit and formal pledge to refrain from using force against Taiwan. Finally, the United States and China agreed to announce, simultaneously on December 15, 1978, that normalization of their relations would begin on January 1, 1979.

Needless to say, the Soviets were not pleased by the Sino-American announcement. During a September 1977 meeting with Carter, Soviet Foreign Minister Gromyko had warned the United States not to engage in the "dirty game" of playing the China card against the Soviet Union.[15] The Soviets were even more upset when Deng accepted the administration's invitation to visit the United States, where he repeatedly castigated the Soviet Union and called for a Sino-American partnership to check Soviet "hegemonism." While the Carter administration was unwilling to conclude an alliance with China, the joint communiqué issued at the end of Deng's meetings with the president stated that the two leaders were united in opposition to "efforts by any country or group of countries to establish hegemony or domination over others"[16]

To show their displeasure with the emerging Sino-American entente, the Soviets stalled SALT. It would be another six months before a SALT II treaty was completed. In addition, the Soviets increased their pressure on China. On November 3, 1978, the Soviet Union signed a friendship treaty with Vietnam. Apparently shielded by their new alliance with the Soviet Union, the Vietnamese launched an all-out invasion of Cambodia on December 25, 1978. Within a month, they occupied most of the country, including Phnom Phen, where they established a puppet government headed by the Cambodian, Heng Samrin.

Vietnam's invasion of Cambodia further aggravated Sino-Vietnamese relations, which were already inflamed by Vietnam's deportation of several hundred thousand ethnic Chinese from Vietnam's cities to so-called new economic zones in the countryside. During Deng Xiaoping's visit to the United States in January 1979, he told Carter that China would punish Vietnam's "aggression" against Cambodia. On February 17, 1979, with the tacit blessing of the Carter administration, China launched an invasion of Vietnam. In sixteen days of fighting, the Chinese army advanced twenty-five miles into Vietnam and then withdrew, publicly expressing satisfaction that China had taught the Vietnamese a lesson.

While the State Department expressed its opposition to both the Vietnamese invasion of Cambodia and the Chinese intrusion into Vietnam, Brzezinski could not conceal his glee over China's action. The Chinese invasion, he said, had demonstrated to the Vietnamese "the limits of their reliance on the Soviets." Not surprisingly, the administration's tacit support for China sidetracked indefinitely its effort to normalize U.S. relations with Vietnam. As Brzezinski proudly bragged, "I shot it down."[17] A normalization effort would not be made again until another Democrat, William Jefferson Clinton, sat in the White House, a decade and a half later.

South Korea

The revival of the Cold War in East Asia was also responsible for the transformation of the Carter administration's policy toward South Korea. Initially, Carter had considered South Korea a worthy target for his human rights policy. During the 1976 presidential election campaign, he had called the government of South Korean President Park Chung Hee a perfect example of a morally repugnant regime that was propped up by U.S. armed forces. On January 26, 1977, in his first press conference after he entered the White House, Carter announced that he would withdraw the 37,000 U.S. ground troops stationed in Korea.

The president's announcement raised a storm of protest in South Korea as well as Japan. It also incited foreign policy hard-liners and senior military officials in the United States, who believed the pullout might encourage North Korea to launch a second invasion of South Korea. Reflecting this view, Major General John Singlaub, chief of staff of U. S. forces in Korea, said publicly that U.S. withdrawal would lead to war. Carter responded by reprimanding Singlaub and recalling him. Defending his military withdrawal plan, Carter argued that a strong South Korea had made another Korean War unlikely.

By 1979, however, the president had changed his mind. Hoping to win Senate approval of the SALT II Treaty, Carter decided he could no longer afford to risk alienating potential Republican supporters by withdrawing U.S. troops from South Korea, and announced his decision on July 20, 1979. He also chose to deemphasize his personal disgust with

South Korea's continued violation of human rights. When Park's successor, Chun Doo Hwan, put the country under martial law in 1980 and used murderous military force to suppress rioting students, the United States issued only the mildest expression of concern. South Korea had become another example of realism triumphing over Carter's idealism.

The Middle East

The Middle East also remained an important theater of the Cold War during the Carter years, despite the president's initial desire to make the region one in which the Soviet Union and the United States could cooperate. Unlike his predecessors, Carter was willing to proceed from the assumption that the unresolved Palestinian issue was at the heart of the Middle East problem. He was the first president to admit publicly that any lasting settlement of the Arab-Israeli conflict would have to recognize the right of the Palestinian people to a homeland of their own.

Accordingly, the Carter administration decided to shift from the limited goals of Kissinger's shuttle diplomacy, in which the United States had negotiated only with Egypt, Syria, and Israel, to a comprehensive approach that would include not only the major parties to the Arab-Israeli conflict, including representatives of the PLO (who would be a part of a single Arab delegation) but also the Soviet Union, which Kissinger had succeeded in excluding from his talks. Both Carter and Vance believed that the Soviet Union must have a role in the negotiations, if only to diminish its inclination to undermine a comprehensive settlement. They also hoped that Soviet participation in a Middle East settlement would stimulate progress in SALT as well. On October 1, 1977, Vance and Gromyko issued a joint U. S.–Soviet statement proposing guidelines and a procedure for Arab-Israeli negotiation of a comprehensive settlement. The talks were scheduled to begin in Geneva no later than December 1, 1977.

Unfortunately, Israel was unwilling to support the comprehensive peace approach. The Israeli parliamentary election of May 1977 brought to power a new government, headed by Menachem Begin, the leader of the Likkud Party, that had no intention of recognizing either a Palestinian homeland or the PLO as the representatives of the Palestinians. Both the Likkud government and the American Jewish community reacted with hostility to the prospect of Soviet participation in the Middle East peace process. The new Israeli government, however, was not about to turn down a peace initiative pushed so strongly by the United States, Israel's only protector. Consequently, on September 19 Israeli Foreign Minister Moshe Dayan agreed to participate in a Geneva conference, subject to certain conditions designed to preserve the Israeli position.

Instead of rejecting the comprehensive approach openly, the Israelis undermined it clandestinely. Before the Geneva conference could begin, the Israelis offered Egypt a separate peace, one that would leave the other Arab parties, and especially the PLO, out in the cold. Unknown to the

Carter administration, in November 1977 Israel offered to return to Egypt the Sinai Peninsula territory that it still held in exchange for Egyptian recognition of Israel and acceptance of a peace treaty. Realizing that Israeli intransigence on the Palestinian problem would block its resolution at Geneva, and eager to secure the return of the Sinai as well as U.S. economic backing, Sadat decided to accept the Israeli conditions. In November 1977 he flew to Jerusalem to sign a peace treaty with his former enemy.

Sadat's decision to make peace with Israel won the enthusiastic endorsement of President Carter, but it also drove the other Arab states into opposition, and thereby killed the possibility of a comprehensive Middle East peace settlement. The Soviets also were angry. They suspected that the demise of the comprehensive approach was, if not instigated by the United States, then at least facilitated by the strong support it received from the Carter administration. On November 29, 1977, Gromyko publicly attacked the Sadat visit. He also informed the United States that the Soviet Union would not participate in a Cairo conference to which Sadat had invited the Soviets and other Arab parties, who also declined to participate. As a result, when the Mid-East peace talks began, they involved only Egypt, Israel, and the United States.

The Israeli-Egyptian talks culminated in a summit meeting at Camp David in September 1978 and a final peace treaty that was signed in March 1979. However, while the peace process ended the state of war between Egypt and Israel, it did not solve the problems created by the continued Israeli occupation of the Golan Heights and East Jerusalem as well as the Israeli refusal to recognize the Palestinian right to a homeland of their own.

Although the Camp David accord provided for the granting of "autonomy" to the Palestinians by Israel, in practice this meant nothing. Israeli Prime Minister Begin held steadfastly to a definition of Palestinian autonomy limited largely to municipal affairs. Under no circumstances, he said, would he permit Palestinian self-determination. Indeed, the Begin government refused to even deal with the PLO, the only organization capable of governing an autonomous Palestinian political entity. Moreover, in the aftermath of the peace treaty, the Begin government pushed ahead with additional Jewish settlements on the West Bank, thereby reinforcing with deeds its declaration that it would never allow a Palestinian state to arise.

Carter's support for the Egyptian-Israeli peace negotiations not only helped scuttle the comprehensive approach to the Arab-Israeli conflict, it also represented a return to the Middle Eastern containment policy pursued by the Nixon and Ford administrations. Its chief features called for denying the Soviets any role in the peace process, ignoring the PLO (Brzezinski characterized the new U.S. policy as "bye-bye PLO"), and putting no meaningful pressure on Israel to be more flexible on the Palestinian issue.

The new Carter policy in the Middle East also represented a return to Kissinger's goal of building a bloc of pro-Western states in the region by various means, including arms sales and economic aid. This bloc would emphasize Egypt and Israel, but also include Saudi Arabia and Iran. In fiscal year 1978, Iran, Israel, and Saudi Arabia alone received nearly three-quarters of all U.S. arms shipments to the entire Third World. The fact that, for the first time, a U.S. administration was willing to sell arms to Arab regimes, equal in quantity and sophistication to those it sold to Israel, shocked both Israelis and American Jews, but the new policy paid dividends for the United States. A major byproduct of the U.S. rapprochement with the moderate Arab states was Sadat's promise to defend the oil-rich states of the Persian Gulf region, a service that was beyond Israel's capacity to perform.

Needless to say, the exclusion of the Soviet Union from the Middle East peace process did nothing to promote détente between the superpowers. In fact, after détente completely collapsed, in the wake of the Soviet occupation of Afghanistan in late 1979, the Soviets pointed to the change in America's Middle East policy as a major factor prompting them to pursue their own interests in the region without regard for the concerns of the United States.

SALT II and the Vienna Summit

Not surprisingly, the continuing decline of détente in 1978 adversely affected the pace of the SALT II negotiations, and ultimately undermined the Carter administration's ability to gain ratification of a treaty after it was signed during the following year. The announcement, in December 1978, that Sino-American relations would be normalized, the Chinese invasion of Vietnam that month with only the mildest of American protests, and Deng's visit to Washington in January 1979, left the Soviet leaders in no mood to make compromises on SALT. On the U.S. side, the overthrow of the shah of Iran in January 1979 deprived the United States of intelligence-gathering stations in that country that were an important way of verifying Soviet compliance with the SALT II Treaty. This was a development opponents of the treaty were quick to exploit in their effort to scuttle it.

Thus, it was not until March 1979 that the ice in Soviet-American relations finally thawed enough to permit a breakthrough in SALT, which culminated in the announcement that a Carter-Brezhnev summit meeting would be held in Vienna in early June to sign SALT II.

Shortly before the Vienna summit, on June 8, 1979, Carter announced a major defense decision that he hoped would gain Republican support for the SALT II Treaty. He approved the production and deployment of 200 mobile MX ICBMs. In so doing, the president reversed his earlier (December 1977) decision rejecting full-scale production of the missile. Privately, Carter admitted that the decision to deploy the MX sickened him. "It was a nauseating prospect, with the gross waste of money going into nuclear weapons of all kinds," he confided to his diary.[18] But without the missile, he believed, there would be little chance of persuading the Senate to approve the SALT II Treaty.

At long last, in a glittering ceremony in Vienna's Hofburg Palace on June 18, 1979, Carter and Brezhnev signed the SALT II agreements. SALT II placed both qualitative and quantitative restrictions on strategic nuclear weapons. The principal quantitative restrictions called for an equal aggregate ceiling of 2,400 launchers for strategic nuclear delivery vehicles, including ICBMs, SLBMs, heavy bombers, and air-to-surface ballistic missiles with a range in excess of 600 kilometers (this ceiling would be lowered to 2,250 by January 1, 1981). The agreement also established sublimits of 1,320 for MIRVed ICBMs and aircraft armed with cruise missiles whose range is greater than 600 kilometers, 1,200 for MIRVed ICBMs and SLBMs, and 820 for MIRVed ICBMs alone. Among the qualitative restrictions was a ban (until December 1981) on the deployment of mobile launchers, ground- and sea-launched cruise missiles with ranges greater than 600 kilometers, and the flight-testing and deployment of air-launched cruise missiles. The treaty also limited the substitution of more technologically advanced missiles for less advanced missiles and prohibited the conversion of "light" ICBM launchers into "heavy" ICBM launchers.

The SALT II agreement also contained a number of provisions dealing with verification. Article 2 of the treaty, for example, contained definitions for ICBMs, SLBMs, and heavy bombers and described the characteristics of strategic cruise missiles and MIRVs. It also defined heavy and light missiles with reference to specific systems on both sides—a first for SALT.

At the Vienna summit Carter and Brezhnev discussed a prospective SALT III agenda. They agreed that both sides should halt production of nuclear weapons and reduce existing stockpiles, but Brezhnev insisted that other countries, particularly China and America's NATO allies, also must be involved in the negotiations. The Soviet leader also insisted that U.S. forward-based systems (primarily fighter-bombers stationed in Western Europe and on aircraft carriers plying the waters near the Soviet Union) be included in the next round of the talks. He disappointed Carter by stating that all strategic factors must be considered before further reductions were made and, for that reason, he felt that the 5 percent annual reductions proposed by Carter would not be advisable.

Returning to Washington on June 18, Carter gave a spirited defense of the treaty before a joint session of Congress. He tried to placate liberals, who argued that SALT II did not do enough to end the nuclear arms race, by arguing that the agreements would make the competition "safer and more predictable, with clear rules and verifiable limits, where otherwise there would be no rules and no limits." He attempted to satisfy conservatives by emphasizing that for the first time a SALT agreement had placed "equal ceilings on the strategic arsenals of both sides, ending a previous numerical imbalance in favor of the Soviet Union." He also tried to assure conservatives that America had the means to verify Soviet compliance: "Were the Soviet Union to take the enormous risk of trying to violate this treaty . . . ," the president promised, "there is no doubt that we would discover it in time to respond fully and effectively."[19]

In the end, however, Carter was unable to translate the successful negotiation of SALT II into a ratified treaty. As with earlier arms control efforts, SALT II was overwhelmed by external events. In early July 1979, U.S. intelligence officials began to leak information that they had detected a brigade of Soviet combat troops in Cuba. The Soviets responded to the congressional furor over the news by insisting that the only Soviet soldiers in Cuba were there to train Cuban troops—a function the Soviets had performed for seventeen years. By pledging to keep Cuba under close surveillance, establish a full-time Caribbean military task force, and increase economic aid to friendly nations, Carter finally succeeded in defusing the incident.

The administration also felt compelled to increase military expenditures to gain support for the treaty. On November 9, the Senate Foreign Relations Committee approved the agreement by a vote of 9 to 6, ominously still less than the two-thirds that would be needed for final passage by the full Senate. It is also quite likely that the Soviet leadership concluded that there was little chance that the treaty would be approved by the Senate. Without the SALT II Treaty, and considering that other détente-related issues were going nowhere, the Soviets had little remaining incentive to keep détente alive. Their invasion of Afghanistan began only a month later.

Nicaragua

The new Latin American economic assistance program that Carter announced in October, in response to the Cuban brigade incident, came too late to save the Nicaraguan dictatorship of Anastasio Somoza. The Somoza government was overthrown in July 1979 by a primarily Marxist movement that styled itself the Sandinista Front for National Liberation (FSLN). Before its overthrow, the Carter administration had pressured the Somoza regime to improve its human rights record and initiate reforms. In June 1979, when Somoza's collapse appeared imminent, the administration even tried to persuade the Organization of American States to intervene in Nicaragua to prevent the inevitable Sandinista victory. But the OAS, for the first time in its history, refused to comply with a U.S. request for hemispheric intervention. As a result, Somoza was forced to flee the country the following month.

Compelled to make the best of a bad outcome, and to prevent Nicaragua from becoming another Cuba, the administration belatedly attempted to befriend the Sandinistas. During the latter part of 1979, the administration approved $262 million in World Bank and Inter-American Development Bank loans to Nicaragua. It also offered the new government an economic aid package worth $75 million. But by the time the Congress approved the aid program, in June 1980, a number of developments in Nicaragua—the Sandinista government's decision to postpone free elections until 1985, its signature on a trade agreement with Moscow, and the resignation from the government of moderate members like Violeta Chamorro and Alfonso Robelo—had convinced many in the United States that Nicaragua was indeed going the way of Cuba.

U.S.–Nicaragua relations approached the breaking point in 1980 after the Sandinistas began assisting revolutionaries in El Salvador who were attempting to overthrow that country's military government. The Carter administration responded by funneling as much as $1 million in covert funds to anti-Sandinista "Contra" forces in Nicaragua. Shortly before he left office in January 1981, Carter was considering the termination of all U.S. aid to Nicaragua. However, he left that decision to his successor, Ronald Reagan, who would not only stop U.S. aid to Nicaragua but also make the overthrow of the Sandinista government his own personal obsession.

Long-Range Tactical Nuclear Weapons

Even though the Soviets and the Americans agreed on limiting strategic nuclear weapons, another category of nuclear weapons, the long-range tactical nuclear weapons force (LRTNF), that is nuclear-armed aircraft and missiles with a range of between 3,000 and 5,500 miles, proved difficult to control. Included in this category were the Pershing 2 ballistic missile and the Tomahawk ground-launched cruise missile (GLCM). The NATO allies wanted to deploy these missiles because they feared that, with the codification of superpower nuclear parity in the SALT II Treaty, the United States would be reluctant to threaten nuclear retaliation against the Soviet Union in the event of Soviet military action directed solely against Western Europe.

The West European allies also wanted the new U.S. missiles to counter deployment of new Soviet SS-20s, land-mobile missiles that were armed with three warheads each. NATO had nothing comparable to the Soviet SS-20, and, after Carter in April 1978 refused to deploy in Europe U.S.-made enhanced radiation weapons (ERWs, popularly called "neutron bombs," which were designed to kill enemy troops primarily with intensive neutron radiation rather than explosive blast, thereby producing minimal damage to surrounding structures), the alliance's capacity to threaten nuclear retaliation with any intermediate-range nuclear weapons was considered inadequate.

Obviously, the Soviets were not pleased with the prospect of additional U.S. nuclear weapons pointed at them, particularly because the SS-20s were not targeted on the U.S. homeland, while the U.S. LRTNFs deployed in Western Europe could hit targets on Soviet territory. In October 1979 Brezhnev threatened to target Soviet SS-20s on West European nations that agreed to deploy the new U.S. missiles, but he added a proposal to negotiate the missile issue, provided that NATO refrained from deploying the U.S. missiles.

Both the Soviet warning and negotiation offer were ignored by the West. On December 12, 1979, NATO decided to deploy 572 Pershing 2 and Tomahawk cruise missiles in Western Europe. However, in what would be called a "double-track" approach, NATO offered to start negotiations immediately with the Soviet Union on limiting theater nuclear systems, but only after NATO had built enough LRTNFs to match those of the Soviet Union. The Soviet leaders reacted angrily to the NATO deployment decision, and they refused to negotiate the LRTNF issue until the decision was reversed. Thus, by late 1979, only six months after the Vienna summit, the prospects for détente again looked dim.

Iran

Détente was dealt a much harsher blow as a result of two crises that erupted in the Middle East, one in Iran, the other in Afghanistan. The crisis in Iran was triggered by the overthrow of Shah Mohammed Reza Pahlavi (whom the CIA helped restore to the throne in 1953) in January 1979, by forces loyal to the Shi'ite religious leader Ayatola Ruholla Khomeini. A number of factors were responsible for the shah's downfall. They included the opposition of Islamic fundamentalists to his effort to modernize the country, his ruthless oppression of the opposition, and his close ties to the United States.

Over the years, one U.S. administration after another had considered the shah's Iran a vital bulwark against Soviet expansion toward the Persian Gulf. Iran was also a major source of oil, not only for the West but for Israel (Iran did not participate in the Arab embargo oil). Because of the service rendered to the West by Iran, the United States provided the shah's regime with billions of dollars worth of sophisticated weaponry. In the process, Iran's military establishment became one of the most powerful in the region.

For these reasons, and in spite of the shah's horrible human rights record, Carter, like his predecessors, embraced the Iranian monarch. In a visit to Tehran at the end of 1977, Carter proclaimed that "Iran under the great leadership of the shah" was "an island of stability in one of the more troubled areas of the world."[20] Carter approved nearly all the shah's requests for advanced aircraft, tanks, and other weapons, as well as nuclear power plants. In early September 1978, just after hundreds of rebelling Iranians had been shot by the shah's U.S.-equipped soldiers, Carter took time out from his Camp David summit meetings with Sadat and Begin to telephone his support to the Iranian ruler. The call did not prevent the shah from fleeing the country, on January 16, 1979, never to return. Three weeks later, on February 9, Khomeini assumed leadership of the country.

Relations between the Carter administration and the new regime were strained, but they reached the crisis stage on November 4, 1979, when sixty-three Americans on the staff of the U.S. embassy in Tehran were taken hostage by Iranian militants. In exchange for releasing the hostages, the militants demanded that the Carter administration return the shah, who had been admitted to the United States for treatment of cancer, which would eventually kill him (in July 1980). Because Carter refused to hand over the shah, the U.S. embassy personnel were held hostage until the very end of his presidency. Carter's defeat by Ronald Reagan in the presidential election of 1980 was in no small part due to the failure of a military expedition sent by the president to free the hostages in April 1980. The rescue attempt, which was urged by Brzezinski, was opposed by Vance, who resigned in protest and was replaced by Senator Edmund Muskie (Dem.–Me.)

The replacement of America's strongest ally in the Persian Gulf region with a hostile Islamic republic constituted one of the greatest foreign policy setbacks for the United States during the entire Cold War. Carter's "loss" of Iran was comparable to Truman's "loss" of China and Johnson's inability to win the Vietnam War, both of which seriously damaged both presidents. With Iran no longer an "island of stability," the Carter administration, and Zbigniew Brzezinski in particular, feared that the Soviets might try to fill the vacuum left by the disappearance of a friendly Iran. The Soviet invasion of Afghanistan on December 27, 1979, only six weeks after the U.S. embassy was seized in Tehran, seemed to confirm that fear.

Afghanistan

The Soviet invasion of Afghanistan, rather than being an offensive thrust to the Persian Gulf, was prompted primarily by the defensive mindset of the Kremlin leadership. The Soviets wanted to preserve the Marxist regime that had come to power in Afghanistan as the result of a bloody coup in April 1978. The coup had triggered a primarily Islamic resistance movement, the Mujahedeen, which caused the Soviets to fear that the unrest in Afghanistan could spread to Muslim areas within the Soviet Union itself. The Soviets claimed their invasion had been in response to an invitation by Afghan President Babrak Karmal, whom the Soviets had installed only one day before the invasion began. The Soviets said that the Afghan-Soviet Friendship Treaty of 1978 obliged them to protect the country from its external enemies, meaning the United States, China, and Pakistan.

Despite Brzezinski's warning that the Soviets might invade Afghanistan, the invasion nevertheless shocked President Carter. Feeling betrayed, he said the invasion of Afghanistan taught him more about the nature of the Soviet government than anything he had known of them before.

Overreacting, he called the Soviet action "the greatest threat to peace since the Second World War."[21] Seemingly paralyzed by his inability to free the Iranian hostages, pummeled by conservative criticism of both his foreign and domestic policies, and facing a difficult reelection campaign the following year, Carter was more receptive than ever to Brzezinski's hard-line reasoning. If the United States did not react vigorously, the national security adviser warned, the Soviet Union would be able to drive on to the Persian Gulf and take control of the vital oil resources of the region. For Brzezinski, the Soviet invasion of Afghanistan was a direct consequence of the administration's refusal to react forcefully to their intervention in Ethiopia two years earlier.

Carter responded by abruptly scrapping détente and restoring the old containment policy. He sharply cut back the sale of high technology (primarily computers and other electronic devices) to the Soviets, placed an embargo on U.S. grain sales to the Soviet Union, and announced the withdrawal of the United States from the forthcoming Moscow Olympic games. He also asked the Senate to postpone indefinitely its consideration of the SALT II Treaty, a move that effectively killed any chance of ratifying the agreement.

In a throwback to the Truman and Eisenhower Doctrines, the president promulgated the Carter Doctrine. In his January 23, 1980, State of the Union address, Carter promised that the United States would defend the Persian Gulf region. He announced that his administration would build a military force capable of rapid deployment to the Persian Gulf. He also proposed that all men between the ages of eighteen and twenty-six be required to register for a future draft, a program President Nixon had terminated in 1973 when the United States switched to a volunteer army. Carter also asked for annual increases of 5 percent in real military spending, rather than the 3 percent that had been his goal since 1977.

To shore up the barrier to Soviet expansionism in Central Asia, Carter gave in to Brzezinski's pressure to play the China card more vigorously by approving an expansion of the U.S.–Chinese defense relationship. As a result, the Chinese were permitted to purchase the kind of military hardware and high technology now denied the Soviets. In addition, China was granted most-favored-nation trade status, a privilege denied the Soviet Union.

In addition to deepening the Sino-American relationship, Carter attempted to restore amicable relations with Pakistan, which had been frayed by the human rights violations of the government of Mohammed Zia ul-Haq. Zia came to power in 1978, when a military coup overthrew the democratically elected government of Zulfikar Ali Bhutto. Ignoring international pleas for clemency, the Zia government executed Bhutto the following year.

U.S.–Pakistani relations had also been strained by Pakistan's effort to acquire a nuclear weapons capability in defiance of American and international policies on nonproliferation. In April 1979 the Carter administration had responded to Pakistan's nuclear weapons program by terminating U.S. aid programs to that country. However, all of this was forgotten in the aftermath of the Soviet invasion of Afghanistan. Aid to Pakistan was restored, and the country became a major base of supply to, and sanctuary for, the Mujahedeen resistance in Afghanistan.

The U.S.–Pakistani rapprochement adversely affected the administration's effort to improve its relationship with India, which, under the leadership of Prime Minister Morarji Desai, was attempting to reduce its dependence on the Soviet Union. In 1977 Carter and Desai had signed a statement, known as the Delhi Declaration, reaffirming the intention of both countries to adhere to the principles of human rights and democracy. In addition, Carter had approved the sale of uranium to India in violation of the spirit, if not the letter, of the U.S. Nonproliferation Act, which prohibited the transfer of nuclear materials to countries, like India, that refused to fully accept the safeguard system of the International Atomic Energy Agency (IAEA). The Carter administration argued that it could not afford a political breakdown in relations with India at a time when tensions in southern Asia were increasing.

However, the administration's tilt toward China, and its resumption of military and economic aid to Pakistan, was more than the newly improved U.S.–Indian relationship could bear. In May 1980 the government of Indira Ghandi, who had replaced Desai as prime minister, announced that it would acquire $1.6 billion worth of arms from the Soviet Union. In December Gandhi received Leonid Brezhnev in New Delhi, where the two leaders issued a statement condemning outside interference in the affairs of Southwest Asia, an indirect reference to the Carter Doctrine.

The Triumph of Brzezinski

While the failed mission to rescue the U.S. embassy hostages was the immediate cause of Vance's resignation, the abandonment of détente in favor of containment was the underlying cause. Although Vance realized that the invasion of Afghanistan warranted a strong U.S. defensive commitment to the Persian Gulf region, he did not believe that the U.S.–Soviet relationship should be permitted to deteriorate to the point of open hostility. Nor did he believe that other U.S. interests, particularly SALT, should be sacrificed on the altar of Afghanistan. By 1980 Vance's views were a minority position in the administration. Though he attempted to find issues on which the Soviet Union and the United States could cooperate, his recommendations were rarely implemented. In March 1980, for example, Vance asked Carter for permission to talk with Gromyko to see if they could reduce Soviet-American tensions. Carter said no. It was another indication that Brzezinski, and not the secretary of state, had the president's ear. Vance's resignation followed the next month.

Vance's successor, Senator Edmund Muskie, was no more successful in challenging Brzezinski's dominance over the administration's foreign policy. Although Carter promised Muskie that he would be the principal foreign policy spokesman for the administration, the new secretary of state discovered, in August 1980, that he had not been consulted or informed about Presidential Directive 59, which Carter had approved the previous month. This directive not only placed new emphasis on a counterforce nuclear targeting doctrine, that is, one that targeted military installations, it also authorized the largest arms procurement program in thirty years. By the early fall of that year, Muskie was saying publicly that, if Carter was reelected, he would stay on only if major changes were made in the way foreign policy was managed. Ronald Reagan's election would deny him that opportunity.

The Soviets were shocked by the implications of the new targeting doctrine outlined in PD-59. Coming on the heels of the administration's decisions to deploy Pershing 2 and Tomahawk missiles in Europe, construct an MX missile system, and indefinitely shelve the SALT II Treaty, the Soviets regarded PD-59 as tantamount to a rejection of nuclear parity, the very foundation of détente. The Soviets threatened to accelerate their own nuclear weapons programs to counter what they perceived as a U.S. attempt to reacquire nuclear superiority.

America's NATO allies were also dismayed by the administration's abandonment of détente. The Europeans realized that a rapid deployment force committed to the Persian Gulf would have to rely heavily on U.S. forces stationed in Europe and assigned to NATO. They feared that the redeployment of these forces to the Gulf would reduce the combat strength of the alliance in its primary theater of operation, Europe. Moreover, the Europeans, unlike the Americans, viewed the invasion of Afghanistan more in regional than in global terms, and they were more alarmed by the breakdown of détente, which had done much to ease tensions in Europe, than were the Americans. Said West German Chancellor Helmut Schmidt, "We will not permit ten years of détente and defense policy to be destroyed."[22] Only Canada, Norway, Turkey, and West Germany joined the U.S. boycott of the Moscow Olympic games.

Nor were the Europeans willing to endure the economic sacrifices that were required by the punitive U.S. policy toward the Soviets. Indeed, instead of joining the Americans in applying economic sanctions against the Soviet Union, the Europeans went out of their way to conclude trade expansion agreements with the Soviets. As a result, while Soviet-American trade declined by 60 percent in 1980, Soviet trade with Western Europe increased substantially (by 100 percent with France and 65 percent with West Germany).

The Demise of Arms Control

Although the Carter administration remained cool to the idea of resuming arms negotiations with the Soviet Union in the aftermath of Afghanistan, the approaching presidential election and pressure from America's NATO allies, who wanted to reduce tensions with the Soviet Union, prompted the administration to change its mind. In an attempt to avoid killing the SALT II Treaty once and for all, the administration offered to observe the ceilings established by the unratified treaty as long as the Soviets agreed to do so as well. On this basis, the unratified treaty escaped extinction and was observed by both sides until 1986, when the Reagan administration finally declared it dead.

The superpowers did attempt to revive the LRTNF talks. In September 1980 the Soviet Union backed off its earlier position of refusing to negotiate on LRTNF until NATO rescinded its decision to deploy the U.S. Pershing 2 and Tomahawk missiles. The talks began in Geneva the following month, but the preliminary round, which lasted from October 16 to November 17, 1980, ended in a stalemate. To preclude deployment of the Pershing 2s and Tomahawks, the Soviets proposed that all LRTNF be frozen at their then current levels, which meant that they were willing to stop deploying SS-20s but were unwilling to reduce their number. The Americans clearly, however, wanted an agreement that would permit at least partial deployment of the new NATO missiles, and they were prepared to reduce their number only in exchange for a reduction in the number of the SS-20s. The deadlock in the talks was not ended before Carter left office in January 1981.

The LRTNF talks were not the only negotiations that were stalemated when Carter left office. The Vienna-based Mutual and Balanced Force Reduction (MBFR) Talks were also deadlocked. One of the of basic reasons was the inability of the two sides to achieve a mutually acceptable database. The Warsaw Pact set its total ground and air personnel at 987,300, of which 805,000 were in ground forces. But NATO estimated the pact's total ground force strength at 962,000 personnel, some 157,000 more than the pact's figure. Without an agreed-upon database, it was impossible for the Vienna negotiators to come to an agreement on the size of the limitations that would take place.

The superpowers were also unable to conclude the Comprehensive Test Ban Treaty (CTBT). Until 1978 progress on the CTBT had been substantial. In March 1977 Brezhnev accepted in principle the American demand for on-site inspections to monitor compliance with the CTBT. In November of that year, the Soviets also gave up their insistence that peaceful nuclear explosions be excluded from the ban. Another major breakthrough was achieved early in 1978 when the United States, Britain, and the Soviet Union agreed in principle to allow up to ten seismic monitoring stations to be placed on each country's territory to facilitate verification. Prompted in part by these Soviet concessions, on May 20, 1978, Carter authorized his negotiators to seek a five-year total ban on all nuclear testing. It was the consensus among the negotiators that a treaty could be concluded that year.

But, as negotiators in the Kennedy administration learned in the early 1960s, when the superpowers were also close to concluding a CTB agreement, the opposition of the military-industrial complex could prove too strong to overcome. Opponents of the CTBT in Congress, the Pentagon, and the Department of Energy argued that a five-year ban on testing would reduce the reliability of America's existing nuclear warheads—a position that was vigorously rejected by more than a few arms control advocates. Nevertheless, Carter's sensitivity to conservative charges that he was "soft on defense" and a "unilateral disarmer" were instrumental in persuading him, in September 1978, to reduce the duration of the ban from five to three years. Throughout 1979 the United States continued to change its position, leading the Soviets to suspect that the Americans really were not interested in a CTBT. Ultimately, it was the decline of détente that gave greater political weight to those who opposed a CTBT.

Yet another failed arms control effort was the attempt to ban anti-satellite (ASAT) weapons systems, that is, weapons designed to destroy surveillance satellites. After raising the matter in March 1977 and gaining Soviet agreement to ASAT negotiations, the administration decided that it needed to develop an American ASAT capability before it could begin talks with the Soviets, who already had a marginal but operational capability. As a result, the first meeting with the Soviets, in Helsinki, did not take place until May–June 1978. It was followed by two other meetings, one in Bern, Switzerland, in January–February 1979 and another in Vienna in April–June 1979. A fourth meeting that was scheduled for early 1980 was canceled by the Carter administration in retaliation for the Soviet occupation of Afghanistan. The talks did not resume before Carter left office.

The effort to demilitarize the Indian Ocean was another victim of détente's decline. The demilitarization talks, which had begun in June 1977 and continued into early 1978, were overtaken by the crisis in the Horn of Africa. The formal U.S. proposal, made in October 1977, called for both sides to refrain from increasing the prevailing level of its naval deployments, or changing the general pattern of deployment, and acquiring new bases in the region of the Indian Ocean. But the conflict between Ethiopia and Somali in the fall of 1977, and the absence of a significant U.S. naval presence in the region, caused the administration to lose interest in an Indian Ocean demilitarization agreement. Thus, when the Soviet Union moved to resume the talks, in the wake of the Somali-Ethiopian crisis, the United States declined to do so. Instead, in the following October Carter boasted that the United States had a reinforced naval presence in the Indian Ocean. Needless to say, the president's announcement only certified what had been known for some time: the Indian Ocean demilitarization talks were dead.

The superpower talks to limit the transfer of conventional arms to Third World countries (CAT), which began in December 1977, also collapsed before détente's demise. Carter had initially believed that curtailing arms transfers to Third World countries would reduce the conflicts in these countries as well as the opportunities for superpower confrontation.

Consequently, in May 1977 the president announced that he was initiating a unilateral policy of restraint on arms transfers. However, the crises in Africa and elsewhere eroded the president's desire to end all arms transfers to the Third World. As a result, the United States proposed that only arms shipments to Latin America and sub-Saharan Africa should be prohibited. The Soviet Union wanted to ban transfers to West Asia (including Iran) and East Asia (including China and South Korea) as well. As superpower tensions increased during 1978, and the United States found it necessary to counter the expansion of Soviet influence in the Third World, the administration lost all interest in CAT, and the talks came to an end in December 1978.

As détente faded, Moscow's incentive to accommodate Western sensibilities on the human rights issue also disappeared. Andrei Sakharov was sent off to internal exile in Gorky, a city some 250 miles east of Moscow. The Soviets were also unwilling to cooperate with the West at the November 1980 review conference of the Helsinki Final Act in Madrid. The West found the Soviets and their East European allies in noncompliance with the human rights guarantees contained in basket three of the Helsinki accord. The Soviet representatives simply countered U.S. criticism of Soviet human rights violations by citing civil rights abuses of African Americans and American Indians in the United States. By their response, the Soviets clearly indicated that, with the demise of détente, their cooperation in keeping the Helsinki process alive could no longer be taken for granted. But with the November 1980 election victory of Ronald Reagan, who had also publicly expressed doubts about the Helsinki process, there was no guarantee that the United States would continue to participate either.

Assessment: The Carter Presidency

Carter entered the White House in 1977 with the hope that he could revive détente. He adhered strongly to that goal for three years, basing his public rhetoric not on Cold War themes but on the hope for international cooperation in solving pressing global problems, such as the spread of nuclear weapons, regional conflicts, and human rights violations. Despite some notable foreign policy achievements, including the Panama Canal treaties, the Camp David accord, the normalization of relations with the People's Republic of China, and the negotiation of the unratified SALT II Treaty, Carter left office with his Soviet policy in shambles.

To be sure, Carter bears a large share of the responsibility for the failure of détente. His initial SALT II proposal, the comprehensive plan, was a needless aggravation that was in part responsible for the delay in completing a SALT II treaty, a delay that proved fatal to its ratification. His support for human rights in the Soviet empire, while admirable, antagonized the Soviets and made their cooperation on other issues hard to obtain. The blatant manner in which the administration played the China card, with Brzezinski trying to outdo Deng Xiaoping's anti-Soviet rhetoric, incited the Soviets further. The administration's exclusion of the Soviet Union from the Middle East peace process only confirmed Soviet fears that it could derive no benefit from cooperating with the Carter administration. The Soviet decision to invade Afghanistan was the logical outcome of that belief.

The Soviets, however, were equally, if not more, responsible for the collapse of détente. The Soviet leadership, old and inflexible, could not abandon their ideological conflict with the United States, despite its desire to acquire the benefits of détente. Its involvement in Angola, Ethiopia, Indochina, and Afghanistan served no vital Soviet interest commensurate to the benefits of developing better relations with the United States. As the Soviet Union declined economically, the Soviet leadership felt compelled to present the nation as a revolutionary power, if only to provide some legitimacy to the monopoly of power enjoyed by the Communist Party. The flexibility that would be displayed by Mikhail Gorbachev, only a half a decade later, was not a characteristic of the Soviet leadership in the late Brezhnev era. Unlike Gorbachev, Brezhnev put the worst possible interpretation on U.S. actions. In so doing, he undercut those in the Carter administration, like Vance, who wanted an accommodation with the Soviet Union, while he strengthened those, like Brzezinski, who were eager for confrontation.

Soviet inflexibility was demonstrated, among other ways, not only in the strategic arms negotiations but also in the LRTNF and MBFR talks. Gorbachev was able to resolve these nuclear arms issues by demonstrating a much greater degree of imagination and flexibility than the Brezhnev politburo was capable of displaying. On the other hand, the ultimate price of Gorbachev's reforms was the collapse of the Soviet empire and with it the Communist Party, consequences that Brezhnev was able to stave off for another decade.

8

The Reagan Cold War, 1981–1989

Ronald Reagan: The Cold War Victor?

Like the overwhelming majority of America's Cold War presidents, Ronald Reagan entered the White House in January 1981 with almost no background in national security affairs. Before entering the political arena, he had been in movies and in television. His only direct military experience occurred during World War II, when he served in the armed forces making training and documentary films. His first and only elected political position prior to the presidency was the governorship of California, a position he held from 1966 to 1974. However, unlike most of his predecessors, Reagan was not particularly eager to master national security issues. This was demonstrated repeatedly during his presidency by his inability to explain them in any detail.

Reagan's knowledge of communism and the Soviet Union was also very limited. It was based almost entirely on personal experience rather than intellectual study. As the president of the Screen Actors Guild in the late 1940s, Reagan fought what he believed was a communist effort to take over the motion picture industry, an experience that made him deeply suspicious of anything communist, particularly the Soviet Union. In his most celebrated statement, on March 8, 1983, Reagan called the Soviet Union an "evil empire."[1]

Needless to say, Reagan had little use for détente, which he had called "a one-way street" that favored only the Soviet Union.[2] The economic concessions that his predecessors had been prepared to grant the Soviet Union, Reagan believed, would have propped up an inefficient economic system, an oppressive political structure, and a menacing military establishment. The centerpiece of détente, the SALT II Treaty, Reagan charged, was a "flawed" agreement that perpetuated a margin of Soviet nuclear superiority over the United States.

Before engaging the Soviets in nuclear arms negotiations, Reagan demanded that the Soviets agree to massive reductions in the size of their nuclear arsenal. Paradoxically, he insisted that his administration had to increase the size of the U.S. nuclear arsenal in order to close a "window of vulnerability," that the alleged nuclear superiority of the Soviet Union had created for the United States. As a consequence, Reagan spent the first years of his presidency engaging the Soviet Union in an arms-building race rather than in an arms reduction contest.

Nevertheless, in 1987, Reagan would sign the first major arms reduction agreement of the entire Cold War era, the INF Treaty. During his second term he held five summit meetings with a Soviet leader — more than any other president — and shortly before leaving the presidency in January 1989, Reagan would visit Moscow and place his arm around the leader of the "evil empire," Mikhail Gorbachev, and call him a man with whom the United States could do business.

What accounts for this startling transformation in the attitude of Ronald Reagan toward the Soviet Union? Was it, as his supporters argue, Reagan's willingness to engage the Soviet Union in a massive arms race that forced the Soviets to, in effect, "sue for peace"? Or was the end of the Cold War due to other factors, such as the statesmanship of Mikhail Gorbachev, who forced the U.S. president to accept détente, as Reagan's critics argue?

The Reagan Grand Strategy

The shallowness of Reagan's knowledge of the Soviet Union helps to explain the turnabout that occurred during his second term in office. A more doctrinaire president would have found it difficult, if not impossible, to transform America's Soviet policy as Reagan did after 1984.

Lacking substantive knowledge of national security affairs, Reagan was forced to rely on his advisers to a much greater extent than most other Cold War presidents. During his first term, the overwhelming majority of his primary national security advisers were anti-Soviet hardliners, drawn heavily from the Committee on the Present Danger, the nucleus of conservative opposition to the SALT II Treaty. The Committee on the Present Danger believed that the Soviet Union had not only acquired a first-strike capability, it also contended that the Soviets were prepared to use it.

The scenario that committee members envisioned was one in which the Soviets attacked only U.S. and allied military installations and then threatened to attack America's cities if the United States retaliated. To prevent such nuclear blackmail, the committee insisted, the United States must have the ability to engage the Soviets at all levels of nuclear conflict, tactical as well as strategic, and have the capability to do so on an extended timetable.

While the existence of a window of vulnerability was later (in 1983) directly refuted by a presidential commission (headed by Brent Scowcroft), it provided the rationale for the greatest peacetime military buildup in U.S. history. Between 1981 and 1986, the Pentagon's budget rose from $171 billion to $376 billion. Major strategic nuclear weapons systems that had been shelved by Carter, such as the B-1 bomber, were revived, and the deployment of the MX ICBM and the Trident submarine was accelerated. The development of new ballistic missile defense (BMD) systems and antisatellite weapons (ASAT) was also undertaken. However, the bulk of the military spending during the Reagan years went to conventional forces. The Navy planned to increase its size from 454 to 600 ships, including 15 aircraft carrier groups.

Reagan and his advisers not only wanted to close the perceived window of vulnerabilty, they also wanted to use an arms race—one that would emphasize America's technological superiority—to strain and bankrupt the Soviet economy. "I intended," Reagan recalled in his memoirs," to let the Soviets know that we were going to spend what it took to stay ahead of them in the arms race." [3]

As outlined in national security directives that were signed by the president in 1982 and 1983, the Reagan strategy toward the Soviet Union amounted to what a senior White House official called "a full-court press."[4] Instead of assisting the Soviet Union in maintaining an inefficient economic system with U.S. trade and credits, the Reagan administration intended to disrupt the Soviet economy by denying it critical resources, hard currency earnings from oil and natural gas exports, and access to Western high technology.

The Reagan administration's military buildup and economic squeeze undoubtedly increased the strain on the Soviet economy, and thereby contributed to the collapse of the Soviet Union a decade later—although how much it did so is still a matter of debate. But Reagan's military and economic policies also put enormous stress on the U.S. economy as well, primarily because the expanded defense spending was not financed by increased taxation (income taxes were reduced during Reagan's first term) or balanced by commensurate cuts in domestic spending (the Democratic-controlled Congress refused to make them). As a consequence, the national debt more than doubled during Reagan's presidency, from $1 trillion in 1980 to $2.5 trillion by 1988.

The Reagan Doctrine and the Third World

The Reagan administration considered the Soviet Union, rather than indigenous factors such as poverty, overpopulation, political corruption, and the like, to be the underlying cause of the tensions in the Third World.

Whether through direct action or through proxies, the Soviet Union, the Reagan people believed, was determined to expand its influence in the Third World.

Accordingly, rather than cooperating with the Soviet Union to resolve Third World crises, as the Carter administration initially attempted to do, the Reagan administration sought to reverse Soviet gains in the underdeveloped regions, by supporting anticommunist forces struggling against Marxist regimes overtly or, where that was not possible, covertly. The administration intended to overcome the Vietnam "syndrome," which had made U.S. intervention in the Third World exceedingly unpopular with the American people and Congress.

In Poland, the CIA advanced covert economic assistance to the Solidarity labor movement, led by Lech Walesa. In Angola, U.S. aid began to flow to the UNITA forces of Jonas Savimbi, which were trying to overthrow the country's Cuban-supported Marxist government. The CIA also sent more than $2 billion worth of weapons and economic assistance to the Mujahedeen guerrillas fighting the Marxist government of Afghanistan.

But the principal area of interest to the Reagan administration in the Third World was the Central American–Caribbean region. As elsewhere in the Third World, Reagan ignored the view that the political instability of the region was indigenous, that is, the consequence of low commodity prices, unjust land distribution, and extremes of wealth and poverty. Although the administration, through the Caribbean Basin Initiative, offered U.S. aid as an incentive for economic reform in the region, the assistance that was provided, primarily through private enterprise channels, was so small that it had almost no impact.

Rather than focusing on local conditions, Reagan fixed the blame for Central America's problems on the external virus of communism, spread and abetted by the Soviets and their Cuban proxies. By creating puppet regimes in Central America, the president warned, Moscow and Havana intended to choke off America's lifeline to the outside world. What was needed to combat the threat was not more U.S. economic aid but military assistance to the anti-Marxist elements in the region.

The most blatant application of the Reagan Doctrine occurred in the Caribbean island-nation of Grenada. Prompted by the overthrow and murder of that country's Marxist leader, Maurice Bishop, by another Marxist faction, the president, on October 22, 1983, ordered 1,900 U.S. troops to liberate Grenada from a "brutal gang of leftist thugs."[5] The U.S. forces were supplemented by 300 troops from the Organization of Eastern Caribbean States, which feared that Grenada would become a base for Marxist revolutionaries in the region.

After the U.S. forces quickly defeated the Marxist forces, representative government was restored to the island. The Reagan administration bragged that it had reversed the Vietnam syndrome by demonstrating that the United States would resist, with military force if necessary, the expansion of communism in the hemisphere. However, some, including the president's friend British Prime Minister Margaret Thatcher, condemned the U.S. invasion as an act of aggression against a sovereign nation.

The major concern of the Reagan administration, however, was Nicaragua, not Grenada. Indeed, the overthrow of Nicaragua's Marxist Sandinista government, led by Daniel Ortega, became a personal obsession of the president. In December 1981 Reagan authorized spending $19 million to assist a 500-man military force, called the Contras, to undermine the Nicaraguan economy, as a prelude to overthrowing the Sandinista government. The Sandinistas responded by declaring a state of emergency, requesting Soviet assistance to combat the Contras, and appealing to the World Court to restrain the United States. After the Court condemned the United States for aggressive actions against Nicaragua, the Reagan administration abrogated a 1946 pledge to accept the court's compulsory jurisdiction in such cases. The administration also intensified its assistance to the Contras.

The opposition of the Congress prevented wider U.S. involvement in the Nicaraguan conflict. Because neither the Congress nor the American people were prepared to support the administration's crusade against the Sandinistas, the administration was forced to use subterfuge to circumvent criticism of its Nicaraguan policy. When members of Congress raised questions about the scope and purpose of the U.S. covert operations in Nicaragua in 1982, CIA director William Casey falsely assured them that neither the Reagan administration nor the Contras sought to overthrow the Sandinista regime.

Congress responded by passing the first of a series of amendments introduced by Representative Edward Boland, (Dem.–Mass.). The first Boland amendment, which was passed by the House of Representatives 411 to 0, capped CIA aid to the Contras at $24 million, and stated that none of it was to be used to overthrow the Nicaraguan government. In early April 1984 the mining of Nicaraguan ports and harbors by Americans working for the CIA prompted Congress to pass an even more restrictive amendment. It barred the CIA or "any other agency or entity involved in intelligence activities" from aiding the Contra guerrillas. Congressman Boland called the prohibition "air tight with no exceptions."[6]

In response to the Boland amendments, members of Reagan's National Security Council staff, led by Marine Lieutenant Colonel Oliver North, with the support of the NSC's director, Robert McFarland, and his deputy and successor, Admiral John Poindexter, attempted to circumvent the congressional restrictions on military aid to the Contras. Through the spring and early summer of 1986, North attempted to carry out "Operation Rescue," which called for covertly selling arms to Iran in an attempt to free U.S. hostages seized by pro-Iranian terrorists in Lebanon. The profits derived from the sale of the arms to Iran were diverted to the Contras. However, after a U.S. transport plane was shot down by the Sandinistas on October 5, 1986, the Iran-Contra coverup rapidly unraveled. After congressional hearings, a grand jury indicted McFarland, North, Poindexter, and other involved persons.

McFarlane later testified that he had kept President Reagan, Vice President George Bush, Secretary of State George Shultz, and Defense Secretary Caspar Weinberger well informed about the Iran-Contra operation. Shultz personally warned the president that his order to circumvent Congress by soliciting foreign funds might constitute an "impeachable offense." Reagan responded by saying that, if the story ever got out, "we'll all be hanging by our thumbs in front of the White House."[7] Later, Reagan admitted that he had authorized arms shipments to Iran, allegedly to win influence with moderates in the Iranian government, but he denied any involvement in the illegal transfer of the arms sales proceeds to the Contras. North, in his memoirs, argued that "President Reagan knew everything" but added that "the president didn't always know what he knew."[8]

The Demise of Human Rights

The principal intellectual support for the Reagan Doctrine was provided by Jeane Kirkpatrick, a political scientist who had criticized Carter's human rights policy because it undermined governments friendly to the United States. In a 1979 article, Kirkpatrick made a distinction between "authoritarian" as opposed to "totalitarian" governments.[9] She argued that at least the possibility of democratic reform existed in countries ruled by authoritarian noncommunist governments, but not in those that were under communist control. The United States, she said, should not let the human rights violations of authoritarian regimes preclude U.S. aid to them. It was important to provide the aid not only to combat the spread of communism but also to encourage the growth of the democracy in the region.

Reagan responded warmly to Kirkpatrick's ideas. He appointed her U.S. ambassador to the Union Nations. There she frequently criticized UN agencies and many Third World states for not supporting U.S. actions without question. To show his dislike for the UN, Reagan withheld financial support to the world body and suspended U.S. participation in the United Nations Economic, Scientific, and Cultural Organization (UNESCO).

The Reagan administration also implemented Kirkpatrick's recommendation to support pro-American authoritarian regimes. It refused to impose sanctions on the white, racist regime in South Africa or to criticize human rights abuses perpetrated by pro-U.S. governments in El Salvador, Guatemala, Chile, Haiti, the Philippines, and Pakistan. Only after it had become clear that dictators might be toppled by indigenous leftist forces, as in the case of Ferdinand Marcos of the Philippines and Haiti's Jean-Claude ("Baby Doc") Duvalier, did Reagan agree to withdraw U.S. support from them.

Reagan's enthusiasm for democracy grew in proportion to his need to obtain approval from Congress for aid for the Nicaraguan Contras and the pro-American government of El Salvador. The latter was headed by a democratic reformer, José Napoleón Duarte, the leader of the country's Christian Democratic Party, but his reforms were opposed by right-wing, paramilitary, death squads who murdered an estimated 60,000 unarmed Salvadoran civilians between 1979 and 1985, including the Roman Catholic bishop of San Salvador, Oscar Romero. The Reagan administration downplayed the terrorism of the death squads and instead emphasized the reforms that the Duarte government attempted to implement.

By 1983, however, Reagan began to call for free elections in Central America. He also authorized the establishment of the National Endowment for Democracy to promote the growth of democratic institutions in the region. More importantly, the administration sent clear messages to the military establishments in the region that overthrowing civilian governments would mean a cutoff of U.S. aid. Despite the new emphasis on democracy, the military dominated every Central American country except Costa Rica at the time Reagan left the White House.

The Reagan Doctrine, International Terrorism, and the Middle East

Despite the Reagan administration's willingness to sell arms, albeit covertly, to the "terrorist" Iranian government, it took a strong public stand against international terrorism. Again ignoring indigenous factors contributing to terrorism, such as the Arab-Israeli conflict, the administration considered the Soviet Union to be the primary initiator, or at least major supporter, of international terrorist activities. The United States accused the Soviets of backing an assassination attempt on Pope John Paul II, who was severely wounded by a Bulgarian assailant in May 1981, although the CIA concluded in a 1983 study that there was no firm evidence linking the Soviets to the plot.

However, during the Reagan administration, as before, the hotbed of international terrorism in the Middle East, not the Balkans. In 1986 the administration took military action against a Soviet client, the Libyan strongman Colonel Muammar el-Qaddafi, whom it accused of backing terrorist activities throughout the Middle East and Western Europe.

In March 1986, in a replay of a U.S.–Libyan clash in 1981, the United States carried out a naval exercise in the Gulf of Sidra. Predictably, U.S. aircraft were fired upon, this time by SA-5 long-range antiaircraft missiles recently acquired from the Soviet Union. The United States responded by attacking the SA-5 radars and sinking three Libyan patrol craft. Libya retaliated in turn by directing a terrorist bomb attack on a Berlin discotheque in which two people were killed and dozens injured, including more than fifty Americans. Nine days later the United States bombed targets in Libya, including Qaddafi's residential compound. Although Qaddafi escaped death, one of his daughters was killed in the attack.

Although the Soviet Union did not consider Libya an ally, the Libyans were long-time Soviet arms customers. Consequently, the Soviets strongly criticized the U.S. attacks, but they did nothing more to help the Libyans. The forceful U.S. reaction, combined with the steep decline in oil prices after 1986, helped to restrain Qaddafi's support for international terrorism.

In the Middle East, as elsewhere in the Third World, the Reagan administration ignored, at least initially, the indigenous causes of political and social instability. The most important cause of the region's instability was the continuing conflict between Israel and the Palestinians. At first, the administration tried to fashion an alliance of Israel and the moderate Arab regimes—Egypt, Jordan, and Saudi Arabia—to check the expansion of Soviet influence in the region. However, the moderate Arab states refused to cooperate militarily with Israel as long as the Israelis refused to negotiate with the PLO.

Moreover, after Anwar Sadat was assassinated in 1982 (by Muslim fundamentalists who opposed his rapprochement with Israel), his successor, Hosni Mubarek, was reluctant to embrace Israel. Mubarek was acutely aware that Sadat's approach to Israel had cost him his life and isolated Egypt from the Arab world. Mubarek not only hoped to live a long life, he also wanted to restore Egypt to its rightful place in the Arab community. At the same time, Egypt's ties with Israel became particularly embarrassing to the Egyptians after the Israelis invaded Lebanon in June 1982, in an attempt to destroy a growing PLO military presence in that country.

In late 1982 the United States intervened militarily in Lebanon after Palestinian refugees in camps near Beirut were massacred by Christian fanatics. The U.S. forces were supplemented by troops from France, Italy, and Britain, but the motives for the allies' intervention differed from those of the Reagan administration. The allies were motivated primarily by humanitarian conerns—they wished to avert another Palestinian massacre—while the United States was primarily interested in propping up the pro-Western government of Amin Gemayel.

However, in September 1983, U.S. forces came into conflict with Gemayel's opponents, the Syrian-supported Druze militia. Seeing the Druze as the pawns of the Syrians, who were themselves clients of the Soviets, the Reagan administration ordered U.S. forces to attack Druze targets in Lebanon. The administration intended to demonstrate that it could use force in the Middle East effectively, and thereby break the "Vietnam syndrome." However, on October 23 a terrorist drove a truck bomb into a U.S. military barracks near Beirut. Its detonation killed 241 marines. As a consequence, the U.S. troops were withdrawn from Lebanon early in February 1984. The Gemayel government, which Reagan had sworn to defend, was compelled to accept a Syrian-imposed peace.

The Israeli invasion of Lebanon compelled the Reagan administration to address the Arab-Israeli conflict. When it did so, in September 1982, its peace plan essentially reaffirmed U.S. support for the Camp David accord, which was a product of joint negotiations between the Israelis and the Egyptians alone, without the participation of either the Soviet Union or the PLO. The Reagan plan proposed self-government for the Palestinians in association with Jordan, an idea that was rejected by both the Israelis and the Palestinians. Little progress was made toward resolving the conflict until 1988 when, after decades of rejecting Israel's legitimacy, Palestinian leader Yassir Arafat responded to U.S. suggestions by declaring that the PLO accepted Israel's right to exist. Neither Arafat nor Israeli leaders, however, were able to agree on terms for establishing a Palestinian state during the remainder of Reagan's presidency.

The Persian Gulf

While the Reagan administration was reluctant to become involved in the Israeli-Palestinian conflict, it did not have to be persuaded to intervene in the Persian Gulf. The strategic importance of this region to the United States had been established during Truman's presidency, but the region took on even greater importance during Reagan's tenure in office after the Soviet invasion of Afghanistan in 1979 and the eruption of war between Iraq and Iran in September 1980.

As early as December 1980, one month after Reagan's election, the Soviet Union approached the United States and suggested that they take a common approach to the problems in the Gulf region. The interests of both superpowers in the area overlapped in many ways; both wanted to end the Iraqi-Iranian war and both, from 1982 onward, supported Iraq. But since the Reagan administration believed that the United States should confront, not cooperate with, the Soviets in the Third World, no serious attempt was made to find a common approach to the war. Instead, the Reagan administration tried to play one side off against the other, in the expectation that such a policy would produce a stalemate in the conflict, and thereby prevent either belligerent from dominating the region.

Nevertheless, the administration tilted more heavily toward Iraq than Iran because it hoped that U.S. aid to the Iraqis would end their dependence on the Soviet Union, and also enable Iraq to serve as a bulwark against Iranian expansion in the Gulf region. Thus, the administration removed Iraq from its list of terrorist countries and provided the Iraqis with credit and intelligence data concerning Iranian troop dispositions. By the time of George Bush's inauguration in 1989, trade between the United States and Iraq had grown to $3.6 billion a year. In addition, the administration encouraged U.S. allies to sell Iraq conventional arms and high-tech equipment, some of which was used by the Iraqis to develop ballistic missiles and the components of chemical, biological, and nuclear weapons.

The Reagan administration's goal of weaning Iraq away from the Soviet Union failed, primarily because the Iraqis refused to abandon a reliable ally, the Soviet Union, for a suitor that was offering, at best, an uncertain commitment. Moscow responded to the U.S. policy by increasing its assistance to Iraq, making that country the largest Third World export market for Soviet arms. In 1985 and 1986 Moscow sold Baghdad more than $3 billion worth of arms and equipment.

In spite of the administration's preference for refraining from military action in the Gulf crisis, the United States became deeply involved in the defense of Persian Gulf shipping lanes, a policy that caused it to clash militarily with both Iran and Iraq. On January 13, 1987, Kuwait asked the United States to protect its vessels (by reflagging them under U.S. registry) after they were attacked by Iranian air and naval forces. The Kuwaitis added that the Soviet Union had already offered to protect their ships. Prompted by a desire to keep the Soviets out of the Persian Gulf, the administration agreed in March 1987 to reflag eleven Kuwaiti vessels, and the following month, it increased the U.S. naval presence in the Gulf to keep the area open to international shipping.

Tragically, the enhanced U.S. naval presence in the Gulf contributed to the loss of additional lives, both civilian and military. In May 1987 an Iraqi fighter pilot, confusing the destroyer U.S.S. *Stark* for an Iranian ship, attacked it with two missiles, killing thirty-seven U.S. sailors. A clear indication of the administration desire to secure Iraq as a counterweight to Iran was its mild reaction to the attack. The United States accepted the compensation offered by Iraq's president, Saddam Hussein. A year later, the captain of the U.S.S. *Vincennes* mistakenly shot down an Iranian passenger plane killing over 100 civilians. In retaliation, in December 1988 Iranian, Syrian, or Libyan agents placed a bomb on a Pan Am flight from London, killing 270 people.

The Reagan Doctrine and East Asia

During Reagan's first years in office, U.S. relations with the other communist giant, China, also deteriorated. Reagan had criticized Carter's rapprochement with China, even though it was motivated largely by a desire to check Soviet influence in East Asia. Reagan even favored restoring the U.S. alliance with Taiwan, promising to sell the Taiwanese weapons regardless of China's opposition. Defense Secretary Weinberger called Taiwan an "unsinkable aircraft carrier" that would enable the United States to project its naval power to the far reaches of the western Pacific.[10]

By contrast, the administration, at least initially, did not view China as a potential ally. The Chinese had little or no navy, an obsolescent air force, almost no capacity for high-tech weaponry, and an antique missile arsenal. Therefore, China was considered incapable of countering the growth of Soviet strategic influence in the Far East, particularly in Indochina, where the Soviets had befriended Vietnam and its puppet ally Cambodia.

Moreover, the Reagan administration did not believe it could count on Chinese support if the United States engaged in another conflict with

North Korea. To preclude that possibility, the Reagan administration planned to increase the U.S. military presence in South Korea by adding some 1,600 soldiers to the 37,000 already there. The North Koreans responded by stating that the situation could "expand into a nuclear war."[11] The North Koreans also felt compelled to reinforce their old ties with the Soviets, which had deteriorated in the previous two decades. However, the Soviets, who opposed the creation of a strong, reunited Korea did not give the North Koreans the degree of support they sought.

The North Koreans were also enraged by the Reagan administration's attempt to "remilitarize" Japan, a country that had committed aggression against both Koreas as well as China. Weinberger called on the Japanese to develop the capacity to defend the air space and the sea lanes up to one thousand miles from their country, a responsibility the Japanese accepted in 1981. The Japanese also agreed to provide South Korea with $4 billion in loans and credits. Japanese Prime Minister Yasuhiro Nakasone even went as far as calling for a revision of Article 9 of the Japanese constitution, which requires Japan to renounce war and the maintenance of war potential.

While Japan's parliament refused to take this step, in 1986 it did approve a small increase in Japan's defense budget beyond the ceiling of 1 percent of GNP that Japan had established. The intensification of Japan's defensive effort alarmed the Chinese, and the North Koreans, and contributed further to the deterioration of Sino-American relations early in the Reagan administration. By 1983 the Chinese were condemning the United States, as well as the Soviet Union, for seeking world "hegemony."

The Chinese were not the only ones who were alarmed by the new direction in Japanese defense policy. In a major address in September 1983, Yuri Andropov, who succeeded Brezhnev upon his death in October 1982, condemned the Reagan administration's effort "to revive Japanese militarism and attach it to the [Western] bloc's military-political machine."[12] As a way of balancing the growth of Japanese military power, both the Chinese and the Soviets began talks to repair their relations. The talks led to increased trade between the two countries and the resumption of Soviet technical assistance to China. Concerned about the thaw in Sino-Soviet relations, the Reagan administration felt compelled to reverse its policy toward China and, as Weinberger put it during a visit to that country in 1983, seek to enlist the Chinese government in "strategic cooperation" with the United States.[13]

In the end, the Sino-American rapprochement was a product of both powers' realization that they had more to gain from cooperation than confrontation. The United States needed China's help in supporting the Mujahedeen guerrillas fighting in Afghanistan, and the Chinese leaders appreciated the potential benefits of U.S. technology, trade, and loans. As a result, the two nations reached an accord in August 1982 that recognized the right of the United States to sell weapons to Taiwan in return for an American promise to "reduce gradually its sales."[14] On May 21, 1983, the administration reciprocated by reclassifying the list of U.S. exports denied to China in order to support China's economic modernization program.

The revival of the Sino-American relationship was celebrated during Reagan's visit to China in April 1984, his first presidential visit to a communist country. Reagan's trip seemed to be a replay of Nixon's journey to China in 1972. Reagan told the Chinese that China and the United States had a common interest in opposing military expansionism, particularly the Soviet intervention in Afghanistan and Vietnam's domination of Cambodia. Tass, the Soviet news agency, accused China of joining President Reagan's anticommunist crusade.

Nevertheless, after his reelection victory, Reagan, unlike Nixon, seldom mentioned the world's largest communist nation, and relations between the two countries remained, if not friendly, at least not hostile. China, Secretary of State George Shultz concluded, remained "a giant crippled by its ideology." He recalled later, "So long as China pursued that ideology, there would need be restraints on the kind of relationship it could have with the United States."[15]

The Reagan Doctrine and Europe

While Reagan came to appreciate the benefits of cooperation with China, he could not, at first, bring himself to the same transformation with respect to the Soviet Union. In March 1982 the president signed a national security decision directive, NSDD-32, which declared that the United States would seek to "neutralize" Soviet control over Eastern Europe. One way it sought to do this was by encouraging the liberalization of the Soviet Union's East European satellite states.

While the Reagan administration was successful in emboldening the Polish labor movement, Solidarity, with covert economic assistance, there was little it could do to reverse the imposition of martial law in Poland during December 1981. That action was taken by the Polish army, under the leadership of General Wojciech Jaruzelski, to avert a Soviet invasion designed to crush Solidarity. On December 23, 1981, the Reagan administration reacted by imposing economic sanctions on Poland as well as the Soviet Union. The Polish communists obviously believed that U.S. sanctions, while painful, were a small price to pay for heading off Soviet military intervention in their country.

In spite of the Reagan administration's inability to reverse the imposition of martial law in Poland, it kept up the pressure on the Soviets and their satellite states. On June 8 in an address to the British Parliament, Reagan said he wanted the Western nations to undertake a "crusade for freedom" that would promote democratic ideals and efforts to build democratic infrastructures around the world. The president also said that the Russian people were not immune to the demands for greater freedom. Pravda responded by warning that Reagan's anticommunist crusade could result in a "catastrophe."[16]

Nevertheless, Reagan continued to call for the expansion of freedom in Eastern Europe, declaring in August 1984 that the United States would not passively accept "the permanent subjugation of the people of Eastern Europe." He also rejected "any interpretation of the Yalta agreement [of 1945] that suggests American consent for the division of Europe into spheres of influence."[17] However, the Reagan administration was not prepared to start a war with the Soviet Union over Eastern Europe. The liberalization of the Soviet satellites, Shultz said, must be a gradual process.

The West European allies of the United States, on the other hand, had little use for the Reagan administration's blatant effort to undermine Soviet control of Eastern Europe. The allies realized that détente had not only reduced tensions in Europe, it had also opened up Eastern Europe to Western trade. The West Germans, in particular, saw their détente policy (*Ostpolitik*) as critical to the improvement of conditions in East Germany and the eventual reunification of Germany. Consequently, while they cooperated with the U.S. economic sanctions on Poland, they did not impose sanctions on the Soviet Union.

The West Europeans, as a whole, also did not support the Reagan Doctrine in the Third World. Both France and Spain refused to allow U.S. warplanes to fly over their territory on their way to bombing Libya in 1986. Instead of trying to overthrow Marxist regimes in the Third World, the European allies preferred to offer the Soviets economic concessions as an incentive to modify their behavior in the underdeveloped regions of the world. As a consequence, the West Europeans not only refused to participate in the U.S. sanctions policy, they resisted the Reagan administration's effort to isolate the Soviet Union economically as well as diplomatically.

The allies were particularly incensed by the Reagan administration's effort to scuttle a European project to build a pipeline that would extend 3,500 miles from the Soviet natural gas fields in western Siberia to Western Europe. On December 29, 1981, in the wake of the imposition of martial law in Poland, the president prohibited the sale of U.S. pipeline technology to the Soviet Union. Six months later, on June 18, 1982, Reagan ordered that any European firm operating on a U.S. license or any American subsidiary operating in Europe must break all pipeline contracts. The administration argued that the collapse of the Siberian pipeline project would deprive the Soviets of a way of blackmailing the Western Europeans, whose dependence on Soviet natural gas would increase from 15 to 20 percent, as well as earning some $10 billion in hard currency.

The West Europeans, however, regarded the pipeline project not only a source of cheap energy but also a major East-West economic link that supported European détente. They were especially aggravated by the fact that the ban on pipeline technology was imposed after the Reagan administration had given the Europeans the impression that the United States would not implement such restraints on trade but only tighten the terms of credit available to the Soviet Union.

To add fuel to the fire, shortly after the Reagan administration called upon the Europeans to cancel the pipeline project, it signed a new grain sale agreement with the Soviets, primarily to win the support of U.S. farmers during the approaching congressional election. It seemed to the Europeans that the Americans expected them to bear an inequitable share of the burden of waging economic warfare on the Soviet Union. Not surprisingly, the Europeans flatly refused to cancel their participation in the Soviet pipeline project. As a result, on November 13, 1982, five painful months after the extended sanctions had been imposed by the United States, they were removed. In the end, rather than causing a modification of Soviet behavior, the U.S. sanctions only exacerbated intra-allied relations.

Nuclear Weapons Control

The West European public was even more upset by the Reagan administration's nuclear buildup. So were an increasing number of Americans. In June 1982, in what was called the largest protest meeting in U.S. history, between one-half and three-quarters of a million people jammed Central Park in New York City to support an end to the nuclear arms race. Three months earlier, Senator Edward Kennedy joined Republican Senator Mark Hatfield in introducing a resolution in the Senate calling for a freeze on the testing and deployment of new nuclear weapons. The Roman Catholic bishops of the United States also began writing a pastoral letter on nuclear weapons, completed in 1983, that condemned first-strike weapons, such as the MX missile, and called for a nuclear freeze.

With its nuclear buildup increasingly threatened by growing hostility in the Congress and the nation, the Reagan administration tried to kill the freeze issue by co-opting it. It supported a resolution sponsored by Representative William S. Broomfield (Rep.–Mich.), calling for a freeze at equal and substantially reduced levels, in effect permitting the Reagan nuclear buildup to continue. On August 5, 1982, the House voted for the Broomfield resolution 204 to 202. A year later, however, a resolution calling for a mutual and verifiable freeze as well as talks on intermediate-range weapons and strategic weapons passed in the House by a hefty margin of 278 to 149.

In spite of the administration's deep-seated dislike for arms control, pressure from the Congress, the burgeoning antinuclear movement, and the NATO allies compelled it to engage in nuclear arms negotiations with the Soviet Union. In 1981 the administration offered the "zero-option plan" as its intermediate-range nuclear forces (INF) proposal. It called for the United States to cancel plans to deploy its Pershing 2s and Tomahawks in return for Soviet dismantling of all intermediate-range missiles, that is, the SS-4s, SS-5s, and SS-20s.

Not surprisingly, the Soviets rejected the zero option. While requiring both sides to eliminate all their INF, the zero option would have left unaffected other NATO-theater nuclear weapons deployed in Western Europe, including 108 medium-range Pershing 1 missiles and U.S. dual-capable fighters. The Soviet counterproposal called for an immediate freeze on long-range INF deployments followed by a two-thirds reduction in their numbers by 1990. The Soviet proposal was quickly turned down by the United States and its NATO allies because it would have maintained the Soviet superiority in IRBMs and also because it included British and French systems in the U.S. total.

Both governments displayed more flexibility on the INF issue during 1982 and 1983. On December 21, 1982, Brezhnev's successor, Yuri Andropov, offered to reduce the number of SS-20s that were aimed at Western Europe from 243 to 162, a figure that matched the combined total of British and French ballistic missiles. He also proposed redeploying the remaining SS-20s at sites about 700 miles further east, on the far side of the Ural Mountains. The offer was rejected immediately by Washington, London, and Paris, not only because it included British and French forces in the limits and precluded the deployment of the new U.S. missiles but also because the allies feared that mobile SS-20s stationed beyond the Urals could easily be moved back to positions in the western part of the Soviet Union.

However, on March 30, 1983, Reagan gave in to allied pressure and moved away from the zero option. In its place, he offered an "interim agreement" that would allow equal numbers of American and Soviet warheads "on a global basis," at the "lowest possible levels."[18] Nevertheless, on April 2 the Soviets rejected the new U.S. offer. They insisted that French and British forces must be included in the limitations, and they rejected the concept of global ceilings because it would have included Soviet missiles deployed in eastern Asia.

On October 26, 1983, shortly before the first U.S. cruise missiles were due to arrive in Britain, Andropov again altered the Soviet position. He proposed to reduce Soviet SS-20 deployments in Europe to 140, a figure that was reduced to 120 in November, and to halt further SS-20 deployments in the Far East. In exchange, he demanded the cancellation of the Pershing 2 and Tomahawk deployments and a freeze on the level of British and French nuclear forces.

By this time, however, the administration wanted to avoid doing anything that would delay the imminent deployment of the first U.S. cruise missiles in Europe; consequently, it rejected the Soviet offer. On November 23, one day after the West German Bundestag voted to reaffirm support for the NATO missile deployments, the Soviets terminated the INF talks without agreeing to a date for their resumption.

The Strategic Arms Reduction Talks (START), as SALT was renamed, also languished during Reagan's first term in office. The administration's initial (1982) START proposal was so lopsided in favor of the United

States that it obviously was designed to be rejected. It called for even
deeper cuts in the number of Soviet missiles and warheads than those proposed by the Carter administration, and rejected by the Soviets, in 1977.

Under the Reagan proposal, ICBMs and SLBMs for both sides
would have been reduced to an equal level of 850 missiles over a five- to
ten-year period. The size of the proposed reductions was roughly one-
half the then current U.S. level of about 1,700 delivery vehicles but
almost two-thirds of the total Soviet force of roughly 2,350 launchers.
One analyst, John Newhouse, argued that the aversion to dealing with
the Soviet Union was so great in some quarters of the Reagan administration that "only reductions—deep ones—justified the unnatural act of
negotiations with the enemy on so vital a subject."[19]

Not surprisingly, the Soviets rejected Reagan's proposal. Brezhnev
then countered with a call for a nuclear freeze that would take effect as
soon as the talks began. Later, in mid-1982, the Soviets tabled a proposal
that would have preserved the structure of SALT II, but also reduced
launcher ceilings to 1,800. The Soviet proposal also called for specified
limits on the total number of nuclear weapons, including cruise missiles
and other bomber armament, and modest reductions in the SALT II
MIRV sublimits. However, because the Soviet proposal did not go far
enough, and was tied to the willingness of the United States to cancel its
INF deployments, it was unacceptable to the Reagan administration. As a
consequence, when the INF talks collapsed in November 1983, so too
did START.

The KAL Tragedy

The collapse of START and the INF talks came in the wake of one of the
most traumatic events of the Cold War, the Soviet interception and shooting down of a South Korean passenger airplane. The plane, Korean Air
Lines flight 007, strayed far off course en route from Alaska to Seoul on
the night of August 31, 1983. It then flew for some distance over Soviet
territory, nearing a secret missile test site on the Kamchatka Peninsula. A
Soviet fighter pilot shot down the craft just before it exited Soviet air
space, killing all 269 people on board, including a member of Congress.

Reagan reacted by calling the Soviet action an "act of barbarism."[20]
Soviet leaders, he insisted, deliberately and callously destroyed a civilian
aircraft without warning. U.S. intelligence intercepts of Soviet communications, however, showed that local air-defense commanders did not at
first realize they were tracking a civilian airliner, believing instead that it
was a U.S. spy plane that had earlier flown near Soviet air space to spy
upon the missile range. This conclusion subsequently was supported by a
report of the UN International Civil Aviation Organization.

Nevertheless, even after receiving the transcripts of U.S. electronic
intercepts, Reagan persisted in condemning the Soviet Union for the
tragedy. He later admitted that the incident "gave badly needed impetus

in Congress to the rearmament programs and postponed [congressional] attempts to gut our efforts to restore American military might."[21] A September 1983 national security decision directive (NSDD-102), which was subsequently declassified under a Freedom of Information Act request, revealed that the administration also intended to use the incident as "an opportunity to reverse the false moral and political 'peacemaker' perception that the [Soviet] regime has been cultivating."[22]

The Soviets, not surprisingly, reacted to the U.S. attacks as further proof that the Reagan administration was more interested in confrontation than détente. On September 28 Andropov accused the administration of pursuing a "militarist course that represents a serious threat to peace."[23] The KAL incident demonstrated vividly how seriously relations between the two countries had declined.

"Star Wars"

Soviet suspicion that the Reagan administration was more interested in building nuclear weapons than in reducing their numbers was reinforced by Reagan's decision, in March 1983, to undertake a five-year, $26-billion program for research and development of a nationwide ballistic-missile defense system (BMD). Although the program was officially called the Strategic Defense Initiative (SDI), the media quickly dubbed it "Star Wars," the title of a popular science fiction movie. While the administration initially considered several approaches to a BMD, all of them envisioned the creation of a multilayered defense system in which ground- and spaced-based weapons, including beam and particle weapons, lasers, and homing rockets, would attack Soviet ballistic missiles and their warheads before they could strike U.S. targets.

Reagan acknowledged that achievement of this goal would be no small accomplishment. An effective nationwide defense would have to intercept and destroy virtually all of the roughly 10,000 nuclear warheads that the Soviets were capable of committing to a major strategic attack. But to Reagan, even if SDI did not offer a total defense for the entire country, it certainly offered more protection against enemy missiles than existed at that time. In addition, Reagan felt that SDI made a lot more sense than the suicidal strategy of mutual assured destruction.

The administration had another, more ambitious goal for Star Wars. Retired Lieutenant General Daniel O. Graham stated that SDI would "severely tax, perhaps to the point of disruption, the already strained Soviet technological and industrial resources."[24] At the very least, argued Edward Teller, the father of the American hydrogen bomb and a strong supporter of SDI, the program would force the Soviets to increase their military expenditures beyond what they could reasonably afford. If it did that alone, Teller stated, "we would have accomplished something."[25]

But Star Wars' critics did not buy even its least ambitious goals. They asserted that the Soviets could easily take a number of countermeasures that would render SDI ineffective. The Soviets could simply increase the number of their deployed ballistic missiles, load some of them with duds, and overwhelm the American BMD. For every ruble the Soviets might spend on such relatively inexpensive countermeasures, the United States would have to spend millions of dollars on devices that could differentiate between real warheads and duds.

Nevertheless, the Soviets clearly were extremely upset by SDI's potential to destabilize the nuclear balance. Even a partially effective SDI, they realized, would give the side that struck first an advantage over the defender. The aggressor could hope to destroy the overwhelming majority of the defender's offensive forces in a first strike and then mop up most of those that managed to be launched with an even partially effective BMD. Even Reagan admitted that SDI could have offensive potential, but he added, "I don't think anyone in the world can honestly believe that the United States is interested in such a thing or would ever put itself in such a position."[26] His pledge to share SDI technology with the Soviet Union, which the Soviets never took seriously, seemed to be an implicit recognition that unilateral U.S. deployment of strategic defenses might be destabilizing.

SDI's critics feared that it would force the Soviets to expand their own ABM system, thereby triggering a dangerous and expensive escalation of the nuclear arms race in a new theater, space, where it had been prohibited by existing Soviet-American treaties, including the Limited Test Ban Treaty of 1963, the Outer Space Treaty of 1967, and the ABM Treaty of 1972.

The ABM Treaty specifically included a provision requiring the parties "not to develop, test or deploy ABM systems or components that are sea-based, air-based, space-based, or mobile land-based." The deployment of SDI, its critics argued, would not only abrogate the ABM Treaty, it would also lead to the removal of all constraints on offensive missiles. The Soviets would be unlikely to reduce their ballistic missile force while the United States was building a ballistic missile defense system. In other words, the construction of a nationwide American BMD program would spell the end of the effort to reduce the numbers of nuclear weapons.

In what seemed to be an attempt to prepare the nation for an abrogation of the ABM Treaty, the Reagan administration accused the Soviets of repeatedly violating not only that treaty but the various other arms control agreements concluded between the two nations. A presidential report to Congress in January 1984 listed, among other alleged Soviet violations, construction of a "phased-array radar" at Krasnoyarsk in the central Soviet Union. This Soviet action, the administration charged, constituted a violation of the ABM Treaty, which bars construction of radar stations and other equipment, except at national borders, that could enhance a country's defense against incoming missiles or serve as an early warning system. While the Soviets initially denied the American accusations, they later admitted (in 1989) that the Krasnoyarsk installation did violate the ABM Treaty; they then agreed to dismantle it.

In spite of the concerns of the Soviets and arms reduction advocates, the Reagan administration pushed ahead with SDI, spending almost $17 billion on research between 1983 and 1989. However, SDI achieved few effective results. The much-touted x-ray laser failed to work, as did other components of SDI. In addition, the *Challenger* shuttle disaster in January 1986, in which all the crew members were killed, raised serious questions about U.S. ability to put SDI's components in space. Nevertheless, the administration remained optimistic, even to the extent of rigging one test of an SDI component, the Homing Overlay Experiment (HOE), on June 10, 1984. The administration apparently was not only trying to fool the Soviets about SDI's potential but the Congress as well.

Reagan's New Approach

For a variety of reasons, during the latter half of his first term, Reagan began to display a much more flexible attitude toward the Soviet Union than he had initially. For one thing, nuclear arms reduction was increasingly a popular issue and Reagan was an astute politician who knew how to alter his position to adapt to changing public opinion. Furthermore, late in 1982 the president decided that he would run for a second term, in 1984. He apparently realized that he would have to make some adjustment in his approach to the Soviet Union to enhance his reelection chances. By 1983 Reagan could rationalize a more conciliatory approach to the Soviet Union on the grounds that his nuclear buildup was well under way, and thus the United States could now negotiate with the Soviet Union from a position of strength.

Another factor that was responsible for Reagan's changing attitude toward the Soviet Union was his own increasing sensitivity to the destructive power of nuclear weapons. Late in 1983 and again in early 1984, the president was advised by CIA Director Casey that a NATO exercise to simulate procedures for the release of nuclear weapons, called Able Archer, had alarmed the Soviet intelligence agency (the KGB) and presumably the Kremlin leadership as well. In his memoir, Reagan admitted that he was surprised to have learned that the Soviet leaders were genuinely afraid of an American nuclear attack.[27]

In addition, by his own surprising admission, Reagan said that he was unaware of the Soviet Union's heavy reliance on land-based missiles until after START had begun and therefore did not appreciate why the Soviets so vehemently rejected his initial START proposal. The very shallowness of Reagan's knowledge of nuclear weapon issues — and indeed of the Soviet Union itself — contributed greatly to the relative ease with which he transformed himself into an arms reduction advocate late in his first term.

Also contributing to the change in Reagan's approach to the Soviet Union was the appointment of George Shultz as secretary of state in June 1982. Shultz replaced Alexander Haig, who was fired by the president when he ran afoul of Reagan's White House staff. Although a member of the Committee on the Present Danger, Shultz demonstrated a much more realistic attitude toward the strategic nuclear balance than the hard-liners in the Reagan administration. He believed that the nuclear forces of the two superpowers were roughly equal and that, therefore, the United States could negotiate safely with the Soviets on issues that both nations had a mutual interest to resolve.

Shultz's conversion of Reagan to détente, however, was an uneven and necessarily gradual process, primarily due to the strong opposition of administration hard-liners. NSC director William Clark, Shultz wrote in his memoir, "categorically opposed U.S.–Soviet contacts" and often countered Shultz's memoranda to the president with memos from hard-liners on the NSC staff, which Vice President George Bush told Shultz were "absolutely vicious." While Reagan, encouraged by Mrs. Reagan, supported Shultz, he at first refused to confront the hard-liners on the issue of improving relations with the Soviet Union. Shultz could only conclude that "the president was a prisoner of his own staff."[28]

Defense Secretary Weinberger and CIA director Casey also opposed negotiations with the Soviets. Shultz wrote that "Bill Casey's ideological bent for foreign policy issues was so strong that I worried about the objectivity of his and his agency's intelligence assessments." The line of analysis the CIA was circulating dovetailed with the Defense Department's overemphasis on the Soviet military buildup. "Both painted a picture of a mighty nation confronting us everywhere—confident, unchanging, and determined," Shultz recalled. "I did not agree. The picture they conjured up of the Soviet Union did not match the reality I saw."[29] On several occasions, Shultz was so discouraged by the infighting and Reagan's wavering that he offered his resignation, but he was always persuaded to stay by the president.

Shultz was gradually successful in persuading Reagan to take a more flexible approach toward the Soviet Union. On January 16, 1984, the president delivered an uncharacteristically conciliatory speech in which he said a new U.S.–Soviet dialogue should concentrate on three broad areas: (1) the reduction and eventually elimination of force in regional conflicts, (2) the reduction of nuclear arsenals, (3) the creation of a better working relationship "marked by greater cooperation and understanding."[30] But the Soviets did not immediately grasp the new Reagan line. They believed that the president's new approach was merely "electioneering."

Another reason for the reluctance of the Soviets to respond to the Reagan turnabout was a change in the Kremlin's leadership following the death of Yuri Andropov (due to kidney failure) on February 9, 1984. Four days later, Andropov was succeeded by Konstantin U. Chernenko, another old-guard member of the Politburo. Although Chernenko restated Soviet dedication to peaceful coexistence, it was not until late June 1984 that the Soviet leadership displayed any willingness to resume negotiations with the United States. By then it was obvious even to the Kremlin leaders that their decision to walk out of the INF talks and

START in November 1983 had been a major blunder. The move had not deterred the Americans from continuing their new INF deployments, and it had also taken the pressure off Washington to proceed with arms control talks.

Reagan also was prompted to resume negotiations with the Soviets by the approaching presidential election. The Democratic nominee, Walter Mondale, criticized the administration's inability to conclude any major arms control agreements with the Soviet Union. Mondale promised that, if elected, he would be ready to begin nuclear arms control talks with the Soviets six months after his inauguration. Until negotiations could begin, he said, he would initiate a unilateral freeze on deploying U.S. nuclear weapons.

Partly to steal Mondale's thunder, and partly to ensure continued congressional funding for the administration's nuclear weapons programs, which was made contingent on Reagan's willingness to engage seriously in arms control talks, the president adopted a more positive attitude toward arms reduction talks with the Soviets. In a speech to the UN General Assembly on September 24, 1984, he proposed the establishment of a new Soviet-American negotiating framework, eventually dubbed the Nuclear and Space Arms Talks (NST), which would combine the three major nuclear weapons talks—INF, START, and the antisatellite weapon talks (ASAT)—under one umbrella. The umbrella concept, Reagan said, would make it difficult for a stalemate in one of the negotiations to disrupt progress in the others.

After Reagan's reelection victory in November, the Soviets agreed to participate in the new talks. They obviously were intent on doing all they could, even to the point of agreeing to resume talks on strategic weapons and INF, to halt the threat of a nuclear arms race in space, which SDI threatened to produce.

However, during the first two rounds of the new talks, which began in March 1985 and ended in July, little progress was made. Although there were sharp differences between the two sides on several issues, the main obstacle was "Star Wars." The administration again proposed major reductions in strategic and intermediate-range nuclear weapons but refused to discuss limitations on ballistic missile defenses. Without them, the Soviets refused to make any reductions in offensive strategic and theater weapons.

Mikhail Gorbachev's "New Thinking"

Just as it appeared that the new nuclear arms talks might fail, they received a major impetus from the elevation to power of a new, relatively young (54), and dynamic Soviet leader, Mikhail Gorbachev. Intelligent, articulate, and suave, Gorbachev stood in marked contrast to his unimaginative and heavy-handed predecessors.

Gorbachev's rise to power from relative obscurity was a result of the critical and, as subsequent events would demonstrate, fatal problems inherent in the Soviet system, problems that had become glaringly obvious by the mid-1980s. The root cause of the Soviet breakdown was directly related to deep-seated structural problems in the Soviet system. The most significant weakness was the Soviet economy. Low productivity, enormous waste, planning mistakes, and constant shortages had restrained Soviet growth rates for decades. But the economic crisis became critical when the Soviet economy could no longer produce or absorb the technological innovations, particularly computer technology, that were the basis of economic expansion in the advanced industrial countries. As a result, the gap between Soviet economic output and that of the leading industrial countries widened in the 1980s for the first time in postwar history.

The acute Soviet economic crisis was aggravated by an increasingly pervasive social crisis, which was exemplified by rising alcoholism, worker absenteeism, and infant mortality rates. Relative to the needs of its population the Soviet Union underinvested in social services, which were characterized by shortages and poor quality. The deficiencies in consumption, in turn, generated popular dissatisfaction, undermined incentives, and contributed to low worker morale, as well as the production of inferior goods. It is not surprising that the Soviet Union could not compete effectively in the world market. As a consequence, the Soviet Union was compelled to rely primarily on arms sales and exports of oil and natural gas to earn hard currency.

The growing Soviet military establishment also placed enormous stress on the Soviet economy. During the Brezhnev period, when defense spending in Western and Eastern Europe averaged between 2 and 5 percent, and that of the United States was about 6 to 7 percent of GNP, the defense share of Soviet GNP rose from 12–14 percent in 1965 to 15–17 percent in 1985. (Some sources, which used different estimates of Soviet GNP, put the total as high as 25 percent, representing an enormous burden on the industrial sector.)[31]

The Soviet Union's defense burden was supplemented by the rising cost of maintaining its satellite empire and supporting client states in the Third World. While the number of countries under communist control expanded during the Brezhnev era, most of them were relatively underdeveloped and consequently heavily dependent on Soviet assistance. The estimated "costs of empire," expressed as a share of Soviet GNP, rose from about 1 percent in 1971 to 3 percent in 1980. Not surprisingly, the decline of the Soviet economy undermined the ideological foundation of the entire Soviet system and contributed to the declining appeal of communism in the underdeveloped world.

Gorbachev realized rather quickly that existing Soviet obligations in the Third World would have to be scaled down and new commitments avoided. He decided to cut back on Soviet assistance to Marxist forces in Nicaragua, Cambodia (Kampuchea), Angola, and Ethiopia, and to terminate the costly and inconclusive Soviet military involvement in Afghanistan.

Not surprisingly, he also saw arms reduction as the key element in improving the Soviet image in the West. An end to the arms race would not only reduce Soviet defense expenditures, it also would reduce tensions with the West and thereby encourage much-needed Western economic assistance to the Soviet Union.

The implementation of Gorbachev's "new thinking" compelled him to revise long-held Marxist-Leninist propositions about the character of Soviet policy and the nature of international relations. He rejected the Marxist-Leninist precept that the clash between communism and capitalism was historically inevitable. As Khrushchev had first admitted, the existence of nuclear weapons made class war between the superpowers a suicidal proposition. But it was not only the danger of nuclear war that caused Gorbachev to abandon the Marxist-Leninist concept of class warfare. The fact was, as Gorbachev clearly realized, communism was not only no longer destined to triumph over capitalism, it was directly responsible for the crisis facing the Soviet Union.

Gradually, Gorbachev attempted to give communism a new face, one emphasizing universal human values, such as freedom and self-preservation, rather than the necessity of class conflict. Though continuing to affirm the ideological differences between East and West, Gorbachev insisted that they were superseded by the need for international cooperation. Moreover, coexistence was no longer conceived as an interlude before an inevitable conflict, but rather as a permanent component of the relationship between the communist and the capitalist worlds.

To demonstrate the sincerity of his intentions, Gorbachev had to be honest about the Soviet Union's responsibility for the Cold War, but he placed most of the blame on Josef Stalin. He accused Stalin of contributing to the outbreak of World War II by signing the Nonaggression Pact with Hitler in 1939 and admitted that Stalin's annexation of the Baltic states in 1940 was an aggressive action. This admission eventually helped to undermine Soviet control over these states and, ultimately, contributed to the disintegration of the Soviet Union itself.

In addition, in a speech on July 25, 1988, Soviet Foreign Minister Eduard Shevardnadze criticized Gorbachev's immediate predecessors. He enumerated Soviet mistakes, such as the Afghan debacle, the feud with China, the long-standing underestimation of the European Community, the costly arms race, the 1983–1984 Soviet walkout from the Geneva arms control talks, and the decision to deploy the SS-20s.

By altering the ideological foundation of Soviet foreign policy as well as the bases of Soviet defense strategy, Gorbachev in effect was declaring that he was prepared to end the Cold War. The West's leaders, however, with the exception of British Prime Minister Margaret Thatcher, were slow to accept Gorbachev's olive branch.

Reagan, in fact, resisted Gorbachev's blandishments longer than most Western leaders. By most accounts, including her own, Nancy Reagan played an important part in persuading the president to open up to

Gorbachev. She believed that a relaxation of Cold War tensions would solidify her husband's place in history. In a "dangerous world," she later remarked, it was "ridiculous for the two heavily armed superpowers to be sitting there and not talking to each other." Mrs. Reagan also admitted that, while she did "push Ronnie a little," he "would never have met Gorbachev if he hadn't wanted to."[32] By mid-1985 Reagan clearly was willing to try to charm Gorbachev as much as the new Soviet leader was mesmerizing the world.

A False START

The first Reagan-Gorbachev meeting took place in Geneva in November 1985. Although substantive progress at the summit was limited, the two leaders were able to establish a genuine sense of rapport, and they committed themselves to continuing their dialogue as a way of improving U.S.–Soviet relations.

However, Gorbachev was not content with the slow pace of the dialogue. To spur the talks, in January 1986 he proposed a plan calling for the complete elimination of nuclear weapons by the year 2000. He suggested that, as a first stage, the United States and the Soviet Union should reduce their theater nuclear forces to zero—a proposal that suggested that the Soviets might retreat from their insistence on keeping enough SS-20s to counter French and British strategic nuclear forces. Although there was some movement on the arms issue in the first half of 1986, the stalemate persisted.

Gorbachev then invited Reagan to come to a brief meeting designed to break the logjam. Reagan agreed and the meeting took place in Reykjavik, Iceland, in October 1986. Although billed as a preparatory meeting, Gorbachev arrived with detailed proposals that turned the Reykjavik meeting into a full-scale summit. The Soviet leader offered a START proposal calling for reductions, over a five-year period, in the number of warheads carried by ballistic missiles and air-launched cruise missiles (ALCMs) to 6,000 and the number of long-range missiles and bombers to 1,600. (At the time of the Reykjavik summit, the Soviet Union had 2,500 missiles and bombers, and the United States about 2,100.) Gorbachev then raised his offer to utopian heights, proposing the abolition of all nuclear weapons within ten years. Surprisingly, considering that Reagan had not consulted his allies, whose defense rested heavily on nuclear weapons, the president responded positively to Gorbachev's proposal.

The Soviet leader insisted that his nuclear disarmament proposal was contingent on continued strict adherence to the ABM Treaty, which required that ballistic missile defense (BMD) research be confined to the laboratory. Reagan expressed his willingness to abide by the ABM Treaty but only for an additional ten years. During that period both sides would eliminate all their offensive ballistic missiles. Then they would be free to deploy defensive systems. Reagan favored a much looser interpretation of the ABM Treaty, one that would have permitted extensive testing and development of BMD outside the laboratory, thereby permitting the United States to continue to develop SDI. Said Reagan: "SDI is not now, nor will it ever become, a mere bargaining chip. I've said for a long time that the doctrine of mutual assured destruction, what's called MAD, is downright immoral."[33] Reagan also said that, if SDI worked, the United States would share it with the Soviet Union. Gorbachev expressed doubt that the United State would share SDI technology, considering that it was denying the Soviet Union oil-drilling technology.

As a result of the superpowers' inability to reach an agreement on SDI, a START agreement was not concluded before Reagan left office in 1989. What was equally worrisome to more than a few observers was the administration's decision in 1986 to abandon the unratified SALT II Treaty limits, which the United States had observed until then. In late 1986 the administration decided to deploy air-launched cruise missiles on B-52 bombers, thereby putting the United States over the SALT II limits. As a result of this abandoning of SALT II, there were no longer any agreed limits on the amount of offensive strategic nuclear weapons either side could deploy.

Reducing the Risks of War in Europe

While Reagan and Gorbachev failed to conclude a START agreement, they did complete the INF Treaty. However, almost all the concessions that were required to make the treaty possible were made by Gorbachev. At the Reykjavik summit, he agreed to a global limit of 100 INF warheads for each of their countries, with the Soviet deployments restricted to Asia and America's to the United States. Gorbachev also accepted Reagan's insistence on strict verification measures, including, for the first time ever, on-site inspection. He also agreed to exclude British and French missiles from the limits. On February 28, 1987, in another major concession, Gorbachev decided to accept the zero option without tying it to a BMD agreement. In effect, Gorbachev had capitulated to Reagan's demand to eliminate all U.S.–Soviet INF missiles in Europe.

Still, one last major obstacle to an INF agreement remained. West German Chancellor Helmut Kohl insisted that short-range missiles (those with ranges below 500 kilometers) must also be included in the treaty in order to eliminate the 300-kilometer-range Soviet Scud missiles that were aimed at his country. In response, the Soviets demanded that all short-range nuclear warheads be included in the treaty, specifically those deployed on seventy-two aging Pershing 1A missiles stationed in West Germany.

On August 26, 1987, Kohl accepted the Soviet condition. He stated that, once the United States and the Soviet Union had completely eliminated their intermediate-range missiles, Bonn would destroy its Pershing 1As and would not seek to replace them with another kind of missile. After several remaining issues were cleared up, an INF treaty was finally

initialed by Shultz and Shevardnadze at Geneva on November 24. Two
weeks later, on December 8, it was signed by Reagan and Gorbachev in a
Washington summit.

The INF Treaty was a historic arms control measure. For the first
time, the United States and the Soviet Union had agreed not only to
reduce their nuclear arsenals but also to eliminate an entire category of
nuclear weapons. The INF Treaty banned all land-based missiles with a
range of 1,000–5,500 kilometers as well as short-range and intermediate-
range nuclear forces (SRINF), that is, land-based missiles with a 500–1,000
kilometer range. In signing the treaty, the United States committed itself
to dismantling 429 Pershing 2 and Tomahawk missiles already deployed
and an additional 430 missiles that were not deployed. The Soviet Union
agreed to eliminate 857 deployed missiles and an additional 895 in stor-
age, for a total of 1,752 missiles. Altogether, the treaty committed the
United States to dismantle just under 1,000 warheads and the Soviet
Union over 3,000. Although the missiles were to be destroyed at specified sites, the treaty permitted the nuclear material in their warheads to be
reprocessed for other purposes. The treaty was ratified by the Supreme
Soviet on May 29, 1988, one day before Reagan's arrival in Moscow for
his final summit as president.

While the superpowers were negotiating the INF Treaty, they also
attempted to reduce the risks of a conventional conflict in Europe. In
1978 France proposed the creation of a Conference on Disarmament in
Europe (CDE), in which all the CSCE states would be participants. The
negotiations would consist of two phases. The first would consider confidence-building measures (CBMs), that is, steps designed to increase crisis
stability and foster increased sharing of military information, and thereby
promote the reduction of tensions in Europe. A second phase of the talks
would consider actual force reductions. The French CDE plan proposed
that the zone covered by the talks should stretch from the Atlantic to the
Urals, an area considerably larger than that addressed by the Helsinki
CBMs, which extended only 250 kilometers into Soviet Union.

The Soviets responded to the French suggestion by requesting that
CBMs cover an area of the Atlantic Ocean comparable in size to the area of
the Soviet Union that would be covered by the agreement. But since the
Western powers did not want the Warsaw Pact monitoring NATO rein-
forcement operations, they refused to permit the inclusion of naval exercises
in an agreement unless they were an integral part of land maneuvers. In the
end it was decided to limit the agreement to "the whole of Europe" as far as
the Urals and to include air and sea operations only if they were related to
land operations. This basic plan was adopted by the Madrid Conference of
the CSCE (which met from November 1980 until September 1983), and
in January 1984 the CDE opened in Stockholm, Sweden.

Little progress was made during the first two years of the CDE. However, on August 19, 1986, a breakthrough was achieved when the Soviets
announced that the Warsaw Pact countries were ready to accept manda-

tory inspections of CBMs. The breakthrough made possible the signing of the Stockholm accord by the thirty-five member countries of the CSCE on September 19, 1986. It reinforced provisions of the Helsinki Final Act affecting military activities in Europe. Among other things, it doubled the time required for the pre-notification of major military exercises to 42 days and prohibited military maneuvers exceeding 75,000 troops unless they were announced two years in advance. The Stockholm document also strengthened verification capabilities, including on-site inspections without the right of refusal, subject to a passive quota of three inspections per year. This represented the first time in history that the Soviets accepted mandatory on-site inspections of its territory, thereby setting the stage for the on-site inspection feature of the INF Treaty.

In addition to diminishing the risk of a surprise attack, Gorbachev was also interested in reducing the actual size of conventional forces in Europe. On April 18, 1986, he proposed the creation of a new forum to replace the unproductive MBFR talks and recommended that it deal with conventional force reductions in all of Europe, from the Atlantic to the Urals. The new talks, eventually called the Conventional Force Talks in Europe (CFE), would include the twenty-three NATO and Warsaw Pact states. In February 1987 Gorbachev pressured the West to cut its forces substantially by announcing that Soviet forces would be reduced in size and restructured to a purely defensive configuration based on the principle of "reasonable sufficiency."

In addition, on December 7, 1988, Gorbachev announced that, within two years, the Soviet Union would unilaterally reduce its total armed forces by 500,000 troops (about 10 percent of the total). The Soviets also would remove 10,000 tanks from the area between the Atlantic and the Urals, including 5,000 from East Germany, Czechoslovakia, and Hungary. In all, six tank divisions totaling 2,000 tanks would be disbanded and 50,000 troops would be withdrawn from these three countries. Subsequently, Soviet Foreign Minister Shevardnadze announced that the Soviets would also remove the short-range nuclear systems associated with the six tank divisions to be withdrawn from Central Europe. Shortly after the Gorbachev announcement, several East European governments announced cuts of their own.

The implication of these Soviet actions was that the Brezhnev Doctrine (which held that no socialist countries would ever be "lost" to the West) was null and void. It would take a few years, however, before the inhabitants of these countries realized the full implications of this very significant change in Soviet policy. Coming on the heals of the INF Treaty and the unilateral reduction of the Soviet armed forces, and the beginning of the Soviet retreat from the Third World, the demise of the Brezhnev Doctrine persuaded all but the most hard-line Westerners of Gorbachev's determination to end the Cold War.

Nevertheless, Reagan kept up the pressure on the Soviets to withdraw from Eastern Europe. In a visit to West Berlin in June 1987, he called upon Gorbachev to tear down the Berlin Wall. He also continued to condemn communist violations of human rights and repeated his earlier calls for freedom in the Baltic states and the withdrawal of the Soviet Union's armed forces from the rest of Eastern Europe.

The Soviet Retreat from the Third World

The president also kept up U.S. pressure on the Soviets to withdraw completely from the Third World. On August 29, 1987, Reagan again called for the Soviets to stop assisting the Sandinista government in Nicaragua, and in his January 25, 1988 State of the Union address, Reagan said there could be no settlement of the Afghanistan problem until the Soviets withdrew all their troops from that country.

During Reagan's last year in office, Gorbachev accelerated the Soviet retreat from the Third World. An agreement was signed by the conflicting Afghan parties on April 14, 1988, with the United States and the Soviet Union acting as its guarantors. The agreement required the withdrawal of Soviet troops between May 15, 1988, and February 15, 1989. In addition, in May 1988, after considerable Soviet urging, Vietnam announced that it would withdraw half of its total forces from Cambodia (about 50,000 troops) by the end of that year. In December 1988 Soviet and American negotiators brokered an end to the conflict in Angola and Namibia. The agreement required the withdrawal of all foreign troops, that is, Cuban soldiers as well as South African forces, from Angola by July 1, 1991, and called for negotiations between the warring parties (which began in June 1989). It also provided for free elections to end Namibia's struggle for independence, a status that was granted Namibia by South Africa in March 1990.

In a speech at Vladivostok in July 1986, Gorbachev also said he also was prepared to end the long Sino-Soviet conflict. He proposed negotiations to resolve the Amur-Ussuri River border dispute and indicated that he would reduce the number of Soviet troops in Mongolia. In addition to beginning the withdrawal of Soviet troops from Afghanistan in 1988, he began the reduction of Soviet forces in Soviet Siberia. These steps made possible the Sino-Soviet rapprochement that occurred before Gorbachev left office. In May 1989 Gorbachev became the first Soviet leader to visit China since Nikita Khrushchev, over three decades earlier.

Gorbachev also attempted to repair Soviet relations with Israel and Egypt. Moscow restored diplomatic relations with Israel, which had been broken during the Six-Day War. Egypt, for its part, allowed the Soviets to reopen their consulates in Alexandria and Port Said. In 1988 Egypt also endorsed Moscow's calls for an international conference on the Middle East and asserted that the Soviet Union should play a leading role in such a conference.

Reagan's Curtain Call

Reagan's appearance in Moscow during June 1988 was a clear indication that the end of the Cold War was finally possible. When asked if he still considered the Soviets the "focus of evil in the modern world," Reagan responded, "They've changed." [34] He attributed the change in part to the leadership of Gorbachev and the trust that had developed between the two leaders as a result of their four summit meetings. The president even embraced the Soviet leader at Lenin's tomb.

In Moscow, the two sides discussed human rights and Jewish emigration, freedom of religious practice in the Soviet Union, trade issues, and regional conflicts in Angola, the Middle East, Central America, Cambodia, and Vietnam. They also discussed steps to provide for the prior notification of missile tests and a verification protocol to make possible U.S. ratification of the 1974 Peaceful Nuclear Explosions Treaty, which prohibited nonmilitary nuclear explosions above 150 kilotons. Later, on September 15, 1988, the president would announce that the United States and the Soviet Union had signed a treaty to establish nuclear risk reduction centers in Washington and Moscow. Their purpose would be to avoid conflicts resulting from an accident, misinterpretation, or miscalculation. While the Moscow conference ended on a positive note, START remained unfinished when Reagan turned the White House over to his successor, George Bush.

Reagan also continued to pressure Gorbachev for more reforms, particularly in the area of human rights. In a speech at Moscow State University, he spoke about the value of freedom and its links to many other aspects of life, such as art and technology. He said that he and Gorbachev wanted to have student exchange programs involving thousands of students a year. On December 3, 1988, Reagan was generally optimistic about the superpower relationship, saying that he was looking forward to the day when the Berlin Wall would be torn down and the works of Alexander Solzhenitsyn would be published in the Soviet Union.

By the end of his term, Reagan took satisfaction in the progress he and Gorbachev had made in improving Soviet-American relations. In December 1988 Reagan and President-elect Bush met Gorbachev again, in New York, where the three leaders posed for pictures in front of the Statue of Liberty. Gorbachev had just delivered a dramatic speech before the UN General Assembly in which he appealed for the de-ideologizing of international relations, supported democracy and human liberty, rejected class warfare and the use of force, and announced a unilateral 10 percent reduction in the Soviet Union's armed forces.

On January 17, 1989, Shultz and Shevardnadze signed the CSCE Vienna Declaration and agreed that Moscow would be the site of a human rights conference in 1991. In Vienna Shultz welcomed changes that had taken place in the Soviet Union since the signing of the 1975 Helsinki Final Act. Among other things, he mentioned the end to the

Soviet jamming of radio broadcasts, the release of more than 600 political prisoners, including some Helsinki monitors, and the change in Soviet emigration policies. However, Shultz did criticize some Eastern European nations for continuing to violate the 1975 Helsinki Final Act. Nevertheless, it was on an optimistic note that the Reagan-Gorbachev era came to an end on January 20, 1989.

Did Reagan Win the Cold War?

The fact that, for all practical purposes, the Cold War ended during Ronald Reagan's presidency has led some to conclude that he was primarily responsible for the U.S. "victory" over the Soviet Union. The so-called Reagan victory school holds that his administration's military and ideological assertiveness during the 1980s was primarily responsible for the end of the Cold War, the demise of communism in Europe, and ultimately the collapse of the Soviet Union itself. As the president put it on December 16, 1988, the changes taking place in the Soviet Union were in part the result of U.S. firmness, a strong defense, healthy alliances, and a willingness to use force when necessary. Moreover, as he boasted, he had been more than willing to point out the differences in the American and Soviet political systems at every opportunity. In addition, his supporters have asserted that the "full-court press" launched by the administration during Reagan's first term, which included a military buildup capped by SDI, the denial of technology to the Soviet Union, and the administration's counteroffensive in the Third World, delivered the "knock-out punch" to a system that was internally bankrupt "and on the ropes."[35]

Others attribute the end of the Cold War to Reagan's desire to prevent a nuclear conflagration. This view asserts that the president never liked nuclear weapons as offensive instruments and that with his SDI program he demonstrated his disdain for deterrence, at least deterrence based on the mutual assured destruction doctrine (MAD). Reagan's goal to eliminate all offensive nuclear weapons, his supporters argue, made possible the INF Treaty. Reagan failed to conclude a START treaty before he left office only because the Soviets refused to accept a defensive deterrent strategy, the basis of SDI, as a better alternative to MAD.

However, not everyone, including this author, accepts the argument that the Reagan administration was primarily responsible for the end of the Cold War. In fact, probably no one, especially the president, expected that the administration's policies ultimately would cause the disintegration of the Soviet empire, at least not as quickly as it occurred. Said Reagan: "We meant to change a nation [the United States], and instead, we changed a world. . . . All in all, not bad, not bad at all."[36]

More important as the cause of the Cold War's demise was the internal weakness of the Soviet Union, which, to be sure, the policies pursued by the Reagan administration exacerbated. By the time Reagan entered the White House, the Soviet economy had sunk into such a state of stagnation that it was obvious that communism had failed and a radically new approach was required.

No one realized this more than Mikhail Gorbachev. Even though there never was much likelihood that SDI would render Soviet missiles ineffective, he nevertheless was obliged to take seriously America's technological potential and the strategic impact of even an imperfect defense. He also realized that the Soviet Union had insufficient economic strength to compete with the United States in another technological arms race. Nor could the Soviet Union continue to expend its resources competing with the United States in the Third World.

Pressed by his country's economic weakness and alarmed by the increasing risks of a nuclear war, Gorbachev was more than willing to attempt to end the Cold War. Its resolution would enable him to reduce his country's expensive military establishment as well as obtain badly needed economic assistance from the West. Accordingly, Gorbachev changed the ideological content and declared goals of Soviet foreign policy and moved away from the concept of international class war toward a vision of peace and cooperation with the West.

While Reagan was willing to improve relations with the Soviet Union, George Shultz must be given credit for the hard work and skill that was required to bring it off, in the face of much opposition from hard-liners within the administration. Yet it was neither Shultz nor Reagan, but rather Gorbachev, who made the major concessions that were needed to achieve success. The INF negotiations, for example, were concluded successfully primarily because of the concessions Gorbachev made, in the face of considerable opposition from hard-liners within his own government and military.

Reagan may have had a genuine revulsion for nuclear weapons, but it was not at all obvious in the policies he adopted and pursued during his first and much of his second term. His disinclination to embrace détente was due to his own limited knowledge of nuclear weapons technology and strategy as well as his reluctance to offend the hard-liners in his administration, who had the expertise that the president lacked but not the same revulsion for nuclear weapons. Reagan had to be encouraged into running the risks of negotiating with the Soviets by his wife, Nancy Reagan, and by Secretary of State George Shultz.

Public and congressional opinion also had much to do with the Reagan's turnabout. The Democratic-controlled Congress made its continued support of pet administration military programs contingent on Reagan's willingness to negotiate seriously with the Soviets. The Congress, in turn, was influenced by an American public that was increasingly susceptible to the warnings of the anti-nuclear weapons movement about the perils of the Reagan military buildup.

Neither Congress nor the American people gave much support to Reagan's crusade against communism, particularly in the Third World. Reagan's ability to conduct that crusade was weakened even more during his last two years in office by waning public and congressional support for large-scale defense increases and, above all, by the Iran-Contra affair, which threatened to destroy Reagan's presidency. In other words, Reagan needed a new approach to the Soviet Union, in part, to divert attention from the Iran-Contra fiasco. While he did not need a new U.S.–Soviet relationship as much as Gorbachev did, the revival of détente late in his presidency did win Reagan public accolades he sorely needed in the aftermath of the Iran-Contra affair. The Reagan-Gorbachev love-in was, in fact, an example of how necessity can make the strangest of bedfellows. Thanks to détente, and the unwillingness of the Congress to press ahead with impeachment proceedings, Reagan left office as one of the most popular presidents in this century.

The fact that Reagan was the reluctant recipient of Gorbachev's advances, nevertheless, does not diminish the importance of his contribution to ending the Cold War. Reagan did not have to support Shultz's efforts to improve U.S. relations with the Soviet Union, nor did he have to accept Gorbachev's concessions. Instead, he could have followed the same hard-line policies he had initiated at the beginning of his first term, even if, as was possible, this would have led to Bush's defeat in the 1988 presidential election.

While the consequences of continued confrontation with the Soviet Union would have been hard to predict, it undoubtedly would have made Gorbachev's attempted transformation of the Soviet system even more difficult than it was. A continuation of the confrontational approach could also have produced a hard-line reaction against the Soviet leader much sooner than it occurred, and perhaps one more successful than was the attempted coup against Gorbachev in August 1991. Reagan's acceptance of Gorbachev's new thinking, in effect, bought time for the Soviet leader and, more importantly, allowed the embryonic Soviet democratic movement to gain a firmer hold among the Russian people, at least firm enough to contribute to the failure of the hard-liners' coup.

Still, the price the United States paid during the Reagan years to "win" the Cold War was high. His decision to cut taxes while initiating the largest and most expensive peacetime military buildup in U.S. history, combined with Congress' refusal to cut domestic spending, contributed to an enormous increase in the national debt. Moreover, pressing domestic problems—the decline of the nation's infrastructure, the increase in crime, educational inequity, and others too numerous to list here—were ignored. Future generations of Americans will have to pay the bill for Reagan's "victory" in the Cold War.

9

George Bush and the End of the Cold War, 1989–1991

Reagan's Successor

The presidency of George Bush, who succeeded Ronald Reagan in January 1989, witnessed the end of the Cold War, the collapse of communism in Eastern Europe, and the disintegration of the Soviet Union itself. During Bush's presidency, the development of a new, post–Cold War relationship between the United States and what would become the successor states to the Soviet Union began. The new relationship would be characterized by cooperation rather than the confrontation that had been the hallmark of the Cold War.

Ironically, considering the important role that he would play in building the new Soviet-American relationship, Bush was slow to pick up the baton of détente. Gorbachev, in his speech before the United Nations on December 7, 1988, had challenged the then president-elect to end the Cold War. Not only did he announce a massive, unilateral reduction of Soviet armed forces and the withdrawal of ten divisions from Eastern Europe, he also challenged the United States to cooperate with the Soviet Union in resolving conflicts around the world, particularly in Afghanistan, Cambodia, Nicaragua, and Angola. Gorbachev also recommended that a revived United Nations should be the instrument of superpower cooperation in creating a new world order.

In late January 1989 former Secretary of State Henry Kissinger urged Bush to boldly seize the initiative from Gorbachev by proposing the withdrawal of all Soviet forces from Eastern Europe. Privately, Gorbachev's close aid, Aleksandr Yakovlev, warned Kissinger that Bush's refusal to support Gorbachev would strengthen the hands of communist hard-liners who were increasingly criticizing the Soviet leader for abandoning socialism and selling out to the West.

Bush expressed fascination with Kissinger's proposal but did not pursue it. The president believed that Reagan had become too enthusiastic about détente in the last years of his presidency and consequently too willing to outdo Gorbachev in demilitarizing the world. Reagan's Reykjavik bid to eliminate all nuclear weapons, without consulting America's NATO allies in advance, was the most startling example of the kind of one-upmanship Bush was determined to avoid. As a result, the new president said he would slow the tempo of détente, at least until a comprehensive review of America's Soviet policy, which he authorized on February 15, was completed.

It was not until May 12 that the review was finally unveiled by the president. Reflecting his cautiousness, it was embarrassingly thin on recommendations for improving U.S.–Soviet relations. Its most impressive initiative was a proposal for reviving the "Open Skies" plan, which had first been proposed by President Eisenhower in 1955. The plan called for reciprocal aerial reconnaissance of Soviet and U.S. territory. Observing that, in the past, friendly overtures from the Soviets were usually followed by increased international tensions, Bush challenged Gorbachev to demonstrate his commitment to change by withdrawing Soviet support from Cuba and Nicaragua, tearing down the Iron Curtain, reducing the size of Soviet armed forces further, and permitting greater emigration from the Soviet Union.

While Bush expressed support for Gorbachev's efforts to reform the Soviet system, key administration officials questioned the wisdom of tying the United States too closely to any Soviet leader. Secretary of Defense Richard Cheney, for one, publicly predicted, on April 29, 1989, that Gorbachev's reforms would fail, and Deputy Secretary of State Lawrence Eagleburger said it was not America's responsibility to ensure that they would not.

By this time, observers on both sides of the Atlantic, including even former President Reagan, were criticizing Bush for what they believed was his excessively cautious pursuit of détente. During the previous month, George Kennan, the originator of the containment theory, told the Senate Foreign Relations Committee that the time for regarding the Soviet Union as a military opponent had "clearly passed."[1] Kennan's comments evoked a standing ovation from his audience.

The NATO allies also were pressuring Bush to be more flexible toward the Soviet leader. French President François Mitterrand and West German Chancellor Helmut Kohl, in particular, blamed Bush for losing the contest of public opinion to Gorbachev. The Soviet leader had captured the public's imagination with a proposal to follow up the INF Treaty with an agreement to remove short-range nuclear forces (SNF) from the European theater, but the Bush administration initially rejected the idea.

Defense Secretary Cheney described the proposed SNF talks as a "dangerous trap" that would strip NATO of its nuclear deterrent capability.[2]

Nevertheless, Gorbachev kept the pressure on Bush. In mid-May he announced that the Soviet Union would eliminate 500 nuclear warheads unilaterally from its European arsenal. He also proposed more generous cuts in conventional weapons at the CFE talks, which had begun in March 1983. Increasingly, Bush's cautious approach was becoming a source of divisiveness within the Atlantic alliance, with the allies pressing the administration to grasp the opportunity offered by Gorbachev to end the Cold War.

By late May 1989 Bush realized that Gorbachev had succeeded in making him look like the primary obstacle to détente. In an attempt to gain the initiative, the president unveiled his own plan to reduce military forces in Europe. At the Brussels NATO summit in late May, he proposed 15 percent cuts in NATO and Warsaw Pact conventional forces and 20 per reductions in total U.S. and Soviet military personnel in Europe. The president's proposal also called for a ceiling of 275,000 troops in the respective European forces of the United States and the Soviet Union.

Bush announced that he was postponing a decision on whether to proceed with the modernization of the Lance short-range missiles, which were deployed by the United States in West Germany. In addition, he expressed his administration's willingness to hold SNF talks with the Soviet Union but stipulated that these negotiations would be deferred until after a CFE agreement was concluded. The Bush initiatives, which represented the beginning of the end of his cautious approach to the Soviet Union, were well received both in Western and Eastern Europe.

The Revolutions of 1989

The rapidly changing situation in Eastern Europe also pressured the Bush administration to achieve an accommodation with the Soviet Union. On July 6 Gorbachev called for a "common European home" and formally rejected the Brezhnev Doctrine, which had been formulated to justify Soviet intervention in Czechoslovakia in 1968. He also stressed the importance of arms control, human rights, the rule of law, and the protection of the environment.[3]

During a trip to Poland and Hungary that month, Bush challenged Gorbachev to put those principles into practice. "There cannot be a common European home," he said, "until all within it are free to move from room to room."[4] Noting that the reform government of Hungary had begun dismantling the barbed-wire fence along its border with neutral Austria, Bush exclaimed to a crowd in Mainz, West Germany, "Let Berlin be next! Let Berlin be next!"[5]

Yet while Bush publicly called for the liberation of Eastern Europe, during his visits to Poland and Hungary he made it clear that he was in no hurry to see that day come. Fearing that the rapid collapse of the Iron

Curtain would increase U.S. tensions with the Soviet Union—if it did not prompt Kremlin hard-liners to overthrow Gorbachev—Bush gave his support to General Wojciech Jaruzelski, who had imposed martial law in Poland in 1981. The Polish people, who for the most part considered Jaruzelski a Soviet stooge, showed their displeasure for Bush's stand by turning out to greet him in much smaller numbers than they had on his previous visit two years earlier.

Despite the disgust of the Polish people for Bush's support for Jaruzelski, the general did prove to be an important element in the peaceful transformation that occurred in Poland during 1989. Earlier that year, Jaruzelski had invited the banned Solidarity Party to join in a communist-led coalition government. Jaruzelski's offer was motivated by a desire to obtain increased Western financial assistance to help reverse Poland's deteriorating economic situation. In exchange, Solidarity agreed to accept continued communist control of the secret police, the military, and the presidency, to which Jaruzelski was reelected by the Polish parliament, by a one-vote margin, on July 19.

To the surprise of the communists, however, in the June 4 election Solidarity won 160 of the 161 contested seats in the lower house of the Polish parliament and 99 of the 100 contested seats in the upper house. But instead of forming a parliamentary coalition with the Communist Party, as was expected, Solidarity leader Lech Walesa persuaded his party to ally itself with two small, noncommunist parties that had been coerced into alliances with the communists in the past. As a result, the Solidarity-led coalition named the new prime minister, Tadeusz Mazowiecki, on August 24, 1989. Mazowiecki would head the first noncommunist government in Eastern Europe since the democratic government of Czechoslovakia had been overthrown in 1948.

Significantly, Gorbachev facilitated this peaceful transfer of power in Poland. In a much publicized telephone conversation on August 22, he advised the Polish communist leader Mieczyslaw Rakowski to support the Mazowiecki government. Gorbachev's refusal to use Soviet troops to reverse the results of the election demonstrated that the Brezhnev Doctrine was indeed dead. It was replaced, said Soviet foreign ministry spokesman Gennadi Gerasimov, by the "Sinatra Doctrine," a reference to the song "My Way" that was popularized by the American singer Frank Sinatra.[6] In other words, Gerasimov said, each East European state would be free to go its own way in determining the nature of its political system.

Gorbachev had a variety of motives for not intervening militarily in Poland. For one, he realized that if the communist regimes in Eastern Europe failed to initiate meaningful reforms, riots would result and the Soviet army would be called upon to reestablish order. He could not afford to comply with such a request and still hope to obtain badly needed economic aid from the West. On July 29, 1989, U.S. Secretary of State James Baker III had warned Shevardnadze that the Soviet Union could not use troops to maintain communism in Poland and still expect to end the Cold War with the United States. Nor could Gorbachev ignore the lesson of Afghanistan, where the Soviets had waged a costly war since 1979 only to withdraw in defeat ten years later (the withdrawal was completed in February 1989).

Determined to avoid future Afghanistans, Gorbachev pressured the satellite regimes to implement their own versions of perestroika (reform) in the hope that they would then acquire a semblance of popular legitimacy that would preclude the necessity of Soviet military intervention. But Gorbachev had vastly underestimated the extent to which the moral bankruptcy of communism had destroyed any possibility of its being legitimized in Eastern Europe. He also clearly did not anticipate the extent of the changes that were destined to occur in Eastern Europe during the next year. What began as an effort to reform communism in Eastern Europe would end with its collapse and, ultimately, the disintegration of the Soviet Union itself.

The Hungarian Communist Party did attempt to emulate Gorbachev's reform program, but to no avail. On January 11, 1989, the communist-dominated Hungarian parliament legalized freedom of assembly and freedom of association for noncommunist groups. It legalized independent political parties a month later. On April 8 Janos Kadar, who had been installed as the leader of the Communist Party after the bloody 1956 revolution, was ousted from power. On May 2 Hungary became the first Soviet bloc country to open its border with Western Europe. In September the communist government and the newly created opposition parties agreed to participate in free elections, which were scheduled for March 1990. In preparation for the election, on October 7 the Communist Party formally disbanded itself and reformed itself as a new Socialist Party. However, the renamed Communist Party received only 9 percent of the vote in the March 25, 1990, parliamentary election, thereby enabling the democratic opposition parties to establish a new noncommunist government under the leadership of Jozsef Antall of the Democratic Forum.

One unanticipated consequence of Hungary's democratization was a massive influx into the country of thousands of East Germans. They had taken advantage of Hungary's open border with Austria, hoping they could emigrate to West Germany. The exodus from East Germany demonstrated the depth of popular discontent with the hard-line communist regime of Eric Hoenecker. When Gorbachev visited Berlin on October 7, 1989, he was cheered by its oppressed citizens. Gorbachev warned the East German Politburo that it could not continue to isolate itself from the people and expect to survive.

On October 18, after demonstrations rocked Leipzig, East Germany's second largest city, Honecker was replaced by Egon Krenz, the long-time party secretary for internal security issues. Krenz attempted to stop the exodus of East Germans from the country by ending restrictions on travel to the West, but the move only encouraged more East Germans to flee. As a result, in a stunning move on November 9, the East German government opened the Berlin Wall. Hundreds of thousands of East Germans immediately poured into West Berlin.

A day after the wall was breached, a worried Gorbachev dispatched a message to Bush expressing his fear that events were moving too rapidly in Germany. He called for urgent consultations with the other three former occupation powers—Britain, France, and the United States—and insisted on being a part of any discussions regarding Germany's future. After consulting America's European allies, Bush sent back a vague reply to Gorbachev emphasizing the importance of German self-determination but not, at this point, accepting the Soviet demand for a role in deciding the future of Germany.

Despite the efforts of the new East German government to gain popular acceptance, demonstrations in the country only intensified. On December 1, 1989, the communist regime buckled and surrendered its monopoly of power. Two days later, Krenz resigned and was replaced by a moderate communist, Hans Modrow, who immediately promised free elections in early 1990. As in Poland and Hungary, the East German election, on March 18, 1990, resulted in a communist defeat. In April 1990 East Germany's first noncommunist government was formed by a coalition of the Christian Democrats and the Social Democrats. The new prime minister, Lothar de Mazière, who favored the rapid reunification of the two Germanys, negotiated an agreement with West Germany's Chancellor Kohl for their economic merger on July 2, 1990.

By November 1989 the events in Poland and East Germany had emboldened the small democratic opposition groups in Czechoslovakia. On November 17 thousands of young people congregated in the main square of Prague to demand recognition of their human rights. Two days later, an estimated 200,000 people demonstrated in the capital, demanding free elections and the resignation of the hard-line communist leaders. On November 24 Communist Party General Secretary Milos Jakes resigned. Fours days later, after millions of Czech workers staged a general strike, the government pledged to allow noncommunist parties to organize freely. On December 10 a new cabinet, with noncommunists in the majority, was sworn in by hard-line President Gustav Husak, who immediately resigned. Husak was replaced as president by the dissident leader Vaclav Havel on December 29, 1989.

The new interim government rapidly dismantled the communist system. It scheduled free elections in June 1990 and opened the Austrian border. Havel also promised that all Soviet troops would be withdrawn from Czechoslovakia by the end of June 1991. In the June 1990 election, the communists received only 14 percent of the parliamentary vote, while Havel's Civic Forum Party won 47 percent. The Civic Forum then formed a coalition government with the new Christian Democratic Party, which received 12 percent of the vote. No communists sat in the new government.

Bulgaria was also affected by the events in the rest of Eastern Europe. On November 9, 1989, the day the Berlin Wall was opened, Bulgaria's communist politburo removed Todor Zhivkov, who had been the party's leader since 1961, and replaced him with Foreign Minister Petar T. Mladenov. Under Mladenov and his successors, the reform communists were able to hang on to power in Bulgaria for more than a year before finally being overtaken by democratic forces.

The transition from communism in Romania was far bloodier than in any other satellite state. In December 1989 hundreds of Romanians were killed by state security forces in the city of Timisoara when they demonstrated against the government's attempt to evict the dissident priest Lazslo Tokes from his church. The killings provoked even larger demonstrations. Nicolae Ceausescu, the long-time, much-hated Romanian president, was jeered in a mass demonstration in Bucharest on December 21. Sensing that he was losing control after military units began supporting the demonstrators, Ceausescu and his wife attempted to flee the country the next day. They were captured and summarily executed by the army on December 25.

Ceaucescu's fate demonstrated the wisdom of hard-line leaders elsewhere in Eastern Europe who decided not to resist the revolutions. Crucial to their decision to yield without a fight was their knowledge that no military support would be coming from Moscow. When Gorbachev did not intervene to save communism in strategically important East Germany, which hosted the best Soviet divisions, some 380,000 troops, he demonstrated that he would not act to prevent its collapse anywhere else in Europe. By the end of 1989, communism in Eastern Europe was finished.

The Malta Summit, December 1989

The events in Eastern Europe served as an important backdrop to the strategic arms reduction talks (START), which resumed in Geneva in mid-June 1989. However, the talks made little progress until Secretary of State Baker met with Soviet Foreign Minister Eduard Shevardnadze in September 1989 at Baker's ranch, near Jackson's Hole, Wyoming. In a major concession to the United States, Shevardnadze told Baker that the two nations could complete and sign a START treaty even if they had not agreed on limits for the American SDI program. In another significant concession, Shevardnadze told Baker that the Soviet Union would dismantle the giant phased-array radar at Krasnoyarsk in Siberia, which the United States had long charged was a violation of the ABM Treaty. Baker and Shevardnadze also issued a joint statement committing the United States and the Soviet Union to work for the completion of a treaty banning chemical weapons.

At their Jackson Hole meeting, Baker and Shevardnadze also made the initial arrangements for a Bush-Gorbachev summit, which would be held in Washington in the spring of 1990. However, Bush decided not to wait that long to see the Soviet leader. On October 31 the White House announced that the president and Gorbachev would have an "informal meeting" off the coast of Malta on December 2 and 3, 1989.

Before joining President Bush in Malta, Gorbachev traveled to Italy. He called upon Pope John Paul II, who, in addition to being the head of the Roman Catholic Church, was a Pole and an arch-foe of communism. Addressing the pontiff as "Your Holiness," Gorbachev invited him to visit the Soviet Union. He also agreed to reopen diplomatic relations with the Vatican and promised that the Soviet Union would soon pass a new law guaranteeing religious freedom for all believers.

The Malta summit convened alternately on U.S. and Soviet warships, both of which were rocked by a severe storm. Bush and Gorbachev resolved to make progress in START, the CFE talks, and negotiations to reduce chemical weapons. The president also promised to move "beyond containment" in the U.S. approach to the Soviet Union. He proposed steps to normalize U.S.–Soviet trade, including granting the Soviet Union most-favored-nation status, credits, and observer status in the General Agreement on Tariffs and Trade (GATT), thus helping to bring the Soviet Union into the world economic structure. Gorbachev was clearly pleased by Bush's economic concessions and responded by reaffirming his promise to turn the Soviet economy "sharply toward cooperation with other countries, so that it would be part and parcel of the world economic system."[7]

Gorbachev also pledged to work with the United States in ending conflicts in the Third World. He agreed to support free presidential elections in Nicaragua and to halt Soviet arms shipments to the El Salvadoran rebels. Two months later, when the ruling Sandinistas lost the election in Nicaragua, the Soviet Union accepted the new government of Violeta Barrios de Chamorro. However, Bush could not get Gorbachev to abandon Fidel Castro. Gorbachev said he had tried to persuade Castro to adopt some form of perestroika, "but we cannot dictate to him."[8]

Nor, at Malta, did the two sides make any progress on the German issue, which served as another unavoidable backdrop to the talks. Gorbachev ignored Bush's proposal to hold the Olympic games in Berlin in the year 2004. He viewed the president's suggestion as an attempt to trap him into recognizing the inevitability of Germany's reunification, with Berlin once again its capital.

In spite of their differences, the most important result of the Malta summit was the cooperative dialogue Bush and Gorbachev established. It was the first time, Gorbachev said later, that he had felt that he could trust Bush not to embarrass him with excessive demands for concessions in Eastern Europe. Two years later, then Soviet Foreign Minister Alexander Bessmertnykh recalled, "If it were not for Malta, the Soviet Union would never have so smoothly surrendered its control of Eastern Europe and the Baltics."[9] President Bush, for his part, said that the United States no longer considered the Soviet Union an enemy. Not surprisingly, some historians have called the Malta summit the symbolic end of the Cold War.

The Continuing Decline of the Soviet Union

As 1990 dawned, and U.S. policy toward the Soviet Union shifted its focus from going beyond containment to moving beyond the Cold War, growing problems within the Soviet Union increasingly affected the U.S.–Soviet relationship. Above all, perestroika had not only failed to produce any visible improvement in the Soviet economy but had contributed to its decline. A report by U.S. intelligence agencies in April 1990 stated that the Soviet economy was in a "near crisis" state, with only slight prospects of improvement.[10] A CIA assessment blamed the economic collapse on a variety of factors, including the anachronistic centralized planning structure, the inefficient agricultural system, and the virtual absence of advanced computer technology. In addition, natural disasters, such as the earthquake in Armenia in 1988, and human errors, such as the Chernobyl nuclear reactor fire in 1986, squeezed already limited Soviet resources.

While the collapse of communism was largely a result of factors beyond Gorbachev's control, the Soviet leader was at least partially responsible for its demise. Fearing that a rapid switch to a free-market system would raise prices and unemployment to levels that even the usually docile Soviet public would not accept, Gorbachev refused to take the painful steps necessary to end the economy's tailspin, such as ending government price supports. Instead, for five years Gorbachev initiated half measures, which undermined the centralized planning system without building an effective free-market system to replace it. The consequences were shortages, falling productivity, strikes, and runaway inflation.

Not surprisingly, while Gorbachev's popularity was soaring in the Western world, it plummeted in the Soviet Union. Moreover, Gorbachev had to contend with public opposition, unlike earlier Soviet leaders. At a conference of the Soviet Communist Party in June–July 1988, he had been able to push a new constitution through the Supreme Soviet. One of its major features was a new Congress of People's Deputies, most of whose members would be directly selected by the Soviet people in an election during March 1989.

The election results were a disaster for the Communist Party. One communist establishment figure after another was defeated and replaced by antiparty candidates, the most outstanding of whom was the maverick communist Boris Yeltsin. In a district coterminous with Moscow, Yeltsin received 6 million votes, far more than the party hack who ran against him. In the Baltic republics, nationalist reformers secured the majority of the seats. The election was tantamount to a vote of no confidence in the communist establishment. Although the Communist Party would remain an important element in Soviet politics, it would no longer be a decisive one.

While Gorbachev did not stand for office in the election—a fact his democratic critics emphasized—as head of the Soviet Communist Party, as well as president of the Soviet Union, he was increasingly identified with the party's failures. At a plenum of the Central Committee of the

Soviet Communist Party in December 1989, one hard-line communist after another criticized both Gorbachev and Shevardnadze. "Why did you lose Eastern Europe? Why did you surrender Germany?" they asked. One speaker said that "if capitalists and the Pope praise us, that means we are moving in the wrong direction. . . ."[11]

Gorbachev was also subjected to growing criticism from reformers. On February 3, 1990, hundreds of thousands of Russians marched through Moscow to demand an end to communist domination. Gorbachev responded, two days later, by recommending a change in the Soviet constitution that would end the Communist Party's monopoly of political power. He also called for the creation of a new executive office, the presidency, that would give him more authority and reduce his dependence on the Communist Party. On February 7 the Central Committee voted to give Gorbachev the additional power he desired and accepted the principle of multiparty democracy. On May 29, the eve of Gorbachev's departure for a summit meeting with Bush in Washington, Yeltsin was elected the chairman of the Presidium of the Supreme Soviet of the Russian Federation—in effect, president of Russia. In that post, he would increasingly challenge Gorbachev.

Rising nationalism contributed to the growing instability of the Soviet Union. With the near collapse of the Soviet economic system, the Communist Party could no longer act as the glue that held together the Soviet multinational state. In February 1988 ethnic violence broke out in Soviet Armenia and Azjerbaijan, requiring Gorbachev to dispatch troops to the scene in what turned out to be only a partially successful attempt to restore order.

The greatest challenge to the territorial integrity of the Soviet Union came from Lithuania, which, along with Estonia and Latvia, had been forcibly annexed by Stalin in 1940. On March 11, 1990, the Lithuanian parliament declared the country's independence. In an attempt to prevent the breakup of the Soviet Union, Gorbachev imposed an economic blockade on Lithuania, threatened to rule the republic by presidential degree, and sent Soviet troops to Vilnius, the Lithuanian capital, all in an ultimately unsuccessful attempt to reverse its declaration of independence.

Bush and a Weakened Gorbachev

A crucial question for the Bush administration during 1990 was how much the United States should help Gorbachev to sustain his position. During a visit to Moscow in February 1990, Secretary of State Baker was shaken by Shevardnadze's bleak account of Gorbachev's problems. Baker told his aides, "The odds have got to be against his survival, although we aren't about to say that in public. . . ."[12] The two men discussed the Bush-Gorbachev summit that would be held in Washington that summer. They also agreed to a chemical weapons ban that would embrace all the elements of a plan Bush had proposed the previous September. In addition, Baker offered Shevardnadze some slight concessions for START, including a willingness to restrict air-launched cruise missiles and possibly sea-launched cruise missiles as well, which the administration previously had refused to accept. At the same time, the growing independence movements in some of the Soviet republics made it increasingly difficult for the administration to support Gorbachev. While the United States had traditionally championed the principle of self-determination, and, in particular, had refused to recognize the Soviet annexation of the Baltic republics, the Bush administration believed the political disintegration of the Soviet Union could lead to domestic violence, a deeper economic crisis, and even civil war. An unstable Soviet Union, the administration officials believed, would present a difficult problem for the United States.

Consequently, the Bush administration tried to walk a fine line between supporting self-determination in the republics and urging the peaceful resolution of ethnic differences. On March 29, 1990, Bush sent Gorbachev a letter assuring him that the United States did not want to do anything to inflame the Lithuanian crisis. But he also warned the Soviet leader that the use of force would have a negative impact on Soviet-American relations, and particularly on the administration's effort to end restraints on trade between the two countries. On May 1 the Senate passed a resolution calling for the withholding of trade benefits to the Soviet Union until the embargo on Lithuania had been lifted by Moscow and negotiations with Vilnius had begun.

Responding to this pressure, Gorbachev rescinded the economic embargo on Lithuania shortly before the start of the Washington summit on May 31. This made it possible for the administration, in the following month, to lift many of the controls on the export of high technology to third countries that might reexport items to the Soviet Union. While these measures were of some assistance to the Soviets, they fell far short of granting the Soviet Union most-favored-nation (MFN) trade status, which the Soviets wanted badly. The administration continued to withhold MFN status because the Soviet Union still did not permit the free emigration of Soviet Jews, as required by the Jackson Amendment (even though over 100,000 Jews had been permitted to leave the Soviet Union by 1990). What made the Soviets bristle even more was the fact that, while denying the Soviet Union MFN status on human rights grounds, the administration had renewed MFN status for China, even after the Chinese army had shot hundreds of pro-democracy demonstrators during the Tiananmen Square massacre in June 1989.

The Bush administration was also not particularly generous in the amount of economic aid it was willing to extend the Soviet Union. As Senator Bill Bradley (Dem.–N.J.) pointed out, the $300 million Bush proposed to help the reform movements in Eastern Europe and the Soviet Union was "barely enough to bail out a failed savings and loan institution, much less to jump start national economies that have been dead for decades."[13] Bradley proposed that 1 percent of the U.S. military budget be set aside for East European reconstruction, but there was little support, either in the administration or the Congress for any massive economic aid program to Eastern Europe.

German Reunification

One of the most important aspects of the Washington summit was its contribution to resolving the major remaining East-West problem: the reunification of Germany. Since the fall of the Berlin Wall in November 1989, the two Germanys had moved inexorably toward unification. Gorbachev was alarmed by this process, not only because he believed a reunited Germany would pose a threat to Soviet security but also because he feared that the conservatives in his own country would use it as an instrument to drive him from power.

To prevent German reunification, without alienating the West, the Soviet leader initially proposed a revival of the almost moribund four-power German occupation institutions. He also called for the absorption of the NATO and Warsaw Pact countries into a new all-European system. Shevardnadze also proposed a European referendum on Germany's future, in the hope that substantial opposition in Europe to Germany's reunification would block it. But the results of the March 18, 1990, election in East Germany made the Soviet plan irrelevant. The communists were routed and a noncommunist coalition put into power. German reunification, as a consequence, was only a matter of time.

Faced with this fait accompli, the Soviets shifted their efforts to preventing the membership of a reunited Germany in NATO. The Western powers insisted that only the Germans could decide whether they would remain in NATO, and it was clear to everybody that they desired to do so. To make that prospect more digestible to the Soviets, in January 1990 the Western allies proposed "two-plus-four" talks, including the two German states plus the United States, Britain, France, and the Soviet Union, as a way of resolving the international issues that would be raised by Germany's reunification. On February 13, the Soviet Union accepted the Western proposal, while continuing to oppose membership of a reunited Germany in NATO, and the two-plus-four negotiations began in May 1990.

To provide additional incentive for the Soviets to change their minds on the German issue, Bush gave Gorbachev nine assurances at the Washington summit: (1) NATO military forces would not be placed in the former territory of East Germany, (2) Soviet forces could leave East Germany over a period of several years, (3) the borders of Germany would not extend beyond those of West Germany and East Germany combined, thus assuring Poland that its border on the Oder-Neise line would not be altered, (4) Germany would reaffirm its commitments to neither produce nor possess nuclear, biological, and chemical weapons, (5) Germany would give economic support to the Soviet Union, (6) NATO would conduct a comprehensive review of its conventional and nuclear strategy to fit the changed circumstances, (7) the Conference on Security and Cooperation in Europe would be strengthened, (8) the CFE negotiations would continue, and (9) negotiations on short-range nuclear forces would begin once the CFE Treaty was signed.

The Soviets responded with a counterproposal at the June 22, 1990, meeting of the two-plus-four talks. Shevardnadze called for a "transition period" of three to five years during which time the four allied powers would "set the strength of Germany's armed forces," revamp their structure, to make sure they are "rendered incapable for offensive operations," enforce a "ban on the resurgence of Nazi political ideology," and require "the preservation of memorials commemorating those who were killed in the fight against fascism."[14]

In addition, Shevardnadze said that the Soviet Union wanted evidence of NATO's intention to transform itself into a political, rather than military, alliance. He called for the four powers to reduce their troops in Germany to "token contingents" or withdraw them completely. Shevardnadze's proposal also called for the four powers to remove all of their troops from Berlin within six months after German reunification, although it permitted the 380,000 Soviet troops to remain in the former East Germany. Baker rejected the Soviet proposal immediately and publicly, saying it "would restrict German sovereignty for some years." A united Germany, in Baker's view, should not be "singularized or discriminated against."[15]

On July 6, 1990, the NATO summit in London took additional steps to ease Soviet fears about the membership of a reunified Germany in the Western alliance. Its members approved a declaration proclaiming the end of the Cold War. They also invited the Warsaw Pact states to establish diplomatic liaisons with NATO and asked them to make reciprocal pledges of nonaggression and nonuse of force. The NATO countries also pledged to adopt a new strategy making nuclear forces the weapons of "last resort" in any conflict. They also acknowledged that NATO now needed "far fewer nuclear weapons," particularly "systems of the shortest range," or, SNF.[16]

Just before the NATO summit began, President Bush declared that the United States would withdraw all of its nuclear artillery shells from Europe provided that the Soviet Union responded in kind. He also announced that the United States would not develop a missile to replace the Lance. With the Soviets withdrawing their forces from Eastern Europe, the only targets that remained for NATO SNF were located in the newly democratic states. In effect, the SNF issue had ceased to be a problem.

The London Declaration also endorsed the negotiations for confidence-building measures and conventional force reductions in Europe, and called for a CSCE summit later in the year in Paris to sign a CFE agreement. The London Declaration was promptly praised by Shevardnadze and later Gorbachev. President Bush later disclosed that he was the principal architect of the declaration.

With the assurances provided by NATO's London Declaration and Bush's arms reduction initiatives, and convinced that further delay would only alienate the Germans, Gorbachev, on July 14, 1990, accepted the reunification of Germany as well as its membership in NATO. In exchange, West German Chancellor Helmut Kohl promised to make massive loans and give other forms of economic aid to the Soviet Union. He also agreed to limit the military forces of the reunited Germany to 370,000 personnel (in 1990 the combined forces of the two Germanys stood at 667,000) and assured Gorbachev that there would be no nuclear, biological, or chemical weapons in the German arsenal. The Germans also promised to provide $8 billion for the maintenance and removal of Soviet forces in Germany.

For his part, Gorbachev promised to withdraw Soviet troops from East Germany within four years, and agreed that after reunification all the rights and responsibilities of the four occupation powers would end. In effect, Kohl and Gorbachev brought to an end the long, drawn-out, and often bitter struggle to conclude a peace treaty ending World War II in Europe.

With the Soviets finally backing off, the two Germanys moved toward reunification. On August 23 the East German parliament set October 3 as the date for East Germany's merger with the Federal Republic. On September 12, 1990, the four allied powers from World War II and the two Germanys signed the Treaty on the Final Settlement with Respect to Germany. It stated the terms under which a unified Germany would be integrated into the framework of European security. On October 1 the World War II victors formally surrendered their four-power rights and responsibilities over Germany and Berlin. Two days later, Germany was reunified, and on December 2, 1990, the first freely elected all-German government since the 1920s took office.

Conventional Forces in Europe

While Germany was being reunified and Eastern Europe liberated from communism, NATO and Warsaw Pact members were negotiating conventional force reductions in Vienna. These talks, called the Conventional Forces in Europe negotiations (CFE), had begun on March 9, 1989, one month after the fruitless fifteen-year Mutual and Balanced Force Reduction Talks (MBFR) finally were concluded. The new talks, in which all twenty-three NATO and Warsaw Pact members were represented, were conducted under the auspices of the thirty-five nation Conference on Security and Cooperation in Europe (CSCE).

The basic structure of the CFE Treaty was settled only two months later. In May 1989 the Soviet Union accepted NATO's proposal for equal force ceilings, which meant that the Warsaw Pact would have to dispose of far more weapons than NATO. The Warsaw Pact agreed to NATO's proposal to limit tanks, armored troop carriers, and artillery, but the Eastern alliance insisted that equal limits also be applied to combat airplanes and armed helicopters as well.

In May 1989 President Bush agreed to this condition. However, he also wanted the Warsaw Pact to accept an asymmetrical troop ceiling that favored the United States. In his State of the Union address on January 31, 1990, Bush proposed that the United States and the Soviet Union have no more than 195,000 troops in the central zone of Europe, which included West Germany, Belgium, the Netherlands, Luxembourg, and Denmark. But he wanted the United States to maintain the right to deploy an additional 30,000 troops elsewhere in Europe. The Soviets ultimately accepted this imbalance, provided that the supplementary U.S. troops would be stationed outside the central zone, a condition the United States accepted.

The CFE Treaty was signed on November 19, 1990, at the Paris meeting of the CSCE. The treaty, which was to go into effect in 1994, set limits on five types of weapons. Each alliance was restricted to 20,000 tanks, 30,000 armored combat vehicles, 20,000 artillery pieces, 6,800 combat aircraft, and 2,000 helicopters, and no country could have more than 60 percent of the total. The CFE Treaty established a combination of national technical means of verification, cooperative measures, and on-site inspection to verify compliance with the treaty.

Some critics were concerned that there was no provision in the CFE Treaty for aerial inspection, which the United States had considered crucial for effective verification. It was not until March 21, 1992, three months after the collapse of the Soviet Union, that an open-skies agreement was finally signed by all sixteen NATO countries, the former Warsaw Pact countries, and three of the former Soviet republics: Belarus, Russia, and Ukraine. The treaty required each nation to accept forty-two overflights per year by surveillance aircraft with a variety of photographic and electronic equipment.

The collapse of Soviet military power in Eastern Europe did much to overcome the concerns about the CFE Treaty. In 1990 Hungary and Czechoslovakia had negotiated agreements providing for the total withdrawal of some 123,000 Soviet troops stationed on their soil by mid-1991. In June 1990 Hungary became the first Warsaw Pact country to announce it would pull out of that alliance (by the end of 1991). The other satellite states followed the Hungarian lead and timetable. Then, in a stunning, but not unexpected, move, on February 25, 1991, the Warsaw Pact announced its dissolution, effective by the end of the following month.

By the time the Senate voted on ratifying the CFE Treaty, the agreement had been partly overtaken by events, particularly the Warsaw Pact's demise and the beginning of the Soviet military withdrawal from Eastern Europe. As a result, Senate opposition to the treaty virtually disappeared. On November 25, 1991, that body ratified the CFE treaty by a vote of 90 to 4.

The Paris meeting of the CSCE also served as the culminating act of the reunification of Europe following the revolutionary changes of 1989. On November 21, 1990, the CSCE's member states signed the Charter of Paris for a New Europe. In it they declared that they were "no longer adversaries" and affirmed a "steadfast commitment to democracy based on human rights and fundamental freedoms, prosperity through economic liberty and social justice, and equal security for all countries."[17]

The New World Order

As multilateral diplomacy was rapidly winding down the Cold War in Europe, the United States and the Soviet Union turned their attention toward resolving conflicts in the Third World, particularly in Afghanistan, Cambodia, Central America, South Africa, and the Horn of Africa. However, as on other issues, the Bush administration was slow to accept Gorbachev's invitation to collaborate in ending Third World conflicts.

Even after the last Soviet troops withdrew from Afghanistan in February 1989, the administration continued to supply arms to the Mujahedeen forces, expecting that they would soon overthrow the Marxist government of Mohammad Najibullah. However, the Najibullah regime proved to be remarkably resilient. Even though the Soviet army had completed its withdrawal from the country, the Marxist regime continued to receive Soviet supplies, which helped it to stave off collapse until 1992.

It was only during the summer of 1990, after Iraq had occupied Kuwait and the administration needed Soviet cooperation to isolate the Iraqis, that it accepted the reality that the Afghan civil war had become a stalemate. Thus, in September 1991 the administration accepted Gorbachev's invitation to cut off all arms to both sides, in the hope that the action would lead to a negotiated end to the conflict. Before that could be accomplished, however, internal divisiveness within the Najibullah government led to its collapse in April 1992 and the occupation of Kabul by the Mujahedeen the following month.

The Soviet decision to withdraw from Afghanistan went a long way toward facilitating the end of the Sino-Soviet dispute. In May 1989 Gorbachev traveled to Beijing, where he and Deng Xiaoping announced that border discussions would be intensified. Two years later, during the May 1991 visit to Moscow of Chinese Communist Party leader Jiang Zemin, a preliminary agreement was reached settling the Sino-Soviet border dispute.

The Sino-Soviet rapprochement was motivated partly by the Chinese desire to avoid being isolated by the developing U.S.–Soviet entente, particularly after Sino-American relations deteriorated in the wake of the Chinese crackdown on pro-democracy demonstrators in Tiananmen Square on June 4, 1989. But when the Cold War ended in 1990, so did the rationale for the Sino-Soviet-American triangle. No longer did any of the three powers have to collude with another against the third. In the end, the demise of this triangle was one of the most profound manifestations that the Cold War was over.

Gorbachev took the lead in ending the conflict in Cambodia. In April 1989 he successfully pressured the Vietnamese to announce that they would withdraw all of their troops from Cambodia by September. The Soviets also phased out their military assistance program to Vietnam and began to withdraw their forces from their base at Cam Ranh Bay. Then, in July 1990, the United States agreed to end its assistance to the noncommunist guerrillas and give its support to a coalition of all parties, including the Vietnamese puppet government in Phnom Penh, which the United States had previously tried to exclude. However, it took more than a year to bring the Cambodian parties to an agreement (in October 1991) that effectively ended the civil war.

After the signing of the Cambodian peace accord, the Bush administration opened talks with the Vietnamese on normalizing relations between their two countries. In April 1991 the administration listed its preconditions for recognizing the Vietnamese government. They included a full accounting by Vietnam of U.S. service personnel missing in action and Vietnamese cooperation in implementing the UN peace plan for Cambodia. It was not until 1995, during the administration of Bush's successor, Bill Clinton, that the United States and Vietnam finally established diplomatic relations.

The Bush administration continued its predecessor's effort to collaborate with the Soviet Union in ending the conflicts in Namibia and Angola. The Namibian civil war ended with national elections in November 1989, followed by a grant of independence from South Africa in March 1990. In Angola, both superpowers cooperated to monitor implementation of the December 1988 peace accord. Negotiations between the warring parties began in June 1989 and resulted in an agreement in which the MPLA-dominated government and the UNITA rebels agreed to reduce the size of their armed forces and eventually combine them. All Cuban and South African troops were withdrawn from the country by the end of May 1991 and in the same month, the United States and the Soviet Union agreed to cease supplying arms to the rival Angolan factions. Shortly afterwards, the MPLA disavowed Marxism-Leninism and converted to social democracy, a process that enabled the party to win national elections in October 1992.

Soviet pressure and an attempted, but unsuccessful, military coup against the regime of Hailie Mariam Mengistu in May 1989 (he finally was overthrown in 1991) was instrumental in ending the twenty-eight-year war between Ethiopia and Eritrean rebels. The peaceful negotiation of the war received added impetus from former President Jimmy Carter's mediation effort in September 1989. Soviet–U.S. pressure also led to an Ethiopian–Eritrean agreement in 1990 to reopen the Red Sea port of Massawa and permit food deliveries to millions of refugees.

The Soviet Union also took steps to end the civil war that had been raging in Mozambique. On one side of that conflict was President Joaquim Chissano's Mozambique Liberation Front, known by its Portuguese acronym FRELIMO, and on the other were the South African–backed rebels of the Mozambican Resistance Movement or RENAMO. In June 1989 the Soviets announced that they would withdraw nearly all of their military advisers from the war-torn country by the end of 1990. Moscow's planned withdrawal was an important factor behind President Chissano's decision to negotiate a peaceful settlement of the civil war. Like the MPLA in Angola, FRELIMO would scrap its orthodox communist ideology in favor of democratic socialism.

As a part of his effort to end Third World confrontations with the United States, Gorbachev put new emphasis on the peaceful resolution of Central America's conflicts. During a visit to Havana in April 1989, he informed Fidel Castro that the Soviet Union would no longer support Cuba's effort to export revolution. Nor, the Cuban leader was informed, could the Soviet Union afford to continue to subsidize Soviet- Cuban trade, particularly the higher-than-world-market price the Soviets paid for Cuban sugar imports. He encouraged Castro to cooperate with the United States as a way out of the squeeze the Soviet Union was compelled to place on the Cuban economy.

As another step to reduce Cuba as an area of Soviet-American tension, Gorbachev told Secretary of State Baker in September 1991 that the 2,800-man military brigade, which the Soviets had stationed in Cuba since the 1960s, would be withdrawn. Withdrawal of the Soviet brigade began in late 1991 and was completed by June 1993. By that time, the Soviet Union had ceased to exist. Obviously, Gorbachev's retreat from Cuba did nothing to endear him to Fidel Castro.

Gorbachev also moved to end the civil war in Nicaragua. In January 1989 he unilaterally stopped military aid to Nicaragua's Sandinista government and, the following month, endorsed a regional peace plan adopted by the Central American presidents (the Contadora Plan). The Soviets persuaded the Sandinistas to conduct elections in February 1990. Combined with the Bush administration's decision to withdraw U.S. support from the Contras, the Soviet action was instrumental in finally bringing an end to the Nicaraguan conflict.

On March 16, 1991, the United States and the Soviet Union also promised to work together to end the civil war in El Salvador, a goal that was achieved with the signing of a peace accord in January 1992.

The Kuwait War, August 1990–February 1991

Without a doubt, the most important test of the new Soviet-American collaborative relationship in the Third World occurred in the Persian Gulf, a region where both superpowers had vital and, for a long time, incompatible national interests. Events in the region again reached the crisis level on August 2, 1990, when the armed forces of Iraq invaded neighboring Kuwait and quickly conquered the oil-rich emirate.

President Bush almost immediately announced his determination to reverse Iraq's aggression. His response was motivated primarily by his desire to keep the oil of the Persian Gulf region out of the hands of Iraqi President Saddam Hussein, but he also viewed the crisis as an opportunity to collaborate with the Soviet Union in building a new world order based on the principles of the UN Charter. Bush considered Hussein just the kind of villain who could force "civilized nations" to see the importance of stopping "another Hitler."[18]

Gorbachev was eager to cooperate with the United States in reversing Iraq's conquest of Kuwait. By this time, late summer 1990, he was more desperate than ever to get Bush's aid in obtaining international financial help for the collapsing Soviet economy. While in Moscow during the allied military buildup, Baker reported that Gorbachev, with a hard winter approaching, said to him: "We need help. . . . Can you help get some money from the Saudis for us?" The Saudis came through with a $4 billion line of credit.[19]

However, Gorbachev was also acutely aware that hard-liners in the Communist Party and the Soviet military would be very critical of any effort on his part to work with the United States against Iraq, the most important Soviet client in the Gulf region. Nevertheless, Gorbachev decided that even supporting clients as important as Iraq did not supersede the paramount requirement of obtaining Western assistance to save the Soviet economy and, indeed, the Soviet Union itself. Still, he could not ignore the opposition of the hard-liners. Accordingly, he tried to circumvent it by working with the United States against Iraq under the mantle of the United Nations. To facilitate the Soviet Union's collaboration, or at least neutrality, on August 3 Secretary of State Baker assured Shevardnadze that President Bush was not preparing to take unilateral military action against Iraq. Only then did the Soviet foreign minister agree to a joint statement condemning the Iraqi invasion. On August 6 the Soviets also voted to implement a UN embargo on arms shipments to Iraq.

On that same day, Bush decided to dispatch U.S. forces to Saudi Arabia, in Operation "Desert Shield," to check a possible advance of the Iraqi army into that oil-rich kingdom. The president assured the Soviets that this mission was "wholly defensive" and promised that the United States would not initiate hostilities with Iraq. As a result, on August 25 the Soviets supported a UN resolution authorizing the use of whatever means were necessary, including military action, to enforce the embargo on Iraq. However, primarily because of opposition from the Soviet military, Gorbachev refused to accept a U.S. invitation to send military forces to the Gulf region.

The Bush administration was not very disappointed by Gorbachev's refusal to cooperate militarily with the UN, but it was determined to ensure that the Soviets would continue to refrain from obstructing it.

Consequently, in early September it hastily proposed a summit with Gorbachev to coordinate superpower policy during the crisis. Gorbachev accepted the U.S. invitation and on September 9 Bush met with the Soviet leader in Helsinki. There they issued a joint statement supporting all UN resolutions against Iraq and acknowledging the possible need for additional action. Bush had succeeded in keeping Gorbachev in line in the Persian Gulf crisis.

Another significant element in the joint statement issued by both leaders at Helsinki was an agreement that, after the objectives of the UN resolutions had been achieved, the two countries would work together actively to resolve all remaining conflicts in the Middle East, particularly the Arab-Israeli-Palestinian conflict. In effect, Bush was overturning the previous Cold War policy of the United States, which had attempted to keep the Soviet Union out of the Middle East.

Although Gorbachev had gone along with the U.S.-led action against Iraq, he did so in the face of increasing criticism from the hard-liners in the Politburo, the Soviet parliament, and the military who argued that he and Shevardnadze were much too willing to please the Americans. The Soviet military, in particular, became increasingly restive as 200,000 U.S. troops were massed in Saudi Arabia, only seven hundred miles from the Soviet border. General Vladimir Lobov, Chief of Staff of the Warsaw Treaty Organization, suggested that the United States might have in mind extending "its forces along the Soviet Union's southern flank, establishing a bridgehead from which to control Middle East oil flows and put pressure on Moscow."[20]

In an attempt to mollify the hard-liners, and over the strong objections of Shevardnadze, Gorbachev permitted Yevgeni Primakov, an "Arabist" member of the Soviet foreign ministry, to undertake a mission designed to achieve a diplomatic settlement of the crisis. However, Primakov was unsuccessful in persuading Iraq to withdraw from Kuwait. As a result, on November 29 the Soviet Union voted to support a UN Security Council resolution authorizing the use of force to compel Iraq to withdraw from Kuwait.

UN-authorized military action against Iraq began on January 17, 1991, when the United States and its allies launched an air attack on Iraqi targets. While the Soviet Union did not obstruct the U.S.-led military action against Iraq, Gorbachev continued his efforts to persuade Saddam Hussein to withdraw from Kuwait. On February 21, however, he felt compelled to telephone Bush to tell him that his latest effort to do so was unsuccessful. As a consequence, two days later, on February 23, the allies launched the ground war against Iraq, Operation Desert Storm. To the surprise of most people, the allied forces quickly (in less than seventy-two hours) routed the Iraqi forces in Kuwait and southern Iraq, and suffered only very light casualties in the process. By contrast, the Iraqis lost thousands of soldiers and tanks and were forced to retreat rapidly across the Iraq-Kuwait border.

To this day, Bush is criticized for not permitting the allied forces to take Baghdad and overthrow Hussein. The president, however, did not want to destroy Iraq's armed forces completely because he wanted to retain Iraq as a barrier against Iran. Nor did he want the United States to assume the economic burden of feeding and policing an occupied Iraq. But equally important, Bush was pressured by Gorbachev to avoid the humiliating defeat of a Soviet client state. In a telephone conversation with the president, Gorbachev warned that U.S.–Soviet relations were "very fragile." Unless the coalition leaders showed a "great sense of responsibility," he said, the improvement that had occurred in international relations could be seriously jeopardized.[21]

Realizing that the Soviet president's assistance would be required on other issues, such as START and CFE, Bush was unwilling to do anything to contribute to Gorbachev's further weakening. Moreover, throughout the Gulf crisis, Bush's first priority had been the eviction of the Iraqi army from Kuwait. With that objective achieved, the president thought he could afford to accommodate Gorbachev's wishes. Consequently, on February 24, only four days after the operation began, the president called a halt to the military action, thereby enabling Hussein to retain power in Baghdad, although the Iraqi leader would be severely constrained by the UN sanctions and other restrictions. After meeting with Gorbachev in the Kremlin in April 1991, Baker echoed the Soviet leader's sentiments when he told reporters that the warming Soviet-American relationship had "gone through a test recently, and it [had] survived."[22]

The Decline of Gorbachev

But by April 1991 there was considerable doubt about Gorbachev's own ability to survive. During the fall of 1990, the Soviet leader vacillated between trying to please the reformers and showing loyalty to the conservatives in an increasingly desperate attempt to hold the political center. In August 1990 he accepted a Yeltsin-drafted plan to bring about a free-market economy in 500 days. The plan would delegate considerable economic power to the republics, including taxation, control of natural resources, hard currency, and proceeds from trade, the administration of agricultural privatization, and price reform. However, Gorbachev withdrew his support from the plan after belatedly realizing that its implementation would have eliminated the need for a centralized economic structure. This, in turn, would have undermined the rationale for maintaining the Soviet Union, and having a Soviet president—which appeared to be the very intent of Yeltsin's plan.

By scuttling the 500-Day Plan, Gorbachev again cut his ties to the reformers and was forced to rely even more heavily than before on the old communist establishment (apparatchiks), but by this time the old guard was thoroughly disgusted with Gorbachev. Throughout the fall of 1990, rumors of a right-wing coup against him swept through Moscow, rumors that were fueled by military maneuvers outside the capital.

In an attempt to appease the hard-liners, Gorbachev appointed a number of them to key positions in the government. In November 1990 he named former KGB general Boris Pugo to be his new interior minister. The following month, he appointed an old-style economist who was deeply hostile to radical reform, Valetin Pavlov, as his prime minister. An undistinguished party apparatchik, Gennady I. Yanayev, was named vice president. Alarmed by Gorbachev's turn to the right, Soviet Foreign Minister Shevardnadze resigned on December 20, 1990, after warning that a dictatorship was coming.

During the winter of 1991, Shevardnadze's prediction appeared to be coming true. In January, Gorbachev approved a hard-liner plan for what turned out to be a bloody, but nevertheless unsuccessful, attempt to overthrow the pro-independence government of Lithuania. In the same month, Gorbachev removed liberal journalists from state television and radio. In February soldiers were briefly assigned to patrol the streets of Moscow. The following month, hard-liners tried to remove Yeltsin from the Russian presidency by impeaching him, but they were thwarted by mass demonstrations for Yeltsin. On March 28 more than 100,000 people marched and chanted in support of Yeltsin, and they denounced, not the hard-liners in the Supreme Soviet, but Gorbachev. The strength of the reformers, combined with the willingness of the hard-liners to turn back the clock, alarmed the Soviet leader, and again pushed him to the left.

In an attempt to appease the restive Soviet nationalities and regain the favor of reformers as well, Gorbachev tried to arouse public support for preserving the Soviet Union. He initiated a nationwide referendum, which was conducted on March 17, 1991, in which the Soviet people were asked to approve the proposition that the Soviet Union should be preserved "as a renewed federation of equal sovereign republics in which human rights and freedoms of all nationalities will be fully guaranteed."[23] With a popular majority supporting this vague formulation, Gorbachev hoped to be able to claim a democratic mandate to redefine the Soviet Union in his own way and according to his own timetable.

However, in a clever move, Yeltsin persuaded the Russian parliament to append to Gobachev's referendum a separate proposal calling for the establishment of a popularly elected Russian presidency, a step Gorbachev refused to implement at the Soviet level. While Gorbachev's referendum was approved by 70 percent of the Soviet voters, Yeltsin's proposal received a favorable vote from 85 percent of the Russian voters. As a consequence, the Russian Congress of People's Deputies set the presidential election for June 12. Yeltsin won. From his new, strengthened position, the popularly elected Yeltsin continued to pressure the unelected Soviet president to move toward democracy and capitalism.

Faced with Yeltsin's growing power and alarmed by the reactionaries in the Communist Party and the Soviet military, Gorbachev embraced democracy, radical economic reform, and greater autonomy for the republics within a new union. Pushed by Gorbachev the Supreme Soviet, on July 1 and 5, approved the denationalization of three-quarters of Soviet industry. On July 8 the nine Slavic and Muslim republics that were expected to compose the new union approved a comprehensive economic reform plan, which Gorbachev would present to the London summit meeting of the Western Group of Seven industrial democracies (the G-7) on July 17.

Gorbachev and the West

In London, Gorbachev hoped to obtain substantial Western economic assistance to help him revive the ailing Soviet economy, as well as his own declining prestige back home, but he was disappointed by the response of the Western leaders. Not only did they not offer him any meaningful economic assistance, they even denied his request for full Soviet membership in the International Monetary Fund, instead offering associate membership.

Gorbachev was reportedly angered and humiliated by the tepid Western response to his plea for economic aid. He quite justifiably put most of the blame for the stinginess of the G-7 on President Bush. While Bush and most of his advisers wanted to provide economic support to Gorbachev, they suspected that it would be wasted by the inept and corrupt Soviet bureaucracy. Moreover, the United States was in a recession, and Bush was being criticized for being more willing to help foreigners than he was his own people. Consequently, the administration virtually ignored a proposal by a Harvard University study group for a "Grand Bargain" in which major U.S. economic assistance to the Soviet Union would be tied to radical market reform of the Soviet economy.

Instead of backing such a generous economic aid program, the Bush administration gave only meager economic assistance to the Soviets On June 3 the president announced that he would extend a waiver he had granted on the Jackson-Vanik restrictions for another year. On June 11 he announced a $1.5 billion credit to the Soviet Union for agricultural purchases, and on June 18 Baker cautiously outlined limited plans for economic assistance to reforms in the Soviet Union.

Still, the London G-7 summit was not a complete failure for Gorbachev. In London he and Bush finally agreed, after nine long years of negotiations, on a START accord, which was signed by both leaders during a Moscow summit on July 29–31, 1991. The treaty required each party to reduce the number of their deployed strategic warheads to no more than 6,000 and their launchers (missiles and bombers) to a maximum of 1,600. (At the end of 1990 the United States had slightly fewer than 12,778 strategic warheads on 1,876 launchers, and the Soviet Union had 10,880 warheads on 2,354 launchers.) In a major concession to the United States, the Soviet Union agreed to cut in half (to 154) the number of their "heavy" SS-18 ICBMs and to allow them to carry no more than 1,540 warheads. The Soviets also accepted a 50 percent reduction in the throw-weight (payload capacity) of their ICBMs and SLBMs. By 1990 total Soviet throw-weight for these missiles was about 12 million pounds, while that of the United States was 4.4 million pounds.

While Bush announced in Moscow that the United States would ratify the bilateral trade agreement and consider granting the Soviet Union most-favored-nation trade status, Bush remained notably cautious in helping the Soviets economically. Most-favored-nation status and a modicum of Western economic aid were not granted until the following year. The Moscow summit also advanced various joint programs, including measures to revive cooperative space exploration and others to facilitate technical economic cooperation, aviation security, and disaster assistance.

Bush and Gorbachev again agreed to cooperate in trying to end regional conflicts. They announced that the United States and the Soviet Union would jointly sponsor an international conference on the Middle East, one that, hopefully, would end the Arab-Israeli conflict. The two leaders also called for a negotiated resolution of the war in Yugoslavia, which had erupted after four Yugoslav republics—Slovenia, Croatia, Bosnia, and Macedonia—declared their independence.

After the Moscow summit, in another effort to prop up the tottering Soviet leader, President Bush traveled to Kiev, the capital of the Ukrainian republic. There he tried to convince the Ukrainians of the wisdom of working with Gorbachev to preserve the Soviet Union. To Bush's dismay, his suggestion, which was not accompanied by any reference to the ideal of national self-determination, did not endear him to the Ukrainian people. Critics in the United States quickly labeled Bush's statement his "Chicken Kiev" speech.

The August Coup

Gorbachev's return to the left, and particularly his acceptance of a new, more democratic union treaty, prompted the hard-liners to take action against him. Because the treaty called for a new national cabinet that would be selected by the republics, the hard-liners realized that the treaty would cost them their jobs. At first, they tried to circumvent the Soviet president legally. On June 17 Prime Minister Pavlov requested that the Soviet parliament to give his cabinet emergency powers to initiate legislation and issue decrees, without Gorbachev's approval. A week later, on June 28, Gorbachev persuaded the parliament to reject Pavlov's "constitutional coup" by a vote of 262 to 24.

The day before the parliamentary vote, President Bush sent a message to Gorbachev warning him that the right-wingers were planning a coup against him. The warning originated with the reform mayor of Leningrad, Gavril Popov, and was passed on to the president by way of the U.S. ambassador to Moscow, Jack Matlock. Gorbachev, believing he was indispensable to the hard-liners, since he thought he shielded them from the reformers, brushed off the warning.[24]

At the same time, Gorbachev did move to reduce the power of the hard-liners by reforming the Communist Party. At a Central Committee plenum on July 25–26, 1991, he called the Leninist-Stalinist-Brezhnevite model of socialism "bankrupt" and declared that socialism and the market were not only linked but "indivisible"—a heresy to orthodox Communists who still regarded the two economic systems as incompatible. He also mentioned plans to create a democratic Soviet Communist Party as an alternative to the existing conservative one. The plenum approved Gorbachev's draft reform program and agreed to submit it to a party congress later in the year. Before that congress could convene, however, the events of August would contribute to the party's demise.

Shortly before the union treaty was scheduled to be signed (on August 20), Gorbachev left Moscow for his annual vacation in the Crimea. His absence from the capital gave the hard-liners an opportunity to overthrow him, in what was almost a replay of Nikita Khrushchev's removal from power while he was on vacation in the Crimea in 1964. On August 19 an eight-member "State of Emergency Committee" led by Vice President Yanayev and including hard-line KGB and military officials, all of whom were appointed to their posts by Gorbachev, declared that the Soviet leader had been removed from power "for health reasons." (In fact, Gorbachev was in good health but under house arrest in the Crimea.) The committee declared a six-month state of emergency to "restore law and order."[25] State radio announced that the signing of the new union treaty, scheduled for the next day, would not take place.

For a variety of reasons, however, the coup against Gorbachev failed. One reason was Yeltsin's decision to resist it. The Russian president climbed a tank outside the parliament building (called "the White House") and denounced the emergency committee as illegal. Thousands of Muscovites rallied to Yeltsin's side, erecting barricades around the White House to protect it from the forces of the hard-liners. But the pivotal reason for the coup's failure was the refusal, or failure, of KGB troops to obey the orders of the coup's leaders to storm the Russian parliament. The armed forces, a majority of whom had voted for Yeltsin in the June election, also refused to move against him. In fact, some Soviet units came to the defense of the White House.

Underestimating the extent of the popular support for democracy, and antipathy for communism, and realizing that they could not rely upon the military to overthrow Yeltsin, the coup leaders quickly gave up their enterprise. On August 21 Soviet troops withdrew from the center of Moscow, and Yeltsin reported that the leaders of the unsuccessful coup were under arrest, with the exception of Interior Minister Victor Pugo, who had committed suicide. The same day, the Congress of Peoples Deputies announced that the emergency committee had been disbanded.

Thus, what had begun as a coup within the Communist Party was transformed into one of history's major revolutions.

On August 22 a fatigued and disheveled Gorbachev returned to Moscow and declared that he was in full control of the government. Gorbachev clearly thought that he could restore his brand of reform communism, but he failed to realize how much had changed in Moscow and other Soviet cities while he had been under house arrest in the Crimea. The collapse of the coup did not restore the status quo; it destroyed the very foundation of the central authority that, ironically, the conspirators had attempted to preserve.

Yeltsin did not wait for Gorbachev to regain his balance. On August 21 the Russian president labeled the Communist Party the organizing and inspiring force behind the coup, suspended its activities in Russia, and seized its property. Yeltsin also vetoed the new ministers appointed by Gorbachev and forced him to accept those he himself nominated. He then publicly humiliated the Soviet president by frequently interrupting Gorbachev's address before the Russian parliament. In other republics, the local leadership, in almost all cases comprising the former communist leaders, followed suit and banned or suspended the Communist Party.

After realizing, belatedly, how the public mood had changed, Gorbachev tried to distance himself from the Communist Party. On August 24 he resigned as the party's general secretary, disbanded its Central Committee, and ordered the Council of Ministers to resign. He then instructed the Congress of Peoples Deputies to take control of the party's property and banned the party's activities within the central government and the security organs. On August 29 the Congress voted (283 to 29 with 52 abstentions) to suspend all Communist Party activities in the Soviet Union until the party's role in the coup was investigated. While the party itself was not abolished immediately, the events of August spelled the end of communism in the Soviet Union.

The Demise of the Soviet Union, August–December 1991

During September 1991, after reluctantly participating in the Communist Party's funeral, Gorbachev again turned his attention to preserving the Soviet Union and, with it, his job as Soviet president. On September 5 he announced the establishment of a new transitional government, which was composed of the president of the Soviet Union (Gorbachev), the Supreme Soviet, and the State Council, consisting of Gorbachev and the presidents of the Soviet republics. One of its first acts, on September 6, was to recognize the independence of the three Baltic states: Latvia, Lithuania, and Estonia. On September 12 officials of the Baltic nations and the twelve remaining Soviet republics agreed to maintain a collective defense framework and joint control over the Soviet nuclear arsenal. On October 1 the Soviet republics agreed to form an economic union. They also drafted a new union treaty that initially appeared to offer the basis for a confederation of ten sovereign states (less Moldova and Georgia). However, the draft treaty was subject to the willingness of Ukraine, the most populous non-Russian republic, to stay in the union. That question would be answered on December 1, when Ukraine conducted a referendum on independence.

Despite Gorbachev's and Yeltsin's efforts to preserve some form of union, the centrifugal force of nationalism that was released by the coup and the demise of communism proved much too strong to overcome. One republic after another followed the lead of the Baltic states and declared their independence. On December 1, 90 percent of the Ukrainians who voted approved independence. Without Ukraine, Yeltsin decided, there was no point in trying to preserve the union. On December 8 he joined the presidents of Ukraine and Belarus in deciding to supplant the Soviet Union with the "Commonwealth of Independent States." and on December 21 eight other republics joined the new commonwealth. On December 18, Yeltsin announced that Ukraine and Belarus (and later Kazakhstan) had agreed to transfer their nuclear missiles to Russia. On December 25 Gorbachev resigned the presidency of the Soviet Union and transferred control of the Soviet Union's nuclear weapons to Yeltsin. The next day, the Supreme Soviet met for the last time and dissolved itself. On December 31, 1991, the Soviet Union formally ceased to exist.

Bush and the End of the Soviet Union

President Bush was slow to condemn the coup against Gorbachev, and he did so only after Yeltsin pleaded with him to intervene. In his initial

Successor States of the Soviet Union, 1992

reaction, early on August 19, the president called the coup "a disturbing development" and said that its leaders had taken over by "extra-constitutional means." Later that day Bush issued a statement branding the coup "unconstitutional" and supporting Yeltsin's demand for Gorbachev's restoration to his post of Soviet president.[26]

Once Gorbachev was restored to power, however, Bush was reluctant to accept, let alone support, the eclipse of the Soviet leader by Yeltsin. The president clearly preferred to see Gorbachev remain in power rather than risk the uncertainties of his demise. Bush also delayed recognizing the independence of the Baltic states; he recognized them, on September 2, only after other nations had done so and it was inevitable that Gorbachev would have to do so as well. Bush's pro-union, pro-Gorbachev stance earned him considerable criticism. He was faulted for placing his personal prestige behind a leader who was trying to save communism and the Soviet empire rather than behind the leading democrat (Yeltsin) who was trying to bring them down.

President Bush did, however, demonstrate boldness in ending the nuclear arms race. On September 27, 1991, the president announced that the United States would remove or destroy all tactical nuclear weapons that were deployed in Europe and Asia and on U.S. warships. He also said the United States would abandon plans to deploy mobile MX and Midgetman missiles. Moreover, he announced that he was ordering an end to the twenty-four-hour-alert status of U.S. strategic bombers as well as those missiles, about 600 ICBMs and SLBMs, that were scheduled for deactivation under the START Treaty. He called on the Soviet Union to negotiate additional arms control measures, including an agreement eliminating all land-based ICBMs with multiple warheads (MIRVs).

Yet while Bush initiated steps to end the offensive nuclear arms race, he refused to abandon the ostensibly defensive SDI antiballistic missile program (although he supported it in a much scaled down version of the initial Reagan program). He invited Gorbachev to begin negotiations to revise the ABM Treaty to permit the limited deployment of a nonnuclear, antiballistic missile systems without undermining the credibility of existing deterrent forces.

Gorbachev responded by announcing reciprocal reductions in the Soviet nuclear arsenal, including a decision to begin the dismantling of Soviet tactical nuclear weapons. This pleased U.S. officials, who were deeply worried that the Soviet Union's tactical nuclear weapons might fall into the hands of terrorists or some hard-line Soviet general determined to embarrass Gorbachev. Indeed, one of Bush's main reasons for continuing to support Gorbachev was his desire to ensure that Soviet nuclear weapons would be under secure control in the event that the Soviet Union broke up. Gorbachev also expressed a willingness to consider modifying the ABM Treaty to permit limited deployment of SDI, but he said he would do so only if the United States agreed to share SDI technology with the Soviet Union. SDI was an issue that was not resolved before the Soviet Union expired.

Nevertheless, the Bush and Gorbachev arms control and reduction initiatives in September and October 1991 were a major step beyond the ceilings set in the START Treaty. They provided the basis for the even deeper strategic arms cuts, roughly two-thirds of their pre–START I numbers, that the United States and Russia would accept in the START II agreement, which Bush and Yeltsin signed in January 1993, shortly before Bush left office.

NATO also took additional steps to wind down the Cold War late in Gorbachev's presidency. On November 8, 1991, the alliance's ministers agreed to change NATO's military doctrine to reflect the fact that an invasion from the East was no longer likely. The ministers abandoned the alliance's "forward defense" doctrine, which had envisioned a defense of West Germany on its border with East Germany.

However, NATO turned a cold shoulder to the idea, advanced by Yeltsin on December 20, 1991, that Russia should be permitted to join the Western alliance as an equal partner. The new warmth in East-West relations was not enough to melt decades of suspicion and distrust of the Soviet (and soon to be) Russian military. The alliance would only go as far as offering Russia, as well as the other former Soviet republics and Warsaw Pact members, associate status with NATO in the so-called Partnership for Peace.

Before the Soviet Union expired, Bush and Gorbachev took additional steps to end the Cold War in the Third World. On September 13, 1991, the Soviet Union and the United States agreed to stop all arms transfers to their clients in Afghanistan (by January 1, 1992). In the same month, Moscow indicated that it would make further cutbacks in Soviet assistance to Cuba, Vietnam, and its other client states. On October 23 the Soviet Union joined the United States and China in the conclusion of a Cambodian peace settlement. On December 2 the United States and the Soviet Union jointly urged the warring parties in El Salvador to conclude a settlement. When they did so, the agreement complemented the earlier one ending the Nicaraguan conflict.

The two powers also took steps to resolve the conflict in the Middle East. On October 18 Secretary of State Baker and Soviet Foreign Minister Boris Pankin (who had succeeded Bessmyrtnykh in the wake of the unsuccessful August coup) invited the parties in the Arab-Israeli conflict to attend an international conference on the Middle East. Bush, Gorbachev, and other heads of state were in attendance when the conference convened in Madrid, Spain, at the end of that month. To provide further impetus to Israel to negotiate with the PLO, the UN General Assembly voted on December 16 to repeal the November 1975 resolution equating Zionism with racism. Although the Soviets had voted for the resolution when it was first passed, they now supported its repeal.

Gorbachev's willingness to cooperate with the United States in the Third World, as elsewhere, was motivated by a desire to obtain desperately needed Western economic assistance. The administration responded by approving insurance guarantees for trade with the Soviet Union, which were designed to overcome the reluctance of American banks to fund grain credits to the United States. On October 1 Bush also granted an additional $585 million in credits to the Soviet Union beyond the amount the banks were prepared to extend. On December 20 Bush approved a further $1.25 billion in grain credits and a token $1 million in humanitarian assistance to the Soviet Union. However, public and congressional opposition to the idea of extending massive economic assistance to the Soviet Union while the U.S. economy was in recession prevented Bush from giving Gorbachev the amount of aid he wanted.

In November 1991 Congress passed, and the president signed, a bill sponsored by Senators Sam Nunn (Dem.–Ga.) and Richard Lugar (Rep.–Ind.) authorizing the United States to spend up to $400 million in fiscal year 1992 to help the Soviet Union destroy nuclear, chemical, and other weapons, and establish verifiable safeguards against the proliferation of such weapons. After the breakup of the Soviet Union, Nunn-Lugar assistance was granted to Russia, Ukraine, Belarus, and Kazakhstan. This assistance made possible the implementation of both START treaties.

An Assessment of the Bush Administration's Soviet Policy

On Christmas Day 1991 President Bush, in an address to the American people, praised Gorbachev "for his intellect, vision, and courage" and credited him for ending the Cold War. The president also said that the demise of the Soviet Union was a "victory for democracy and freedom." [27]

To be sure, the U.S. "victory" in the Cold War had come about largely as a result of developments within the Soviet Union, rather than as the direct consequence of U.S. policies. The collapse of the Soviet economy was at the heart of the Soviet Union's demise; it destroyed what little faith in communism remained among the Soviet people. Gorbachev's attempt to reform communism, and in particular his effort to institute limited democracy both in Eastern Europe and the Soviet Union, enabled communism's critics to delegitimize it. Once communism, the glue that held together the Soviet empire, was removed both the satellites and the constituent republics of the Soviet Union used the opportunity to go their own way.

Nevertheless, Bush did play an important role in ending the Cold War. In spite of the excessive caution that he displayed in responding to Gorbachev's overtures early in his presidency, Bush facilitated the dramatic concessions that Gorbachev was compelled to make, which finally made possible the conclusion of the Cold War. Bush provided the necessary assurances that Gorbachev needed to accept the membership in NATO of a reunified Germany (although the enormous financial assistance granted to the Soviet Union by West Germany was also a critical factor). In addition, by proceeding slowly and delicately on the independence of the Baltic states, Bush provided Gorbachev with some breathing space on the issue. This facilitated the Soviet leader's effort to separate himself from the hard-line crackdown on Lithuania and eventually made it possible for him to rejoin the reformers. Furthermore, while Bush was tardy in supporting the Soviet leader during the unsuccessful coup, his arms control initiatives after Gorbachev was restored to power ensured that, after the Soviet Union did disintegrate, the transfer of Soviet nuclear weapons to Yeltsin's control was accomplished without tragic consequences.

Bush, indeed, was niggardly in the amount of economic assistance he was willing to extend to the Soviet Union. However, considering the magnitude of the Soviet Union's economic weakness, it is difficult to conceive the amount of Western economic assistance that would have been required to avert the country's disintegration. Indeed, it is doubtful that any amount would have been enough to overcome the popular disgust with communism as well as the revival of nationalism, within the Soviet empire. Saving the Soviet Union, in the end, was neither within the capacity, nor apparently the national interest, of the United States. The demise of the Soviet Union was lamented only by Gorbachev and the last of the die-hard Soviet nationalists.

Conclusion

A Legacy of Expansionism

According to the conventional view, the Cold War began in the waning months of World War II, but the roots of the superpower competition are centuries old, going back to the very infancy of the American nation. Both Russia and America were expansionist nations whose peoples each believed they possessed a special mission in history. While all nations, no doubt, see themselves as fulfilling a unique mission in history, the missions of the United States and Russia achieved global dimensions during the twentieth century.

Czarist Russia spread orthodox Christianity as well as Russian political, economic, and cultural hegemony across Asia to the Pacific Ocean, into South-Central Asia, and as far west into Central Europe as its powerful neighbors, particularly Germany, would permit. The United States, which began as an English settlement at Jamestown, Virginia, in 1607, also has a history of expansionism. Americans saw their mission as one of spreading certain ideals, including democracy, free enterprise, and technological progress, across the vast North American continent and far beyond that.

Yet while republican and democratic America found the autocratic Russian monarchy repulsive, for most of the common history of the two nations—with the exception of the disagreement over Alaska, which was resolved peacefully in 1867—Russian and American interests did not collide.

The Wilsonian Legacy: Ideological Conflict

The Bolshevik Revolution changed the relatively cordial relationship between Russia and America. When the Bolsheviks came to power in Russia during November 1917, they expected, as devoted Marxists, that the workers of the world, including those in the United States, would follow Russia's lead and overthrow their capitalist-dominated governments. Capitalists of the world, including those in the United States, feared that that possibility could happen.

Accordingly, the capitalist nations treated Soviet Russia as a threat virtually from the first days of its existence. President Woodrow Wilson not only refused to recognize the Bolshevik regime, he worked to overthrow it. Bolshevism was ideologically repulsive to Wilson. He considered it a threat to the new world order he intended to establish after the world war, which would be characterized by international cooperation, collective security, self-determination, and open markets. Bolsheviks committed to the violent overthrow of capitalism and democracy obviously had no place in the new international order Wilson envisioned.

Therefore, Wilson authorized the sending of covert U.S. economic aid to the anti-Bolshevik forces in Russia and the dispatch of U.S. troops to Archangel and Vladivostok. To be sure, Wilson's decision to intervene militarily in the Russian civil war was prompted primarily by a desire to reestablish the eastern front against the Germans, as well as preclude Japanese territorial aggrandizement in Siberia. But Wilson also hoped that a by-product of such action would be the revival of the kind of democratic movement that ruled Russia briefly during the brief tenure of the Provisional Government.

The military intervention of the capitalist powers in Russia only reinforced Bolshevik fears that they, and not the Germans, were its primary targets. Even though unsuccessful in toppling the Soviet regime, Western military intervention in the Russian civil war planted in the minds of Soviet leaders a lasting fear of capitalistic encirclement and, for a long time thereafter, a belief in the inevitability of war between communism and capitalism.

Nevertheless, in the aftermath of the Bolshevik victory in the Russian civil war, both Lenin and Stalin tried to play down the ideological differences that divided the two systems. They badly needed Western economic assistance to rebuild Soviet Russia's infrastructure. In addition, during the thirties Stalin needed U.S. diplomatic assistance in creating a balance of power strong enough to check the aggressive tendencies of Germany and Japan.

However, the Republican administrations of the 1920s and early 1930s continued the Wilsonian policy of not recognizing the Soviet regime. While there was some private, and in some cases very beneficial, American economic activity in the Soviet Union during the 1920s, economic and political contacts with the Soviet government during the period were virtually nonexistent.

Franklin Roosevelt and the Grand Alliance

Franklin D. Roosevelt entered the White House in March 1933 determined to reverse his predecessors' Soviet policy. Not only had it failed to change the internal structure of the Soviet Union, it had not prevented other countries from establishing diplomatic relations with the Soviet government. The Wilsonian policy had also kept the United States from fully exploiting the Soviet market, which looked increasingly inviting to American entrepreneurs as the U.S. economy slid deeper into the Great Depression. More importantly, Roosevelt believed that the Soviet Union could play a crucial role in checking the aggressive ambitions of both Germany and Japan.

While Roosevelt recognized the Soviet government in 1933, the benefits that both sides expected to gain from the new relationship never materialized. Perhaps the most important reason was the inability of Roosevelt, because of the strength of isolationist sentiment in the United States, to participate with the Soviet Union in the creation of an effective collective security system. In retaliation, Stalin dragged his feet on a settlement of the old Russian debt to the United States and, then, to add insult to injury, revived Comintern activity in the United States.

Even worse from the Western perspective, Stalin, after being rebuffed by the British and French, made a separate deal with Hitler in August 1939 by signing the German-Soviet Nonaggression Pact. The agreement not only enabled Hitler to begin World War II, it also permitted the Soviet Army to occupy the Baltic states and eastern Poland. Stalin's "perfidy" convinced most Americans that he could not be trusted.

But Roosevelt was not moved by anti-Soviet hostility. While he was not ignorant of the oppressive nature of the Soviet regime, he believed that he could deal with Stalin as a realist rather than a revolutionary. Moreover, after Germany invaded the Soviet Union in June 1941, Roosevelt believed that the Red Army could tie down most of the German army, thereby saving Britain, and possibly precluding direct U.S. military involvement in the war. Therefore, Roosevelt did all he could to prevent a Soviet defeat, including sending billions of dollars in Lend-Lease aid to the Soviet Union. After the United States entered the war in December 1941, Roosevelt worked hard to maintain the Grand Alliance.

Even when the Soviet Union was on the verge of defeat, however, issues arose that strained the new U.S.–Soviet relationship. For example, Roosevelt failed to deliver a promised second front in France until June 1944, three years after the German invasion of the Soviet Union began. But perhaps the most important problem that strained the Grand Alliance throughout the war, and eventually contributed to its demise after the Axis powers were defeated, was determining the postwar territorial boundaries of Eastern Europe. After avoiding the issue for as long as he could, to keep the allies united against Germany, Roosevelt, at the Tehran conference in 1943 and again at the Yalta conference in February 1945, tacitly recognized the Soviet annexation of the Baltic states and formally agreed to altered boundaries for Poland.

Roosevelt attempted to cover his engagement in realpolitik with a mantle of moralism. He persuaded Stalin to sign the Declaration on Liberated Europe and, in effect, permit free elections in the states of Eastern Europe. In this way, Roosevelt paid lip service to Wilsonian idealism, while recognizing that there was little to be done, short of war, to dislodge the Soviets from the areas they had occupied.

Much to the dismay of Western observers, the Soviets violated the Declaration on Liberated Europe within two weeks of signing it by forcing a subservient government on Romania. Stalin had little confidence in the ability of the United Nations to keep the peace. What he wanted was a wide buffer zone of pro-Soviet states between Germany and the Soviet Union. In Stalin's mind, self-determination, open markets, and all the other paraphernalia of American idealism were peripheral to this paramount goal.

While Roosevelt may have overestimated his ability to influence the Soviet dictator, he never completely counted on gaining Stalin's trust. He demonstrated this, among other ways, by refusing to share the atomic bomb with the Soviets. But, despite the personal doubts Roosevelt may have had about the future prospects for Soviet-American relations, he never publicized them, fearing they might break up the Grand Alliance before the Axis powers were defeated. Roosevelt's success in papering over his differences with the Soviet Union preserved the Grand Alliance until his death, but he also gave Stalin the impression that Soviet occupation of Eastern Europe was acceptable to the United States, as long as it could be made palatable to American public opinion. In this sense, Roosevelt was Stalin's accomplice in the Soviet occupation of Eastern Europe.

Truman and Containment

Clearly, the ideological differences that had made Soviet-American relations difficult before World War II, when both countries were relatively weak militarily and isolated from world affairs as well, were bound to be aggravated after both nations emerged from that conflict as the world's major military powers. During the Second World War these ideological differences, and the suspicion and distrust they engendered, were submerged by the mutual U.S. and Soviet need to cooperate to defeat the common enemy, but the defeat of the Axis powers allowed the old negative perceptions to take precedence once again.

Initially, Harry Truman tried to follow Roosevelt's conciliatory approach toward the Soviet Union. But pressure from hard-liners within his administration and the Republican Party, who were agitated by the Soviet occupation policy in Eastern Europe and attempted intimidation of Turkey and Iran, compelled Truman to revert to a confrontational Soviet policy early in 1946. He pressured the Soviets to withdraw from Iran and in the Truman Doctrine, declared his intention to extend economic and military aid to Turkey and Greece. With the Marshall Plan the

Truman administration initiated a massive economic aid program to the nations of Europe with the expectation that the reconstruction of capitalism in the region would halt the expansion of communism.

The growing U.S. antagonism toward the Soviets was fueled by a number of other problems. The two sides were unable to agree on several German issues, including reparations, the German-Polish border, and the political and economic nature of a reunited German state. Nor could they agree on an international arrangement for the control of atomic energy. These failures not only promoted distrust between the superpowers, they also helped to make a nuclear arms race inevitable. Their inability to resolve these and other issues also helped to make the United Nations a focus of Cold War confrontation, rather than a forum for the resolution of international differences.

As revisionist historians have asserted, economic factors were important in explaining the breakdown of the Grand Alliance. The United States did attempt to use economic leverage to modify Soviet behavior, for example, with Truman's suspension of Lend-Lease and rejection of a U.S. loan. Not surprisingly, the Soviets were led to believe that the Americans had a sinister motive in offering the Marshall Plan, that is, the manipulation of Soviet domestic and foreign policies, particularly the undermining of Soviet control of Eastern Europe. As a result, the Soviet Union rejected the Marshall Plan and compelled its satellite states to follow suit.

The Soviet rejection of the Marshall Plan, the communist coup in Czechoslovakia, and the Soviet blockade of Berlin reinforced an emerging Cold War consensus in the United States. It held that, if America again withdrew into isolation, Western Europe would again fall under the domination of an aggressive power, and U.S. military forces would again have to fight on the continent. This realization was primary in persuading the United States to join the North Atlantic alliance in 1949.

To be sure, the Truman administration did exaggerate its estimate of Soviet military strength to win public support for its commitment to NATO. In fact, the Soviet Union demobilized the vast majority of its forces after the war and had roughly the same amount of troops available to attack Western Europe as the NATO nations had to defend themselves.

A Soviet invasion of Western Europe was not a realistic possibility at the end of World War II. The Soviet Union was greatly weakened by that conflict and was in no position to engage in a protracted military conflict with the United States, particularly when they considered the U.S. nuclear weapons advantage. Still, the memory of Pearl Harbor and the explosion of the first Soviet atom bomb in 1949 convinced Americans that it was better to err on the side of exaggeration than to underestimate another enemy.

Moreover, the possibility of communist subversion of Western governments, as the Czechoslovak coup had demonstrated, was real. American fears of Soviet "proxy" expansion were reinforced by the "fall" of China in 1949 and the North Korean attack on South Korea the following year. By then, the Truman administration, as well as the American people, were convinced that the Soviet Union was an aggressive power determined to dominate the world.

The rise of McCarthyism, with its charge that Truman was soft on both the internal and external communist threats, added to the sense of vulnerability the American people felt. Consequently, any realistic assessment of the Soviet threat was politically impossible, indeed almost treasonable, during the Truman era, and long after.

The Truman administration concluded that the United States must build up its military forces and contain communist aggression wherever it occurred. The administration refused to recognize Communist China and undertook to protect Taiwan. It also intervened in the Korean War and provided military and economic aid to Taiwan, Thailand, and French Indochina. The Truman administration also built a network of alliances in the Pacific with Japan, Australia, and New Zealand. By the time Truman left office in 1953, the foundations for the next four decades of the Cold War were firmly in place.

The Expansion of Containment to the Third World

With the status quo frozen in Europe, the Third World quickly became the main arena of U.S.–Soviet competition. To prevent the spread of communism into the underdeveloped world, the United States often allied itself with dictatorships rather than the forces of reform. During the Eisenhower administration, the CIA assisted the shah of Iran to regain his throne, helped to overthrow an agrarian reform government in Guatemala, and prepared plans for the overthrow of Fidel Castro in Cuba.

The United States also expanded its application of the containment doctrine in the Middle East during Eisenhower's administration. It helped to create the Central Treaty Organization (CENTO) and proclaimed (in the Eisenhower Doctrine) a willingness to intervene militarily to prop up pro-Western governments in the region. It demonstrated its determination to do so in 1958 by sending U.S. Marines to Lebanon and by supporting the British in upholding the government of King Hussein of Jordan.

Eisenhower applied the containment doctrine in the Far East as well. In 1954 the United States concluded an alliance with Taiwan and created the Southeast Asia Treaty Organization (SEATO), which engaged the United States in the defense of Thailand, Pakistan, South Vietnam, Laos, and Cambodia against "communist aggression."

The Soviets were also responsible for the intensification of the Cold War during the Eisenhower years. Nikita Khrushchev's pompous boasting about the inevitability of communism's triumph irked Americans. His willingness to engage in "rocket diplomacy" helped to fuel the nuclear arms race, and his eagerness to challenge U.S. interests around the world contributed to the expansion of the Cold War in the Third World.

Khrushchev's aggressiveness was motivated not only by a desire to take advantage of an opportunity to expand Soviet influence but also by the perceived need to fend off a growing challenge from China for leadership of the communist movement.

For a variety of reasons—political, economic, and even psychological—John F. Kennedy could not ignore Khrushchev's challenges, particularly the Soviet leader's pledge to assist "liberation" movements in the Third World. Thus, Kennedy approved the Eisenhower-initiated CIA plan to overthrow Castro. Its humiliating failure in the Bay of Pigs invasion helped set the stage for the greatest superpower confrontation of the Cold War, the Cuban missile crisis. Kennedy also permitted the CIA to overthrow the Lumumba regime in the Congo. And he expanded the U.S. commitment to South Vietnam, and in the process created the military forces that would enable his successor, Lyndon Johnson, to enter the Vietnam quagmire.

Johnson's inability to defeat the North Vietnamese was a turning point in the history of the U.S. containment policy. His failure in Vietnam destroyed the domestic consensus, which had prevailed since the Truman administration, that the United States must intervene wherever possible to resist the expansion of communism. The collapse of that consensus compelled Johnson to withdraw from the presidential campaign of 1968. It also forced his successor, Richard Nixon, to pull American combat forces out of Vietnam, a process that was completed in 1973. The consequent collapse of South Vietnam two years later was the bitterest defeat experienced by the United States during the entire Cold War.

The Nuclear Arms Race

The nuclear arms race also intensified and prolonged the Cold War. The United States came to rely heavily on nuclear weapons to contain communism during the Eisenhower administration, primarily because they were relatively inexpensive to construct and deploy compared to conventional forces.

After the Soviets began to produce nuclear weapons and, in the 1950s, the means to deliver them to U.S. targets, nuclear weapons became even more important to the United States. They were considered necessary not only to deter a Soviet nuclear attack on the American homeland and on U.S. allies but also to counter a wide variety of other communist challenges. The United States made nuclear threats during the offshore islands crises with China in the 1950s, the Berlin crises of 1948 and 1961, the Cuban missile crisis in 1962, and the Arab-Israeli war of 1973.

The willingness of the United States to engage in nuclear diplomacy was based on the overwhelming nuclear superiority it possessed until the 1970s. With the exception of ICBMs and ABMs, the United States led the Soviet Union in developing and deploying every major strategic nuclear

weapons system. To Americans, nuclear superiority was not only a requirement of national security but a matter of national supremacy. To the Soviets, U.S. nuclear superiority was a threat to their continued existence.

Each postwar administration experienced pressure to build more
nuclear weapons from the military-industrial complex, which included the
Pentagon, defense contractors, scientists in the nation's nuclear weapons
labs, and politicians with defense industries in their districts or an ax to
grind with the administration in power. To raise congressional support for
increased defense spending, the military-industrial complex capitalized
repeatedly on the public's fear of the Soviet Union with exaggerated estimates of Soviet capabilities. The result was one weapon's gap scare after
another: the bomber gap and then the missile gap in the late fifties, the
ABM gap in the late 1960s, the throw-weight gap in the 1970s, and the
space weapons gap in the 1980s.

The Soviets felt compelled to keep up with their more technologically
advanced adversary, and, in time, they succeeded in matching in number
if not quality virtually every major U.S. nuclear weapon. Paradoxically,
the ultimate and inevitable result of this action-reaction cycle was an
increase in both American and Soviet insecurity. The more nuclear
weapons the Americans targeted on the Soviet Union, the more nuclear
weapons the Soviets aimed at the United States.

The Failure of U.S.–Soviet Détente

The ever-increasing risks of nuclear war, not to mention the expense, produced by the nuclear arms race motivated the Kennedy, Johnson, and
Nixon administrations to pursue détente with the Soviet Union. In the
wake of the almost catastrophic Cuban missile crisis, the United States
and the Soviet Union signed the first significant nuclear arms control
agreements, the Limited Test Ban Treaty and the Nuclear Nonproliferation Treaty. But the high point of détente occurred during the Nixon
administration. Nixon and Brezhnev signed the SALT I agreement, a
major U.S.–Soviet trade accord, and the Agreement on the Prevention of
Nuclear War, among other détente-related accords. Nixon also began the
normalization of U.S. relations with China.

For a variety of reasons, however, détente also began to fall apart during the Nixon years. Basically, the Soviets did not see improved relations
with the United States as a reason to discontinue giving support to Soviet
client states, such as Vietnam, Syria, Egypt, and Cuba, or to Marxist
movements elsewhere in the Third World, such as in Angola. As a consequence, American politicians, particularly conservatives, began to question how the United States was benefiting from détente. They argued
that U.S.–Soviet economic agreements subsidized an inefficient Soviet
economy, thereby enabling the Soviet Union to augment the size and
quality of its military establishment. Conservatives responded by blocking
the ratification of the U.S.–Soviet trade agreement and imposing addi-

tional restrictions on the SALT II agreement. American liberals, on the other hand, were angered primarily by what they considered to be Nixon's misuse of presidential war powers. They reacted by stopping the funding of U.S. combat activities in Indochina, passing the War Powers Act, and restricting covert operations by the CIA. Nixon and his successor, Gerald Ford, argued that Congress had deprived the United States of both the carrot and stick by which they had attempted to regulate Soviet behavior.

Jimmy Carter tried to revive détente during his presidency. He hoped to enlist Soviet cooperation in solving pressing global problems, such as the growth of nuclear weapons, regional conflicts, and human rights violations. However, Carter left office with U.S.–Soviet relations at their lowest point since the Cuban missile crisis.

Carter was partially responsible. His mishandling of the SALT II negotiations delayed the completion of a treaty and allowed time for other events, notably the Soviet invasion of Afghanistan, to undermine support for its ratification. His support for human rights in the Soviet empire made Soviet cooperation on other issues hard to obtain, and the blatant manner in which the administration normalized U.S.–Chinese relations incited the Soviets further. The administration's exclusion of the Soviet Union from the Middle East peace process only confirmed Soviet fears that it could derive no benefits from cooperation with the Carter administration. The Soviet decision to invade Afghanistan was an outcome of that belief.

The Soviets, however, were primarily responsible for the collapse of détente. The inflexibility of the Soviet leadership under Brezhnev was demonstrated not only in the Strategic Arms Limitation Talks but also in the LRTNF and MBFR talks. Brezhnev was also unable to desist from competing with the United States in the Third World; this competition inevitably drained the Soviet Union's resources and contributed to its ultimate collapse. As the Soviet Union declined economically, the Soviet leadership felt all the more compelled to pose as a revolutionary power, if only to provide some legitimacy to the monopoly of power enjoyed by the Soviet Communist Party. But the price it paid for doing so was steep: the next American president, Ronald Reagan, would push the Soviet Union much harder than Carter did, in fact, to the brink of collapse.

The End of the Cold War

The "full-court press" launched during Reagan's first term—which included a military buildup capped by the Strategic Defense Initiative, the denial of economic assistance to the Soviet Union, and a willingness to challenge the Soviet Union in the Third World—did force the Soviets to consider the prospect of having to expend resources they did not have. But, the Cold War came to an end primarily because of the inherent weaknesses in the Soviet system, not the pressure the Reagan administration brought to bear upon it. Simply put, the Soviet economic system had failed to support the Soviet empire. The economic failure, in turn, undermined popular support for communism, not only in the Soviet Union and Eastern Europe but also in Marxist client states in the Third World, making it that much more difficult for the Soviets to compete with the United States in the underdeveloped world.

Mikhail Gorbachev tried to make changes in Soviet domestic and foreign policies, and even abandoned long-held Marxist principles, in an attempt to reverse the economic and social decline of the Soviet Union. He initiated economic reforms, perestroika, and permitted greater freedom of expression, glasnost, to try to overcome hard-line opposition. He also tried to end the exorbitantly expensive arms race with the United States. He proposed meaningful arms reductions and pressured Reagan and Bush to accept them. The INF Treaty was one result. A START treaty was another. Gorbachev also began the Soviet retreat from the Third World.

Nevertheless, the forces that Gorbachev's reforms unleashed only made collapse of the Soviet Union inevitable. Greater freedom of expression permitted democratic and nationalistic forces to arise in opposition to the communist monopoly of power. It also provoked a hard-line reaction that culminated in the failed coup of August 1991 and the disintegration of the Soviet Union itself.

After an initially cautious approach to Gorbachev, President Bush wisely facilitated the demise of the long-time U.S. adversary. He provided the assurances that Gorbachev needed to accept German reunification. He also did not push the Soviet leader too hard on the issue of self-determination for the subject nationalities of the Soviet Union. His forbearance helped Gorbachev to separate himself from the hard-line crackdown on Lithuania and eventually to rejoin the reformers. Furthermore, while Bush was tardy in supporting the Soviet leader during the unsuccessful coup, his arms control initiatives after Gorbachev was restored to power ensured that the transfer of Soviet nuclear weapons to Russian President Boris Yeltsin's control was accomplished without incident.

Who "Won" the Cold War?

With the demise of the Soviet Union in December 1991, Bush could argue, as he did, that the West had won the Cold War. Not only was Soviet communism gone but under Boris Yeltsin a new Russia had emerged that was committed to democracy and the free market system.

Still, the price the West, and particularly the United States, paid to fight the Cold War was high. Tens of thousands of U.S. military personnel, and many more friendly soldiers and civilians, were killed in the hot conflicts of the Cold War, especially in Korea and Vietnam.

The Cold War also altered American political institutions. The increased requirements of national security contributed to the growth of the so-called imperial presidency, and the abuse of presidential powers, of which the Watergate affair was the most sordid example. As the worst abuses of Watergate demonstrated, even the most cherished principles of American democracy were endangered by the requirements of national security.

The Cold War was also expensive in dollars. The United States and the Soviet Union both spent heavily on weapons of war, and on military and economic aid to allies and client states. The U.S. national debt had risen to $4 trillion by the end of the Cold War. While much of the debt was due to Congress's refusal to reduce domestic spending and ensure adequate taxation to maintain it, massive military spending was also responsible. To finance the burgeoning national debt, the United States was forced to become a debtor nation for the first time in seventy years.

During the Cold War, America's economic infrastructure also suffered. Important elements of the nation's transportation system, such as roads and bridges, were allowed to decay. Investment in other key areas of an advanced industrial economy—education, job training, and nonmilitary research and development—was also inadequate. As a result, the United States was at an increasing disadvantage in competing commercially with other countries—notably Japan and Germany—that were not compelled to invest as heavily in their military establishments, primarily because the United States was assuming a portion of the expense of their defense. As a result, these two World War II losers became America's leading economic competitors during the late Cold War era. Another price the American people paid for winning the Cold War was the relative neglect of pressing social problems. The effects are still visible in the nation's inner cities, where slums, crime, widespread unemployment, and welfare dependence are the rule rather than exception.

In some ways the most damaging effect of the Cold War, on both the Soviet and the American people, and many others as well, was psychological. The Cold War engendered fear and suspicion. It helped to provide a rationale for maintaining a Stalinist state in the Soviet Union, long after Stalin himself was gone, as well as brutal dictatorships in both communist and noncommunist countries elsewhere in the world.

Fear and suspicion of communism, in turn, terrified countless Americans and ruined more than a few careers of people who were only suspected of being Communists. Moreover, the Cold War, and specifically U.S. participation in the Vietnam conflict, divided the American people as no other issue had since the Civil War. Afghanistan was the Soviet Vietnam.

In addition, the superpower competition, especially during the Cuban missile crisis, almost produced a nuclear war, one that could have destroyed the life of the planet. While that outcome, fortunately, was avoided, the fear of nuclear war afflicted two generations of Americans and Soviet citizens, not to mention countless other inhabitants of the world.

Clearly, there is much truth in Gorbachev's statement that both the Soviet Union and the United States *lost* the Cold War. The people of both nations lost much in waging it, even if the Soviet Union as an entity disappeared and the United States emerged triumphant.

Paradoxically, there are some who almost miss the Cold War. While there were numerous conflicts between the United States and the proxies, allies, or clients of the Soviet Union during the Cold War, there was no general war between the two superpowers because both realized that such a conflict could very well be humanity's last. For this reason, historian John Lewis Gaddis has called the Cold War the era of "the Long Peace."

Fearing an all-out nuclear war, both sides sought to maintain a stable balance of power. Not only did the two superpowers check each other, they also kept other potentially destabilizing forces under control. The United States helped to keep Germany and Japan in line, and the Soviet Union kept a lid on the ethnic rivalries of Eastern Europe and Central Asia. The negative consequences of the Soviet Union's decline and ultimate demise can be seen in the mass slaughter of civilians in Bosnia, Azerbaijan, Armenia, and Chechnya.

In the aftermath of the Cold War, as Somalia, Haiti, and Bosnia have demonstrated, the burden of maintaining the world's peace has fallen even more heavily on the United States. This helps to explain why the Clinton administration has worked very hard to enlist Russian support for NATO's peace-keeping role in Bosnia. It is an ironic legacy to U.S. "victory" in the Cold War.

Was there any alternative to the Cold War? Clearly, no. The competition between the two nations was inevitable given their respective manifest destinies to expand their political, cultural, economic, and influence. In so doing, both states sought security from real and imaginary enemies and, in the process, established colonies, client states, and allies to protect themselves.

But a more important reason for the inevitability of the Cold War, beyond the two parties' common sense of vulnerability, was the incompatibility of their ideologies. This was evident as early as the Bolshevik Revolution, when both Lenin and Wilson realized that genuine cooperation between the two systems was impossible. After the defeat of the common Russian-American enemy in World War II, Germany, the earlier ideological animosity between the two countries revived and deepened. Only after Mikhail Gorbachev demonstrated a willingness to abandon the decades-old ideological conflict did the end of the Cold War and the beginning of genuine Russian-American cooperation finally become possible.

That the Cold War did not destroy humanity is providential. Another cause for optimism is that, despite all the challenges it faced during the Cold War, American democracy survived the struggle. With any luck, democracy will also take hold in Russia and the other former Soviet republics. That, in the end, may be the most beneficial consequence of the Cold War.

Still, while Russian-American relations have improved considerably since the end of the Cold War, much of the old friction that characterized that era is again threatening the new relationship. The economic hardships endured by the Russian people in the transition toward a free-market economy have been more severe and unequal than was expected. The result has been a decline not only in public support for capitalism but also the democratic system that is trying to bring it about. This probably explains the good showing of the Communist Party in the Russian parliamentary election in December 1995, in which the communists received the largest percentage of seats, roughly 22 percent.

Russian nationalism has also revived, as was demonstrated by the good showing of the ultranationalist party (headed by Vladimir Zhirinovsky) in the Russian parliamentary election (11 percent of the seats). The Russian nationalist movement has been spurred not only by popular disappointment with Yeltsin's economic program but also by the demise of Russia as a superpower. Russians of all political stripes were offended by the refusal of NATO to accord Russia full membership in the alliance. Now most Russians adamantly oppose the extension of NATO to the other states of Eastern Europe that have requested membership in the alliance, particularly Poland, Czechoslovakia, and Hungary.

Unfortunately, the survival of democracy in Russia is not a sure thing, despite the reelection of Yeltsin in 1996. Its demise and replacement by a more aggressively nationalist, and less democratic and capitalistic, Russia could again revive the Cold War.

Notes

Introduction: The United States and Czarist Russia

1. Miroslav Nincic, *Anatomy of Hostility: The U.S.–Soviet Rivalry in Perspective* (1989), 86.

2. Thomas Jefferson, *The Writings of Thomas Jefferson*, A. A. Lipscomb and A. E. Bergh, eds., memorial edition, 20 vols. (1907), 19:142–144.

3. Ibid., 11:290–292.

4. John Lewis Gaddis, *Russia, the Soviet Union, and the United States: An Interpretive History*, 2nd ed. (1990), 10–11.

5. James Buchanan, *The Works of James Buchanan*, John Bassett Moore, ed. (1908–11) 2:199.

6. John Lewis Gaddis, *The Long Peace: Inquiries into the History of the Cold War* (1987), 5.

7. E. A. Adamov, "Russia and the United States at the Time of the Civil War," *Journal of Modern History* 2 (December 1930), 601–602.

8. Gaddis, *Russia, the Soviet Union, and the United States*, 21.

Chapter One. The United States and the Bolshevik Revolution, 1917–1933

1. Woodrow Wilson, *War and Peace* (1927), 1:13.

2. U.S. Department of State, *Foreign Relations of the United States: 1918, Russia* (1931–32), 1:258. Hereafter cited as *FRUS*, followed by appropriate subtitle of volume.

3. Robert Lansing, *War Memoirs* (1953), 340.

4. *New York Times*, December 5, 1917.

5. Lansing, 342.

6. C. K. Cumming and Walter W. Pettit, *Russian-American Relations: March 1917–March 1920* (1920), 65.

7. Ray Stannard Baker and William E. Dodd, eds., *The Public Papers of Woodrow Wilson*, 6 vols. (1925–27), 5: 159–160.

8. *The Papers of Woodrow Wilson*, Arthur S. Link, ed. (1984), 65.

9. Leonid I. Strakhovsky, *American Opinion about Russia, 1917–1920* (1961), 50.

10. William A. Williams, "American Intervention in Russia, 1917–1920," (part 2), *Studies on the Left* 4 (Winter 1964), 40.

11. Strakhovsky, 55.

12. Cumming and Pettit, 81–82.

13. *FRUS: 1918, Russia*, 1:395.

14. George F. Kennan, *Soviet–American Relations, 1917–1920*, vol. 1: *Russia Leaves the War* (1958), 516.

15. David R. Francis, *Russia from the American Embassy* (1921), 230.

16. FRUS: *1918, Russia*, 2:30.

17. Ibid., 42.

18. *FRUS: The Lansing Papers, 1914–1920* (1940), 2:355.

19. *FRUS: 1918, Russia* 2:67.

20. Robert J. Maddox, *The Unknown War with Russia: Wilson's Siberian Intervention* (1977), 39.

21. Strakhovsky, 59.

22. *FRUS: 1918, Russia*, 2:81.

23. Ibid., 88.

24. George F. Kennan, *Soviet-American Relations, 1917–1920*, vol. 2: *The Decision to Intervene* (1960), 100.

25. *FRUS: 1918, Russia*, 2:116–117.

26. John W. Long, "American Intervention in Russia: The North Russian Expedition, 1918–19," *Diplomatic History* 6 (Winter 1982), 50.

27. *FRUS: 1918, Russia*, 2:160.

28. *FRUS: Lansing Papers*, 2:361–362.

29. *FRUS: 1918, Russia*, 2:476.

30. *FRUS: Lansing Papers*, 2:360.

31. W. B. Fowler, *British–American Relations, 1917–1918* (1969), 179–180.

32. *FRUS: Lansing Papers*, 2:363.

33. *FRUS: 1918, Russia*, 2: 245–246.

34. Peyton C. March, *The Nation at War* (1932), 116–126.

35. *FRUS: 1918, Russia*, 2:287–290.

36. Ibid., 351.

37. Basil Dmytrysin, *USSR: A Concise History* (1965), 91.

38. *FRUS: 1918, Russia*, 2:324.

39. Ibid., 395.

40. Betty Miller Unterberger, "Woodrow Wilson and the Bolsheviks: The 'Acid Test' of Soviet–American Relations," *Diplomatic History* 11 (Spring 1987), 85.

41. Ibid., 87.

42. Long, 61.

43. Louis Fischer, *The Soviets in World Affairs* (1951), 1:150.

44. Richard K. Debo, *Revolution and Survival: The Foreign Policy of Soviet Russia, 1917–1918* (1979), 388.

45. Ibid.

46. *FRUS: 1919, Russia* (1937), 15.

47. Jane Degras, ed., *Soviet Documents on Foreign Policy* , 2 vols. (1951), 1:135.

48. *FRUS: 1919 , Russia,* 57.

49. Ibid.

50. Betty Miller Unterberger, "Woodrow Wilson and the Russian Revolution," in Arthur S. Link, ed., *Woodrow Wilson and a Revolutionary World, 1913–1921* (1982), 84.

51. Frederick S. Calhoun, *Power and Principle: Armed Intervention in Wilsonian Foreign Policy* (1986), 240.

52. *Congressional Record,* 65th Cong., 3rd sess., February 14, 1919, pt. 4:3334–3342.

53. *FRUS: 1919, Russia,* 617.

54. Lloyd C. Gardner, *Wilson and Revolutions, 1913–1921* (1970), 53.

55. *FRUS: 1920* (1936), 3:466.

56. Strakhovsky, 114–115.

57. Degras, 1: 221–224.

58. Katherine A. S. Siegel, "Technology and Trade: Russia's Pursuit of American Investment, 1917–1929," *Diplomatic History* 17 (Summer 1993), 393.

59. Degras, 2:408.

60. John Lewis Gaddis, *Russia, the Soviet Union, and the United States: An Interpretive History,* 2nd ed. (1990), 108.

61. Long, 67.

Chapter Two. Franklin D. Roosevelt and the Grand Alliance, 1933–1945

1. *FRUS: 1933* (1949) 2:794–795.

2. *FRUS: 1933,* 2:805–814.

3. Gaddis, *Russia, the Soviet Union, and the United States,* 121.

4. Edward M. Bennett, *Recognition of Russia: An American Foreign Policy Dilemma* (1970), 192.

5. Thomas R. Maddux, *Years of Estrangement: American Relations with the Soviet Union, 1933–1941* (1980), 23.

6. Edward M. Bennett, *Franklin D. Roosevelt and the Search for Security: American–Soviet Relations, 1933–1939* (1985), 45.

7. *FRUS : Soviet Union, 1933–39* (1952), 245.

8. Gaddis, *Russia, the Soviet Union, and the United States,* 126.

9. *FRUS : Soviet Union, 1933–39,* 265.

10. George F. Kennan, *Memoirs: 1925–1950* (1967), 57.

11. *FRUS : Soviet Union, 1933–39,* 310.

12. Bennett, *Franklin D. Roosevelt and the Search for Security,* 136–137.

13. Kennan, 74.

14. Fraser J. Harbut, *The Iron Curtain: Churchill, America, and the Origins of the Cold War* (1986), 34.

15. Kennan, 137–141.

16. Joseph Davies, *Mission to Moscow* (1941), 493, 496.

17. Raymond H. Dawson, *The Decision to Aid Russia, 1941: Foreign Policy and Domestic Politics* (1959), 108.

18. *FRUS: 1941* (1958), 1:832.

19. U.S. Department of State, *Bulletin* 5 (1941), 366.

20. Winston S. Churchill, *The Second World War*, vol. 4: *The Hinge of Fate* (1950), 327.

21. Robert E. Sherwood, *Roosevelt and Hopkins: An Intimate History* (1948), 563.

22. *FRUS: 1942*, (1942), 3:598.

23. Churchill, 4:744.

24. Orville H. Bullitt, ed., *For the President, Personal and Secret: Correspondence Between Franklin D. Roosevelt and William C. Bullitt* (1972), 575–579.

25. William C. Bullitt, "How We Won the War and Lost the Peace," *Life*, August 30, 1948, 94.

26. John Lewis Gaddis, *The United States and the Origins of the Cold War, 1941–1947* (1972), 64–65.

27. Robert Dallek, *Franklin D. Roosevelt and American Foreign Policy, 1932–1945* (1979), 439.

28. Warren F. Kimball, *Churchill and Roosevelt: The Complete Correspondence,* 3 vols. (1984), 3:371.

29. FRUS: *The Conferences at Malta and Yalta* (1955), 973.

30. William D. Leahy, *I Was There* (1950), 315–316.

31. *FRUS: The Conferences at Malta and Yalta* , 770.

32. Beatrice B. Berle and Travis B. Jacobs, eds., *Navigating the Rapids, 1918–1971: From the Papers of Adolf A. Berle* (1973), 477.

33. *FRUS: 1945* (1967), 5:194–196.

34. Kimball, 3:629–630.

35. Frederick W. Marks III, *Winds over Sand: The Diplomacy of Franklin Roosevelt* (1988), 177, 173.

36. Gaddis, *Russia, the Soviet Union, and the United States* , 167.

Chapter Three. Truman and Containment, 1945–1953

1. John Lewis Gaddis, *The United States and the Origins of the Cold War, 1941–1947* (1972), 267.

2. *Time*, February 18, 1946, 25–26.

3. Gaddis, *The United States and the Origins of the Cold War,* 300.

4. Harry S. Truman, *Memoirs*, vol. 2: *Years of Trial and Hope* (1956), 95.

5. *FRUS: 1946* (1969) 7:524, 529–532.

6. *Vital Speeches of the Day* 12 (March 15, 1946), 326–329.

7. Robert L. Messer, *The End of an Alliance: James Byrnes, Roosevelt, Truman, and the Origins of the Cold War* (1982), 190.

8. *Vital Speeches of the Day* 12 (March 15, 1946), 329–332.

9. Messer, 185.

10. *Public Papers of the Presidents of the United States: Harry S. Truman, 1947* (1963), 178–179.

11. Gaddis, *The United States and the Origins of the Cold War,* 352.

12. U.S. Department of Defense, *History of the Secretary of Defense*, Alfred Goldberg, gen. ed., vol. 1: Steven L. Rearden, *The Formative Years, 1947–1950* (1984), 13–14.

13. Michael H. Hunt, "Mao Tse-tung and the Issue of Accommodation with the United States," in Dorothy Borg and Waldo Heinrichs, eds., *Uncertain Years: Chinese-American Relations, 1947–1950* (1980), 215.

14. U.S. Department of State, *U.S. Relations with China* (1949), 358.

15. U.S. Department of State, *Bulletin* 22 (January 23, 1950), 111–118.

16. *Congressional Record*, 81st Cong., 1st sess., August 22, 1949, pt. 15:A5451–5453.

17. *Congressional Record*, 81st Cong., 1st sess., September 9, 1949, pt. 10:12, 755, 758.

18. Hunt, 221.

19. U.S. Department of State, *Bulletin* 22 (March 27, 1950), 468.

20. Andrew J. Rotter, *The Path to Vietnam: Origins of the American Commitment to Southeast Asia* (1987), 120–121.

21. Norman A. Graebner, *America as a World Power: A Realist Appraisal from Wilson to Reagan* (1984), 175.

22. *FRUS: 1950* (1977) 1: 235–292.

23. Michael Schaller, *The United States and China in the Twentieth Century*, 2nd ed. (1990), 135–136.

24. Bevin Alexander, *The Strange Connection: U.S. Intervention in China, 1944–1972* (1992), 98.

25. *FRUS: 1950*, 7:174–177.

26. Truman, 2:333.

27. Philip C. Jessup, *The Birth of Nations* (1974), 10.

28. David R. Kepley, *The Collapse of the Middle Way: Senate Republicans and the Bipartisan Foreign Policy, 1948–1952* (1988), 127.

29. Rotter, 211.

30. *The Pentagon Papers: The Defense Department History of United States Decisionmaking on Vietnam*, Senator Gravel edition (1971), 1:384–390.

31. Arthur Schlesinger, Jr., "Origins of the Cold War," *Foreign Affairs* 46 (October 1967), 47.

32. Lloyd C. Gardner, Arthur Schlesinger, Jr., and Hans J. Morgenthau, *The Origins of the Cold War* (1970), 94–95.

33. For an example, see Nikolai V. Sivachev and Nikolai N. Yakovlev, *Russia and the United States*, Olga Adler Titlebaum, trans. (1979).

34. Michael Parenti, *The Sword and the Dollar: Imperialism, Revolution, and the Arms Race* (1989), 147.

35. Ibid.

36. Gabriel Kolko and Joyce Kolko, *The Limits of Power: The World and United States Foreign Policy, 1945–1954* (1972).

37. Fred L. Block, *The Origins of International Economic Disorder: A Study of United States International Monetary Policy from World War II to the Present* (1977), 10.

38. Parenti, 148.

39. John Lewis Gaddis, "The Emerging Post-Revisionist Synthesis on the Origins of the Cold War," *Diplomatic* History 7 (Summer 1983), 171–190.

40. Robert L. Pollard, *Economic Security and the Origins of the Cold War, 1945–1950* (1985), 244.

41. Melvyn P. Leffler, *A Preponderance of Power: National Security, the Truman Administration, and the Cold War* (1992).

Chapter Four. Eisenhower and the Globalization of the Cold War, 1953–1961

1. *Vital Speeches of the Day* 19 (May 1, 1953), 421.

2. Chester J. Pach, Jr., and Elmo Richardson, *The Presidency of Dwight D. Eisenhower*, rev. ed. (1991), 64.

3. *Public Papers of the Presidents of the United States: Dwight D. Eisenhower, 1953* (1960), 447. Hereafter cited as *EPP*.

4. Pach and Richardson, 71.

5. Charles C. Alexander, *Holding the Line: The Eisenhower Era, 1952–1961* (1975), 30.

6. Charles F. Bohlen, *Witness to History, 1929–1969* (1973), 371.

7. John Lewis Gaddis, *Strategies of Containment: A Critical Appraisal Of Postwar American National Security Policy* (1982), 149–150.

8. James Shepley, "How Dulles Averted War," *Life* 40 (January 16, 1956), 78.

9. Lawrence S. Wittner, *Cold War America: From Hiroshima to Watergate* (1974), 145.

10. Chalmers Roberts, *The Nuclear Years: The Arms Race and Arms Control, 1945–1970* (1970), 41.

11. *EPP: 1953*, 484–486.

12. Morris H. Morley, *Imperial State and Revolution: The United States and Cuba, 1952–1986* (1987), 41–42.

13. Townsend Hoopes, *The Devil and John Foster Dulles* (1973), 230.

14. Frederick W. Marks III, "The Real Hawk at Dienbienphu: Dulles or Eisenhower?" *Pacific Historical Review* 59 (August 1990), 297–322.

15. Robert A. Divine, *Eisenhower and the Cold War* (1981), 48.

16. Lord Moran (Charles McMoran Wilson), *Winston Churchill: The Struggle for Survival, 1940–1965* (1966), 543.

17. Alexander, 81.

18. *FRUS: 1952–1954* (1985), 14:354.

19. Robert D. Schulzinger, *American Diplomacy in the Twentieth Century* (1990), 240.

20. *FRUS: 1954*, 14:831.

21. Alexander, 97–98.

22. Lester A. Sobel, ed., *Russia's Rulers: The Khrushchev Period* (1971), 81.

23. John Lewis Gaddis, *The Long Peace: Inquiries into the History of the Cold War* (1987), 189.

24. John Emmett Hughes, *The Ordeal of Power* (1963), 217.

25. *EPP: 1957* (1957), 6–16.

26. U.S. Department of State, *Documents on Disarmament, 1945–1959* (1960), 2:1121–1125.

27. Arnold L. Horelick and Myron Rush, *Strategic Power and Soviet Foreign Policy* (1966), 49.

28. Divine, *Eisenhower and the Cold War*, 147–148.

29. Richard D. Mahoney, *JFK: Ordeal in Africa* (1983), 38.

30. Ibid., 41.

31. Alexander, 287.

Chapter Five. Kennedy and Johnson: Confrontation and Cooperation, 1961–1969

1. Richard J. Walton, *Cold War and Counterrevolution: The Foreign Policy of John F. Kennedy* (1972), 9.

2. Arthur M. Schlesinger, Jr., *A Thousand Days: John F. Kennedy and the White House* (1965), 303.

3. Bruce Miroff, *Pragmatic Illusions: The Presidential Politics of John F. Kennedy* (1976), 64.

4. *Public Papers of the Presidents of the United States: John F. Kennedy, 1961* (1962), 304. Hereafter cited as *KPP.*

5. Louise FitzSimons, *The Kennedy Doctrine* (1972), 70.

6. Stephen G. Rabe, "Controlling Revolutions: Latin America, the Alliance for Progress, and Cold War Anti-Communism," in Thomas G. Paterson, ed., *Kennedy's Quest for Victory: American Foreign Policy, 1961–1963* (1989), 112.

7. Schlesinger, 348.

8. Nikita S. Khrushchev, *Khrushchev Remembers: The Last Testament*, Strobe Talbott, ed. and trans. (1974), 565.

9. Schlesinger, 334.

10. Ibid., 374.

11. Ibid., 391.

12. Ibid., 482–483.

13. Maxwell D. Taylor, *The Uncertain Trumpet* (1959), 146.

14. Khrushchev, 494.

15. Robert Kennedy, *Thirteen Days: A Memoir of the Cuban Missile Crisis* (1969), 67.

16. Schlesinger, 810–811.

17. *KPP: 1962*, 806–809.

18. Schlesinger, 841.

19. FitzSimons, 127.

20. Theodore C. Sorenson, *Kennedy* (1965), 705.

21. William J. Medland, *The Cuban Missile Crisis of 1962: Needless or Necessary?* (1988), 147–148.

22. *KPP: 1963*, 459–464.

23. FitzSimons, 15.

24. *KPP: 1963*, 890–894.

25. Bernard J. Firestone, *The Quest for Nuclear Stability: John F. Kennedy and the Soviet Union* (1982), 149–150.

26. John Wilson Lewis and Xue Litai, *China Builds the Bomb* (1988), 10.

27. Lester A. Sobel, ed., *Russia's Rulers: The Khrushchev Period* (1971), 325.

28. Robert M. Slusser, *The Berlin Crisis of 1961: Soviet–American Relations and the Struggle in the Kremlin, June–November 1961* (1973), 341.

29. Schlesinger, 479.

30. Jacob D. Beam, *Multiple Exposure* (1978), 139.

31. John F. Kennedy, *The Strategy of Peace*, Allan Nevins, ed. (1960), 89.

32. *The Pentagon Papers, New York Times* edition (1971), 98–99, 118–119.

33. Charles Bartlett, "Portrait of a Friend," in Kenneth W. Thompson, ed. *The Kennedy Presidency* (1985), 16.

34. Thomas G. Paterson, "Introduction: John F. Kennedy's Quest for Victory and Global Crisis," in Paterson, *Kennedy's Quest for Victory*, 21.

35. Thomas J. Noer, "New Frontiers and Old Priorities in Africa," in Paterson, *Kennedy's Quest for Victory* , 253.

36. Ibid., 257.

37. Richard D. Mahoney, *JFK: Ordeal in Africa* (1983), 214–215.

38. Noer, 276.

39. Walton, 219.

40. Eric Goldman, *The Tragedy of Lyndon Johnson* (1968), 378.

41. Lyndon B. Johnson, *The Vantage Point: Perspectives of the Presidency, 1963–1969* (1972), 18.

42. Walter LaFebre, "Latin American Policy," in Robert A. Divine, ed., *The Johnson Years*, vol. 1: *Foreign Policy, the Great Society, and the White House* (1987), 69.

43. Ibid.

44. Tom Wicker, *JFK and LBJ: The Influence of Personality upon Politics* (1968), 205.

45. George C. Herring, *America's Longest War: The United States and Vietnam, 1950–1975,* 2nd. ed. (1986), 141.

46. "Joint Resolution to Promote Maintenance of International Peace and Security in South-east Asia" (PL-88–488, August 10, 1964), *U.S. Statutes at Large* 78:384.

47. Michael Schaller, *The United States and China in the Twentieth Century,* 2nd. ed. (1990), 165.

48. Kwan Ha Yim, *China and the U.S. 1964–72* (1973), 143–144.

49. Ibid., 145.

50. Harold Wilson, *The Labour Government, 1964–70: A Personal Record* (1971), 359–365.

51. Larry Berman, *Lyndon Johnson's War: The Road to Stalemate in Vietnam* (1989), 191.

52. Herring, 210.

53. Ibid., 213.

54. U.S. Arms Control and Disarmament Agency, *Documents on Disarmament, 1968* (1969), 655.

55. Thomas J. Schoenbaum, *Waging Peace and War: Dean Rusk in the Truman, Kennedy, and Johnson Years* (1989), 483.

Chapter Six. Nixon, Ford, and Détente, 1969–1977

1. *Public Papers of the Presidents of the United States: Richard M. Nixon, 1969* (1971), 3. Hereafter cited as *NPP*.

2. Richard M. Nixon, "Asia after Vietnam," *Foreign Affairs* 46 (October 1967), 121.

3. Henry A. Kissinger, *White House Years* (1979), 224–225.

4. *NPP: 1972* (1973), 376–379.

5. Ibid., 379.

6. Henry A. Kissinger, "The Viet Nam Negotiations," *Foreign Affairs* 47 (January 1969), 211–234.

7. *NPP: 1969,* 901–909.

8. Richard Nixon, *RN: The Memoirs of Richard Nixon* (1978), 407.

9. U.S. Arms Control and Disarmament Agency, *Documents on Disarmament, 1973* (1974), 271–283.

10. U.S. Congress, Senate Committee on Foreign Relations, *Hearings: Strategic Arms Limitations Agreements,* 92nd Cong., 2nd sess., 1972, 394.

11. Nixon, 701.

12. Nguyen Tien Hung and Jerrold L. Schecter, *The Palace File* (1986), 124.

13. Kissinger, *White House Years,* 1399.

14. Nixon, 721.

15. George C. Herring, *America's Longest War: The United States and Vietnam*, 2nd ed. (1986), 253.

16. Ibid., 254.

17. *Weekly Compilation of Presidential Documents,* January 29, 1973, 45–64.

18. Marilyn Blatt Young, *The Vietnam Wars, 1945–1990* (1991), 278.

19. Hung and Schecter, 144.

20. U.S. Arms Control and Disarmament Agency, *Documents on Disarmament,* 1973 (1974), 283–285.

21. *Time,* January 27, 1975, 35.

22. U.S. Arms Control and Disarmament Agency, *Documents on Disarmament,* 1974 (1975), 750–761.

23. Gary Hess, "The Unending Debate: Historians and the Vietnam War," *Diplomatic History* 19 (Spring 1994), 255.

24. Henry A. Kissinger, *Diplomacy* (1994), 701.

25. Robert D. Shulzinger, *Henry Kissinger: Doctor of Diplomacy* (1989), 206.

26. John Stoessinger, *Henry Kissinger: The Anguish of Power* (1976), 109.

27. Michael A. Genovese, *The Nixon Presidency: Power and Politics in Turbulent Times* (1990), 150.

28. Ibid.

29. Gerald Ford, *A Time To Heal: The Autobiography of Gerald R. Ford* (1979), 373.

30. *New York Times,* July 16, 1975.

31. Henry A. Kissinger, *Years of Upheaval* (1982), 243–245.

Chapter Seven. Carter and the Decline of Détente, 1977–1981

1. Dan Caldwell, *The SALT II Treaty Ratification Debate* (1991), 291.

2. Cyrus Vance, *Hard Choices: Critical Years in America's Foreign Policy* (1983), 27–28.

3. Zbigniew Brzezinski, *Power and Principle: Memoirs of a National Security Adviser, 1977–1981* (1983), 520.

4. Srinivasmi Chary, "Principled Pragmatism: Carter, Human Rights, and Indian–American Relations," in Herbert D. Rosenbaum and Alexej Ugrinsky, eds., *Jimmy Carter: Foreign Policy and Post-Presidential Years* (1994), 246.

5. Vance, 51.

6. Ibid., 49–50.

7. Jimmy Carter, *Keeping Faith: Memoirs of a President* (1982), 259–260.

8. Vance, 89.

9. Brzezinski, 186, 189.

10. Marilyn Blatt Young, *The Vietnam Wars, 1945–1990* (1991), 303.

11. Ibid.

12. Gaddis Smith, *Morality, Reason, and Power: American Diplomacy in the Carter Years* (1986), 89.

13. Richard C. Thornton, *China: A Political History, 1917–1980* (1982), 60.

14. Smith, 88.

15. Ibid., 89.

16. Ibid., 93.

17. Young, 310.

18. Carter, 241.

19. U.S. Arms Control and Disarmament Agency, *Documents on Disarmament, 1979* (1982), 231–238.

20. Carter, 473.

21. *Weekly Compilation of Presidential Documents,* 16 (January 1, 1980), pt. 1:40–41.

22. Raymond L. Garthoff, *Détente and Confrontation: American–Soviet Relations from Nixon to Reagan* (1985), 978.

Chapter Eight. *The Reagan Cold War, 1981–1989*

1. *Public Papers of the Presidents of the United States: Ronald Reagan, 1983* (1984), 364. Hereafter cited as *RPP.*

2. *Christian Science Monitor,* June 3, 1976, 15.

3. Ronald W. Reagan, *An American Life* (1990), 267.

4. Robert Sheer, *With Enough Shovels: Reagan, Bush and Nuclear War* (1982), 7. See also Christopher Simpson, ed., *National Security Directives of the Reagan and Bush Administrations: The Declassified History of U.S. Political and Military Policy, 1981–1991* (1995), 62–64.

5. David Locke Hall, *The Reagan Wars: A Constitutional Perspective on War Powers and the Presidency* (1990), 181.

6. Michael Schaller, *Reckoning with Reagan: America and Its President in the 1980s* (1992), 152.

7. Ibid., 153.

8. Oliver L. North, *Under Fire: An American Story* (1991), 12, 14.

9. Jeane Kirkpatrick, "Dictatorships and Double Standards," *Commentary* 68 (November 1979), 34–45.

10. Bruce Cumings, "American Hegemony in Northeast Asia: Security and Development," in Morris H. Morley, ed, *Crisis and Confrontation: Ronald Reagan's Foreign Policy* (1988), 91.

11. Ibid., 105.

12. Ibid., 89.

13. Ibid., 88.

14. *New York Times,* September 29, 1983.

15. George P. Shultz, *Turmoil and Triumph: My Years As Secretary of State* (1993), 398.

16. *Weekly Compilation of Presidential Documents,* (1982), pt. 2:764–770.

17. Ibid., vol. 20 (1984), pt. 3:1132.

18. Ibid., vol. 19 (1983), pt. 1:479.

19. John Newhouse, *War and Peace in the Nuclear Age* (1989), 34.

20. Schaller, 133.

21. Ibid., 134.

22. Simpson, 321.

23. Raymond L. Garthoff, *The Great Transition: American–Soviet Relations and the End of the Cold War* (1994), 128.

24. *World Press Review* 30 (June, 1983), 22.

25. *New York Times,* November 5, 1983.

26. *Weekly Compilation of Presidential Documents* 21 (1985), pt. 3:172.

27. Reagan, 588–589.

28. Shultz, 275, 490, 267.

29. Ibid., 490, 711.

30. *Weekly Compilation of Presidential Documents* 20 (1984), pt. 1:40–45.

31. Christopher Mark Davis, "Economic Influences on the Decline of the Soviet Union as a Great Power: Continuity Despite Change," in David Armstrong and Erik Goldstein, eds., *The End of the Cold War* (1990), 90.

32. Schaller, 171.

33. *Weekly Compilation of Presidential Documents* 23 (1987), pt. 2:321.

34. *RPP: 1988* (1990), 716.

35. Daniel Deudney and G. John Ikenberry, "Who Won the Cold War?" *Foreign Policy* 87 (1992), 123–138.

36. Wilbur Edel, *The Reagan Presidency: An Actor's Finest Performance* (1992), 300.

Chapter Nine. George Bush and the End of the Cold War, 1989–1991

1. Michael R. Beschloss and Strobe Talbott, *At the Highest Levels: The Inside Story of the Cold War* (1993), 50.

2. *New York Times*, April 25, 1989.

3. Ibid., July 7, 1989.

4. *Weekly Compilation of Presidential Documents* 25 (1989), pt. 3:1034.

5. Ibid., pt. 2:814.

6. Beschloss and Talbott, 134.

7. Raymond L. Garthoff, "The Bush Administration's Policy toward the Soviet Union," *Current History* 90 (October 1991), 313.

8. Beschloss and Talbott, 156.

9. Ibid., 165.

10. *New York Times*, April 21, 1990.

11. Robert. G. Kaiser, *Why Gorbachev Happened: Triumphs and Failure* (1991), 308.

12. Beschloss and Talbott, 179–180.

13. Peter G. Boyle, *American–Soviet Relations: From the Russian Revolution to the Fall of Communism* (1993), 240.

14. Constantine C. Menges, *The Future of Germany and the Atlantic Alliance* (1991), 112.

15. Ibid., 112–113.

16. *New York Times*, July 7, 1990.

17. *Weekly Compilation of Presidential Documents* 26 (November 26, 1990), pt. 4:1868–1869, 1871–1873.

18. Beschloss and Talbott, 255.

19. James A. Baker III, *The Politics of Diplomacy, Revolution, War, and Peace, 1989–1992* (1995), 294.

20. Robert Legvold, "The Gulf Crisis and the Future of Gorbachev's Foreign Policy Revolution," in Frederic J. Fleron, Jr., Erik P. Hoffman, and Robin F. Laird, eds., *Contemporary Issues in Soviet Foreign Policy: From Brezhnev to Gorbachev* (1991), 828.

21. Beschloss and Talbott, 341.

22. Ibid., 344.

23. Ibid., 350.

24. For the details, see ibid., 398–401.

25. *New York Times*, August 20, 1991.

26. John B. Dunlop, *The Rise of Russia and the Fall of the Soviet Empire* (1993), 216.

27. *Weekly Compilation of Presidential Documents* 27 (1991), pt. 4:1883–1884.

Suggested Readings

General Histories

Among the excellent general surveys of U.S.–Soviet relations since 1917 are John Lewis Gaddis, *Russia, the Soviet Union and the United States: An Interpretative History*, 2nd ed. (1990); Peter G. Boyle, *American-Soviet Relations: From the Russian Revolution to the Fall of Communism* (1993); and Miroslav Nincic, *Anatomy of Hostility: The U.S.–Soviet Rivalry in Perspective* (1989). A classic revisionist view is provided by William A. Williams, *American-Russian Relations, 1781–1947* (1952). A Soviet perspective is provided by Nikolai Sivachev and Nikolai Yakolev, *Russia and the United States* (1979). See also David Shavit, *United States Relations with Russia and the Soviet Union: A Historical Dictionary* (1993).

General surveys of Soviet foreign policy are offered by Adam B. Ulam, *Expansion and Coexistence: Soviet Foreign Policy, 1917–1973*, 2nd ed. (1974) and Joseph Nogee and Robert Donaldson, *Soviet Foreign Policy Since World War II*, 3rd ed. (1988).

For overviews of U.S. diplomacy, see Robert D. Schulzinger, *American Diplomacy in the Twentieth Century*, 3rd ed. (1994), and John Spanier and Steven W. Hoo, *American Foreign Policy*, 13th ed. (1995). Both have excellent bibliographies. For revisionist interpretations, see Michael Parenti, *The Sword and the Dollar: Imperialism, Revolution, and the Arms Race* (1989), and William A. Williams, *The Tragedy of American Diplomacy* (1962).

Introduction: The United States and Czarist Russia

Among the surveys of Russian-American relations before the Bolshevik Revolution are three dated works: Foster Rhea Dulles, *The Road to Teheran: The Story of Russia and America, 1781–1943* (1944); Thomas A. Bailey, *America Faces Russia: Russian-American Relations from Early Times to Our Own Day* (1950); and William A. Williams, *American-Russian Relations, 1781–1947* (1952).

More recent studies of early Russian-American relations include Nikolai N. Bolkhovitinov, *The Beginnings of Russian-American Relations, 1775–1815*, Elena Levin, trans. (1975), and *Russia and the American Revolution* (1976); Nina N. Bashkina et al., eds., *The United States and Russia: The Beginnings of Relations, 1765–1815* (1980); and Norman Saul, *Distant Friends: the United States and Russia, 1763–1867* (1991).

Chapter One. The United States and the Bolshevik Revolution, 1917–1933

For U.S. policy during the era of Bolshevik Revolution, see Arno J. Mayer, *Wilson vs. Lenin: Political Origins of the New Diplomacy, 1917–1918* (1958); Linda Killen, *The Russian Bureau: A Case Study in Wilsonian Diplomacy* (1983); George F. Kennan, *Soviet-American Relations, 1917–1920*, 2 vols. (1956–1958), and *Russia and the West Under Lenin and Stalin* (1961); Betty Miller Unterberger, *America's Siberian Expedition, 1918–1920: A Study of National Policy* (1956), and *The United States, Revolutionary Russia and the Rise of Czechoslovakia* (1989); Lloyd C. Gardner, *Safe for Democracy: The Anglo-American Response to Revolution, 1913–1923* (1984); Robert J. Maddox, *The Unknown War with Russia: Wilson's Siberian Intervention* (1977); Leonid L. Strakhovsky, *American Opinion about Russia, 1917–20* (1961), and *The Origins of American Intervention in Northern Russia, 1918* (1937); Benjamin D. Rhodes, *The Anglo-American Winter War with Russia, 1918–1919* (1988); Richard Goldhurst, *The Midnight War: American Intervention in Russia, 1918–20* (1978); and John Silverlight, *The Victors' Dilemma: American Intervention in the Russian Civil War* (1978).

Soviet policy is examined in Richard K. Debo, *Revolution and Survival: The Foreign Policy of Soviet Russia, 1917–1918* (1979) and *Survival and Consolidation: the Foreign Policy of Soviet Russia, 1918–1921* (1992).

For the era of nonrecognition, 1921–1933, see Joan Hoff-Wilson, *Ideology and Economics: U.S. Relations with the Soviet Union, 1918–33* (1974), and Peter G. Filene, *Americans and the Soviet Experiment, 1917–33* (1967).

Chapter Two. Franklin D. Roosevelt and the Grand Alliance, 1933–1945

An excellent survey of Roosevelt's diplomacy is provided by Robert Dallek, *Franklin D. Roosevelt and American Foreign Policy, 1932–1945* (1979).

For the period between U.S. recognition of the Soviet Union and World War II, see Donald G. Bishop, *The Roosevelt-Litvinov Agreements: The American View* (1965); John Richman, *The United States and the Soviet Union: The Decision to Recognize* (1980); Thomas R. Maddux, *Years of Estrangement: American Relations with the Soviet Union, 1933–1941* (1980); Edward M. Bennett, *Recognition of Russia: An American Foreign Policy Dilemma* (1970) and *Franklin D. Roosevelt and the Search for Security: Soviet-American Relations, 1933–1939* (1985); and Hugh De Santis, *The Diplomacy of Silence: The American Foreign Service, the Soviet Union, and the Cold War, 1933–1947* (1980).

For Soviet diplomacy, see Jonathan Haslam, *Soviet Foreign Policy, 1930–33* (1983), and *The Soviet Union and the Struggle for Collective Security in Europe, 1933–39* (1984); Jiri Hochman, *The Soviet Union and the Failure of Collective*

Security, 1934–1938 (1984); and Geoffrey Roberts, *The Unholy Alliance: Stalin's Pact with Hitler* (1989).

Various aspects of Roosevelt's wartime Soviet diplomacy are examined in Warren F. Kimball, "*The Most Unsordid Act*": *Lend-Lease, 1939–1941* (1969); Raymond H. Dawson, *The Decision to Aid Russia, 1941: Foreign Policy and Domestic Politics* (1959); George C. Herring, *Aid to Russia, 1941–1946: Strategy, Diplomacy, and the Origins of the Cold War* (1973); Richard W. Steele, *The First Offensive, 1942: Roosevelt, Marshall and the Making of American Strategy* (1973); Mark A. Stoler, *The Politics of the Second Front* (1977); Robin Edmonds, *The Big Three: Churchill, Roosevelt and Stalin in Peace and War* (1991); Edward M. Bennett, *Franklin D. Roosevelt and the Search for Victory: American–Soviet Relations, 1939–45* (1990); Robert Beitzell, *The Uneasy Alliance: America, Britain and Russia, 1941–1943* (1973); and Gabriel Kolko, *The Politics of War, 1943–1945* (1968).

For the wartime strains in the Grand Alliance, see John Lewis Gaddis, *The United States and the Origins of the Cold War, 1941–1947* (1972); Paul D. Mayle, *Eureka Summit: Agreement in Principle and the Big Three at Tehran, 1943* (1987); Lynn Ethridge Davis, *The Cold War Begins: Soviet-America Conflict over Eastern Europe* (1974); Diane Shaver Clemens, *Yalta* (1970); John L. Snell, ed., *The Meaning of Yalta: Big Three Diplomacy and the New Balance of Power* (1956); and Russell D. Buhite, *Decisions at Yalta: An Appraisal of Summit Diplomacy* (1986).

Anglo-American relations with the Soviet Union are dealt with in William Hardy McNeil, *America, Britain, and Russia: Their Cooperation and Conflict, 1941–1946* (1970); Terry H. Anderson, *The United States, Great Britain, and the Cold War, 1944–1947* (1981); Fraser J. Harbutt, *The Iron Curtain: Churchill, America, and the Origins of the Cold War* (1986); and Steven Merritt Miner, *Between Churchill and Stalin: The Soviet Union, Great Britain, and the Origins of the Grand Alliance* (1988).

For Roosevelt's and Churchill's wartime correspondence, see Warren F. Kimball, *Churchill and Roosevelt: The Complete Correspondence, 1939–1945*, 3 vols. (1984).

Stalin's wartime diplomacy is examined in Vojtech Mastny, *Russia's Road to the Cold War: Diplomacy, Warfare, and the Politics of Communism, 1941–1945* (1979)

Chapter Three. Truman and Containment, 1945–1953

Surveys of the period after World War include Walter LaFeber, *America, Russia, and the Cold War, 1945–1992*, 7th ed. (1993); Thomas G. Paterson, *Meeting the Communist Threat: Truman to Reagan* (1988); Adam B. Ulam, *The Rivals: America and Russia since World War II* (1971); and Bernard A. Weisberger, *Cold War, Cold Peace: The United States and Russia since 1945* (1984). See also Joseph M. Sircusa, ed., *The American Diplomatic Revolution: A Documentary History of the Cold War, 1941–1947* (1977), and Thomas H. Etzold and John Lewis Gaddis, eds., *Containment: Documents on American Policy and Strategy, 1945–1950* (1978).

A massive, in-depth study of the Truman era is Melvyn P. Leffler, *A Preponderance of Power: National Security, the Truman Administration, and the Cold War* (1992).

Among the numerous studies on the breakdown of Soviet-American relations during the Truman administration are Hugh Thomas, *Armed Truce: The Beginning of the Cold War, 1945–46* (1987); Daniel Yergin, *Shattered Peace: The Origins of the Cold War and the National Security State* (1977); Deborah Welch

Larson, *Origins of Containment: A Psychological Explanation* (1985); Lisle A. Rose, *Dubious Victory: The United States and the End of World War II* (1973), and *After Yalta: America and the Origins of the Cold War* (1973); Gabriel Kolko and Joyce Kolko, *The Limits of Power: The World and United States Foreign Policy, 1945–1954* (1972); Barton J. Bernstein, ed., *Politics and Policies of the Truman Administration* (1970); Thomas G. Paterson, *On Every Front: The Making of the Cold War* (1979), and *Soviet-American Confrontation: Postwar Reconstruction and the Origins of the Cold War* (1973); Robert L. Messer, *The End of an Alliance: James Byrnes, Roosevelt, Truman, and the Origins of the Cold War* (1982); James L. Gormly, *The Collapse of the Grand Alliance, 1945–1948* (1987); and Frank Kofsky, *Harry S. Truman and the War Scare of 1948* (1993).

For an introduction to the historiography of the Cold War, see J. Samuel Walker, "Historians and Cold War Origins: The New Consensus," in Gerald K. Haines and J. Samuel Walker, eds., *American Foreign Relations: A Historiographical Review* (1981), 207–236. See also Robert James Maddox, *The New Left and the Origins of the Cold War* (1973).

The role of the atomic bomb in the early Cold War is examined in Gregg Herken, *The Winning Weapon: The Atomic Bomb and the Cold War, 1945–1950* (1980); Martin J. Sherwin, *A World Destroyed: The Atomic Bomb and the Grand Alliance* (1975); Gar Alperovitz, *Atomic Diplomacy: Hiroshima and Potsdam*, expanded and updated ed. (1985), and *Decision to Use the Bomb* (1995), and David Holloway, *Stalin and the Bomb: The Soviet Union and Atomic Energy, 1939–1956* (1994).

The economic aspects of Truman's foreign policy are discussed in Robert A. Pollard, *Economic Security and the Origins of the Cold War, 1945–1950* (1985); Michael J. Hogan, *The Marshall Plan: America, Britain, and the Reconstruction of Western Europe, 1947–1952* (1987); and John Gimbel, *The Origins of the Marshall Plan* (1976).

For U.S. policy toward Germany, see Frank Ninkovich, *Germany and the United States: The Transformation of the German Question since 1945* (1988); Bruce Kuklick, *American Policy and the Division of Germany* (1972); Avi Shlaim, *The United States and the Berlin Blockade, 1948–1949: A Study in Crisis Decision-Making* (1983); John Gimbel, *The American Occupation of Germany: Politics and the Military, 1945–1949* (1968); and Rolf Steininger, *The German Question: The Stalin Note of 1952 and the Problem of Reunification*, Mark Cioc, ed., and Jane T. Hedges, trans. (1990).

The creation of NATO is examined in Timothy P. Ireland, *Creating the Entangling Alliance: The Origins of the North Atlantic Treaty Organization* (1981); Don Cook, *Forging the Alliance: NATO, 1945–1950* (1989); Lawrence S. Kaplan, *The United States and NATO: The Formative Years* (1984); and Ronald E. Powaski, *Toward an Entangling Alliance: American Isolationism, Internationalism, and Europe, 1901–1950* (1991).

For Soviet policy, see William O. McCagg, Jr., *Stalin Embattled: 1943–1948* (1978); William Taubman, *Stalin's American Policy: From Entente to Détente to Cold War* (1982); and Albert Resis, *Stalin, the Politburo, and the Onset of the Cold War, 1945–1946* (1988).

The beginnings of containment in the Near East are discussed in Bruce Robellet Kuniholm, *The Origins of the Cold War in the Near East: Great Power Conflict and Diplomacy in Iran, Greece, and Turkey* (1980), and Mark Lytle, *Origins of the Iranian-American Alliance, 1941–1953* (1987).

For the Far East, see Marc S. Gallicchio, *The Cold War Begins in Asia: American East Asian Policy and the Fall of the Japanese Empire* (1988).

Sino-American relations are discussed in June M. Grasso, *Harry Truman's Two-China Policy, 1948–1950* (1987); Russell D. Buhite, *Soviet-American Relations in Asia 1945–54* (1981); Akira Iriye, ed., *The Origins of the Cold War in Asia* (1977); William W. Stueck, Jr., *The Road to Confrontation: American Policy Toward China and Korea, 1947–50* (1986); and David Allan Mayers, *Cracking the Monolith: U.S. Policy Against the Sino-Soviet Alliance, 1949–1955* (1986).

For the Korean War, see James L. Matray, *The Reluctant Crusade: American Foreign Policy in Korea, 1941–50* (1985); Peter Lowe, *The Origins of the Korean War*, 2 vols. (1986–1990); Burton L. Kaufman, *The Korean War: Changes in Crisis, Credibility and Command* (1986); Bruce Cummings, ed. *Child of Conflict: The Korean-American Relationship, 1943–53* (1983); Callum A. MacDonald, *Korea: The War before Vietnam* (1987); Rosemary Foot, *The Wrong War: American Policy and the Dimensions of the Korean Conflict, 1950–53* (1985) William W. Stueck, Jr. *The Korean War: An International History* (1995); John Merrill, *Korea* (1989); and Alexander Bevin, *Korea* (1987).

For early U.S. involvement in Vietnam, see Gary R. Hess, *The United States' Emergence as a Southeast Asian Power, 1940–1950* (1988), and Lloyd Gardner, *Approaching Vietnam, 1950–1954* (1988).

For the Red Scare and McCarthyism, see Richard M. Fried, *Nightmare in Red: The McCarthy Era in Perspective* (1990); Robert M. Griffith, *The Politics of Fear: Joseph R. McCarthy and the Senate*, 2nd ed. (1987); Richard M. Freeland, *The Truman Doctrine and the Origins of McCarthyism* (1972); Stanley L. Kutler, *The American Inquisition: Justice and Injustice in the Cold War* (1982); Ronald Radosh and Joyce Milton, *The Rosenberg File: A Search for the Truth* (1983); and Allen Weinstein, *Perjury: The Hiss-Chambers Case* (1978).

Chapter Four. Eisenhower and the Globalization of the Cold War, 1953–1961

For an overview of the Eisenhower foreign policy, see Robert A. Divine, *Eisenhower and the Cold War* (1981); Richard A. Melanson and David Mayers, eds., *Reevaluating Eisenhower: American Foreign Policy in the1950s* (1986); Charles C. Alexander, *Holding the Line: The Eisenhower Era, 1952–1961* (1975); Chester J. Pach, Jr., and Elmo Richardson, *The Presidency of Dwight D Eisenhower*, rev. ed. (1991); and H. W. Brands, Jr., *Cold Warriors: Eisenhower's Generation and American Foreign Policy* (1988).

Dulles' diplomacy is discussed in Townsend Hoopes, *The Devil and John Foster Dulles* (1975); Richard H. Immerman, ed., *John Foster Dulles and the Diplomacy of the Cold War* (1990); and Frederick W. Marks III, *Power and Peace: The Diplomacy of John Foster Dulles* (1993).

Eisenhower's intervention in Iran is discussed in Richard W. Cottam, *Iran and the United States: A Cold War Case Study* (1988), and Mark Gasiorowski, *U.S. Foreign Policy and the Shah: Building a Client State in Iran* (1991).

For U.S. intervention in Guatemala, see Piero Gleijeses, *Shattered Hope: The Guatemalan Revolution and the United States, 1944–1954* (1991), and Richard H. Immerman, *The CIA in Guatemala: The Foreign Policy of Intervention* (1982).

Eisenhower's policy toward Indochina is examined in Lawrence S. Kaplan, Denise Artaud, and Mark R. Rubin, eds., *Dien Bien Phu and the Crisis of Franco-American Relations, 1954–1955* (1990); David L. Anderson, *Trapped by Success: The Eisenhower Administration and Vietnam, 1953–1961* (1991); and James Cable, *The Geneva Conference of 1954 on Indochina* (1986).

For Latin America, Stephen G. Rabe, *Eisenhower and Latin America: The Foreign Policy of Anticommunism* (1988). For Africa, see Madeleine G. Kalb, *The Congo Cables: The Cold War in Africa from Eisenhower to Kennedy* (1982).

The nuclear test ban talks arms are discussed in Robert A. Divine, *Blowing in the Wind* (1978). The event that disrupted those talks is examined in Michael R. Beschloss, *Mayday: Eisenhower, Khrushchev, and the U-2 Affair* (1986).

For Soviet policy, see Nikita S. Khrushchev, *Khrushchev Remembers* (1970), and *Khrushchev Remembers: The Last Testament* (1974), both translated and edited by Strobe Talbott. See also Carl A. Linden, *Khrushchev and the Soviet Leadership* (1990); Arnold L. Horelick and Myron Rush, *Strategic Power and Soviet Foreign Policy* (1966), and Lincoln P. Bloomfield, Walter C. Clemens, Jr., and Franklyn Griffiths, *Khrushchev and the Arms Race: Soviet Interests in Arms Control and Disarmament, 1954–1964* (1966).

Chapter Five. Kennedy and Johnson: Confrontation and Cooperation, 1961–1969

Two very readable surveys of Kennedy's presidency are Arthur M. Schlesinger, Jr., *A Thousand Days: John F. Kennedy in the White House* (1965), and Theodore Sorensen, *Kennedy* (1965).

Works dealing more specifically with Kennedy's foreign policy are Alexander L. George and Richard Smoke, *Deterrence and American Foreign Policy: Theory and Practice* (1974); Roger Hilsman, *To Move a Nation: The Politics of Foreign Policy in the Administration of John F. Kennedy* (1967); Thomas G. Paterson, ed., *Kennedy's Quest for Victory: American Foreign Policy, 1961–1963* (1989). Revisionist interpretations are provided by Louise FitzSimons, *The Kennedy Doctrine* (1972); Richard J. Walton, *Cold War and Counterrevolution: The Foreign Policy of John F. Kennedy* (1972); and Bruce Miroff, *Pragmatic Illusions: The Presidential Politics of John F. Kennedy* (1976).

For a very readable account of Soviet-American relations during the Kennedy years, see Michael R. Beschloss, *The Crisis Years: Kennedy and Khrushchev, 1960–1963* (1991).

The Berlin crisis is examined in Norman Gelb, The *Berlin Wall: Kennedy, Khrushchev and a Showdown in the Heart of Europe* (1986); Robert M. Slusser, *The Berlin Crisis of 1961* (1973); and Jack M. Schick, *The Berlin Crisis, 1958–1962* (1971).

Kennedy's problems in Cuba are discussed in Trumbull Higgins, *The Perfect Failure: Kennedy, Eisenhower and the CIA and the Bay of Pigs* (1987); Robert A. Divine, ed., *The Cuban Missile Crisis*, 2nd ed. (1988); William J. Medland, *The Cuban Missile Crisis of 1962: Needless or Necessary?* (1988); Raymond L. Garthoff, *Reflections on the Cuban Missile Crisis*, rev. ed. (1989); James G. Blight, *On the Brink: Americans and Soviets Reexamine the Cuban Missile Crisis*, 2nd ed. (1990).

For Kennedy's military strategy, see Desmond Ball, *Politics and Force Levels* (1981), and Bernard J. Firestone, *The Quest for Nuclear Stability: John F. Kennedy and the Soviet Union* (1982). See also Glenn T. Seaborg and Benjamin S. Loeb, *Kennedy, Khrushchev, and the Test Ban* (1981).

Kennedy's approach to the Third World is examined in Gerard T. Rice, *The Bold Experiment: JFK's Peace Corps* (1986); John M. Newman, *JFK and Vietnam* (1992); William J. Rust, *Kennedy in Vietnam* (1985); and Richard D. Mahoney, *JFK: Ordeal in Africa* (1983).

Among the numerous studies that have appeared on Johnson's Vietnam policy are Larry Berman, *Lyndon Johnson's War: The Road to Stalemate in Vietnam* (1989); Brian Van De Merk, *Into the Quagmire: Lyndon Johnson and the Escalation of the Vietnam War* (1991); George C. Herring, *America's Longest War*, 2nd ed. (1988), and *LBJ and Vietnam* (1994). See also the accounts by Johnson's secretaries of defense, Robert S. McNamara, *In Retrospect: The Tragedy and Lessons of Vietnam* (1995), and Clark Clifford, *Counsel to the President (1991)*, and by his secretary of state, Dean Rusk, *As I Saw It* (1990). For a revisionist account, see Gabriel Kolko, *Anatomy of a War* (1985).

For Johnson and arms control, see Glenn Seaborg, *Stemming the Tide: Arms Control and the Johnson Years* (1987).

For Soviet policy, see Michel Tatu, *Power in the Kremlin: From Khrushchev to Kosygin* (1969), and W. W. Kulski, *The Soviet Union in World Affairs: A Documented Analysis, 1964–1972* (1973).

Chapter Six. Nixon, Ford, and Détente, 1969–1977

Henry Kissinger's memoir in two volumes, *White House Years* (1979) and *Years of Upheaval* (1982), is indispensable to any study of the diplomacy and military strategy of the Nixon-Ford years. Richard Nixon, *RN: The Memoirs of Richard Nixon* (1978), while less detailed, is useful. See also Gerald Ford, *A Time To Heal: The Autobiography of Gerald R. Ford* (1979).

Among the secondary works are Raymond L. Garthoff, *Détente and Confrontation: American-Soviet Relations from Nixon to Reagan*, rev. ed. (1995); Robert S. Litwak, *Détente and the Nixon Doctrine: American Foreign Policy and the Pursuit of Stability, 1969–1976* (1984); Richard C. Thornton, *The Nixon-Kissinger Years: Reshaping America's Foreign Policy* (1989); John G. Stoessinger, *Henry Kissinger: The Anguish of Power* (1976); Seymour Hersh, *The Price of Power* (1983); Walter Isaacson, *Kissinger* (1992); Robert D. Shulzinger, *Henry Kissinger: Doctor of Diplomacy* (1989); Coral Bell, *The Diplomacy of Détente: The Kissinger Era* (1977); Michael A. Genovese, *The Nixon Presidency: Power and Politics in Turbulent Times* (1990); and John Robert Greene, *The Limits of Power: The Nixon and Ford Administrations* (1992).

For Nixon and Ford and Vietnam, see Nguyen Tien Hung and Jerrold L. Schecter, *The Palace File* (1986), and P. Edward Haley, *Congress and the Fall of South Vietnam and Cambodia* (1983). For Nixon and Chile, see Paul Sigmund, *The Overthrow of Allende and the Politics of Chile* (1977).

Soviet military and diplomatic policies are discussed in Stephen S. Kaplan, ed., *Diplomacy of Power: Soviet Armed Forces as a Political Instrument* (1981); Robin Edmonds, *Soviet Foreign Policy: The Brezhnev Years* (1983); William E. Griffith, ed., *The Soviet Empire, Expansion and Détente: Critical Choices for Americans* (1976); Derek Leebaert, ed., *Soviet Military Thinking* (1981); and Harry Gelman, *The Brezhnev Politburo and the Decline of Détente* (1984).

Chapter Seven. Carter and the Decline of Détente, 1977–1981

A number of memoirs provide useful surveys of Carter's foreign and defense policies: Jimmy Carter, *Keeping Faith: Memoirs of a President* (1982); Zbigniew Brzezinski, *Power and Principle: Memoirs of the National Security Adviser, 1977–1981* (1983); Cyrus Vance, *Hard Choices: Critical Years in America's Foreign Policy* (1983).

Secondary works on the Carter era are Gaddis Smith, *Morality, Reason and Power: American Diplomacy in the Carter Years* (1986); Erwin C. Hargrove, *Jimmy Carter as President:* (1988); Burton Kaufman, *The Presidency of James Earl Carter, Jr.* (1993); Coral Bell, *President Carter and Foreign Policy: The Cost of Virtue?* (1980); Alexander Moens, *Foreign Policy under Carter* (1990); Jerel A. Rosati, *The Carter Administration's Quest for Global Community* (1987); Herbert D. Rosenbaum and Alexej Ugrinsky, eds., *Jimmy Carter: Foreign Policy and Post-Presidential Years* (1994); Laurence H. Shoup, *The Carter Presidency and Beyond* (1980); Donald S. Spencer, *The Carter Implosion: Jimmy Carter and the Amateur Style of Diplomacy* (1988).

For Carter's human rights campaign, see A. Glenn Mower, Jr., *Human Rights and American Foreign Policy: The Carter and Reagan Experiences* (1987), and Joshua Muravchik, *The Uncertain Crusade: Jimmy Carter and the Dilemmas of Human Rights Policy* (1986).

For SALT II, see Strobe Talbott, *Endgame: The Inside Story of SALT II* (1979); Roger P. Labrie, ed., *SALT Hand Book: Key Documents and Issues, 1972–1979* (1979); and Dan Caldwell, *The SALT II Treaty Ratification Debate* (1991).

For other special topics, see William Quandt, *Camp David: Politics and Peacemaking* (1986); Gary Sick, *All Fall Down: America's Tragic Encounter with Iran* (1985); Henry Jackson, *From the Congo to Soweto* (1982); David D. Newsome, *The Soviet Combat Brigade in Cuba* (1987); and Thomas T. Hammond, *Red Flag over Afghanistan: The Communist Coup, the Soviet Invasion, and the Consequences* (1984).

For Soviet foreign policy, see Adam B. Ulam, *Dangerous Relations: The Soviet Union in World Politics, 1970–1982* (1983).

Chapter Eight. The Reagan Cold War, 1981–1989

In addition to the memoir of President Reagan, Ronald W. Reagan, *An American Life* (1990), other books bearing on America's Soviet policy are Alexander M. Haig, *Caveat* (1984); Caspar Weinberger, *Fighting for Peace* (1990); and George P. Shultz, *Turmoil and Triumph: My Years as Secretary of State* (1993).

Among the secondary works dealing with U.S. foreign policy during the Reagan administration are Michael Schaller, *Reckoning with Reagan: America and Its President in the 1980s* (1992); Coral Bell, *The Reagan Paradox: American Foreign Policy in the 1980s* (1989); Jeff McMahon, *Reagan and the World: Imperial Policy in the New Cold War* (1985); Morris H. Manley, ed., *Crisis and Confrontation: Ronald Reagan's Foreign Policy* (1988); David Kyvig, ed., *Reagan and the World* (1990); Kenneth A. Oye, Robert J. Lieber, and Donald Rothchild, eds., *Eagle Defiant: United States Foreign Policy in the 1980s* (1983), and *Eagle Resurgent? The Reagan Era in American Foreign Policy* (1987); and Morris H. Morley, ed., *Crisis and Confrontation: Ronald Reagan's Foreign Policy* (1988).

Works dealing more specifically with U.S.–Soviet relations are Raymond L. Garthoff, *The Great Transition: American-Soviet Relations and the End of the Cold War* 1994); Fred Halliday, *From Kabul to Managua: Soviet-American Relations in the 1980s* (1989); Michael Mandelbaum and Strobe Talbott, *Reagan and Gorbachev* (1987); Seweryn Bialer and Michael Mandelbaum, eds., *Gorbachev's Russia and American Foreign Policy* (1988); Thomas W. Simons, Jr., *The End of the Cold War* (1990).

For the Korean airliner incident, see Alexander Dallin, *Black Box: KAL 007 and the Superpowers* (1985), and Seymour Hersch, *The Target Is Destroyed* (1987).

Nuclear issues are discussed in Strobe Talbott, *Deadly Gambits* (1984), and Michael Krepon, *Arms Control in the Reagan Administration.* (1989).

For Reagan's Third World policies, see David Locke Hall, *The Reagan Wars: A Constitutional Perspective on War Powers and the Presidency* (1990).

Reagan and Central America are covered in Roy Gutman, *Banana Diplomacy: The Making of American Policy in Nicaragua, 1981–87* (1988); E. Bradford Burns, *At War in Nicaragua: The Reagan Doctrine and the Politics of Nostalgia* (1987); Peter Kornbluh, *Nicaragua, The Price of Intervention: Reagan's Wars Against the Sandinistas* (1987), and Thomas W. Walker, ed., *Reagan versus the Sandinistas: The Undeclared War on Nicaragua* (1986).

For the Iran-Contra Affair, see Jonathan Marshall, Peter D. Scott, and Jane Hunter, The *Iran-Contra Connection: Secret Teams and Covert Operations in the Reagan Era* (1987).

Gorbachev's policies are discussed in his *Memoirs* (1995) and *Perestroika: New Thinking for Our Country and the World* (1987); Anders Aslund, *Gorbachev's Struggle for Economic Reform* (1989), Robert. G. Kaiser, *Why Gorbachev Happened: Triumphs and Failure* (1991); Raymond W. Duncan and Carolyn McGiffert Ekedahl, *Moscow and the Third World under Gorbachev* (1990); Gerhard Wettig, *Changes in Soviet Policy towards the West* (1991); and Seweryn Bialer and Michael Mandelbaum, eds., *Gorbachev's Russia and American Foreign Policy* (1988). Robert W. Davies, *Soviet History in the Gorbachev Revolution* (1989).

Chapter Nine. George Bush and the End of the Cold War, 1989–1991

The most important memoir to appear on the Bush administration is James A. Baker III, *The Politics of Diplomacy* (1995).

Michael R. Beschloss and Strobe Talbott, *At the Highest Levels: The Inside Story of the Cold War* (1993) is a highly readable account of Bush's Soviet diplomacy. For German reunification, see Constantine C. Menges, *The Future of Germany and the Atlantic Alliance* (1991), and Stephen F. Szabo, *The Diplomacy of German Unification* (1992).

For Soviet policy, see Joseph G. Whelan, *Soviet Diplomacy and Negotiating Behavior, 1988–90: Gorbachev-Reagan-Bush Meetings at the Summit* (1991).

For the decline and collapse of the Soviet Union, see Marshall Goldman, *What Went Wrong with Perestroika?* (1992); Harley D. Balzer, ed., *Five Years That Shook the World: Gorbachev's Unfinished Revolution* (1991); Thomas H. Naylor, *The Cold War Legacy* (1991); David Armstrong and Erik Goldstein, eds., *The End of the Cold War* (1990); Michael Mandelbaum, ed., *The Rise of Nations in the Soviet Union: American Foreign Policy and the Disintegration of the USSR* (1991); Zbigniew Brzezinski, *The Grand Failure: The Birth and Death of Communism in the Twentieth Century* (1989); Charles Gati, *The Bloc That Failed* (1990); and a massive but very readable account by Bush's ambassador to Moscow, Jack F. Matlock, *Autopsy of an Empire* (1995).

Among the works that have appeared on the end of the Cold War are John Lewis Gaddis, *The United States and the End of the Cold War: Implications, Reconsiderations, Provocations* (1992), and Michael Hogan, ed., *The End of the Cold War: Its Meaning and Implications* (1992).

More Specific Topics

For U.S.–Soviet economic relations, see Philip J. Funigiello, *American-Soviet Trade in the Cold War* (1988); James K. Libbey, *American-Russian Economic Relations: A Survey of Issues and References* (1989); Bruce Parrott, ed., *Trade,*

Technology, and Soviet-American Relations (1985); and Colin White, *Russia and America: The Roots of Economic Divergence* (1987). See also Fred L. Block, *The Origins of International Economic Disorder: A Study of United States International Monetary Policy from World War II to the Present* (1977).

Among the many books that have appeared on U.S. intelligence and covert activities, see William Blum, *The CIA: A Forgotten History* (1986); John Prados, *Presidents' Secret Wars: CIA and Pentagon Operations since World War II* (1986); John Ranelagh, *The Agency: The Rise and Decline of the CIA* (1986); and Gregory F. Treverlon, *Covert Action: The Limits of Intervention in the Postwar World* (1987).

For histories of the nuclear arms race, see Ronald E. Powaski, *March to Armageddon: The United States and the Nuclear Arms Race, 1939 to the Present* (1987); McGeorge Bundy, *Danger and Survival* (1988); John Newhouse, *War and Peace in the Nuclear Age* (1989); David Holloway, *The Soviet Union and the Arms Race* (1983); John Wilson Lewis and Xue Litai, *China Builds the Bomb* (1988); Coit D. Blacker, *Reluctant Warriors: The United States, the Soviet Union, and Arms Control* (1987); Patrick Glynn, *Closing Pandora's Box: Arms Races, Arms Control, and the History of the Cold War* (1992); Charles R. Morris, *Iron Destinies, Lost Opportunities: The Arms Race between the USA and the USSR, 1945–1987* (1988).

For the United States and NATO, see Ronald E. Pwaski, *Toward an Entangling Alliance: American Isolationism, Internationalism, and Europe, 1901–1950* (1991), and *The Entangling Alliance: The United States and European Security, 1950–1993* (1993); Anton W. DePorte, *Europe between the Superpowers*, 2nd ed. (1986), John Van Oudenaren, *Détente in Europe: The Soviet Union and the West since 1953* (1991).

For U.S. relations with Japan, see Roger Buckley, *U.S.–Japan Alliance Diplomacy, 1945–1990* (1992).

Sino-Soviet relations are discussed in Warren L. Cohen, *America's Response to China*, 3d ed. (1986); Michael Schaller, *The United States and China in the Twentieth Century*, 2nd. ed. (1990); Bevin Alexander, *The Strange Connection: U.S. Intervention in China, 1944–1972* (1992); Charles R. Kitts, *The United States Odyssey in China, 1784–1990* (1991); Gordon H. Chang, *Friends and Enemies: The United States, China, and the Soviet Union, 1948–1972* (1990).

U.S. policies toward the Third World are covered in H. W. Brands, Jr., *The Specter of Neutralism: The United States and the Emergence of the Third World, 1947–1960* (1989); Gabriel Kolko, *Confronting the Third World* (1988); and Scott Bills, *Empire and Cold War* (1990).

General studies on Vietnam include *The Pentagon Papers: The Defense Department History of United States Decisionmaking on Vietnam*, Senator Gravel edition (1971); Marilyn Blatt Young, *The Vietnam Wars, 1945–1990* (1991); Andrew J. Rotter, *The Path to Vietnam: Origins of the American Commitment to Southeast Asia* (1987); Gabriel Kolko, *Vietnam: Anatomy of a War* (1986); George Kahin, *Intervention* (1986); Stanley C. Karnow, *Vietnam* (1983); William Appleman Williams, et al., *America in Vietnam* (1988); Douglas Pike, *Vietnam and the Soviet Union* (1987); and Richard Dean Burns and Milton Leitenberg, eds., *The Wars in Vietnam, Cambodia and Laos, 1945–1982* (1984).

U.S. policy toward Latin America is discussed in Abraham F. Lowenthal, *Partners in Conflict: The United States and Latin America* (1987); Lars Schoultz, *National Security and United States Policy toward Latin America* (1987); Lester Langley, *America and the Americas* (1989).

For U.S. relations with Cuba, see Wayne S. Smith, *The Closest of Enemies: A Personal and Diplomatic Account of U.S.–Cuba Relations since 1957* (1987); and Morris Morley, *Imperial State and Revolution: The United States and Cuba, 1952–1986* (1987). Soviet-Cuban relations are discussed in Peter Shearman, *The Soviet Union and Cuba* (1987), and W. Raymond Duncan, *The Soviet Union and Cuba* (1985).

Other regional studies are Walter LaFeber, *Inevitable Revolutions: The United States in Central America* (1993); Seth P. Tillman, *The U.S. and the Middle East* (1982); Peter J. Schraeder, *United States Foreign Policy toward Africa* (1994); David A. Dickson, *United States Foreign Policy toward Sub-Saharan Africa* (1985); Zaki Laidi, *The Superpowers and Africa, 1960–1990* (1990), René Lemarchand, ed., *American Policy in Southern Africa.* (1978).

For the social and psychological effects of the Cold War, see Stephen J. Whitefield, *The Culture of the Cold War* (1991), and Ralph K. White, *Fearful Warriors: A Psychological Profile of U.S.–Soviet Relations* (1984).

Index

CPSIA information can be obtained
at www.ICGtesting.com
Printed in the USA
BVHW021557100123
656001BV00030B/7

9 780195 078503